# AWS DevOps Simplified

Build a solid foundation in AWS to deliver enterprise-grade software solutions at scale

**Akshay Kapoor**

BIRMINGHAM—MUMBAI

# AWS DevOps Simplified

Copyright © 2023 Packt Publishing

*All rights reserved.* No part of this book may be reproduced, stored in a retrieval system, or transmitted in any form or by any means, without the prior written permission of the publisher, except in the case of brief quotations embedded in critical articles or reviews.

Every effort has been made in the preparation of this book to ensure the accuracy of the information presented. However, the information contained in this book is sold without warranty, either express or implied. Neither the author, nor Packt Publishing or its dealers and distributors, will be held liable for any damages caused or alleged to have been caused directly or indirectly by this book.

Packt Publishing has endeavored to provide trademark information about all of the companies and products mentioned in this book by the appropriate use of capitals. However, Packt Publishing cannot guarantee the accuracy of this information.

**Associate Group Product Manager**: Preet Ahuja

**Publishing Product Manager**: Vidhi Vashisth

**Book Project Manager**: Neil Dmello

**Senior Editor**: Divya Vijayan

**Technical Editor**: Yash Bhanushali

**Copy Editor**: Safis Editing

**Proofreader**: Safis Editing

**Indexer**: Rekha Nair

**Production Designer**: Shyam Sundar Korumilli

**DevRel Marketing Coordinator**: Rohan Dobhal

First published: September 2023

Production reference: 1080823

Published by Packt Publishing Ltd.

Grosvenor House

11 St Paul's Square

Birmingham

B3 1RB, UK.

ISBN 978-1-83763-446-0

www.packtpub.com

*To my family that completes my world:*

*Rohini, my rock, whose love and encouragement light up every chapter of my life, motivating me to face challenges fearlessly and achieve greater heights.*

*Dr. Rajnish Kapoor and Mrs. Anita Kapoor, my guiding stars, whose blessings, encouragement, and sacrifices have shaped me into who I am today.*

*Manish and Shashi, my pillars of strength, whose presence brings joy and inspiration, motivating me in everything I do.*

*Himank, our little rockstar, whose infectious enthusiasm, curiosity, and laughter continue to brighten our lives. May this book inspire him to reach for the stars and embrace the joy of learning!*

*– Akshay Kapoor*

# Foreword

In the early stage of my career, I was part of a massive project to build a medical logistics software system. The team was big, and my role was multifaceted – application frameworks, security, messaging, you name it. But we were in a rut. Two years passed, and we still hadn't delivered anything to our end users. Why? We were chasing some abstract ideal of "perfect" but had no alignment with our customers' needs. The whole process was complicated – version control alone felt like solving a Rubik's Cube without instructions.

The *aha* moment came during an on-site installation. Cutting out the middleman, we got direct user feedback. That was the eureka moment. Feedback wasn't just something "nice to have"; it was the lifeblood of what we did. From that point on, my core principle has been to shorten the feedback loop between engineers and customers. The outcome was transformative; instead of a two-year feedback loop, I aimed to narrow it down to two months, two weeks, two days, two hours, and less – continually speeding up the process for better software.

Then came 2008 and my introduction to AWS. This was a paradigm shift wrapped in an API call. The exhilaration was palpable. So much so that I had to share it right then and there – I pulled a colleague into my cubicle, and we went from zero to a running Linux instance in five minutes flat. Compared to the old-world slog of six-week lead times and red-tape marathons, this was a seismic shift. AWS was not just another service; it was the cornerstone of a faster, more agile feedback loop.

Now, let's talk about DevOps. It's a term that gets thrown around a lot. What does it mean? Culture, process, tooling? It's all these things. According to AWS, DevOps is a combination of philosophies, practices, and tools that accelerate software delivery. In other words, it speeds things up and fosters a culture of continuous feedback.

So, when I see Akshay orchestrating a foundation grounded in this "continuous feedback" ethos in *AWS DevOps Simplified*, it's more than just gratifying. It's vindicating. He doesn't stop at DevOps principles; he dives into tactical execution, offering a treasure trove of hands-on examples and best practices that can be deployed, well, continuously.

*Paul M. Duvall*

*Director at AWS and author of the Jolt Award-winning book Continuous Integration: Improving Software Quality and Reducing Risk*

# Contributors

## About the author

**Akshay Kapoor** is a software engineer and cloud architect with over a decade of experience in delivering simple solutions for intricate business challenges. He's a continuous learner and loves to share his knowledge. From start-ups to big companies, Akshay understands how tech teams work and how to boost their progress with the innovative use of DevOps and the cloud. At **Amazon Web Services** (**AWS**), he partners with enterprises as a trusted advisor, crafting inventive solutions using AWS services that connect technical strategies with business goals.

He is based in Munich, Germany, and holds a master's degree in computer applications from Thapar University, India. Akshay can be reached on LinkedIn at `https://www.linkedin.com/in/akskap/`.

*I want to thank my wife, Rohini, for her unwavering support throughout the lengthy process of authoring this book; my parents, for instilling in me the values and strength that have shaped this journey; and Manish and Shashi, for their constant motivation and guidance in all endeavors.*

*Thanks to the entire team at Packt for their help and support throughout the process, and the reviewers for their valuable suggestions and feedback.*

## About the reviewers

**Alexander (Melnyk) Schüren**, as a senior solutions architect at AWS, works with customers across all sectors and sizes to modernize and build new applications on AWS. With deep knowledge and expertise in distributed systems, cloud computing, and software development practices, he enables customers to get the best out of the cloud, gain new perspectives, and understand the architectural trade-offs in day-to-day IT.

**Sri Laguduva** is an AWS fanatic and experienced DevOps engineer with a background in business administration and project management. He focuses on automating DevOps with testing, security, and business alignment, resulting in robust solutions for start-ups. He believes in the power of automation for developers and implements the shift-left concept for testing, security, and DevOps. He possesses quick learning skills and the ability to adapt to new tech early, and recently added AI and ML to his DevOps portfolio. Sri is a serial entrepreneur with a start-up connecting customers and service providers in niche sectors, such as the religious and spiritual space. Using Flutter, he has built apps such as SuitApp and Next on Plate and has a constant drive to innovate and explore new horizons in the realm of technology.

*I would like to express my heartfelt gratitude to all those who have contributed to the creation of AWS DevOps Simplified. Special thanks to the author and the dedicated team of editors and reviewers who have put their expertise and effort into making this book a valuable resource. Additionally, I would like to acknowledge the support of my family as I was reviewing this book. I wish all the very best to the author and hope this book is a great success.*

# Table of Contents

Preface — xv

# Part 1: Driving Transformation through AWS and DevOps

## 1

## Accelerating Your DevOps Journey with AWS — 3

| | | | |
|---|---|---|---|
| AWS and DevOps – a perfect match | 4 | CI | 14 |
| Production-like environments | 4 | CD and continuous deployment | 16 |
| Scaling with the cloud | 9 | IaC | 17 |
| DevOps methodologies to accelerate software delivery | 13 | Summary | 17 |
| | | Further reading | 18 |
| Key AWS DevOps services | 14 | | |

## 2

## Choosing the Right Cloud Service — 19

| | | | |
|---|---|---|---|
| The three tiers of cloud offerings | 20 | Understanding your organization's cloud operating model | 24 |
| Infrastructure as a Service (IaaS) | 20 | Focusing on sustaining workloads with the traditional approach | 24 |
| Platform as a Service (PaaS) | 21 | | |
| Software as a Service (SaaS) | 21 | | |
| | | Focusing on optimizing workloads | 24 |
| What to choose when | 22 | Focusing on growth in the cloud | 28 |
| Simplicity versus control | 22 | Key AWS services | 31 |
| Cloud skills and resources | 23 | Abstracting the infrastructure | 31 |
| Business requirements | 23 | Accelerating software delivery with plattform services | 32 |
| Security considerations | 23 | | |

| | | | |
|---|---|---|---|
| Fully managed software services | 32 | Summary | 33 |
| | | Further reading | 33 |

# 3

## Leveraging Immutable Infrastructure in the Cloud — 35

| | | | |
|---|---|---|---|
| Technical requirements | 36 | Navigating your Cloud9 environment | 46 |
| Pets versus cattle | 36 | Working with the test application | 47 |
| Mutable and immutable infrastructure | 37 | Test application | 48 |
| Mutable infrastructure | 38 | Building an AMI with Packer | 49 |
| Immutable infrastructure | 39 | Deploying our test instance | 52 |
| Getting started with AWS | 40 | Securing incoming traffic with security groups | 52 |
| Creating a new AWS account | 41 | Creating the test EC2 instance | 53 |
| Securing your root user credentials | 42 | Terminating the test EC2 instance | 54 |
| Creating additional users | 43 | Summary | 55 |
| Setting up an AWS Cloud9 IDE in your AWS account | 44 | Further reading | 55 |

# Part 2: Faster Software Delivery with Consistent and Reproducible Environments

# 4

## Managing Infrastructure as Code with AWS CloudFormation — 59

| | | | |
|---|---|---|---|
| Technical requirements | 60 | Best practices for using CloudFormation to define enterprise-grade architectures | 68 |
| What is AWS CloudFormation? | 60 | | |
| Key concepts in AWS CloudFormation | 60 | | |
| How CloudFormation works | 64 | Keep templates small and reusable | 68 |
| Permissions delegation for resource management | 65 | Leverage inputs and outputs for cross-stack dependencies | 68 |
| API call logging with CloudTrail | 65 | Leverage other service integrations | 69 |
| How requests flow over the network | 67 | Leverage StackSets for organization-wide stack rollouts | 69 |
| | | Avoid hardcoding parameter values | 69 |
| | | Life cycle policies to protect critical resources | 69 |

| | | | |
|---|---|---|---|
| Reusable resource configurations | 70 | Modules for code reusability | 72 |

## Deciding between Terraform and CloudFormation — 70

| | | | |
|---|---|---|---|
| Third-party provider ecosystem | 70 |
| Mapping a resource definition with a deployment | 71 |
| Support for programming constructs | 71 |
| State management for deployed resources | 71 |
| Better integrations offered by cloud-native services | 71 |

## Hands-on deployment with CloudFormation — 72

| | |
|---|---|
| Network architecture design to support multi-AZ deployments | 73 |
| Hosting a sample web application with an application load balancer and Auto Scaling groups | 81 |

| | |
|---|---|
| Summary | 86 |
| Further reading | 87 |

# 5

# Rolling Out a CI/CD Pipeline — 89

## What is CI/CD? — 90

| | |
|---|---|
| How does CI/CD enable faster software delivery? | 91 |
| Why is continuous deployment hard to implement? | 91 |
| An effective branching strategy is key | 91 |
| Working with feature toggles | 92 |
| Identifying what works best for you | 92 |

## How to choose the best CI/CD solution for your needs — 92

| | |
|---|---|
| Integration with existing tools | 92 |
| On-premises hosting considerations | 93 |
| Open source or commercial offerings? | 93 |

## Enabling continuous integration with CodeCommit and CodeBuild — 93

| | |
|---|---|
| Key features offered by CodeCommit | 94 |
| Automating builds and tests with CodeBuild | 95 |

## Using CodeDeploy to orchestrate deployment workflows in compute environments — 98

| | |
|---|---|
| Key components in CodeDeploy | 98 |
| Key features offered by CodeDeploy | 99 |

## Implementing end-to-end software delivery with CodePipeline — 100

| | |
|---|---|
| Key constructs used by CodePipeline | 101 |
| Triggering actions in other regions | 103 |

## Rolling out a fully automated CI/CD pipeline in your AWS account — 103

| | |
|---|---|
| Creating a base AMI for the application instances | 105 |
| Deploying infrastructure and application stacks | 107 |

| | |
|---|---|
| Summary | 112 |
| Further reading | 113 |

# 6

## Programmatic Approach to IaC with AWS CDK    115

| | | | |
|---|---|---|---|
| Different approaches to managing infrastructure in AWS | 116 | Understanding the different components of the image recognition application | 124 |
| Manual infrastructure management | 116 | Bootstrapping a new CDK project | 125 |
| Automating infrastructure rollouts with scripts | 117 | Bootstrapping the AWS account to enable CDK deployments | 127 |
| Adopting a declarative approach | 117 | Defining CDK constructs for application components | 127 |
| Using infrastructure definition generators | 118 | | |
| Using frameworks that offer high-level abstractions | 119 | Defining Lambda code for orchestrating the application workflow | 130 |
| What is AWS CDK? | 120 | Synthesizing the template | 132 |
| Key concepts in CDK | 121 | Deploying the CDK stack into an AWS account | 133 |
| Development workflow | 122 | Testing the image analysis workflow | 134 |
| Pros and cons of working with CDK | 122 | Summary | 136 |
| Deploying a test application with AWS CDK | 123 | Further reading | 137 |

# Part 3: Security and Observability of Containerized Workloads

# 7

## Running Containers in AWS    141

| | | | |
|---|---|---|---|
| A quick introduction to the container ecosystem | 142 | AWS Elastic Kubernetes Service (EKS) | 146 |
| | | AWS Elastic Container Service (ECS) | 146 |
| What are containers and why do we need them? | 142 | ECS constructs and security features | 147 |
| Docker as a container platform | 143 | Important constructs used by ECS | 147 |
| Scaling containerized deployments beyond simple use cases | 144 | Ensuring a good security posture with ECS | 149 |
| Key responsibilities of container platforms | 145 | Deploying a test application on ECS | 150 |
| AWS services that support running containers in the cloud | 146 | Understanding the test application architecture | 150 |
| | | Defining the CDK stack constructs | 154 |
| | | Preparing the web application code | 159 |
| AWS Elastic Compute Cloud (EC2) | 146 | Preparing the static HTML template | 161 |

| | | | |
|---|---|---|---|
| Bundling all application dependencies together for deployment on ECS | 162 | Summary | 164 |
| Deploying our CDK stack in an AWS account | 162 | Further reading | 165 |

# 8

## Enabling the Observability of Your Workloads  167

| | | | |
|---|---|---|---|
| What is observability? | 168 | Ensure that all components of your system emit events | 175 |
| Benefits of observability | 169 | | |
| Key AWS offerings for monitoring and observability | 170 | Defining your observability strategy for workloads hosted in AWS | 176 |
| Amazon CloudWatch | 170 | Deploying an observability stack for a test application hosted in ECS | 176 |
| Best practices for a solid observability strategy | 172 | Extending the code base for better observability | 178 |
| Build a hierarchy of dashboards | 172 | Deploying the stack in an AWS account | 183 |
| Use consistent time zones across all systems | 174 | Observing data to understand application behavior | 189 |
| Propagate trace identifiers | 174 | Summary | 192 |
| | | Further reading | 193 |

# 9

## Implementing DevSecOps with AWS  195

| | | | |
|---|---|---|---|
| Trade-offs and challenges of security | 197 | Security challenges for operating workloads in the cloud | 203 |
| Lack of ownership | 197 | Test strategies for your AWS workloads | 205 |
| Last step in software delivery | 197 | Important tools for security assessments | 208 |
| The rapid evolution of application architectures | 198 | | |
| Outdated security tools | 198 | Rolling out a test CI/CD workflow for DevSecOps | 209 |
| What is DevSecOps? | 198 | Understanding the target architecture of the DevSecOps pipeline | 210 |
| How is it different from DevOps? | 199 | | |
| Key benefits of DevSecOps | 199 | Understanding the code base | 212 |
| What it means for security professionals | 201 | Deploying the CDK stack in an AWS account | 212 |
| What it means for developers | 202 | Checking the result of security assessments | 214 |
| What it means for the operations team | 202 | Summary | 219 |
| Securing your workloads in AWS | 202 | Further reading | 220 |

# Part 4: Taking the Next Steps

## 10

## Setting Up Teams for Success 223

| | | | |
|---|---|---|---|
| **Building a collaborative team setup and culture** | **224** | Invest in building abstractions that promote best practices | 232 |
| Enable your teams to create more value | 224 | Making injection of failure scenarios a routine practice | 232 |
| Establishing a culture of collaboration and learning | 227 | Aligning technology decisions with business expectations | 233 |
| Measuring the DevOps maturity of your teams | 228 | **Resources for continuous learning and enablement** | **234** |
| De-silo Dev and Ops | 230 | **Driving change from the bottom up** | **235** |
| Blameless post-mortems and RCAs | 231 | Structure your ideas well | 235 |
| **Technology best practices and considerations for success** | **231** | Demonstrate commitment | 235 |
| Right-size the teams based on the technology cognitive load they can handle | 231 | Find collaborators and share good practices | 235 |
| | | **Summary** | **236** |
| | | **Further reading** | **236** |

## 11

## Ensuring a Strong AWS Foundation for Multi-Account and Multi-Region Environments 237

| | | | |
|---|---|---|---|
| **What is a Landing Zone?** | **238** | **Best practices for managing multi-account architectures** | **247** |
| **Key considerations in a Landing Zone** | **241** | Limiting access to the management account | 247 |
| Defining a structure for organizational units and accounts | 241 | Adopting solutions that offer the right balance of ease and control | 248 |
| Focus on cross-account and hybrid networking needs | 245 | Invest in building an Account Vending Machine | 248 |
| Securing the Landing Zone with IAM and security services | 245 | Maintain a separate AWS Organizations organization for platform development | 249 |
| DevOps and config management | 246 | Avoid provisioning any IAM users | 249 |
| Operations | 247 | Prefer no-code or low-code solutions | 250 |

| | | | |
|---|---|---|---|
| Building a Landing Zone with Control Tower and CfCT | 250 | Summary | 255 |
| | | Further reading | 256 |
| Deploying resources with CfCT | 253 | | |

# 12

## Adhering to AWS Well-Architected Principles 257

| | | | |
|---|---|---|---|
| Understanding different components of AWS Well-Architected | 258 | infrastructure and workloads | 263 |
| | | Building resilient and highly available systems | 266 |
| The AWS Well-Architected Framework | 259 | Improving the performance efficiency of your workloads | 269 |
| AWS Well-Architected lenses | 259 | | |
| The AWS Well-Architected Tool | 260 | Minimizing cloud costs while maximizing business value creation | 272 |
| Aligning your architecture with the six focus pillars of the framework | 260 | Building sustainable workloads in the cloud | 274 |
| Operating your workloads with confidence | 260 | Summary | 275 |
| Enhancing the security posture of | | Further reading | 275 |

## Index 277

## Other Books You May Enjoy 290

# Preface

In the realm of technology, a huge shift has occurred in recent years that has reshaped the way businesses operate. Cloud computing, spearheaded by **Amazon Web Services** (**AWS**), has revolutionized the very foundations of IT infrastructure, offering an elastic, on-demand platform for hosting modern software workloads in a cost-efficient and reliable manner. Concurrently, the rise of **DevOps** practices has transformed how security, operations, and software development teams collaborate, aiming for maximum speed, agility, and continuous improvement.

An interconnected web of compute resources spanning the globe and a virtual environment that can be tailored to meet the precise needs of any project is a wonderful world that AWS has brought to life. But the journey to the cloud isn't solely about technology; it's also about the transformative mindset that accompanies this shift. And that's where DevOps comes in. To be successful, organizations must adopt DevOps principles that *align* with cloud-native environments, enabling them to deliver high quality software faster and respond swiftly to market changes.

In this book, we will understand the ways in which AWS and DevOps harmoniously intersect and will delve into the tools, techniques, and mindsets that drive success in both worlds. I believe the best way to comprehend something is to engage with it firsthand; so, the chapters introduce a topic and gradually transition from theory to practice, with each section taking you closer to a solution deployed in your AWS account. The hands-on exercises have been carefully crafted to align with real-life enterprise use cases. You can extend these solutions further, depending on your interests or the needs of your organization.

As we progress through the chapters, I will share my experiences of working with organizations at different stages of their transformation journey, and how AWS and DevOps have helped them during this transition.

So, whether you are a seasoned IT professional seeking to master the cloud or a developer who is eager to reshape the software delivery life cycle, this book is your guide to leveraging the boundless potential that awaits at the intersection of AWS and DevOps.

*Let's dive in!*

## Who this book is for

This book is designed for a diverse range of individuals. Whether you're a seasoned DevOps leader driving AWS adoption, a developer optimizing software delivery, an ops specialist improving software reliability, or a cloud engineering leader, this book has something to offer:

- **Cloud engineering leaders driving transformations through the innovative use of AWS**: The book empowers you with insights to make crucial decisions when hosting workloads on AWS.

You will learn how to select the optimal AWS service tiers, foster cultural shifts with DevOps, set up teams for success, and explore AWS offerings that help derive technical metrics from business KPIs as well as measure them.

- **Software developers and operations specialists**: The book covers essential AWS services to reliably host your software in the cloud and deploy changes in an iterative manner, across multiple AWS accounts and Regions. You will get hands-on with ready-to-use solutions focusing on containers, infrastructure automation, DevSecOps, and observability. You will learn by doing, and evolve solutions to meet personal or organizational needs.

- **DevOps practitioners delving into the AWS world**: The book covers vital AWS services and how they synergize with key DevOps and DevSecOps practices in modern software development. You will dive into the cultural aspects and foundations of team structures that help maintain the same level of agility in the cloud.

## What this book covers

*Chapter 1, Accelerating Your DevOps Journey with AWS*, emphasizes the importance of digital transformation and how DevOps and AWS play a role in this transition. With two examples from the author's own experience, the chapter covers key learnings from each instance and focuses on the need for customer-centricity and prioritizing business outcomes over technology.

*Chapter 2, Choosing the Right Cloud Service*, covers the three service tiers offered by AWS: IaaS, PaaS, and SaaS. Starting with a basic understanding of all three, it delves into the trade-offs between simplicity and control, and the application of these tiers in specific organizational situations. With two real-life examples, it covers the benefits that software teams reap by adopting one of the tiers.

*Chapter 3, Leveraging Immutable Infrastructure in the Cloud*, highlights the importance of infrastructure immutability in the AWS realm and demonstrates how to boost software reliability with a hands-on deployment covering HashiCorp's Packer tool. Most importantly, this chapter unveils an AWS Cloud9 IDE-based toolbox to deploy the hands-on exercises covered throughout the book and serves as an introduction to AWS for new users while learning about security best practices.

*Chapter 4, Managing Infrastructure as Code with AWS CloudFormation*, delves into the benefits of **infrastructure as code** (**IaC**) automation using AWS CloudFormation. After explaining key service constructs, the chapter moves on to good enterprise design strategies for IaC and compares the service with Terraform, another famous infrastructure automation tool from HashiCorp.

*Chapter 5, Rolling Out a CI/CD Pipeline*, lays the foundations for a robust software delivery life cycle backed by **Continuous Integration and Continuous Delivery** (**CI/CD**) practices. It covers typical enterprise challenges in adopting continuous deployment methodologies and suggests some strategies to solve them. Before concluding with a fully automated application delivery pipeline deployment, the chapter covers the integrations offered by all AWS services in the CI/CD space and how to leverage them for maximized benefits.

*Chapter 6*, *Programmatic Approach to IaC with AWS CDK*, introduces different approaches and tools to manage infrastructure resources in AWS, and where AWS CDK fits in. It contrasts the service with other offerings, such as Pulumi and troposphere, and demonstrates the simplicity of spinning up an image recognition application, entirely using CDK.

*Chapter 7*, *Running Containers in AWS*, establishes the relevance of containers and how they make the adherence to microservices patterns and Twelve-Factor design principles an inherent part of your software artifacts. Going deeper into the service constructs of Amazon ECS, an opinionated service, the chapter covers security best practices to ensure least-privileged access in your applications. It builds on the foundations of the previous chapter and leverages AWS CDK to roll out a to-do list manager application, running on containers.

*Chapter 8*, *Enabling the Observability of Your Workloads*, covers the key observability pillars – logs, metrics, and traces – and an approach to measuring and alerting on key health indicators of your workloads hosted in AWS. Through a hands-on example, it demonstrates the integration between AWS services and famous open source platforms – Prometheus and Grafana – as well as the best practices for a solid observability strategy in the cloud.

*Chapter 9*, *Implementing DevSecOps with AWS*, introduces a three-step approach to ensuring a good security posture for workloads hosted on AWS. By enabling you to deploy a CI/CD workflow for DevSecOps, it goes into the practical details of wrapping every stage of the software delivery life cycle with security scans, or in other words, shifting left. There is a heavy focus on leveraging the maturity of open source tools to uncover security risks through static and dynamic testing for the application code, along with the corresponding Dockerfile.

*Chapter 10*, *Setting Up Teams for Success*, identifies the importance of the coordinated integration of both people and technology for continued success. It provides practical tips for organizing your teams, establishing a culture of collaboration, and measuring the DevOps maturity of your organization. On the technology front, it identifies the benefits of building the right abstractions and reducing the cognitive load of developers. Toward the end, it suggests strategies for individuals to drive change from the bottom up.

*Chapter 11*, *Ensuring a Strong AWS Foundation for Multi-Account and Multi-Region Environments*, delves into the intricacies and best practices for managing multiple AWS accounts, a common challenge faced by enterprises. It introduces the concept of a landing zone and the several solutions, services, and deployment frameworks that can be used to build one. An approach leveraging the AWS Control Tower service and the **Customizations for Control Tower** (**CfCT**) framework covers the continued compliance and security of AWS accounts, while managing everything as code.

*Chapter 12*, *Adhering to AWS Well-Architected Principles*, emphasizes the importance of the six pillars of the AWS Well-Architected Framework and how you can use it to evolve your cloud workloads over time. It extends these learnings with best practices under each pillar and sample implementation scenarios for common enterprise use cases.

## To get the most out of this book

You will need to have a foundational knowledge of what DevOps is, combined with a basic understanding of the key AWS offerings – **Identity and Access Management (IAM)**, the AWS console, and the CLI. Ideally, you will have used AWS or another cloud provider in the past to deploy a sample application or a proof of concept, but it's not a hard requirement. The hands-on exercises additionally assume basic software engineering skills to comprehend the ready-to-deploy code available in the book's GitHub repository and work with tools such as `git`, familiarity with the Linux operating system, and a basic understanding of how the web works. To be able to deploy the hands-on exercises, you will require an active AWS subscription and an IAM user with administrator privileges.

| Software/hardware covered in the book | Operating system requirements |
| --- | --- |
| Amazon Web Services (AWS) | Accessed through a web browser (Google Chrome, Safari, Firefox, or Microsoft Edge) |
| Cloud9 IDE – deployed in your AWS account, hosted on a Linux-based server | Linux (managed by AWS) |
| AWS CDK, npm, git, Docker | Linux (pre-installed on the server that hosts the Cloud9 IDE in your AWS account) |

AWS Cloud9 is fully supported on recent versions of Google Chrome, Safari, Firefox, and Microsoft Edge. You will be using Cloud9 to deploy the hands-on exercises in your AWS account. If you are unable to access the service for some reason, please refer to the following link for troubleshooting information: `https://docs.aws.amazon.com/cloud9/latest/user-guide/troubleshooting.html`.

**If you are using the digital version of this book, we advise you to type the code yourself or access the code from the book's GitHub repository (a link is available in the next section). Doing so will help you avoid any potential errors related to the copying and pasting of code.**

## Download the example code files

You can download the example code files for this book from GitHub at `https://github.com/PacktPublishing/AWS-DevOps-Simplified`. If there's an update to the code, it will be updated in the GitHub repository.

We also have other code bundles from our rich catalog of books and videos available at `https://github.com/PacktPublishing/`. Check them out!

## Conventions used

There are a number of text conventions used throughout this book.

`Code in text`: Indicates code words in text, database table names, folder names, filenames, file extensions, pathnames, dummy URLs, user input, and Twitter handles. Here is an example: "Using the Terraform CLI, the developers were able to roll out the entire infrastructure stack using a single `terraform deploy` command."

A block of code is set as follows:

```
InstanceTargetGroup:
  Type: AWS::ElasticLoadBalancingV2::TargetGroup
  Properties:
    HealthCheckEnabled: true
    TargetType: instance
    Protocol: HTTP
    Port: 8080
    VpcId:
      Fn::ImportValue:
        'Fn::Sub': "${NetworkStackName}-vpc-id"}
```

When we wish to draw your attention to a particular part of a code block, the relevant lines or items are set in bold:

```
@app.post("/<id>/delete")
def delete(id):
    if (request.method == "POST"):
        logging.info('Deleting task represented by ID: \'%s\''
',ObjectId(id))
        todos_collection.delete_one({"_id": ObjectId(id)})
        return redirect(url_for('todos'))
```

Any command-line input or output is written as follows:

```
$ npm install
$ cdk synth
```

**Bold**: Indicates a new term, an important word, or words that you see onscreen. For instance, words in menus or dialog boxes appear in **bold**. Here is an example: "In the later chapters, we will learn about the relevant AWS services, such as CloudFormation and **Cloud Development Kit** (**CDK**)."

> **Tips or important notes**
> Appear like this.

## Get in touch

Feedback from our readers is always welcome.

**General feedback**: If you have questions about any aspect of this book, email us at `customercare@packtpub.com` and mention the book title in the subject of your message.

**Errata**: Although we have taken every care to ensure the accuracy of our content, mistakes do happen. If you have found a mistake in this book, we would be grateful if you would report this to us. Please visit `www.packtpub.com/support/errata` and fill in the form.

**Piracy**: If you come across any illegal copies of our works in any form on the internet, we would be grateful if you would provide us with the location address or website name. Please contact us at `copyright@packt.com` with a link to the material.

**If you are interested in becoming an author**: If there is a topic that you have expertise in and you are interested in either writing or contributing to a book, please visit `authors.packtpub.com`.

## Share Your Thoughts

Once you've read *AWS DevOps Simplified*, we'd love to hear your thoughts! Scan the QR code below to go straight to the Amazon review page for this book and share your feedback.

`https://packt.link/r/1837634467`

Your review is important to us and the tech community and will help us make sure we're delivering excellent quality content.

# Download a free PDF copy of this book

Thanks for purchasing this book!

Do you like to read on the go but are unable to carry your print books everywhere? Is your eBook purchase not compatible with the device of your choice?

Don't worry, now with every Packt book you get a DRM-free PDF version of that book at no cost.

Read anywhere, any place, on any device. Search, copy, and paste code from your favorite technical books directly into your application.

The perks don't stop there, you can get exclusive access to discounts, newsletters, and great free content in your inbox daily

Follow these simple steps to get the benefits:

1. Scan the QR code or visit the link below

```
https://packt.link/free-ebook/9781837634460
```

2. Submit your proof of purchase
3. That's it! We'll send your free PDF and other benefits to your email directly

# Part 1
# Driving Transformation through AWS and DevOps

This part underscores the essence of digital transformation and the pivotal roles played by DevOps and AWS. Through real-life examples, you will grasp the significance of customer-centricity and the success linked to focusing on business outcomes over technology. You will also learn about the different service tiers of AWS and how the cloud provider helps realize the benefits of infrastructure immutability. Finally, we'll guide you through setting up your AWS Cloud9 IDE, which enables the deployment of all hands-on exercises covered in this book, in your AWS account.

This part has the following chapters:

- *Chapter 1, Accelerating Your DevOps Journey with AWS*
- *Chapter 2, Choosing the Right Cloud Service*
- *Chapter 3, Leveraging Immutable Infrastructure in the Cloud*

# 1
# Accelerating Your DevOps Journey with AWS

**Digital transformation** is key to the success of any modern business that wants to deliver great products and delight its customers. It involves the integration of digital technologies and solutions across all areas of the organization. To be successful in this journey, the majority of organizations leverage software automation. This helps them stay ahead of their competition, innovate faster, and reduce the lead time to produce something valuable for the end user. However, just moving fast is not sufficient. Moving fast, and executing well, every single time is where the real magic happens.

**Amazon Web Services** (**AWS**) and **DevOps** are two such enablers that spearhead organizations with fast and controlled growth. They are representative of high-performing teams and agile cultures. Both are often misunderstood in different ways.

DevOps is a *human-centered approach* that aims at improving communication between people, while software and automation *contribute* to this goal. It aims at removing silos that block organizations from delivering software faster, and with increased quality. Adopting DevOps requires a change in culture and mindset. The core idea is to remove barriers between development and operations – the two traditionally siloed groups. By frequently communicating with each other, these take complete ownership of their deliverables, often going beyond the scope of their job titles. In some organizations, there might not be any difference between development and operations; they are just seen as one product team that owns the complete life cycle of the software – they build it, they run it.

AWS, on the other hand, is a public cloud provider that helps users get rid of *undifferentiated heavy lifting*. It provides managed services that help you focus on what you do best while it takes care of everything else. However, it is important to understand that the benefit you reap from these services will largely depend on how you use them and the level of AWS expertise within your organization. Some customers end up increasing their costs while others are able to reduce them. Some might make their application architectures more resilient than before, and others may not. In addition, people mostly view the cloud as a replacement for their on-premises IT landscape, but its real value can also be seen during seamless integration with your existing or future platforms. Sometimes, it just sits there, alongside your data centers, providing you with core differentiating capabilities.

To keep it short, DevOps is not just about automation and tools; DevOps is not just about the cloud. There's a lot more to it. But if you are a software professional, using AWS anyway, and want to accelerate your DevOps adoption, this book is for you. We want you to be successful in accelerating your software delivery by using AWS. The intent is not to have answers to all the problems you will ever face, but rather to ensure a strong foundational understanding and strategy that you can apply to a variety of problems on AWS, now and in the future.

In this chapter, we will go through some practical solution implementations and DevOps methodologies and will discuss how AWS fits into the overall picture.

The main topics in this chapter are the following:

- AWS and DevOps – a perfect match
- Key AWS DevOps services

## AWS and DevOps – a perfect match

Gartner's **Cloud Infrastructure and Platform Services** (**CIPS**) Magic Quadrant report (`https://www.gartner.com/doc/reprints?id=1-2AOZQAQL&ct=220728`) positioned AWS as a leader in both their metrics – *Ability to Execute* and *Completeness of Vision*. This speaks volumes about the reliability of the platform in hosting your mission-critical workloads that can adapt to changing customer demands. DevOps methodologies complement this with time-tested ways of working that have a positive impact on the overall IT service delivery.

However, let's not sugar coat this – efficiently operating your enterprise-grade software environments on AWS can be challenging. The cloud provider has been expanding the list of services offered from the beginning. Your usage, implementation, and solid future strategy will be key.

Even before we dive into anything regarding AWS or DevOps, let's first go through some real-life examples, covering aspects that are relevant to any software professional. The idea here is to discuss a few approaches that have helped me over many years of maintaining or writing software. I hope these topics are useful for you as well.

### Production-like environments

While working as a DevOps specialist a few years ago, I was tasked with helping developers in my team to ship features faster. Upon understanding the challenges they faced in the huge monolithic LAMP stack (Linux, Apache, MySQL, and PHP) application, MySQL surfaced as a common pain point across the board. The continuously increasing size of these on-premises production databases (1 TB+) meant that the developers were frequently unaware of the challenges the application would face in the live environment when the production load kicked in. The application (warehouse management system) was used across several countries in Europe, with each country having its own dedicated MySQL instance and read replicas. Every minute of downtime or system degradation directly impacted shipping, packaging, and order invoicing. During that time, the developers were using local MySQL instances to develop and test new features and would later ship them off to staging, followed by production rollout.

With the problem statement clear, a promising next step was to enable them to develop and test in *production-like* environments. This would allow them to see how their systems were reacting to evolving customer usage, and to have a better understanding of the production issues at an earlier stage.

With a strong understanding of Bash scripting (…or at least I thought so) and basic MySQL administration skills, I decided to build shell scripts that could prepare these testbed environments, and refresh them with the most recent production data, on a daily basis. A request for a similar number of new MySQL servers was raised with the on-premises infrastructure team. They provisioned them in a week, set up the operating system, and required libraries for MySQL, before handing over to me my *newly acquired liability*. Moving forward, all maintenance and upkeep of these servers were my responsibility. I later scheduled cronjobs on all these servers to run the scripts created previously. They would perform the following steps at a pre-configured time of the day:

1. Copy the previous day's production backups from the fileserver to the local filesystem.
2. Remove all existing data in the local MySQL database.
3. Dump the new backup data into the local MySQL database.
4. Perform data anonymization and remove certain other confidential tables.

You can see how the different entities communicated in the following figure:

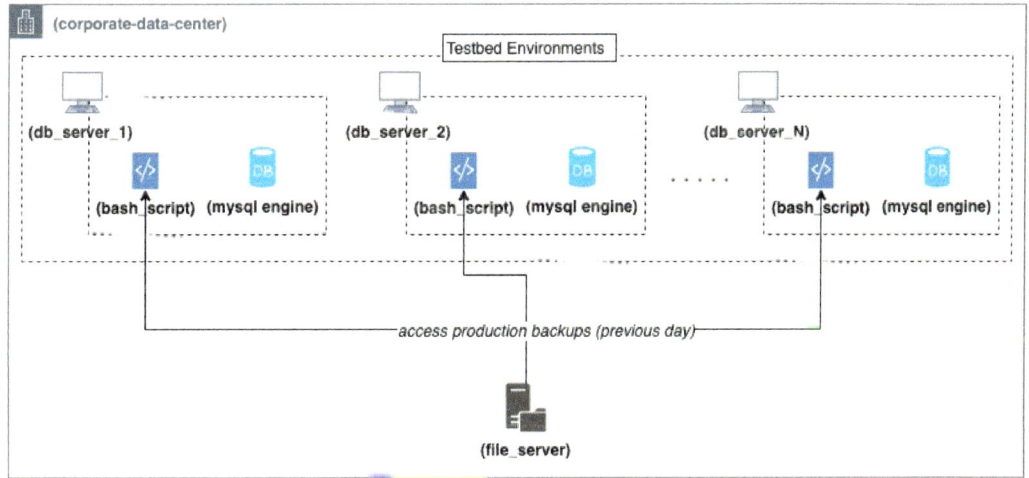

Figure 1.1: Bash scripts to manage database operations

The following day, the developers had recent production replicas available at their disposal, anonymized for development and testing. This was a huge step forward and the developers were excited about this as they were now developing and testing against environments that matched production-level scale and complexity. The excitement, however, was soon overshadowed by new issues. What happens if a particular cronjob execution does not terminate successfully? What if database import takes forever? What if fileservers are not responding? What if the local storage disk is full?

How about a parent orchestrator script that manages all these edge cases? Brilliant idea! I spent the next few days building an orchestrator layer that coordinated the execution of all these scripts. It was not too long before I had a new set of Bash scripting problems to solve: tracking child process executions, exception handling, graceful cleanups, handling kernel signals…the list goes on. Doing all this in Bash was a Herculean task. What started as a simple set of scripts now evolved into a framework that required a lot of investment in time and effort.

Days and weeks passed, and the framework kept evolving. Bugs were identified. New feature requests from the developers were implemented. The framework now had a fancy new name: **Bicycle** – *end-to-end life cycle management for Bash scripts*. Finally, after two months, a YAML config-driven Bash framework came into being that sent error notifications on Slack, executed report attachments via email, orchestrated and measured the entire flow of operations, and was generic enough to be adopted by other teams easily. This was not solely for managing database operations, but rather any collection of Bash scripts put together to accomplish a task, as you can see in *Figure 1.2*:

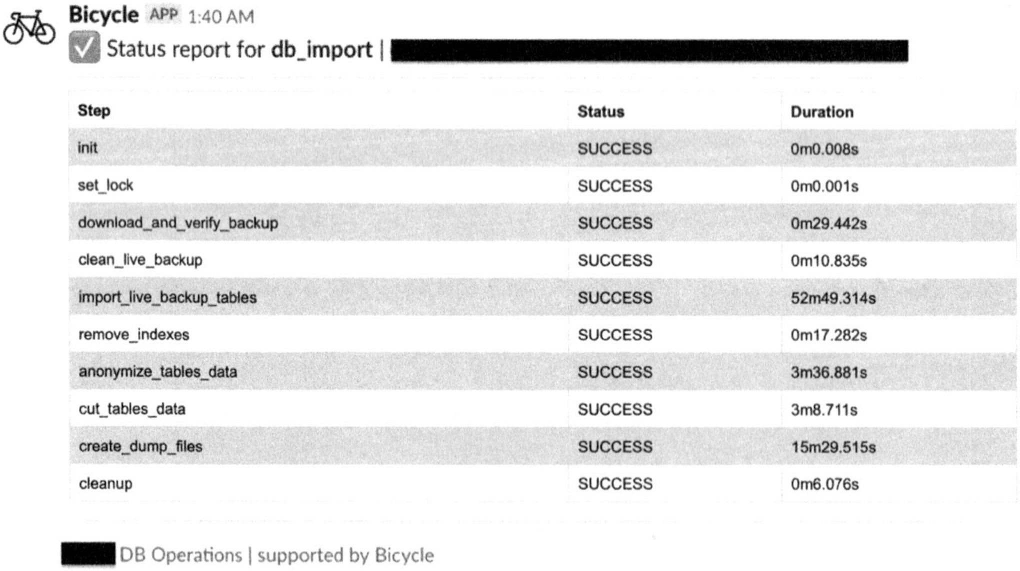

**Bicycle** APP 1:40 AM
✅ Status report for **db_import** |

| Step | Status | Duration |
| --- | --- | --- |
| init | SUCCESS | 0m0.008s |
| set_lock | SUCCESS | 0m0.001s |
| download_and_verify_backup | SUCCESS | 0m29.442s |
| clean_live_backup | SUCCESS | 0m10.835s |
| import_live_backup_tables | SUCCESS | 52m49.314s |
| remove_indexes | SUCCESS | 0m17.282s |
| anonymize_tables_data | SUCCESS | 3m36.881s |
| cut_tables_data | SUCCESS | 3m8.711s |
| create_dump_files | SUCCESS | 15m29.515s |
| cleanup | SUCCESS | 0m6.076s |

▇ DB Operations | supported by Bicycle

Figure 1.2: Bicycle framework – managing the life cycle of Bash scripts

The framework served the team well for two to three weeks and then the next wave of challenges became evident:

- Data import time was increasing exponentially. To execute parallel MySQL threads, I needed more compute power – so, another request to the infrastructure team was needed.
- High I/O operations required more performant disks. To upgrade these, the infrastructure team had to raise a new purchase order and install new SSDs.
- Developers now wanted the capability to be able to maintain the latest $X$ versions of the backups. Where should these be stored?

As you might have noticed already, the framework had matured considerably, but it was as good as the availability, scalability, and reliability of the underlying infrastructure. With underpowered machines, disk capacity issues, and frequent network timeouts, there was only so much the framework could do.

What started as an initiative to increase development velocity soon transitioned into a technology-focused framework. *Were there some technical learnings from this exercise?* A lot. In fact, there were so many that I wrote a *Best Practices for Bash Scripts* blog afterward, which can be found at `https://medium.com/p/17229889774d`. Did it resolve all the problems the developers were facing? Probably not. Before embarking on these lengthy development cycles and going down the rabbit hole of solving technical problems, it would have been better to build a little, test a little, and always challenge myself with the question, *Is this what my customers really need?*

## Knowing your customers (and their future needs)

It's of paramount importance to know the end beneficiary of your work. You will always have a *customer* – internal, external, or both. If you are not clear about it, I would strongly recommend discussing this with your manager or colleagues to understand for whom the solution is being built. It's essential to put yourself in your customer's shoes and approach the problems and solutions from their perspective. Always ask yourself whether what you are doing will address your customers' issues and delight them. It took me at least two or three months to bring the Bash framework up to the desired level of performance and utility. However, a Bash script orchestrator was not something my customers (developers) required. They needed a simple, scalable, and reliable mechanism to reproduce production-like databases. In fact, operating this framework was an additional overhead for them. It was not helping them with what they did best – writing code and delivering business outcomes.

## Focusing on iterative development and failing fast

Another prerequisite for delivering impactful customer solutions is to establish an iterative working model: deliver work into manageable pieces, monitor the success metrics, and establish a feedback mechanism to validate progress. Applying this to the aforementioned situation would have meant that developers had complete visibility of the implementation from the beginning. Collaborating together, we could have defined the success criteria (time to provision production database replicas) at the very start of the process.

This is very similar to the trunk-based development approach used by high-performing software teams. They frequently merge small segments of working code in the main branch of the repository, which greatly improves visibility and highlights problems more quickly.

### Prioritizing business outcomes over technology

As an IT professional, it is very easy to have tunnel vision, whereby the entire focus is on technical implementations. Establishing feedback mechanisms to ensure that the business outcomes are met will avoid such situations and will help with effective team communications while accelerating delivery. This is what DevOps is all about.

### Offering solutions as a service

It is important to take the *cognitive load* off of your customers and offer them services that are operationally light, are easy to consume, and require little to no intervention. This enables them to focus on their core job, without worrying about any add-on responsibilities.

Offering well-documented and easy-to-consume interfaces (or APIs) would have been far easier for the developers in my team rather than onboarding them to learn how to use the custom-built Bash framework. What they really needed was an easy method to provision production-like databases. Exposing them to underlying infrastructure scalability issues and Bash internals was an unnecessary cognitive load that ideally should have been avoided.

Similarly, the on-premises infrastructure team's focus on their *customer* (myself) could have eased my job of requesting new infrastructure resources, without having to go through all the logistics and endure a long wait until something tangible was ready for use.

This is an area AWS excels in. It reduces the cognitive load for the end user and enables them to deliver business outcomes, instead of focusing on the underlying technology. The customer *consumes* the services and has less to worry about when it comes to the availability, scalability, and reliability of the service, as well as the underlying infrastructure. It offers these services in the form of APIs with which the developers can interact, using the tools of their choice.

### Mapping the solution components to the AWS services

One exercise that will often help you when working with AWS is designing your solution, identifying key components, and then evaluating whether some of these un-differentiated tasks can be offloaded to AWS services. It's good practice to compare these choices and to conduct a cost-benefit analysis before adopting the services immediately. Let's dive quickly into the main components of the database replicas' example discussed in the *Production-like environments* section previously, and consider whether AWS services could have been an option to avoid reinventing the wheel:

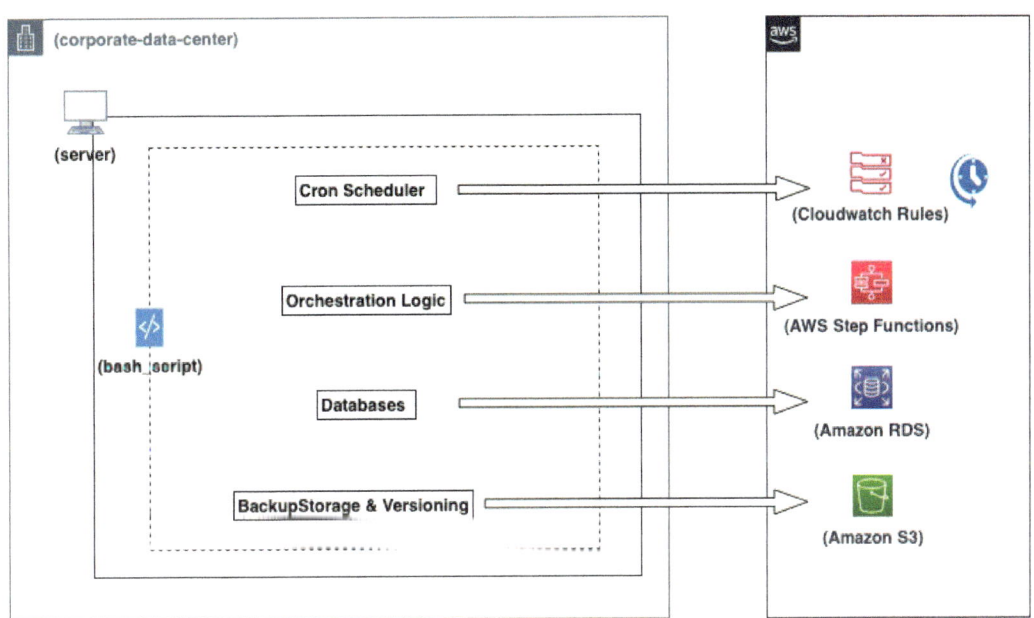

Figure 1.3: Mapping Bash framework components to AWS services

From a timeline perspective, building the entire stack from scratch, as seen in *Figure 1.3*, took around three months, but you can provision similar services in your AWS account in less than three hours. That's the level of impact AWS can have in your DevOps journey. In addition, it's important to understand that you need not go all-in on AWS. If Amazon S3 (data storage and retrieval service) is all that was needed, then retaining the other components on-premises and using AWS as an extension of the solution could also be considered as an approach for solving the problems at hand.

To summarize, understand your needs, evaluate the benefits provided by AWS services, and adopt only what helps you in the long run.

Now, let's discuss another instance in which I helped the same developers scale their continuous integration activities with **GitLab Continuous Integration and Continuous Deliver**, but this time, with AWS. If you have not been exposed to these terms before, continuous integration is a practice that automates the integration of code changes from multiple developers into a single project, and GitLab is a software development platform that helps with the adoption of DevOps practices.

## Scaling with the cloud

The GitLab Continuous Integration and Continuous Delivery suite helps software teams to collaborate better and frequently deploy small manageable chunks of code into production environments. My company at that time was using a self-hosted, on-premises version of GitLab Continuous Integration and Continuous Delivery.

There are three main architectural components of GitLab Continuous Integration and Continuous Delivery that are especially relevant to this discussion:

- **Control plane**: This is the layer that interacts with the end user, so APIs, web portals, and so on all fall into this category. This was owned and managed by the central infrastructure and operations team.
- **Runners**: Runners are the compute environments used by GitLab to run/execute the pipeline stages and the respective processes. As soon as developers commit code to their repository, a pipeline triggers and executes the pipeline stages in sequence by leveraging these compute resources. Due to the heterogeneous project requirements, each team owned and operated their own runners. Based on the technology stacks they worked with, they could decide which type of compute resources would best fit their needs. As a fallback mechanism, there was also a *shared pool* of GitLab runners, which could be used by teams. However, as you can imagine, these were not very reliable in terms of availability and spiky workloads. For example, if you need two cores of CPU and 1 GB RAM for your Java build immediately, the release of an urgent patch to production could be a challenge. Therefore, it was generally recommended to begin with these but to switch to custom-built, self-managed runners when needed.
- **Pipelines**: Lastly, if you have used **Jenkins** or **AWS CodePipeline** in the past, GitLab Pipelines are similar in terms of functionality. You can define different phases of your software delivery process in a YAML file, commit it alongside your code, and let GitLab manage your software delivery from there on.

At that time, I was supporting five to six software projects for the developers of my team. Having started with the shared pool of GitLab runners hosted on-premises, we were able to leverage the compute resources for our needs, for roughly 80-120 builds per day. However, with increasing adoption throughout the company, the resources on these runners would frequently become exhausted, leading to several pipeline processes waiting for execution. Additionally, occasional VM failures meant that all software delivery processes dependent on these shared resources across the company would come to a halt. This was certainly not a good situation to be in. The central ops team added more resources to this shared pool, but this was still a static server farm, whereby my team's build jobs were dependent on how others used these resources.

Having learned from the issues relating to unscalable on-premises infrastructure during the database setup, as discussed previously, I decided to leverage AWS cloud capabilities this time. Discussions with the developers (customers) led to the definition of the following requirements, which were all fulfilled with AWS services out of the box:

- Flexibility to scale infrastructure up/down
- Usage monitoring for the runners in AWS
- Less operational work

Across the entire solution design, the only effort required from my side was the code to register/de-register these runners with the control plane when the compute instances were started or stopped.

The final design (see *Figure 1.4*) leveraged auto-scaling groups in AWS, which is a mechanism to dynamically scale up or trim down the compute resources depending on the usage patterns:

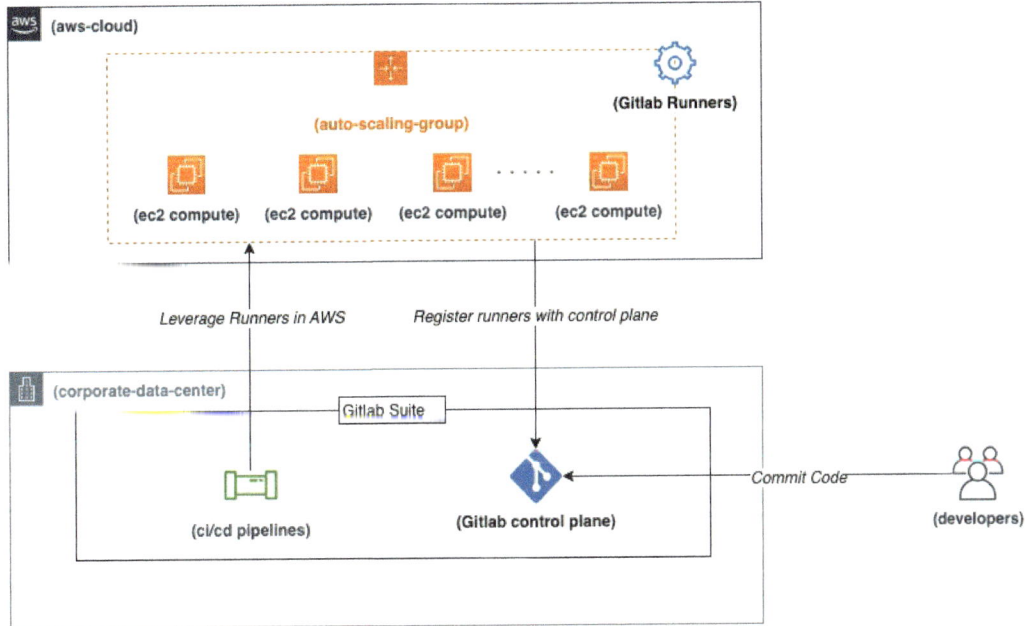

Figure 1.4: GitLab Continuous Integration and Continuous Delivery with runners hosted in AWS

As soon as the new servers were started, they registered themselves with the GitLab control plane.

## *Extending your on-premises IT landscape with AWS*

AWS cloud adoption need not always translate into shutting down data centers and migrating applications through a lift-and-shift approach. The real value lies in starting small, measuring impact, and utilizing cloud offerings as a natural extension to your on-premises IT landscape.

As seen in the previous scenario, the GitLab control plane still continued to remain in the on-premises data center, while the runners leveraged the elasticity of the cloud. This gave the developers immediate benefits in terms of compute selection, scalability, reliability, and elasticity of the cloud. Amazon EC2 is the Elastic Compute Cloud offering, which offers scalable computing capacity for virtual servers, security, networking, and storage. Combining this with the **EC2 Auto Scaling service**, I configured capacity thresholds that allowed us to maintain a default set of runners and scale, with the demand driven by real usage.

Infrastructure management in data centers usually lacks this level of flexibility unless there are interfaces or resource orchestrators made available to the end user for provisioning resources in an automated way.

## Collecting metrics for understanding resource usage

Requirements relating to measuring usage and alerting on thresholds were further simplified with the use of **Amazon CloudWatch**. CloudWatch is a metrics repository in which different AWS services and external applications publish usage data. EC2, like other services, makes data points such as CPU, memory, and storage consumption available, which helps to identify threshold breaches, resulting in the automation of scaling decisions.

Having access to these metrics out of the box is a considerable automation accelerator for two reasons. You need not invest any effort in capturing this data with third-party agents and the close-to-real-time nature of this data helps with dynamic decision-making. Furthermore, AWS also offers native integrations around alarms and service triggers with CloudWatch. So, extending these to usual notification mechanisms, such as email, SMS, or an external API, is generally a low-effort implementation.

## Paying for what you use

AWS offers a pay-as-you-go pricing model. In contrast to this, on-premises resources come with a fixed-priced costing model and require a lot of time and operational effort. Combining this with metrics from CloudWatch, it was possible to automatically scale down the EC2 compute resources during periods of low usage (after work hours and weekends). This further reduced AWS costs by ~20-30%.

Generally speaking, on-premises infrastructure resources are mostly over-provisioned. This is done to maintain an additional buffer of resources, should ad-hoc demand require it. AWS, on the other side, offers the capability to right-size all your resources based on your exact needs at the moment. This is a big win for agile teams to respond to changing customer demands and usage patterns.

## Simplifying service delivery through cloud abstractions

Software technology these days is all about abstractions. This is a topic that we will explore in more depth in *Chapter 2*, *Choosing the Right Cloud Service*. All AWS services abstract the complexity from the end users around operational aspects. As a result, end users are empowered to focus on the differentiating features and business outcomes. Earlier, we discussed the need to take the cognitive load off the developers. AWS makes this a reality, and you can develop proofs of concept, demos, and production-grade applications in hours or days, which previously took months.

## Leveraging the infrastructure elasticity of the cloud

AWS cloud benefits are not limited to procuring more resources when needed but are also about contracting when possible. Of course, this needs to align with the type of workload you plan to run in the cloud. Sometimes, there are known events that would require more resources to handle the increased load, such as festive sales and marketing initiatives. In other cases, when the usage spikes cannot be determined in advance, you can leverage AWS' auto-scaling capabilities, as we did for GitLab runners.

So far, we have discussed two solution implementations and how adopting cloud services gives a big boost to reliability and scalability, leading to better customer outcomes. Next, let's learn about some DevOps methodologies that help accelerate the software delivery process. We will later map these key areas to certain AWS services.

## DevOps methodologies to accelerate software delivery

As we discussed at the beginning of the chapter, successful organizations use software automation to catapult their digital transformation journey.

As highlighted in the 2022 State of DevOps Report by DORA (`https://cloud.google.com/devops/state-of-devops`), DevOps methodologies positively influence your team culture and foster engineering best practices to help you be able to ship software with increased velocity and better reliability. In software engineering, the following principles have been well established and are known to optimize the way teams work and collaborate.

### *Continuous integration*

**Continuous Integration** (**CI**) is a software engineering best practice that advocates the frequent merging of code from all software developers in a team to one central repository. This increases the confidence in and visibility of new features being released to the customers. At the same time, automated tests make releasing code multiple times a day seamless and easy. Developers also get quick feedback regarding any bugs that might have been introduced into the system as a result of implementing features in isolation.

### *Continuous delivery*

**Continuous Delivery** (**CD**) is the practice of producing code in short cycles that can be released to production at any time. Automatically deploying to a production-like environment is key here. Fast-moving software teams leverage CD to confidently roll out features or patches, on demand, with lightweight release processes.

### *Continuous deployment*

Continuous deployment enables teams to automatically release the code to production. This is indicative of high DevOps maturity and rock-solid automation practices. Using continuous deployment, code is automatically deployed to the production environments.

This requires deep integration into how the software stack functions. All ongoing operations and customer requests are automatically taken care of, and the release process is hardly noticeable to the end user.

In later chapters, we will go through some hands-on examples around CI/CD processes and use native AWS services to see things in action.

### Infrastructure as Code (IaC)

Managing AWS infrastructure components with code, using SDKs, APIs, and so on, makes it very convenient to reliably manage environments at scale. Unlike static provisioning methods used on-premises, these practices enable the creation of complete infrastructure stacks with the use of programmable workflows.

This also reduces the ownership silos across the development and operations teams. The developers are free to use familiar programming language constructs and have end-to-end control of the foundational infrastructural elements.

### Effective communication and collaboration

Collaboration between team members is crucial for faster software delivery. It is advisable to have small teams that share a common goal. Amazon uses the concept of the **Two-Pizza Team** rule, which suggests creating a workgroup that is no larger than one that can be fed by two pizzas, so roughly an 8-to-10-member team.

Furthermore, this enables the team to not just deliver software but own it end to end. Operations, deployment, support, and feature development are all owned by the members of this team.

Now, since we have a good understanding of key DevOps methodologies, let's dive into several AWS services that make this a reality in the cloud.

## Key AWS DevOps services

AWS offers managed services that cater to each of these principles. Depending on the organization's operating model, you can deploy these services in your AWS accounts and give autonomy to all team members to leverage the unlimited potential of the cloud.

Feature roadmaps of all these AWS services are strongly driven by customer feedback. This increases the likelihood of enterprise-grade usage patterns being supported out of the box. Imagine use cases such as automatic notifications and deployment triggers as soon as code is committed to a repository, for example. Let's have a deeper look into the variety of offerings that simplify your DevOps adoption in each of the key areas.

### CI

Git workflows are instrumental to the success of any software team. The way they commit code, the comments they use, and how they collaborate across feature requests say a lot about their engineering practices. High-performing teams also ensure quick automated feedback for every single commit that ends up in the central repository. AWS offers three key services to support such requirements.

## AWS CodeCommit

A simple explanation for this would be *Git as a Service*. Git is a distributed version control system that addresses the limitations of the previously used centralized model, such as SVN (Apache Subversion). AWS makes it easier for users to create, operate, and scale Git repositories for their software workloads. Traditionally, on-premises administrators used to provision and manage Git repositories on a self-hosted server. This had its challenges, but with AWS, you just focus on consuming the service for your collaboration needs and everything else is taken care of.

CodeCommit allows you to easily create branches, commit code, and create pull requests for review by your team members. With all AWS offerings, security is the highest priority, and CodeCommit is no different. By default, all data is encrypted at rest and secure transit mechanisms such as SSH and HTTPS are used for any access requirements. For the end user, nothing changes, as they still use the same tooling (the `git` CLI) to communicate with the service endpoints.

Like other services, it also publishes important metrics and events to CloudWatch, which can be used to build automation workflows. Let's check out just some events that might be interesting for your team's collaboration needs:

- Creation of pull requests
- Tracking comments on pull requests
- Pull request merge status changed
- Restriction of access to certain branches only for a set of users

## AWS CodeBuild

Soon after the code is committed to a repository, automated processes are triggered. These might be creating artifacts, running tests, or building container images. CodeBuild is a service that provides a lightweight and scalable execution environment in which certain operations can be performed on the recently committed code. You can configure your build environments with basic configuration details, such as CPU/memory resources and the commands you would like to run.

If you have configured and managed build servers on your own, you can imagine the benefit such managed services bring to the table. You are only charged for the duration for which the builds run, and the service scales automatically to process multiple parallel executions.

Finally, it can also store build artifacts, such as JAR files, executables, or even obfuscated JavaScript files, in locations such as Amazon S3.

### AWS CodeArtifact

This is the artifact repository where your compiled binaries, scripts, and executables can be stored for later consumption. This replaces the need for package managers, which teams generally manage on their own, although they sometimes opt for a remote-hosted offering. Out-of-the-box compatibility with PyPI, Maven, NPM, and so on makes it easy to store your artifacts directly in AWS.

We have just scratched the surface by discussing these services that enable CI. There is more to them, which will be covered in the following chapters.

Next, let's discuss delivery and deployment methodologies, which prepare or deploy builds for production usage.

## CD and continuous deployment

Successful implementations of CI practices allow for the automatic preparation of code release activities. High-performing teams typically automate an integration test suite while practicing CD and continuous deployment. They deploy the code in production-like environments, measure performance, load tests, and evaluate known edge cases before deploying in live environments.

The only difference between CD and continuous deployment is that the former does not automatically promote the artifact to production, and there is no need for rollbacks when failures are detected. Continuous delivery prepares a production-ready build, but the final deployment still requires human intervention. With the increasing maturity of tooling and automation, the teams at some stage start automatically rolling out code to production environments, which is continuous deployment. AWS offers two main services in these areas.

### AWS CodeDeploy

As the name suggests, this is a code deployment service. It provides support for a variety of compute offerings, such as EC2, AWS container services, and even on-premises machines. Furthermore, several deployment strategies control the rollout process for you and back it up with health checks that add to the visibility and reliability of code rollout procedures.

Depending on the application architecture and rollout methodology, one of the following could be used:

- **In-place deployments**: Update code in all instances in the application group followed by a service restart. The scope of change could be controlled by going all in at once or doing a controlled release.
- **Blue-green deployments**: An identical environment is set up and CodeDeploy deploys different versions in both, giving the end user the capability to switch the production traffic when possible and revert when issues are observed.
- **Canary deployments**: This is a deployment strategy in which new code is released in phases. For example, every few minutes, $X\%$ of the servers get the code upgrade, and this continues until a rollback is explicitly performed.

## AWS CodePipeline

CodePipeline is an orchestrator that works with all the services discussed previously. It manages the overall software delivery process and is responsible for invoking certain services, in the defined order.

Using YAML and JSON templates, you can code an automated procedure that can be used to reliably release software every single time. The service shines in terms of native integrations with many other services. This abstracts lots of internal details and lets you focus on application-specific details.

## IaC

With the ever-increasing complexity of software applications, infrastructure requirements have grown exponentially. Managing all these components manually is error prone and subject to human limitations. Using standard tools, SDKs, and APIs, AWS makes it easy to manage the entire IaC. It takes minutes to spin up and tear down infrastructure across an entire AWS region.

AWS offers SDKs in different programming languages such as Python, Go, Ruby, JavaScript, C++, and many more. Using familiar programming syntax, you can develop and operate your entire software stack using code. In the later chapters, we will learn about the relevant AWS services, such as CloudFormation and **Cloud Development Kit** (**CDK**).

## AWS CloudFormation

With JSON or YAML templates, users can define their entire infrastructure stacks and maintain them as code. CloudFormation allows them to build resource dependency graphs automatically and provision all services in the desired order. It further supports multi-region and multi-account rollouts, which is helpful for enterprise-grade AWS landscapes.

## AWS CDK

This is an open source, infrastructure management framework that works using the concept of **constructs** – readymade abstractions for deploying integrated application components. Under the hood, it works with CloudFormation templates but abstracts these details from the end user. It offers native programming language features such as conditionals, composition, and inheritance, which enable the user to apply programming methodologies to infrastructure management. These reusable components can then be shared with other teams in the company. This not only accelerates overall DevOps adoption but also leads to standardized infrastructure solutions for a particular application pattern.

# Summary

In this chapter, we discussed two real-life examples that helped you to compare different approaches to building solutions and to enable your teams. While this highlighted certain drawbacks in the traditional on-premises infrastructure model, you also learned about the practical benefits of using AWS services in the cloud.

Along the way, we also covered some guiding principles that will make your life as a software professional easier. You learned how to think of your end users as customers, align technology offerings to their business outcomes, reduce their cognitive load, and focus on iterative development practices.

With the foundations set, we then dived into important DevOps methodologies that enable software delivery at scale, reliably and securely. Toward the end, you learned about key AWS services that can boost your DevOps adoption and offer enterprise-grade reliability, availability, and security.

In *Chapter 2, Choosing the Right Cloud Service*, we will learn about the different service models offered by AWS and some strategies to decide what works best for your organization.

## Further reading

You can gain a greater insight into AWS service offerings in the continuous integration, continuous delivery, and continuous deployment space by examining the official whitepaper: `https://docs.aws.amazon.com/whitepapers/latest/practicing-continuous-integration-continuous-delivery/welcome.html`

# 2
# Choosing the Right Cloud Service

We all agree that cloud computing has become an integral part of every modern company's IT strategy and that it spearheads its digital transformation. However, it is often an overwhelming task for organizations to decide where to begin and what services to choose while ensuring the right balance of control and simplicity. In *Chapter 1*, *Accelerating Your DevOps Journey with AWS*, we focused on the importance of delivering business outcomes for customers. This is exactly what companies should have in mind as they finalize their cloud strategy. What would best help their teams to continue delivering delightful customer experiences? What would reduce the cognitive load of their software developers and fit their operating model at the same time?

An important categorization to aid this decision-making is the three *cloud service tiers*. They describe how you use the cloud services within your organization and the degree of management you're responsible for in the cloud environment as a customer. Not all the tiers would equally fit your requirements; they can have a positive and negative impact at the same time. On one hand, they abstract the underlying complexity. On the other hand, they can affect your future flexibility in terms of control and change.

In this chapter, we will cover what these three tiers are and the differences between them. Choosing the right tier that aligns with your company's operating model is an important decision for hosting your workloads in the cloud. This influences the operations and flexibility to change, which directly links to how easily you can deliver customer outcomes.

We will cover the following topics:

- The three tiers of cloud offerings
- Understanding your organization's cloud operating model
- How to choose the appropriate tier for hosting your workloads
- Key AWS services

## The three tiers of cloud offerings

Everything is offered *as a service* these days. You might have come across several terms such as **IaaS**, **PaaS**, and **SaaS**, which are part of a bigger trend of offering *X as a service*. Hosting all the hardware and software components of your application stack on-premises requires a lot of effort and time. However, you can selectively offload some of these components to the cloud.

AWS and other cloud providers abstract the underlying infrastructure and platform, thereby only exposing what the end-users want to use. The interesting part is that some of these offerings have now extended beyond the service provider's data center and are offered as a managed service, directly running in customers' on-premises environments in racks managed by AWS. This new cloud trend of hybrid-deployment models is evolving in several domains such as containers, databases, and end-user computing.

Let's have a look into the differentiating capabilities across the three tiers and the degree of service management they offer.

### Infrastructure as a Service (IaaS)

Companies that host their workloads on-premises require lots of investment in terms of IT resources, operations, and costs. Cloud providers such as AWS simplify this by abstracting the complexities of the underlying infrastructure. They manage compute, networking, and storage while offering internet-accessible endpoints to enable automation. In this model, the IT teams still need to manage the operating systems, software dependencies, and the application that runs on top of them. From a cost perspective, this has a huge benefit due to the reduction of investment and planning around infrastructure procurement, maintenance, and operations.

The IT teams have a lot of flexibility and control under this model as they can leverage the SDKs and APIs from the cloud provider for programmatically provisioning resources on demand. They can customize the operating systems, libraries, and pretty much everything that impacts the application behavior and performance. With tools such as **AWS CloudFormation**, **AWS CDK**, and **Terraform**, the users can define their entire infrastructure as code and can apply good code management practices to infrastructure.

Services provided under the IaaS tier are particularly useful for teams adopting DevOps approaches that involve frequent software testing and infrastructure management entirely via code. IaaS offerings can be used to spin up environments whenever you want, scale them up to match the production load, and tear them down again when you no longer need the resources. In terms of service reliability and solid security posture, AWS offers a lot of capabilities at this level.

It is common for IT teams to combine the IaaS offerings with other tooling that helps them efficiently manage the software delivery process, be it configuration management tools, or other deployment automation frameworks, such as the AWS Code suite, which we discussed in the previous chapter.

## Platform as a Service (PaaS)

In a PaaS service model, cloud providers additionally manage the operating system and application integrations on top of the infrastructure. This further abstracts the system internals from the software team, allowing them to focus on business outcomes. With pre-built integrations, all aspects of infrastructure, operations, and configuration management, which is the process of maintaining hardware and software in a desired state, are taken care of by the provider. These platforms, to some degree, are opinionated about the software delivery process and the automation around it. The developers still need to write code, but PaaS takes care of the operations and deployment activities, which results in a seamless merge with the underlying IaaS.

Developers greatly benefit from such offerings as they help them build proof of concepts in no time. In contrast to IaaS, these offerings are generally less flexible to customization and change. It takes time for the developers to get used to the specifics of the framework and what is expected in terms of code structure, configurations, software delivery process, and so on. However, once they have a foundational understanding of the service offered, onboarding time for a new application improves a great deal.

## Software as a Service (SaaS)

This is the most comprehensive form of offering by cloud providers, where the end-user simply consumes application features via APIs or directly through their browser over the internet. The end-user is not responsible for software patches, overall maintenance, and application uptime. The cloud provider, however, needs to take care of security aspects around such offerings. Generally, these are multi-tenant systems with common storage for multiple users.

In some form or the other, we all use SaaS applications these days. Common examples are email and cloud-based file storage. In *Chapter 1*, we discussed the importance of undifferentiated heavy lifting being taken over by cloud services. SaaS excellently fits that concept. The end-user consumes the software application without having to worry about anything else.

This model is the least flexible in terms of change and control, as you are bound by the service boundaries and limitations coming from the provider side. You have less influence on the software features. SaaS is great for companies who don't want to take ownership of applications that they can simply consume as-is and who don't want to reinvent the wheel.

Let's try to visually map our learnings so far to different cloud service tiers and the varied levels of abstraction and control they offer. Different layers are highlighted in *Table 2.1*, where we can see the ones you have to manage in white and the ones managed by cloud provider in blue:

| On-premises | IaaS | PaaS | SaaS |
|---|---|---|---|
| Applications | Applications | Applications | Applications |
| Data | Data | Data | Data |
| Runtime | Runtime | Runtime | Runtime |
| Middleware | Middleware | Middleware | Middleware |
| O/S | O/S | O/S | O/S |
| Virtualization | Virtualization | Virtualization | Virtualization |
| Servers | Servers | Servers | Servers |
| Storage | Storage | Storage | Storage |
| Networking | Networking | Networking | Networking |

Table 2.1: Layers of management under different cloud service tiers

So far, we have covered the underlying principles and abstractions offered by the three cloud tiers. Next, let's have a look into the key questions you should answer when deciding on what works best for your use case.

## What to choose when

Getting started with any of these offerings is fairly simple, but aligning these decisions with long-term success needs several considerations. As we just discussed, these service tiers come with different levels of abstraction. This directly translates to the flexibility you would have in terms of modifications and extensions, should a need arise. Let's take a look at what factors you need to evaluate and the impact they could have.

### Simplicity versus control

Striking the right balance is important to ensure the success and agility of your software teams. The service tier capabilities need to match the software stack you are working with. Whether the team is building a stock trading application or a static website will largely define the level of customization and control they expect from the platform or the underlying infrastructure components. On the other hand, for developing a PoC, developers don't need extensive customization and performance tuning. This is where AWS PaaS offerings such as AWS Elastic Beanstalk could give them a jumpstart while handling all infrastructure details such as load balancers, DNS and EC2 compute instances.

PaaS requires a certain level of adaptation in the application itself for the user to be able to utilize the framework. In some cases, this introduces a cloud provider lock-in as the application cannot be easily migrated as-is to another service provider in the future.

## Cloud skills and resources

IaaS works best for organizations that have the resources and skills to manage the entire application and infrastructure stack on their own. The elasticity of the cloud is what they mostly want to leverage while ensuring a higher level of customization. This offers great flexibility around fine-tuning the application components for maximum performance and control.

It is equally important to highlight that in the absence of cloud skills or resources, the teams can still benefit from the PaaS capabilities by utilizing certain AWS services. This allows them to focus on just writing code. Then, the PaaS layer wires it together with the infrastructure layer by offering additional workflows around code release, integration, and infrastructure scaling.

## Business requirements

Business requirements and priorities can sometimes influence the overall IT strategy in interesting ways. Time-constrained project rollouts and proof of concepts align better with PaaS offerings as there isn't a pressing need for building the entire infrastructure up.

Building another Slack or Mailchimp service is probably not the most important thing you want to focus on. In such cases, signing up for SaaS services is usually the best option. This avoids investing time in things that are not in alignment with the business outcome.

Once a certain size of the organization is comfortable with these PaaS offerings, it paves the way for establishing best practices around these services and sharing them with other teams in the company. If you are time-constrained, have fewer resources, or don't care for a lot of customization but rather wish to get to the market sooner, then PaaS is certainly an option you should look into.

## Security considerations

SaaS offerings are mostly multi-tenant systems, which means that a single instance of the software is used by several customers. Any security breach or threat has a big impact, as customers would lose their data. These systems are also prone to *noisy neighbor* problems, where a faulty tenant can affect the service availability of other customers hosted on the same server.

For applications where data and infrastructure security are absolutely critical, it makes more sense to use IaaS offerings. Organizations then have full control over data encryption, for example, to enhance security posture and meet their regulatory requirements. AWS offers the possibility to use customer-managed encryption keys that ensure a good level of trust around data security and compliance needs.

All these aspects need to be considered in tandem with how your organization operates. What is your organization's operating model? Let's take a deeper look.

## Understanding your organization's cloud operating model

Every organization is structured differently. Typically, there are three working models commonly seen across IT organizations with different levels of cloud and DevOps maturity. Some key behaviors that define which model is in use are as follows:

- Who develops the software?
- Who operates the software?
- Who builds the cloud platform?
- Who operates the cloud platform?

### Focusing on sustaining workloads with the traditional approach

Traditionally, there are dedicated teams that own each of the areas described previously. The software developers build an application and then pass it over to another team for maintenance and operations. Cloud infrastructure also follows a similar pattern where certain teams build, and others run the platform. This setup is indicative of a lack of DevOps maturity and hinders growth and ownership. Software teams that function with such siloed approaches don't have visibility into the challenges faced and the approaches followed by other teams. This also affects the growth and learning of all team members, as new innovative approaches are rarely followed to optimize the processes or solve challenges at scale.

This approach is good enough to sustain IT applications that don't require consistent innovation to delight customers. Regular payroll processing, leave management portals, and so on would fall under this category.

### Focusing on optimizing workloads

Unlike the traditional operating model, software developers can also operate the application in productive environments. However, they don't manage anything in terms of the cloud infrastructure underneath. The infrastructural foundations are still built and operated by a dedicated team.

This allows a certain degree of control and optimization in the software stack and the corresponding business outcomes. Teams with limited cloud skills can leverage the cloud PaaS offerings to be able to operate the applications in the cloud while they establish deeper expertise in other areas.

Let's discuss an example from my past experience working with a team that lacked cloud skills but wanted to leverage innovative cloud offerings to be able to grow in the months and years to come.

## Taking the first steps in the cloud

The software in question was a **CakePHP** web application that was running on-premises. The team faced frequent issues with data-center outages and networking, thereby struggling to meet the dynamic scale of the application.

Aligning with the overall organizational strategy to adopt AWS offerings, the team was obviously looking for some quick wins through the elasticity and endless possibilities offered by the cloud.

> **Note**
> This is a common scenario you will come across when teams are on a transition path from on-premises to the cloud. PaaS clearly stands out in such situations by offering a solid foundation the teams can begin with. It safeguards teams from falling down before they begin.

With the need justified and the challenges well understood, my next step was to explore which AWS service could meet these requirements. AWS Elastic Beanstalk seemed to be a promising candidate. It offered a unique combination of managed operating systems, web servers, programming language runtime, and application servers. The user just needs to design and target the web application to a particular platform, and Beanstalk takes care of the rest.

Creating a new PHP-based Beanstalk application provisioned the following resources out of the box:

- **EC2 instances** – These are the compute servers that host the chosen application platform, in this case, CakePHP.

- **AWS Elastic Load Balancer (ELB) with a custom domain name** – As a security best practice, the EC2 instances are not directly exposed over the internet. Beanstalk additionally configures a Route53 CNAME record, which makes the ELB available on a custom domain name. It forwards incoming requests to the underlying EC2 instances.

- **Security groups (SG)** – SGs are configured at the instance level and the ELB level. They allow the incoming traffic to pass through both components only when specified ports are used.

- **Auto-scaling group** – Depending on application usage metrics, the EC2 instances are configured to automatically scale out or scale in. This allows for adapting the application based on user demand by leveraging cloud elasticity.

- **Amazon S3 bucket** – This is where the user can upload code archives. Post-upload, these are unzipped, and Elastic Beanstalk takes care of provisioning the recent application binaries to the attached servers.

- **CloudWatch Alarms** – Beanstalk also sets up CloudWatch alarms to trigger alerts based on pre-defined load thresholds such as CPU, memory, or network usage.

All of this with just a few clicks in the AWS web console!

As you can see in *Figure 2.1*, an entire environment starting from the infrastructure up until the external domain name was provisioned by the service – that's the power of PaaS:

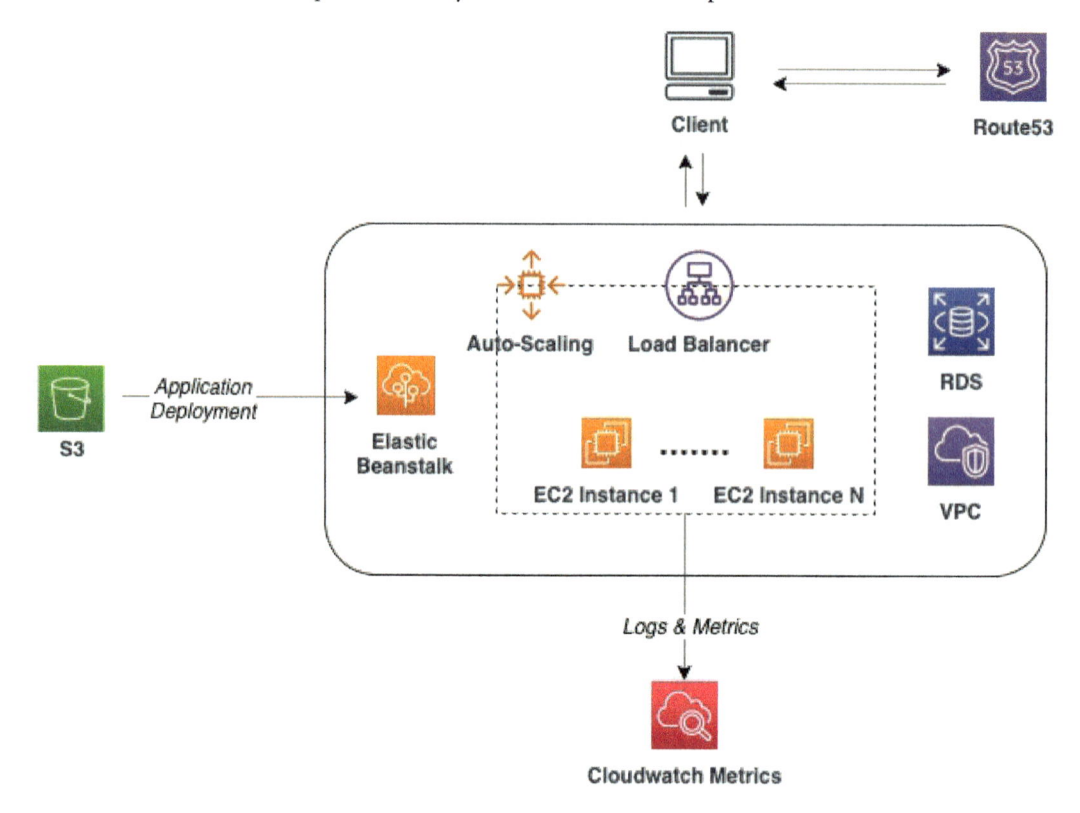

Figure 2.1: Managing applications via AWS Elastic Beanstalk

After playing around for a week or so with the newly provisioned environments, the developers gained the confidence to work with it and migrated their existing codebase to Elastic Beanstalk.

To support data storage in the cloud, an Amazon **Relational Database Service (RDS)** cluster was also spun up that provided data persistence in the cloud. Beanstalk offers possibilities to inject customized environment variables that can then be read inside the application code.

Replicating these application stacks across multiple environments was super easy with the creation of new environments linked to the same parent application. So, within a few hours, the developers had development, staging, and production environments up and running in the AWS cloud. It took around 8-10 days to completely migrate the application from an on-premises static infrastructure to the cloud.

There are a few important areas to assess when selecting a PaaS offering.

## Monitoring

Running an application in production requires visibility in terms of how all layers of the application are functioning. To understand key system behaviors, software developers can derive valuable insights from the metrics supported by the PaaS offering, such as the number of incoming HTTP requests, database response time latencies, and so on.

Beanstalk offers basic or enhanced reporting and monitoring directly in the console. With basic insights such as *target response time*, *CPU utilization* across the fleet, and *total requests*, the platform offers an aggregated view of the application performance that was not available in the systems on-premises. Using the Beanstalk health agent, the service additionally provides interesting insights into the deployment time activities and how they correlate with the application behavior. This was never available in the infrastructure setup on-premises.

With PaaS offerings, you not only meet your basic application needs but get interesting features from the platform based on the provider's experience running workloads of thousands of other enterprise customers, at scale. This level of knowledge and best practices takes a long time to establish when you are managing workloads on your own and starting from scratch.

## Code deployment

For rolling out features in the cloud, Beanstalk offers seamless integration with Amazon S3. You upload the code packages into the storage service, and Beanstalk takes care of the rest. Furthermore, it supports well-established DevOps methodologies to test new functionalities in isolation before rolling them out on all servers.

The team ended up using a *traffic-splitting* deployment policy that gave them the possibility to test new features on a subset of servers, while the live requests were served by others, using the older stable version of the application code.

A modification to any of these configuration settings was as simple as modifying a property in the web console that switched the deployment mode to *rolling* or *all at once*. These deployment modes control the rate of change rollout across your servers: one at a time or all in one go. Implementing similar software delivery capabilities on your own requires a lot of tinkering with various systems, applications, and tools. That is definitely not easy for teams just getting started with cloud.

## Configuration

Modification of any application stack component including software, instances, capacity planning, and so on was possible within the configuration options supported by Elastic Beanstalk. Once the developers were comfortable operating the service via the console, they started rolling out modifications through code as well. Elastic Beanstalk offers the possibility to roll out customizations using its custom configuration files.

This level of understanding and confidence paved the way for easier adoption of automation and tooling, driven by code. In the on-premises world, the developers hardly had any opportunities to own the operations of the software stack. Beanstalk opened the doors for them to not just build but own the application environments, from development to production.

## Operations

A key measure of success for PaaS services is the level of simplicity offered in terms of *Day 2 operations*. If not managed properly, this can lead to software developers either focusing too much time on repeatable, boring tasks, or even worse, the end-user experience takes a hit.

Through AWS EC2 auto-scaling and ELB, Beanstalk offers the capabilities to provision capacity on demand, load balance requests across multiple instances, and scale the application based on application usage metrics.

Starting with a basic set of features, it is very simple for developers to extend the system for future requirements by leveraging the integration points such as custom configuration files and CloudFormation support. However, the cloud platform, that is the AWS accounts, the underlying VPCs, and so on, are still managed by the cloud platform team.

Next, let's dive deeper into a growth-focused operating model that promotes ownership and gives even more control to the application owners.

## Focusing on growth in the cloud

Fast-moving organizations with mature DevOps practices demonstrate this approach to operating in the cloud. The developers not only build and run the software stack but also manage the cloud platform on their own. This is only possible when teams automate most of their tasks, test frequently, and leverage IaaS cloud capabilities to manage the entire infrastructure as code.

In such setups, the cloud platform teams focus on ensuring the right guardrails, compliance, and overall strategy instead of managing the infrastructure for individual teams. Managing multi-account AWS environments at scale is a topic we will cover in a dedicated chapter towards the end of the book.

It is important to understand that not all teams within an organization need to follow the same operating model. It is common for companies to have a mix of all three, based on what the individual application needs and priorities are.

Let's discuss another real-life example where the same team, after gaining relevant cloud skills, went ahead and launched another service in the cloud a few months later. This time, they took care of the entire cloud infrastructure. It is a common progression path observed in companies that adopt PaaS offerings, expand their learning horizons, and later go ahead and control the entire infrastructure using IaaS. These requirements are mostly fueled by the need to control and optimize beyond what PaaS environments would expose to the end user.

## Owning it all in the cloud

PaaS offerings support common application platforms, enterprise-grade frameworks, and much more. However, the application requirements sometimes need more granular control for mission-critical applications, where every single configuration matters.

There was a similar use case, where the team had to roll out a multi-region, high throughput, latency-sensitive application that required custom AMIs (short for Amazon Machine Images, used to provide information to launch EC2 instances), fine-tuned load balancer configurations, optimized disk storage layout, and much more. By leveraging AWS IaaS capabilities, they were able to establish the control they needed while taking benefit of the infrastructure elasticity and cloud awesomeness.

Adoption of IaaS features, at the enterprise scale, is made possible with the likes of **AWS CDK**, **Terraform**, and **CloudFormation**. These frameworks allow for provisioning and controlling AWS resources with the use of structured documents such as YAML, JSON, and **Hashicorp Configuration Language (HCL)**.

For this particular application, the team developed the entire infrastructure with Terraform. It consisted of all components including the load balancer, DNS, compute, and storage. Managing this layer as code allowed them to make use of code version control, followed by pipeline-driven multi-region rollouts. The team created an AMI pipeline using custom AMI builder tools such as Hashicorp's Packer that would build, test, and deploy AMIs in the cloud and make them ready for use by EC2 AutoScaling. In this case, the cloud platform team just focused on provisioning the AWS accounts, allocating network CIDRs, and providing data center connectivity via the AWS Transit Gateway. Everything beyond that was directly configured by the developers to give them flexibility they never had before.

*Figure 2.2* depicts the architectural components managed by the developers by using Terraform:

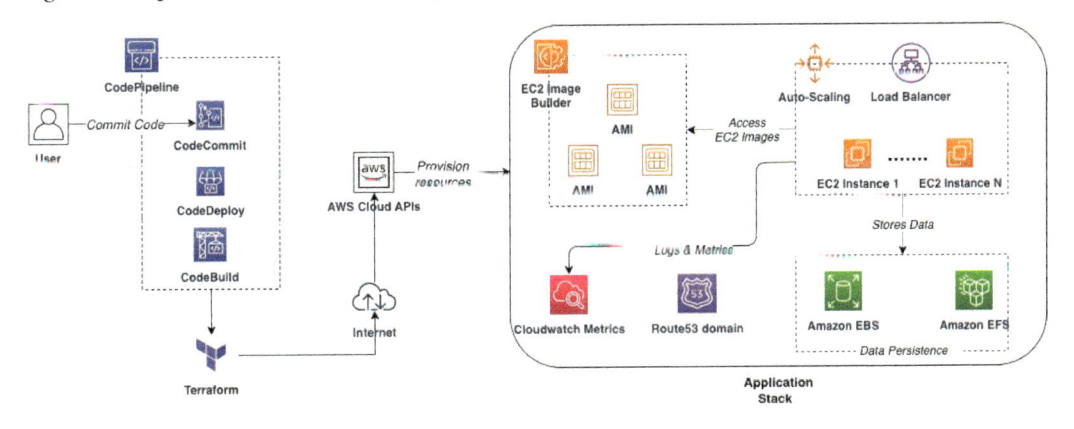

Figure 2.2: Managing the AWS infrastructure with Terraform

Let's contrast the key areas from the Elastic Beanstalk use case that we discussed previously in the *Taking the first steps in the cloud* section.

## Monitoring

Managing all the application components on their own also meant that extensive monitoring capabilities had to be rolled out, alongside the application itself. Basic CloudWatch monitoring sufficed the need for insights into how the infrastructure components were behaving but was not enough for application observability.

By injecting the CloudWatch agent in the AMIs and creating custom parsers for the application logs, the developers were able to publish relevant metrics onto the monitoring dashboard. Once the metrics were available, it was simple for the developers to derive intelligence from them to dissect system behaviors and configure alerts.

The application had tough latency boundaries to be met by all systems participating in the cluster. This required continuous monitoring and alerting for any threshold breaches. With full control over the AMI, the team was able to inject custom utilities that measured the latency across multiple availability zones and later publish them on CloudWatch.

## Code deployment

Using the Terraform CLI, the developers were able to roll out the entire infrastructure stack using a single `terraform deploy` command. This allowed them to easily provision and manage their applications on multiple AWS regions.

Similar to code deployment practices, the infrastructure stack was also rolled out just like any other software component. AWS CodeDeploy and AWS CodePipeline gave the developers CI/CD capabilities to deploy application components across the entire compute cluster.

## Configuration

IaaS services, unlike PaaS, do not offer application configuration features. They simply don't manage anything above the network, compute, and storage. This meant that the developers had to design and deploy their own pipelines for rolling out EC2 IAM images for respective AWS regions. The smallest change inside the operating system, or the application configuration, was rolled out in the form of a new AMI revision.

On the other side, this gave a lot of flexibility to the developers in terms of modifying the Linux kernel parameters, software libraries, and disk storage configurations. AWS, as a cloud provider, only provided APIs to manage infrastructure, and the rest was managed by developers with a mix of AWS and open source tools and frameworks.

## Operations

Beanstalk abstracts many details and offers ready-made integrations and best practices by default. This architecture, however, requires everything to be managed by the developers. The journey to manage all application intricacies led to great AWS learnings amongst the developers, which allowed them to automate all the operations they wanted.

Having discussed the common operating models adopted by organizations, let's have a look at some AWS services commonly used across each of these service tiers.

# Key AWS services

AWS offers several services under each tier. Depending on your target cloud strategy, you can cherry-pick what part of your work you would like to offload to the cloud provider. The following sections highlight the services that are widely adopted by most organizations. Let's start with the infrastructure.

## Abstracting the infrastructure

AWS's core capabilities revolve around infrastructure services that are offered through APIs and SDKs. High-velocity software delivery depends on being able to provision and scale infrastructure resources at the click of a button. Let's discuss some commonly used services.

### Amazon EC2

Amazon **Elastic Compute Cloud** (**EC2**) offers broad computing capabilities that allow the user to choose between different processor types, storage, networking, and operating system. The EC2 family encompasses different services such as **Elastic Block Store** (**EBS**), **Elastic File Storage** (**EFS**), and networking to meet the needs of a variety of applications.

**Elastic Block Store**

This is a high-performance block storage service from AWS used by EC2 compute instances. Applications use it for different use cases such as SAN for I/O intensive applications, relational or non-relational databases, and big data analysis.

**Elastic File Storage**

This is a simple set-and-forget elastic file system that is used to set up cost-optimized storage in the cloud. EFS can scale from gigabytes to petabytes of data without any explicit scaling requests from the user. There are no pre-set limits for the data storage that the user needs to provision. They just pay for what they use.

**Amazon Virtual Private Cloud (VPC)**

Amazon VPC allows users to create a virtual network dedicated to their accounts. This is basically a private space of the AWS data center carved out for the needs of the users.

## Accelerating software delivery with platform services

Platform-as-a-service offerings allow users to focus on managing their applications instead of underlying infrastructure. With this support, the developers can be more efficient in their work and need not worry about capacity planning and software maintenance or patching.

There are two key services worth mentioning that boost application development.

### *AWS Elastic Beanstalk*

From quickly launching web applications to supporting mobile backend APIs, Elastic Beanstalk helps users with end-to-end management of infrastructure and application components. Users commit code to a central repository, and the service takes care of software delivery, basic networking, and monitoring. This allows for rapid expansion and an accelerated go-to-market strategy. It supports a wide range of application platforms in several programming languages.

### *AWS Lambda*

AWS Lambda is a compute service that executes code in a completely managed environment. With automatic scaling, logging, and operating system maintenance, users can just write code and wire together Lambda functions with other AWS services to build an application.

You write your logic as Lambda functions which scale to thousands of requests per second. You pay only for the execution time.

## Fully managed software services

The final tier offers complete abstraction and just offers SDKs and APIs for users to consume the functionality. There is nothing that requires user intervention around operations, deployment, or feature development. These services are used exclusively for very specific business use cases where re-inventing the wheel is not an option.

### *Amazon Chime*

This is a fully managed communication service used by organizations for hosting meetings, conferences, and chat sessions. All enterprise use cases such as managed policies, SSO access, and persistent communications are offered out of the box. Companies that want to build customized experiences can also leverage the SDK to build innovative solutions.

### *Amazon WorkMail*

Amazon WorkMail is a secure, enterprise-ready email and calendar service that operates on different clients such as Outlook, Android, and iOS applications. This can also integrate with existing Active Directory systems.

## Summary

In this chapter, we discussed the three important service tiers offered by cloud providers: IaaS, PaaS, and SaaS. We started with a basic understanding of all three, discussed the different levels of abstraction they offer, and talked about their fitment in specific scenarios. Balancing the needs of the organization, its current cloud skills, and its business goals are key to ensuring that the right service tier is adopted for a particular software stack or team.

We then went on to discuss typical cloud operating models that can co-exist in any organization. In the context of two real-life scenarios, we discussed how software developers leveraged AWS PaaS and IaaS offerings on two separate occasions. Sometimes, it also makes sense to adopt a readymade solution to a common problem by leveraging SaaS solutions. This helps avoid undifferentiated heavy lifting and allows the developers to focus on real customer problems and business use cases.

In the next chapter, we will discuss a mental shift around how we think of infrastructure these days and how AWS supports such an approach with evolving application needs. Furthermore, we will set up your AWS environment with security best practices and go through some real-life hands-on exercises that highlight the benefits of infrastructure automation and the idea of disposability.

## Further reading

If you are interested in establishing a cloud operating model in your organization or want to understand the architectural fundamentals around hosting SaaS offerings on AWS, you can learn more about them here:

- `https://docs.aws.amazon.com/whitepapers/latest/saas-architecture-fundamentals/saas-architecture-fundamentals.html`
- `https://docs.aws.amazon.com/whitepapers/latest/building-cloud-operating-model/building-cloud-operating-model.html`

# 3
# Leveraging Immutable Infrastructure in the Cloud

Among many other benefits of AWS, one that stands out is the ease of provisioning resources in the cloud, dynamically scaling them, and bringing them down again when they're no longer required. This is a big mental shift from how IT resources were perceived and managed on-premises. Software applications have also evolved during this time and the infrastructure advancements have complemented this unprecedented growth.

If you've been in IT for more than a decade, you would agree that every situation around the lack of resources back then was addressed by *vertically scaling up* the existing servers. Adding more memory, storage, or compute solved most of the problems. Servers would be idle for months and years and get in-place upgrades when applications needed to do more. To make the software applications resilient to hardware failures, companies started looking at other options, such as horizontal scaling, also known as *scale-out*. Instead of using big servers to support the application, the idea was to leverage a fleet of commodity hardware that also provided cost benefits. This allowed you to easily replace faulty components in the fleet, which made the applications more resilient to underlying hardware failures and improved their overall availability. However, this introduced a new problem to solve – **configuration management**. Managing such a fleet of servers at scale now required additional tools. Rolling out configuration changes, or software updates, to tens and hundreds of servers posed new challenges.

Operating in the cloud simplifies the problems associated with configuring and managing a large fleet of servers, which has grown beyond what manual procedures can handle. This is going to be the theme of discussion for this chapter, where we will discuss strategies to operate your cloud workloads with reliability and confidence. Towards the end, we will also get our hands dirty with some interesting tools to deploy resources on AWS.

We will cover the following topics:

- Pets versus cattle – an analogy
- Mutable and immutable infrastructure

- Getting started with your AWS account
- Understanding the test application and development toolbox
- Building an AMI and deploying a test instance

Let's begin with an analogy that fits our topic of discussion well.

## Technical requirements

To follow along with this chapter, you will need the following:

- AWS Cloud9 IDE deployed in your AWS account
- Active AWS account subscription
- *Hashicorp's Packer* for AWS AMI creation

## Pets versus cattle

In the old way of doing things, servers were always cared for, lovingly nurtured, and given pet names such as *Atlantis, Raptor, Battlestar*, and so on. These were standalone systems that hosted critical applications, were monitored 24/7, and required administrators to nurse them as soon as issues were identified. The smallest of problems with these systems meant some part of the organization would not function, or external customers would be impacted. The nature of how these systems were perceived and maintained was similar to how we treat **pets** – with utmost care and affection. You cannot just replace them; instead, you must fix the underlying problem and get them healthy again. The application developers also operated with a similar mindset in terms of rolling out changes to these servers. They would keep track of all changes, execute scripts in a particular order, and define runbooks for all expected scenarios. Such an approach to maintaining critical systems introduces fear of the unknown, scope of human errors, and resistance in quickly rolling out changes to all systems. This is only good so long as the workloads are of a manageable size, say 5-10 servers. Once the scale increases, the limitations of scripting, tools, manual changes, and, most important of all, humans kick in. Think about unit-testing your **bash** scripts against all possible permutations and combinations of system libraries available on the target servers. How do you build a rollback mechanism for hundreds or thousands of servers? If these scripts are executed by a human, there is a high probability of common errors, such as running wrong commands in terminals, unintentionally targeting production environments, and typos resulting in loss of data – the list goes on. Not to say that Bash is imperfect, it's just that working with it requires a very good level of understanding and experience. The foundation of these scripts has to be quite strong for the team to be able to reliably evolve them over time.

On the other hand, the new way of operating in the cloud promotes the idea of **infrastructure disposability**. Why modify, fix, and indefinitely maintain something that can be replaced with a brand-new server, at the click of a button? Why nurture existing servers and introduce additional operational overhead, or possibilities of mismatch in system configurations? In this model, organizations typically name their fleet of servers with functional identifiers such as *web001*, *web002*, *web003*, and so on. If *web002* stops functioning, the server would be de-registered from the fleet and then replaced with a healthy new machine. The infrastructure elasticity of the cloud empowers this. Typically, these processes are entirely automated, and the end users, or the operation engineers hardly notice any service interruption. However, this does require some adaptation and architectural considerations in the application design to support such operative procedures. For example, a de-registered server for a stateful application should still complete in-flight work, persist all information to disk, and then prepare for a graceful shutdown. Applications need to be programmed to handle these signals.

As you can see, it all comes down to a shift of mindset where the infrastructure is no longer treated like pets, but more like a *herd of cattle*. If you think of a server that can be easily recreated and replaced at any time, it's part of a herd. If you consider a server indispensable, then it's a pet.

It's important to highlight that maintaining pets in the cloud takes you further away from leveraging the real benefits of the elastic infrastructure. You should be designing your architectures with failure in mind, all the time. What is more important is to architect an application that seamlessly recovers from failures. Once this is ensured, your applications can leverage the cloud in the best way possible.

In the words of AWS's CTO:

> *"Failures are a given and everything will eventually fail over time: from routers to hard disks, from operating systems to memory units corrupting TCP packets, from transient errors to permanent failures. This is a given, whether you are using the highest quality hardware or lowest cost components."*
>
> – Werner Vogels, Chief Technology Officer and Vice President, Amazon

Having covered the foundational differences around how you perceive your infrastructure, let's discuss the benefits offered by **immutable infrastructure** – a key enabler for the adoption of the **cattle mindset**.

# Mutable and immutable infrastructure

Infrastructure resources created on premises, or in the cloud, can either be modified in place or be completely replaced with a new instance. It is usually not a problem to modify the servers, which involves upgrading libraries, rolling out new application code, or changing configuration settings in the early days. However, as your workloads scale, these *in-place* upgrades risk the reliability of the applications and complicate the testing and operational procedures. Before diving into the benefits of the immutable infrastructure, it's important to introduce you to mutable infrastructures and explain their trade-offs. Let's discuss this in the light of a real-life example, where I managed a Java-based web application on a Tomcat web server.

## Mutable infrastructure

This is a traditional **Java** web stack with **web application archives** (**WAR**) files deployed on **Tomcat** web servers. For high availability, four similarly configured machines were wired together to form a cluster and were exposed to the end user through **HAProxy**, a high-performance TCP/HTTP load balancer.

Any system update on the Linux servers, be it a new software rollout, security patch, or an operating system configuration change, was carried out manually by initiating a remote SSH session and executing the required commands. As the application load increased, new servers were added to the *pet fleet*, increasing the count to 10. Manually executing commands was no longer practical, so I started leveraging tools such as **Ansible**. Ansible works by connecting to the managed nodes and injecting small programs known as *Ansible modules*. These modules represent the desired state of the system and they are executed on the host, over SSH by default. This allowed me to automate the manual tasks with a configuration file describing the sequence of commands to be executed. This file was then passed to Ansible along with a server inventory it had to be executed against. From here on, Ansible took over the responsibility of ensuring that all modifications were deployed across every single server in the fleet with a single command. The most important thing to highlight here is that these servers were still *mutable*. Whenever a change had to be rolled out, it was done in place, adding on top of previous modifications. Over time, you continue building, or in other words, *move further away* from the state the server was in when it was freshly provisioned. This is completely ok, so long as the change process is reliable and you don't lose the server itself.

As mentioned in Werner Vogel's quote earlier: "... *failures are a given and everything will fail over time.*" The same happened with this software application stack. Ansible simplified the server fleet management by taking over the heavy lifting involved around SSH and manual command executions. However, it could not circumvent other problems around networking and security. Let's discuss them:

- Random unresponsiveness of Linux package repositories resulted in installation failures.
- Since Ansible was essentially running over SSH, network packet drops resulted in incomplete command executions.
- The indeterministic state of servers further resulted in a unique combination of code and dependencies that hadn't been tested before.
- To fix the intermediate states of servers, developers were required to log into the servers and execute commands. Over time, this introduced additional configuration drift among the servers.
- Having a dependency on developers and operations to SSH into live systems was a security risk.

As you can see, most of these errors would leave a subset of servers in a unique untested state as they would all fail in slightly different ways. This resulted in a lack of reliability and confidence around how those servers would behave until this interim state was fixed. Debugging the 10 servers was still somewhat manageable, but imagine doing this on hundreds and thousands of machines.

Such *half-failed* scenarios contribute to major problems around the following:

- Lack of testability of all possible permutations and combinations
- Complex debugging procedures
- Unreliable software applications

The life cycle of cloud resources is easy to manage and automate through APIs and SDKs provided by cloud providers such as AWS. This has paved the way for the adoption of immutable infrastructure practices – let's see what it is and the benefits it provides.

## Immutable infrastructure

Immutable infrastructure is a strategy that promotes the idea of *replacing* your software components with IT resources instead of *modifying them in-place*. Whenever a change needs to be rolled out, an application or service undergoes a complete redeployment. All the components in the stack, starting from the underlying OS, libraries, dependencies, and the application code, are packaged and deployed as a *discrete unit*.

In the AWS world, one way to adopt the concept of immutable infrastructure is by using EC2 **Amazon Machine Images (AMIs)**. You version and release the entire image with all dependencies baked in. Modifications to the live servers are discouraged as it leads to issues such as configuration mismatch, which eventually affects system stability and reliability. You no longer need to care about the myriad configuration combinations, as we discussed in the context of mutable infrastructures. The users can now test if the entire stack, which represents all the components and dependencies of the application, works or not. The scenarios where it doesn't work surface much earlier in the software delivery process, so it's easy to fix the underlying problem. Furthermore, not requiring direct access to the machines backed by these AMIs increases system reliability and promotes security best practices. With automated testing procedures, this image can also be tested in isolation, followed by replacing the servers in the cattle fleet.

Adopting this approach in the Java web stack allowed us to get rid of all issues around configuration mismatch, security risks, and networking. Combining the AMI concept with Amazon EC2's Auto Scaling service further simplified the rollout of new changes. With an API call, the users could map the entire fleet to a new version of the AMI, gradually replacing all the servers automatically.

There is, however, one important aspect of application design that you need to consider when adopting infrastructure immutability.

*Trade-offs of immutable infrastructure*

Most important of all, applications should not have any dependency on the local state within the server. Any loss of local data should be recoverable and in ideal cases should only be used for performance optimization, such as caching. End user functionality coupled with the local state is bound to suffer because, with the immutable infrastructure, we are promoting the idea of replacing the server at *any time* with a new one.

Another way to solve this is by externalizing data storage and not maintaining any local data at all. Some AWS services in the **Elastic Compute Cloud** (**EC2**) suite that help decouple the compute and storage, and thereby enable the adoption of infrastructure immutability, are **Elastic Block Store** (**EBS**) and **Elastic File Systems** (**EFS**). In AWS, there are two main approaches to defining artifacts for immutable infrastructure:

- **AMI**: In the AWS cloud, AMIs are used to spin up EC2 compute instances. You can easily create multiple instances from the same image to spin up a cluster or use separate images when differing configurations are required for some of the EC2 instances. An AMI defines the block store mappings to specify what volumes will be attached to an instance that uses this image. Additionally, it defines the AWS accounts that would have permission to launch instances using these AMIs. A multi-account AWS strategy typically uses a golden image pipeline to ship enterprise-grade security-hardened images across all member accounts. This is a topic that we will cover in greater detail in later chapters.

- **Container images**: Similar to hardware virtualization technologies such as VMWare, **Docker** defines an image as the template from which multiple lightweight process containers can be created. It is a software virtualization technique that follows a similar principle of immutability. Any change in the software stack, or the operating system dependencies, results in a new Docker image being created. Running containers should never be modified in place.

    In AWS, you can use services such as **Elastic Container Service** (**ECS**) or **Elastic Kubernetes Service** (**EKS**) to manage containers.

While we will cover AWS containerization technologies in greater detail in the following chapters, it would be worthwhile seeing an AMI-backed EC2 instance in action, within your AWS account. Before we get there, let's start by getting your cloud environment ready for the hands-on exercises that follow.

# Getting started with AWS

To use AWS services in the cloud, you need to have an active AWS account subscription. In the following sections, we will sign up for one and ensure the required security measures are in place. Later, we will move on to creating an IAM user for deploying any hands-on exercises covered throughout this book. If you already have an AWS account, you might want to jump to the *Creating additional users* section.

> **Note**
> Please note that the steps listed in the *Creating a new AWS account* section are also available on the *AWS Getting Started* page: `https://docs.aws.amazon.com/accounts/latest/reference/manage-acct-creating.html`. It is advised that you follow the official docs for any updated information and guidance.

## Creating a new AWS account

If you don't have an AWS subscription, you can create a new account at `https://aws.amazon.com` by choosing **Create an AWS account**.

The initial screens will ask for your email address and contact information. Once you've provided that information, the website will ask you to create a root user password, as shown in *Figure 3.1*:

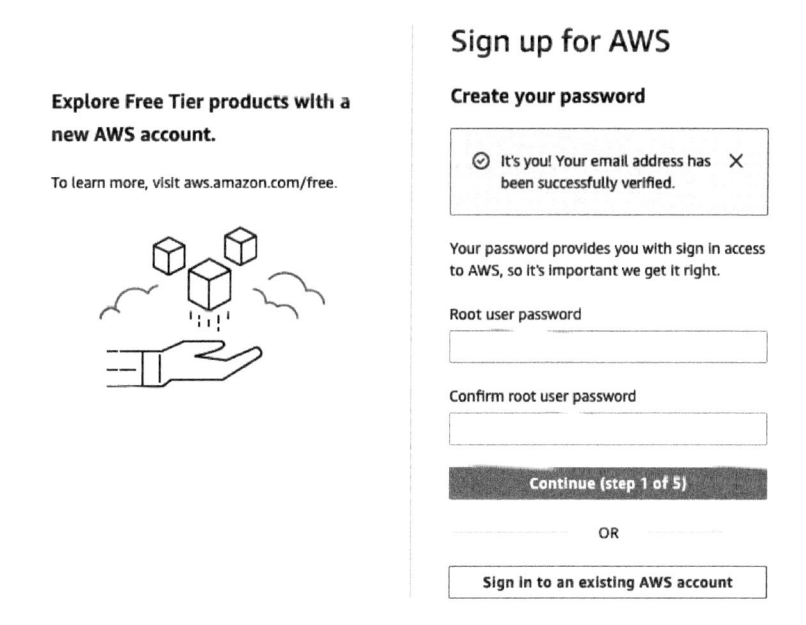

Figure 3.1: Root user credentials during AWS account creation

This is an extremely sensitive credential that should never be shared with anyone else. After the payment details have been successfully verified, you will be asked to select a support plan. For your personal use, I recommend signing up for the **Basic Support** plan, which is intended for developers or users who are just getting started with AWS.

## Securing your root user credentials

As soon as your account is activated, you will receive an email from AWS at your registered email address. You can use your browser to log into your newly created account using the AWS console sign-in page at `https://console.aws.amazon.com/`:

1. After a successful login, you will be greeted with the Console Home page (*Figure 3.2*):

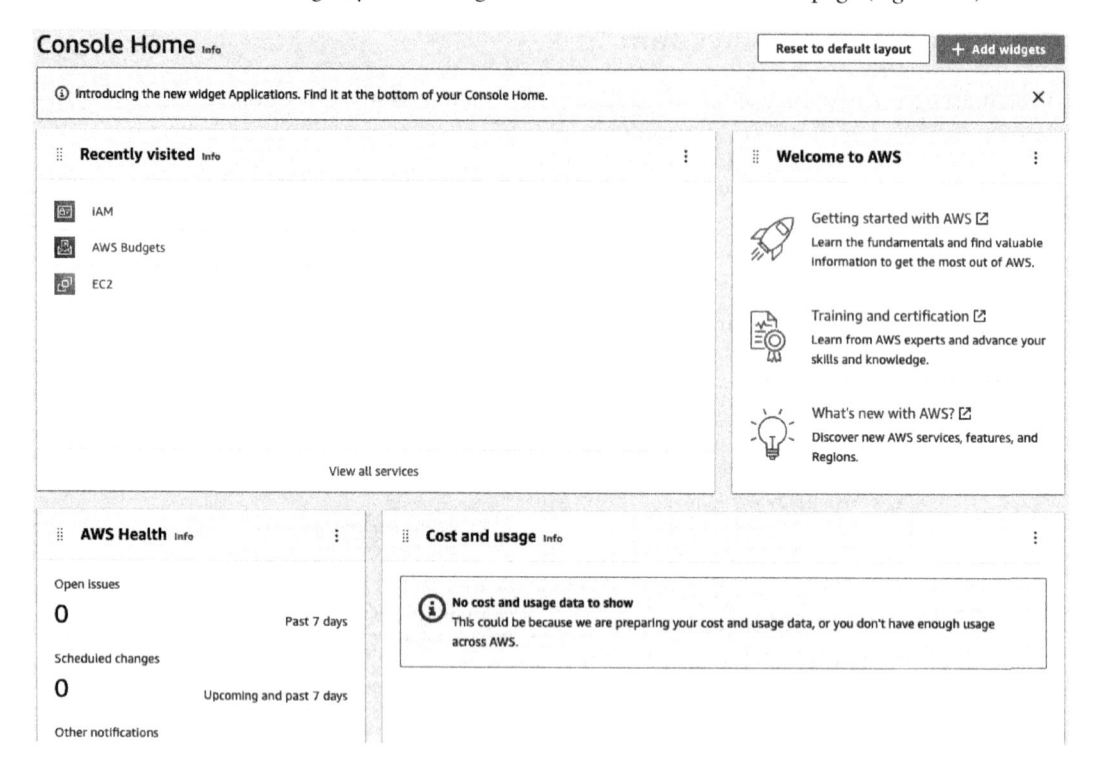

Figure 3.2: AWS Console Home page

2. In the search bar at the top, enter `IAM`, and then select **IAM** in the **Services** section. This will lead you to the IAM dashboard, where you can enable **multi-factor authentication (MFA)** for your root user, thereby adding an additional layer of security.

3. Under **Security Recommendations**, you will be prompted to secure the root user account with MFA. Choose **Add MFA**, then **Active MFA**. You can choose any of the listed options (*Figure 3.3*) as your MFA device. Enterprise companies typically use hardware tokens, but the use of virtual devices, or mobile apps such as **Authenticator**, is equally common these days:

## Manage MFA device

**Name***

aws-devops-simplified-mfa

Maximum 128 characters. Use alphanumeric and '+ = . . @ - _' characters.

Choose the type of MFA device to assign:

- **Virtual MFA device**
  Authenticator app installed on your mobile device or computer

- **Security key**
  Authenticate by using a FIDO security key, such as Yubikey

- **Other hardware MFA device**
  Hardware TOTP token

For more information about supported MFA devices, see AWS Multi-Factor Authentication

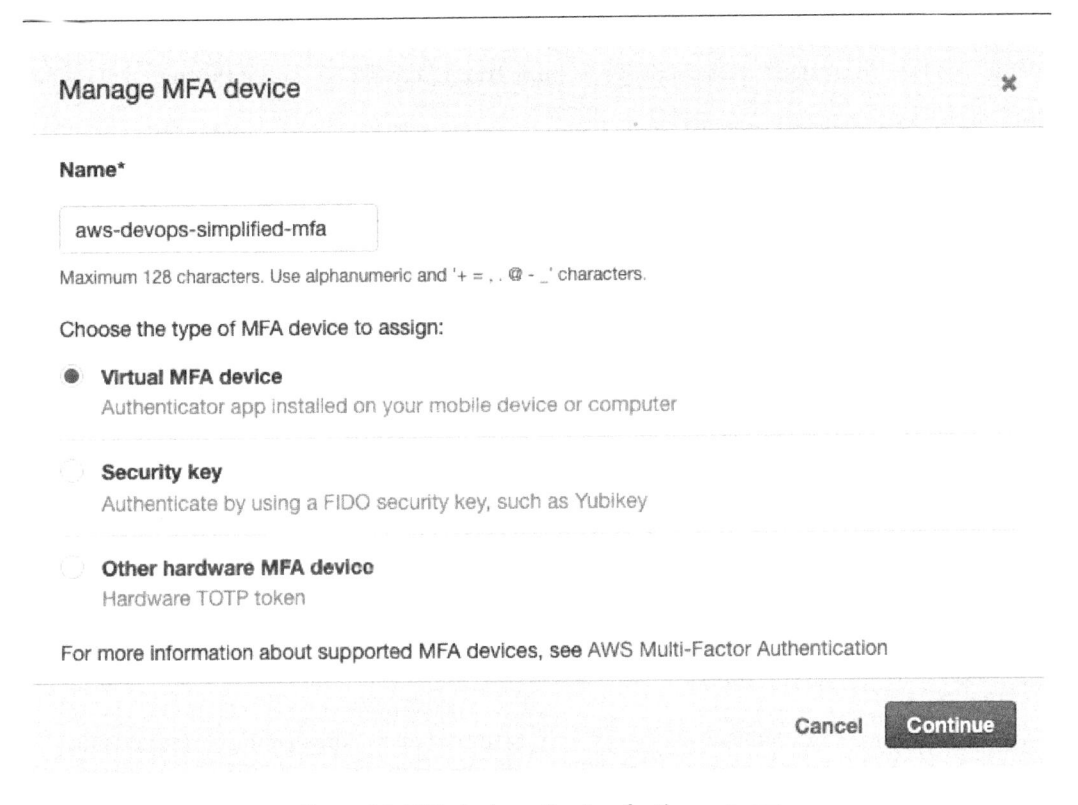

Cancel    **Continue**

Figure 3.3: MFA device activation for the root user

4. After selecting the appropriate device, you can click on **Continue**, which will lead you to the final steps required to connect your device to the account.

This will secure your AWS root account; all future logins will prompt for an additional MFA code.

## Creating additional users

It is a security best practice to **not use your root account** credentials for daily use. AWS recommends creating individual *users/groups*, with least privilege access tied to respective job functions.

For the hands-on exercises in this book, we will create a dedicated IAM user that can then be used to log into the AWS console. Each IAM user has a specific permission assigned to them and they can only make requests to the services defined in the attached policies. AWS offers a set of *managed* permissions based on common job functions, but you can also define a custom IAM policy to tailor the access as per your requirements.

For our needs, we'll create an IAM user with **AdministratorAccess**. Let's look at the steps that follow:

1. In the IAM console, select **Users** in the navigation panel and then click **Add Users**.
2. Enter a username you would like to identify these credentials with. In the following section, **Specify user details**, you can click on the checkbox that provides access to the AWS Management Console. Next, set **Console password** to **Autogenerated password** or type in a **Custom password** property.
3. Click **Next**; you will be taken to the **Set permissions** section, where you can attach an existing AWS policy directly. For our requirements, we will choose **AdministratorAccess** and assign it to the user we are creating.
4. Once the user creation process is complete, you can save your **User name** and **Console password** details, or email the sign-in instructions to an email ID.
5. As a security best practice, let's go ahead and assign an MFA device to this user. You may repeat the MFA steps shown in the *Secure your root user credentials* section or go through the steps provided in the official AWS docs (recommended): `https://docs.aws.amazon.com/IAM/latest/UserGuide/id_credentials_mfa_enable_virtual.html`.

> **Tip**
> Even though we are creating an IAM user here, it's important to note that this is *not* a practice you should be following in your actual AWS environments. From a security standpoint, you should always *federate* into your AWS accounts via some other **identity provider** (**IdP**), such as Azure AD, which should act as the authoritative source of credential management. Setting up an IdP is outside the scope of this book, so for the sake of simplicity, we will proceed with an IAM user. To secure its usage, please ensure that you have set up MFA access, as described previously.

Having created the IAM user for the hands-on exercises in this book, let's set up the customized **AWS Cloud9 integrated development environment** (**IDE**) that I have prepared for you.

## Setting up an AWS Cloud9 IDE in your AWS account

AWS Cloud9 is a cloud-based IDE that allows developers to write, edit, and deploy code from within the AWS console. We will be using it to deploy sample code covered in various chapters throughout this book.

> **Note**
>
> Please note that all the hands-on exercises in this book have been tested in the AWS Frankfurt (eu-central-1) region, using a t3.medium instance type of the Cloud9 environment. It's strongly advised that you use the same region in your AWS console. Furthermore, all activities from this point onwards will incur costs in your AWS account. A **5hrs/day** usage of the t3.medium compute instance costs roughly **7.30 USD** per month, for example. You can reduce these costs further by choosing a low-cost instance type, such as t3.small. Furthermore, it is highly recommended that you set up billing alarms in your AWS account. For instructions, please refer to https://docs.aws.amazon.com/AmazonCloudWatch/latest/monitoring/monitor_estimated_charges_with_cloudwatch.html.

You will use a **CloudFormation** template to perform a one-time installation of the IDE in your AWS account. If you have not used CloudFormation in the past, it is an AWS service that enables you to provision AWS infrastructure deployments predictably and repeatedly. A template is a YAML or JSON formatted file that defines certain AWS resources, as code, and deploys them as one group, known as a **stack**. We will dive into the details of the service in *Chapter 4, Managing Infrastructure as Code with AWS CloudFormation*. Let's proceed with installing the Cloud9 IDE:

1. First and foremost, download the template from this book's GitHub repository onto your local machine: https://github.com/PacktPublishing/AWS-DevOps-Simplified/blob/main/toolbox/cloud9-ide.yaml.

2. In the AWS console, log in with the IAM user we created in the previous section, switch to the eu-central-1 region, and search for the **CloudFormation** service in the search panel at the top.

3. Once you are on the service page, click the **Create stack** dropdown and select the **With new resources (standard)** option.

4. In the **Prepare template** section, select the **Template is ready** option.

5. In the subsequent section, **Specify template**, select **Upload a template file** and upload the file you downloaded in *Step 1*. Click **Next**.

6. Enter any stack name that you want. In the **Parameters** section, you can configure certain properties. However, it is recommended that you use the defaults unless you are sure about the changes you want to make.

7. Continue clicking **Next** until you arrive at the final screen, where you can click on the checkbox that asks for your acknowledgment to create IAM resources. Finally, click **Submit** – your Cloud9 IDE should be ready in 5-10 minutes.

Once the CloudFormation stack has been created, you can go to the Cloud9 service page to access your newly created environment.

## Navigating your Cloud9 environment

Look for the Cloud9 service in the AWS Web Console; you should see an environment on the service page called **AWS-DevOps-Simplified**, ready for you to use. Once you're ready, you can click on the **Open** link, which will load the IDE in your browser.

If you face any problems accessing the Cloud9 environment, please go through the suggestions listed on the troubleshooting page: https://docs.aws.amazon.com/cloud9/latest/user-guide/troubleshooting.html.

Once loaded, your browser page should look similar to *Figure 3.4*, with all the hands-on exercises configured so that you can deploy them in your AWS account:

Figure 3.4: Navigating the Cloud9 environment in your AWS account

Let's take a look at the three highlighted sections in *Figure 3.4*:

1. The navigation panel on the left allows you to browse the code files when you're going through the respective chapters, as well as make edits when needed.

2. Once you open a code file from the left navigation panel, you get a dedicated tab for it on the navigation bar at the top.

3. Cloud9 gives you an integrated Terminal that can be used to execute all the commands given in the hands-on exercises from here onwards. To confirm that it works fine, you can use the following command, which shows the version of the AWS CLI that's installed on the Cloud9 IDE:

```
Admin:~/environment $ aws --version
aws-cli/1.19.112 Python/2.7.18 Linux/4.14.320-243.544.amzn2.
x86_64 botocore/1.20.112
```

With AWS environment access configured, we are all set to proceed with our first hands-on exercise.

> **Note**
> If you are well-versed with `Docker`, and using AWS Cloud9 is not an option for you for some reason, I've also prepared a Docker image `akskap/awsdevopssimplified-toolbox:latest` that you can download on your local machine. All dependencies are pre-installed on this image, and the code for the hands-on exercises is available in the `/opt/aws-devops-simplified` directory. However, it is important to note that you will have to provision a programmatic IAM access key pair so that you can authenticate yourself from inside the Docker container when you're working on the hands-on exercises. From a security standpoint, using Cloud9 is the preferred and recommended option.

## Working with the test application

The test application that we want to deploy demonstrates the immutability offered by EC2 AMIs. We will create an AMI using Hashicorp's packer tool and use it to deploy a test server in our AWS account, in the Frankfurt region. All EC2 instances are deployed in a private network in your AWS account, known as a **Virtual Private Cloud** (**VPC**). Let's run a simple command that lists the default VPC that AWS has created for you in your newly set up account:

```
aws-devops-simplified:~/environment $ aws ec2 describe-vpcs --filters
Name=is-default,Values="true" --region eu-central-1
{
    "Vpcs": [
        {
            "VpcId": "vpc-068adcdab67978302",
            "InstanceTenancy": "default",
            "CidrBlockAssociationSet": [
                {
                    "AssociationId": "vpc-cidr-assoc-08c4cf86102517222",
                    "CidrBlock": "172.31.0.0/16",
                    "CidrBlockState": {
```

```
                    "State": "associated"
                }
            }
        ],
        "State": "available",
        "DhcpOptionsId": "dopt-0f4b0f7b37d374e83",
        "OwnerId": "449569851435",
        "CidrBlock": "172.31.0.0/16",
        "IsDefault": true
    }
  ]
}
```

This VPC ID will soon be used for deploying our test EC2 instance, using the AMI we register in our account. Please note that the resource identifiers, such as `vpc-068adcdab67978302`, as seen in the output, will be different for you as they will reflect the VPC present in your own AWS account.

## Test application

The test application for our use case is a simple Python-based web server implementation that responds to requests on port 8080:

```
# Python 3 server example
from http.server import BaseHTTPRequestHandler, HTTPServer
import time

hostName = "0.0.0.0"
serverPort = 8080

class MyServer(BaseHTTPRequestHandler):
    def do_GET(self):
        self.send_response(200)
        self.send_header("Content-type", "text/html")
        self.end_headers()
        self.wfile.write(bytes("<html><head><title>AWS DevOps Simplified</title></head>", "utf-8"))
        self.wfile.write(bytes("<p>Request: %s</p>" % self.path, "utf-8"))
        self.wfile.write(bytes("<body>", "utf-8"))
        self.wfile.write(bytes("<p>AWS DevOps Simplified - Simple HTTP Server</p>", "utf-8"))
        self.wfile.write(bytes("</body></html>", "utf-8"))

if __name__ == "__main__":
    webServer = HTTPServer((hostName, serverPort), MyServer)
```

```
        print("Server started http://%s:%s" % (hostName, serverPort))

    try:
        webServer.serve_forever()
    except KeyboardInterrupt:
        pass

    webServer.server_close()
    print("Server stopped.")
```

This is a sample web server implementation where Python listens for incoming GET requests on port 8080 and responds with a static string *AWS DevOps Simplified - Simple HTTP Server*. Let's jump into creating a new AMI with a widely adopted automation tool – Hashicorp's **Packer**.

## Building an AMI with Packer

Packer is an open source tool from Hashicorp that automates the process of building system images. It works with all major cloud providers and helps author your *golden images* – templates for your virtual machines in the cloud. It also offers a multi-cloud workflow to define a blueprint for creating images across multiple providers, such as AWS and GCP. For the scope of this chapter, we will focus on creating an AWS-based AMI and starting an EC2 instance off of it.

Packer leverages a JSON template that defines all the configurations for creating your AWS image. Using the CLI, you can target a specific configuration that defines the steps to create an AMI in your AWS account. Once the execution completes, you can simply create an EC2 instance using this standardized template with all software dependencies baked in. Using pre-baked AMIs ensures a good security posture and avoids the need for any modifications post instance creation.

Let's start our AMI build process with `packer`, inside the Cloud9 IDE we used previously. Packer configuration files can be found in the `packer/` folder, inside the `chapter-3` directory. A configuration file called `ami_build.json` pre-exists in the same directory. You will notice that the values for the `vpc_id` and `subnet_id` properties have been automatically updated for you, based on the resource identifiers in your AWS account. Please confirm that the right values are in place before proceeding with the AMI build using `packer`:

```
aws-devops-simplified:~/environment/chapter-3/packer $ packer build
ami_build.json
```

Completing the build gives an AMI ID toward the end that can later be used to provision an EC2 instance. If you observe the output on your local machine, `packer` executes the following steps:

1. Starting with some pre-validations, it creates a temporary SSH keypair in the AWS account to be able to log into the EC2 instance:

    ```
    ==> amazon-ebs: Prevalidating any provided VPC information
    ==> amazon-ebs: Prevalidating AMI Name: aws-devops-simplified-
    ```

```
   packer-1669369661
       amazon-ebs: Found Image ID: ami-076309742d466ad69
   ==> amazon-ebs: Creating temporary keypair: packer_63808f3e-
   c953-c575-6cf6-15543e77f52e
```

2. It creates a temporary security group that allows incoming traffic over port 22 from any IP address:

```
   ==> amazon-ebs: Creating temporary security group for this
   instance: packer_63808f40-9532-928d-ce28-d02bede1b7a8
   ==> amazon-ebs: Authorizing access to port 22 from [0.0.0.0/0]
   in the temporary security groups...
   ==> amazon-ebs: Prevalidating any provided VPC information
   ==> amazon-ebs: Prevalidating AMI Name: aws-devops-simplified-
   packer-1669369661
       amazon-ebs: Found Image ID: ami-076309742d466ad69
   ==> amazon-ebs: Creating temporary keypair: packer_63808f3e-
   c953-c575-6cf6-15543e77f52e
   ==> amazon-ebs: Creating temporary security group for this
   instance: packer_63808f40-9532-928d-ce28-d02bede1b7a8
   ==> amazon-ebs: Authorizing access to port 22 from [0.0.0.0/0]
   in the temporary security groups...
```

3. After the key pair and security group are available, it starts creating a temporary EC2 instance with the source AMI that we provided in the `ami_build.json` file:

```
   ==> amazon-ebs: Launching a source AWS instance...
       amazon-ebs: Instance ID: i-06267de9bb837aa15
   ==> amazon-ebs: Waiting for instance (i-06267de9bb837aa15) to
   become ready...
   ==> amazon-ebs: Using SSH communicator to connect: 18.196.17.104
   ==> amazon-ebs: Waiting for SSH to become available...
   ==> amazon-ebs: Connected to SSH!
```

4. It triggers the provisioning script, `server-provision.sh`, which installs all relevant software (a Python web server, for example) on this instance:

```
   ==> amazon-ebs: Provisioning with shell script: ./scripts/
   server-provision.sh
       amazon-ebs: Loaded plugins: extras_suggestions, langpacks,
   priorities, update-motd
       amazon-ebs: Resolving Dependencies
       amazon-ebs: --> Running transaction check
   ...
   ...
       amazon-ebs: Running transaction test
       amazon-ebs: Transaction test succeeded
       amazon-ebs: Running transaction
```

```
            amazon-ebs: Installed:
            amazon-ebs:   kernel.x86_64 0:5.10.149-133.644.amzn2
            amazon-ebs: Complete!
            amazon-ebs: Loaded plugins: extras_suggestions, langpacks,
    priorities, update-motd
            amazon-ebs: Package wget-1.14-18.amzn2.1.x86_64 already
    installed and latest version
            amazon-ebs: Running scripts as 'ec2-user'
            amazon-ebs: Making scripts executable
            amazon-ebs: Configure ADS Sample Server Service Unit File
    ==> amazon-ebs: Created symlink from /etc/systemd/system/multi-
    user.target.wants/ads-server.service to /etc/systemd/system/
    ads-server.service.
```

5. It stops the instance and creates an AMI based on the instance's state:

```
    ==> amazon-ebs: Stopping the source instance...
        amazon-ebs: Stopping instance
    ==> amazon-ebs: Waiting for the instance to stop...
    ==> amazon-ebs: Creating AMI aws-devops-simplified-
    packer-1669369661 from instance i-06267de9bb837aa15
        amazon-ebs: AMI: ami-09d522b72c0ca8128
    ==> amazon-ebs: Waiting for AMI to become ready...
    ==> amazon-ebs: Skipping Enable AMI deprecation...
```

6. After AMI creation is complete, it terminates the test EC2 instance and removes other temporary resources:

```
    ==> amazon-ebs: Terminating the source AWS instance...
    ==> amazon-ebs: Cleaning up any extra volumes...
    ==> amazon-ebs: No volumes to clean up, skipping
    ==> amazon-ebs: Deleting temporary security group...
    ==> amazon-ebs: Deleting temporary keypair...
    Build 'amazon-ebs' finished after 3 minutes 5 seconds.
    ==> Wait completed after 3 minutes 5 seconds
    ==> Builds finished. The artifacts of successful builds are:
    --> amazon-ebs: AMIs were created:
    eu-central-1: ami-09d522b72c0ca8128
```

This is how immutable infrastructure can be managed within AWS. All dependencies, software packages, and scripts to start the Python web server have been baked into the AMI. This is a discrete artifact that is version controlled and can be used to deploy EC2 instances in AWS. As soon as the instance creation is complete, the *SystemD* scripts start the web server, ready to respond to incoming HTTP GET requests.

To see this working in your web browser, let's quickly create relevant EC2 resources that are needed to bring up a test instance from this AMI.

## Deploying our test instance

To deploy our first EC2 instance using the AMI, we need some prerequisites to be in place. They can be created using the `AWS CLI` inside the Cloud9 IDE.

### Securing incoming traffic with security groups

AWS security best practices recommend a *security-in-depth* approach, where multiple levels of traffic controls allow, or reject, incoming packets. For the sake of simplicity and the scope of this chapter, we will use an instance-level security group that only allows incoming traffic originating from your local machine. Security groups are stateful, which means you don't have to define a corresponding *egress* rule for packets that are allowed by certain *ingress* rules:

1. First, let's see what the public IP address that is used for outgoing internet-bound traffic from your local machine is. A quick way to test this is by running a `curl` command on your local Terminal (not the Cloud9 IDE):

    ```
    → curl ipv4.icanhazip.com
    95.157.36.247
    ```

2. On your machine, you will get a different IP address. This will be used in the EC2 security group to allow incoming traffic on port 8080. From within the Cloud9 IDE, let's create a security group that will be later attached to the EC2 instance:

    ```
    aws-devops-simplified:~/environment/chapter-3/packer $ aws
    ec2 create-security-group --group-name aws-devops-simplified-
    webserver --description "This is a security group that
    allows incoming traffic destined for the webserver" --vpc-id
    vpc-06edc6a5d805901db --region eu-central-1
    {
        "GroupId": "sg-06320d12095603e68"
    }
    ```

3. By default, security groups allow all outgoing traffic from the instance. We just need to add a rule for the incoming TCP traffic on port 8080:

    ```
    aws-devops-simplified:~/environment/chapter-3/packer $ aws
    ec2 authorize-security-group-ingress --group-name aws-devops-
    simplified-webserver --protocol tcp --port 8080 --cidr
    95.157.36.247/32 --region eu-central-1
    {
        "Return": true,
        "SecurityGroupRules": [
    ```

```
            {
                "SecurityGroupRuleId": "sgr-0b38ce903b21e47cb",
                "GroupId": "sg-06320d12095603e68",
                "GroupOwnerId": "643998996127",
                "IsEgress": false,
                "IpProtocol": "tcp",
                "FromPort": 8080,
                "ToPort": 8080,
                "CidrIpv4": "95.157.36.247/32"
            }
        ]
}
```

With the AMI and security group ready, let's move onto creating the EC2 instance.

## Creating the test EC2 instance

1.  With all prerequisites covered, we can proceed with creating the instance:

    ```
    aws-devops-simplified:~/environment/chapter-3/packer $ aws ec2
    run-instances --instance-type t3.micro  --security-group-ids
    sg-06320d12095603e68 --image-id ami-0834874e33262e665 --region
    eu-central-1
    {
        "Groups": [],
        "Instances": [
            {
                "AmiLaunchIndex": 0,
                "ImageId": "ami-0834874e33262e665",
                "InstanceId": "i-00f089cfe084be59a",
                "InstanceType": "t3.micro",
                "LaunchTime": "2022-11-25T10:51:15+00:00",
                "Monitoring": {
                    "State": "disabled"
                },
                "Placement": {
                    "AvailabilityZone": "eu-central-1c",
    . . .
    ```

2.  Once the instance has been created, you can extract the public IP address to test the web application in your browser (*Figure 3.5*):

    ```
    aws-devops-simplified:~/environment/chapter-3/packer $  aws ec2
    describe-instances --region eu-central-1 --profile aws-devops-
    simplified
    . . .
    ```

```
                        "PrivateDnsName": "ip-172-31-6-119.
    eu-central-1.compute.internal",
                        "PrivateIpAddress": "172.31.6.119",
                        "ProductCodes": [],
                        "PublicDnsName": "ec2-18-197-150-199.
    eu-central-1.compute.amazonaws.com",
                        "PublicIpAddress": "18.197.150.199",
                        "State": {
                            "Code": 16,
                            "Name": "running"
    . . .
```

Accessing the public IP address over port 8080 gets us a response from the Python server running on the instance.

Figure 3.5: Accessing the EC2 hosted web server in your browser

## Terminating the test EC2 instance

As of writing this book, AWS offers a free-tier usage policy, which includes a certain number of compute hours that can be used per month, without incurring any costs. Now that we've completed all the tests, it is time to remove the EC2 instance so that we don't exceed this limit:

```
aws-devops-simplified:~/environment/chapter-3/packer $aws ec2
terminate-instances --instance-ids i-00f089cfe084be59a --region
eu-central-1
{
    "TerminatingInstances": [
        {
            "CurrentState": {
                "Code": 32,
                "Name": "shutting-down"
            },
            "InstanceId": "i-00f089cfe084be59a",
            "PreviousState": {
                "Code": 16,
                "Name": "running"
            }
        }
```

        ]
}

## Summary

This chapter laid the foundations of immutable infrastructure and the benefits of adopting this approach for managing software at scale. This is important for delivering solutions with increased reliability and confidence. The same approach can easily be adopted on-premises, but AWS shines in this space as its infrastructure elasticity fits particularly well with such methodologies.

Those of you who have not used AWS before will also benefit from this chapter as we have covered creating an AWS account and security best practices around the usage of root credentials. It also provided some hands-on practice with the AWS CLI, and the toolbox setup. All of this will help you in the upcoming chapters as the hands-on exercises in this book will leverage the tooling baked into the Cloud9 IDE.

Finally, we used tools such as Packer to create an AMI and deployed an EC2 instance hosting the Python web server application. We used some resources such as a default VPC and the subnets that were pre-created by AWS when we set up our account.

In *Chapter 4, Managing Infrastructure as Code with AWS CloudFormation*, we will dive deeper into managing these resources as code.

## Further reading

To learn more about the topics that were covered in this chapter, take a look at the following resources:

- The AWS services offered in the free tier: `https://aws.amazon.com/free/`
- Packer tutorial for building an AWS AMI: `https://developer.hashicorp.com/packer/tutorials/aws-get-started/aws-get-started-build-image`
- AWS security best practices: `https://aws.amazon.com/architecture/security-identity-compliance/`

# Part 2
# Faster Software Delivery with Consistent and Reproducible Environments

This part focuses on the AWS foundations that enhance the software delivery process using consistent and reproducible environments. You will explore the benefits of managing infrastructure as code, learn how AWS CloudFormation works under the hood, and experience the setup of a CI/CD pipeline using AWS-managed services. Taking the learnings further, you will dive into the fundamentals of AWS CDK – a programmatic approach to managing infrastructure in AWS – while deploying an image recognition app in your AWS account.

This part has the following chapters:

- Chapter 4, Managing Infrastructure as Code with AWS CloudFormation
- Chapter 5, Rolling Out a CI/CD Pipeline
- Chapter 6, Programmatic Approach to IaC with AWS CDK

# 4
# Managing Infrastructure as Code with AWS CloudFormation

What does **Infrastructure as Code** (**IaC**) mean? How can we get started with this approach to managing infrastructure resources? Simply put, IaC is an approach to applying software engineering DevOps practices, such as version control, auditability, testing, and pipeline automation, to infrastructure resources. These days, the success of rapidly evolving application architectures largely depends on the stability and elasticity of the underlying infrastructure. Infrastructure can no longer be seen separately from code; rather, *it is code*. AWS offers several capabilities to support this approach. By leveraging services such as **AWS CloudFormation**, you can achieve the same level of automation and reliability as seen in software delivery, also at the infrastructure level. Adopting IaC practices allows software professionals to spend less time on ensuring the reliability, portability, and consistency of the underlying infrastructure, which has a direct positive impact on the software that runs on top of it.

The core idea behind IaC is to prevent the problems associated with **environmental drift**. A commonly adopted DevOps methodology for improving the software delivery pipeline is to use dedicated development, staging, and production environments. To support these software applications in the cloud, developers typically depend on a lot of infrastructure resources, such as load balancers, application servers, firewalls, and databases. Manually configuring them can be a Herculean task. Historically, companies used to build and maintain operational runbooks and document all the steps, but this cannot support the pace of infrastructure change rollout in the cloud. Furthermore, system administrators can easily forget what component configuration was applied in a particular environment, and not others. This results in the environments being out of sync, causing unexpected application behaviors since the software was developed and tested in an environment that differed from how production looked like. Overall, this leads to bad customer experience, unreliable infrastructure, and operational complications.

Managing the complete infrastructure stack as code solves these problems and leads to increased efficiencies around deployment speed and faster feedback cycles. The idea of infrastructure disposability also gets a boost when infrastructure is managed with code. Infrastructure configurations are no longer embedded in the respective systems, but rather available at the surface, allowing everyone to understand and debug communication patterns between different components.

We will cover the following topics in this chapter:

- What is AWS CloudFormation?
- Good design practices when using AWS CloudFormation
- How to choose between Terraform and AWS CloudFormation
- Hands-on exercise to deploy infrastructure and application stacks with AWS CloudFormation

Let's establish a basic understanding of important AWS CloudFormation concepts first before we dive into more advanced topics.

## Technical requirements

For this chapter, you will require the following:

- AWS Cloud9 IDE deployed in your AWS account
- An active AWS account subscription

## What is AWS CloudFormation?

AWS exposes well-defined APIs to manage resources in the cloud. When we trigger a command such as `aws ec2 run-instances`, the CLI invokes the respective **Elastic Compute Cloud (EC2)** APIs in the background to perform desired actions. Enterprise-grade architectures require much more than just the creation of such resources. You want to define inter-dependencies between all the components, adapt the resources based on the environment's type (development/production), seed them with initial data, and control and track any modifications on the entire stack. AWS CloudFormation simplifies all this by allowing the user to define their infrastructure resources with a YAML/JSON template. After adding all the resources to the file, you can manage the entire stack as a single unit. Provisioning and de-provisioning the entire unit is now a matter of running a single CloudFormation command, such as `aws cloudformation deploy --template-file template.yml -stack-name teststack`. That's the power of IaC. Imagine provisioning the same template across multiple AWS accounts (and regions) to have the entire stack replicated with ease. Let's dive deeper into the AWS CloudFormation concepts that are used in the context of a template.

### Key concepts in AWS CloudFormation

There are three fundamental concepts you need to be aware of when using the CloudFormation service to manage infrastructure resources in your AWS account. Let's go through them and identify the CLI commands that you will use when working with each.

## Stacks

When managing IaC, you want to deal with the related resources as a single unit. For example, a three-tier web application will require you to create a set of resources, such as the load balancer, compute instance, and database server. It is ideal to be able to manage them all within a single template. This simplifies the management of the dependencies and stack operations. In CloudFormation terminology, this single unit is what is referred to as a **stack**. A template definition is a prerequisite for AWS CloudFormation to understand the resources you'd like to create and the configurations to be used for those resources.

You can create a stack in your AWS account with the `aws cloudformation deploy` command.

## Change sets

Just like software applications, infrastructure needs to adapt to changing requirements. This results in the modification of stacks that have already been deployed by CloudFormation in an AWS account. Some resources in AWS are *immutable*, which means any modification requires a complete replacement since in-place updates are not possible. To provide a safety net around such operations, CloudFormation allows you to evaluate the impact of your changes before you roll them out. This intermediate stage is known as a **change set**. After a change set has been created, it tells you about the impact of the planned stack update operation on existing resources. If you notice unexpected changes to the resources, you can cancel the update process; otherwise, you can go ahead with the final rollout.

To create a change set, you can use the `aws cloudformation create-change-set` command.

## Template

A CloudFormation **template** is a blueprint of the resources in your infrastructure stack and their dependencies. It is the interface between the infrastructure developer and the service itself. What gets defined here becomes part of a *stack* that CloudFormation will eventually roll out in your AWS account. It is a text file that is consumed by the service to provision resources. When you trigger a CloudFormation deployment, you need to pass a template file as an argument to the CLI command. Within a template, there are several constructs that you can leverage to define your infrastructure components. Let's go through some of them.

### Resources

This is a mandatory section of the template that defines the resources that should be created in your AWS account. It also includes the properties that define specific configurations those resources should have. A simple example could be the creation of an EC2 instance, mapped to a particular security group, and using a specific **Amazon Machine Image (AMI)**:

```
Resources:
  TestEC2Instance:
    Type: AWS::EC2::Instance
    Properties:
```

```
      ImageId: ami-0834874e33262e665
      InstanceType: t3.micro
      SubnetId: subnet-0e4f97bea5c50b873
      SecurityGroupIds:
        - sg-06320d12095603e68
      KeyName: test-key-pair
```

Deploying this template will create an EC2 instance with all the configurations defined under the `TestEC2Instance:` section. You will notice that most of the configurations reference pre-existing resource identifiers. This means that they should be present in the respective AWS account (and region) before you deploy a stack using this template.

> **Tip**
> Most of the AWS services are region scoped and you should take special care about the implications this could have. For example, a public AMI available in `eu-central-1` cannot be referenced in your CloudFormation template when you're deploying a stack in another region. Furthermore, AWS ensures that none of your resources transfer data to another region unless they've been explicitly configured by the user. You should keep this in mind when you're working on architectures that need to comply with strict data residency and compliance needs.

Therefore, please keep in mind that hard-coding configurations is not a good design practice as stack deployments will fail if prerequisites don't exist. Secondly, it's difficult to reuse such templates in other AWS accounts and regions. Security, reusability, and modularity should be at the top of your mind when you're working with them. We will cover some good design practices later in the *Best practices for using CloudFormation to define enterprise-grade architectures* section.

To ensure reusability and a clean design, CloudFormation offers the capability to use **parameters**, which can be defined at runtime. This enables dynamic configuration possibilities and simplifies template maintainability.

## Parameters

These are the values that you pass to your template during stack creation. It helps separate the design from the configuration. You can have defaults, and also provide a list of allowed values, to control what the user can or cannot use. Once the parameters have been defined, it is easy to reference them in the `Resources` section using the `Ref` keyword:

```
Parameters:
  InstanceType:
    Type: String
    Default: t3.micro
    AllowedValues:
      - t3.micro
```

```
            - m5.medium
   ...
   ...
Resources:
  Ec2Instance:
    Type: AWS::EC2::Instance
    Properties:
      InstanceType:
        Ref: InstanceType
   ...
   ...
```

This makes your templates flexible as they can adapt to the values provided at runtime.

## Conditions

**Conditions** provide a control mechanism in your template. Based on a certain condition being `true` or `false`, you could either skip the resource creation altogether or use a different configuration value when deploying the stack. This is useful in situations where you would like different values for development or production, for example:

```
   ...
Conditions:
  SkipResourceCreation: !Equals
    - !Ref Environment
    - dev
   ...
   ...
Resources:
  EC2Instance:
    Type: AWS::EC2::Instance
    Condition: SkipResourceCreation
   ...
```

But what if you would like to block the stack's operation based on the evaluation of certain parameter values? Let's have a look at **rules**.

## Rules

This is an optional section of your template that can be used to evaluate a certain combination of parameter values and block the stack creation or update process. It works around the concepts of a *rule condition* and an *assertion*. If you don't define any condition, then the rule assertion will always be evaluated:

```
Rules:
  testInstanceType:
```

```
      RuleCondition:
        !Equals - !Ref Environment
        - test
      Assertions:
        - Assert:
          'Fn::Contains':
            - - t3.medium
            - !Ref InstanceType
          AssertDescription: 'For a test environment, the instance type
  must be t3.medium'
```

This rule denies stack updates or creation when the instance type is different than t3.medium.

So far, we've covered different ways to pass information to a CloudFormation template. What if we need some information in return after stack operations are complete? This is where **outputs** come into the picture.

### Outputs

These are the values that you would like to retrieve after the stack operations have been completed. You can access them via the console or CLI commands, or reference them in other templates as *imports*. This approach ensures that the templates are of a manageable size as you don't have to put all the resources together in one big file. You can define an output value using the Outputs construct:

```
Outputs:
  InstanceID:
    Description: ID of the EC2 instance
    Value: !Ref EC2Instance
```

As soon as the stack operations are complete, you can access the identifier of the new EC2 instance using the InstanceID key.

The concepts we've covered so far should help you get started with the practical day-to-day usage of the CloudFormation service. To make debugging issues easier, let's discuss the internals of how CloudFormation works under the hood.

## How CloudFormation works

AWS services such as CloudFormation are great at reducing the cognitive load of the end user. A lot of internal details are abstracted, exposing only the functionalities that the users need. However, in certain situations, it's important to understand what the service is internally doing. This not only helps debug problems faster but also gives you a good thinking ground when discussing topics such as security, compliance, and day-to-day operations for your organization.

## Permissions delegation for resource management

By default, AWS CloudFormation uses the permissions of the user that invokes the CLI commands or uses the service directly in the web console. So, in a way, the end user *delegates* authority to the service for temporary use. If you face any permission denial issues, then this is the first thing you should be checking.

For all stack operations, CloudFormation generates temporary security tokens that match the user's IAM permissions. This sequence of actions is highlighted in *Figure 4.1*. Using this token, the service invokes the API endpoints of all services you are creating resources for. For example, if you are creating an EC2 instance in the eu-central-1 region, CloudFormation will use the regional EC2 service endpoint, ec2.eu-central-1.amazonaws.com, and register an instance creation request on your behalf. If required, you can also define a service role in IAM. This role can then be assumed by the service during any stack operation. You can leverage this to scope different permission sets for the service than what the user possesses. This service role needs to be passed as an argument when the stack is first deployed:

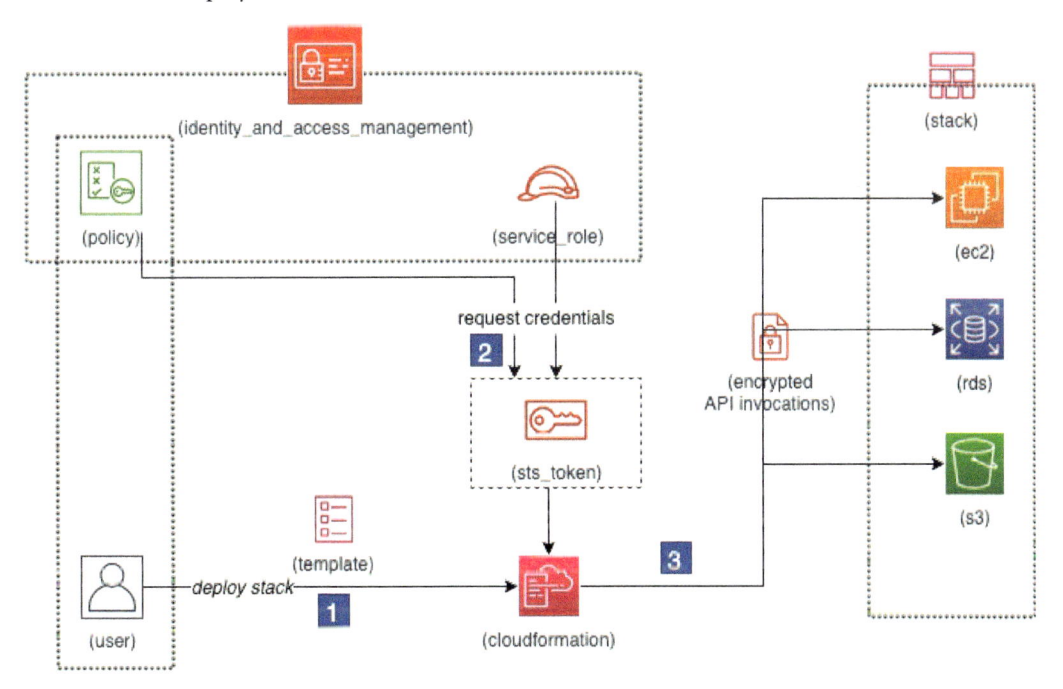

Figure 4.1: Sequence of operations when working with CloudFormation

## API call logging with CloudTrail

Like other AWS services, AWS CloudFormation is integrated with **AWS CloudTrail** for logging its API activities. It's interesting to note how a single CLI command from your Terminal translates into multiple API calls in the background, all targeted toward realizing the infrastructure stack described in your CloudFormation template.

AWS CloudTrail's event history describes all the event payloads from the APIs triggered by the service on your behalf. Let's see what events are logged during the creation of a simple stack:

```yaml
AWSTemplateFormatVersion: 2010-09-09
Description: Demonstrate CloudTrail log integration
Resources:
  MyS3Bucket:
    Type: 'AWS::S3::Bucket'
    Properties:
      BucketName: devops-simplified-cfn-test-bucket
  MyEC2Instance:
    Type: 'AWS::EC2::Instance'
    Properties:
      ImageId: ami-0c956e207f9d113d5
      InstanceType: t3.micro
      SubnetId: subnet-0a09e573bc8792a95
```

Let's deploy our stack in the `eu-central-1` region using the AWS CLI:

```
aws cloudformation deploy \
  --stack-name devops-simplified-test \
  --template-body file://template.yml \
  --region eu-central-1
```

Once the stack has been created, you can see the logged API calls in the CloudTrail console. These are highlighted in *Figure 4.2*:

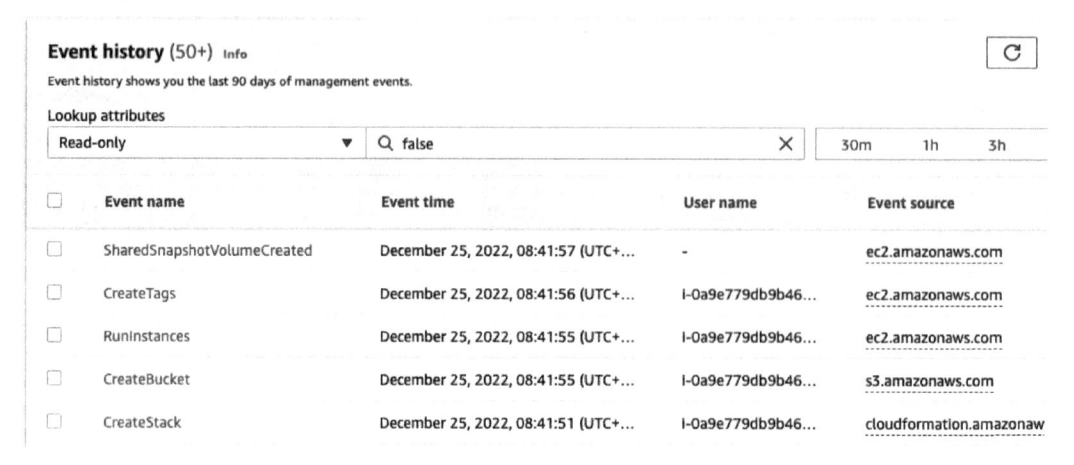

| Event name | Event time | User name | Event source |
|---|---|---|---|
| SharedSnapshotVolumeCreated | December 25, 2022, 08:41:57 (UTC+... | - | ec2.amazonaws.com |
| CreateTags | December 25, 2022, 08:41:56 (UTC+... | i-0a9e779db9b46... | ec2.amazonaws.com |
| RunInstances | December 25, 2022, 08:41:55 (UTC+... | i-0a9e779db9b46... | ec2.amazonaws.com |
| CreateBucket | December 25, 2022, 08:41:55 (UTC+... | i-0a9e779db9b46... | s3.amazonaws.com |
| CreateStack | December 25, 2022, 08:41:51 (UTC+... | i-0a9e779db9b46... | cloudformation.amazonaw |

Figure 4.2: API calls logged in CloudTrail as a result of stack creation

The following sequence of events was logged in CloudTrail:

1. Stack creation triggered by the user resulted in the `CreateStack` event being logged.
2. CloudFormation invoked the respective APIs from the EC2 and S3 services to create the resources defined in the template. These events were logged as `CreateBucket` and `RunInstances`.
3. CloudFormation requested the assignment of relevant tags on the EC2 instance. These tags identify the `stack-name` and `stack-id` properties that created the instance. The event type in this case was `CreateTags`.
4. Finally, we can see the `SharedSnapshotVolumeCreated` event log, which was a result of the EC2 service requesting a volume creation from an existing snapshot.

These audit logs are very important to understand the service behavior and dissect the activities happening behind the scenes. Typically, organizations set up forwarding of CloudTrail trails to a centralized S3 bucket for audit purposes. This data is sometimes also forwarded to **Security Information and Event Management** (**SIEM**) systems.

## How requests flow over the network

Have you ever tried using the `--debug` flag with your AWS CLI commands? When executing CloudFormation commands with this option enabled, you will notice the regional service endpoints being invoked:

```
2022-12-25 10:12:38,034 - MainThread - urllib3.connectionpool - DEBUG
- Starting new HTTPS connection (1): cloudformation.eu-central-1.
amazonaws.com:443
```

These domains resolve to public IP addresses, which means internet connectivity is a prerequisite when executing these commands from within a VPC. Highly regulated environments generally deny all outgoing internet-bound requests. To cater to such requirements, AWS offers a brilliant offering known as **AWS PrivateLink**. This allows you to route these requests to private internal endpoints, removing the need for internet connectivity altogether. However, please be aware that these PrivateLink endpoints cost around $7/month, per AZ, without considering any data transfer costs.

CloudFormation supports the creation of VPC interface endpoints to allow private access mode. Once these have been provisioned in your VPC, service endpoints such as `cloudformation.eu-central-1.amazonaws.com` start resolving to a private IP address. As a result, your requests flow through a private network into the AWS backbone, without any packets traversing the internet.

There is a lot more to the service, but considering the scope of this chapter, I believe what we've discussed so far should set you on a strong foot. When designing enterprise-grade infrastructure architectures, there are a few design principles that you should consider.

# Best practices for using CloudFormation to define enterprise-grade architectures

When it comes to architectural designs spawning multiple accounts, teams, and regions, there are a few guiding principles you should always keep in mind.

## Keep templates small and reusable

When you are just getting started, you work with small templates targeting a minimal set of resources. Over time, the needs of your team and organization grow, which can lead to an uncontrolled expansion of the same template for all future additions. It is a good practice to restrict the scope of these templates based on the team's responsibilities and the applications they own. Managing infrastructure resources for two different applications in the same stack can have adverse effects on the team's agility and introduce dependencies. Furthermore, it also introduces an element of risk as some stack operations can affect all other resources.

Secondly, maintaining small templates promotes reusability. For example, a three-tier web application following all the best practices and organizational security controls could easily be shared with other teams to get them started with a secure and compliant infrastructure baseline.

Managing dependencies between different stacks can be simplified with inputs and outputs.

## Leverage inputs and outputs for cross-stack dependencies

As discussed previously, CloudFormation can export certain resource identifiers for use by other stacks. This can be achieved by defining `Output` parameters and exporting these values with a predefined name. In such cases, the service acts as a message bus facilitating communication between different stacks.

Stacks that import these values use the `Fn::ImportValue` intrinsic function:

```yaml
Resources:
  WebServerInstance:
    Type: 'AWS::EC2::Instance'
    Properties:
      InstanceType: t3.micro
      ImageId: ami-0c956e207f9d113d5
      NetworkInterfaces:
        - GroupSet:
            - Fn::ImportValue
              'Fn::Sub': '${NetworkStack}-SecurityGroupID'
```

In this example, the stack is importing `SecurityGroupID` from another stack whose name is referenced by the `${NetworkStack}` parameter.

## Leverage other service integrations

It is a good practice to avoid including secure data such as passwords, service tokens, and API keys in your templates as they will most likely be added to some code version control. Passing them as parameter values during runtime should ideally be avoided as those values can be identified from the stack inputs. AWS CloudFormation offers integrations with services such as **AWS Secrets Manager** and **AWS Parameter Store** to securely transfer data at runtime. Without building any additional tooling or workflows, you can directly reference those parameter keys in your template and CloudFormation will inject them during stack operations. Of course, appropriate IAM permissions will have to be ensured for CloudFormation to be able to extract those values.

This integration can be used to retrieve the entire secret string or a particular value from the secret. To extract the password value of the `SecureData` secret stored in SecretsManager, you can use the `'{{resolve:secretsmanager:SecureData:SecretString:password}}'` dynamic reference.

## Leverage StackSets for organization-wide stack rollouts

Multi-account and multi-region environments require certain services to be enabled, or resources to be created, as soon as new accounts are vended. It is a good practice to roll out these resources with CloudFormation StackSets. StackSets extend the capabilities of stacks by providing an additional orchestration layer on top of them. You can target individual accounts or a group of accounts within an **organizational unit** (**OU**). StackSets can be a big productivity boost when you want to ensure a minimum baseline of resources in multiple regions and accounts. It helps you link a template definition to intended targets and manages all stack operations from that point onwards.

## Avoid hardcoding parameter values

A rule of thumb for good template design is to not have any hardcoded parameter values. These can be passed at runtime to make a variety of configuration permutations possible. Production installations could use a different instance type than the test/dev environments. CloudFormation conditions can also be used to conditionally roll out certain resources in an environment.

## Life cycle policies to protect critical resources

AWS resources that interact with your on-premises environments or maintain data and state are some examples of critical components. Losing them can result in unexpected application failures or data loss. CloudFormation offers life cycle policies that can safeguard such resources from accidental deletion. One such policy is `DeletionPolicy`, which marks any CloudFormation resource for retention when the stack is deleted. This avoids accidental removal and post-stack deletion as this resource is no longer managed by CloudFormation.

By default, some resources, such as `AWS::RDS::DBCluster`, go through a snapshot process before they are removed, but this is something you need to ensure on a per-resource basis.

### Reusable resource configurations

Certain resource combinations represent frequently defined stacks and are a good candidate for reuse. A three-tier web application and a static website hosted in S3 are some examples. **Modules** are one such feature in CloudFormation that allow the end user to publish reusable templates in a centralized registry. This avoids re-inventing the wheel every time a similar stack configuration needs to be provisioned.

Cloud platform teams can use this feature to make certain modules available in the member accounts across the organization. If you've worked with **Terraform** in the past, then you might have used modules there as well. Functionally, they both offer similar benefits around code reuse and modularity.

By now, I am sure you are convinced of CloudFormation's capabilities around managing your AWS infrastructure resources at scale. While it's the official IaC offering from the cloud provider, it's not the only one you can work with. Terraform is another tool that is quite famous in the infrastructure space and offers similar capabilities across other cloud providers, such as Azure and GCP. When starting with AWS, organizations always get into a dilemma about which tool they should go ahead with. Let me make this easy for you.

## Deciding between Terraform and CloudFormation

Terraform is an offering from **Hashicorp** and uses **Hashicorp Configuration Language (HCL)** for resource definitions. It is commonly adopted by organizations working with multiple cloud providers as it offers a standard templating scheme. Functionally, it works just like CloudFormation – that is, it directly consumes underlying service APIs from the cloud provider. Other benefits such as code version control, change tracking, and automation are more or less similar to what we already covered in the context of CloudFormation.

Getting started with either of the two to manage sizeable workloads is easy. The difference comes to the surface when you're dealing with a huge number of resources in a multi-account, multi-region organizational structure. Let's discuss some areas where these tools are uniquely positioned.

### Third-party provider ecosystem

Terraform lets you manage much more than just AWS resources. With support for over 1,000+ providers, you can additionally manage things such as **Active Directory**, **Kubernetes Helm Charts**, **GitHub/GitLab** repositories, RedisCloud instances, and so on. This is a big benefit when you want to codify not just your cloud components but other infrastructure services as well. The standard configuration language improves the user experience as you can use the same configuration syntax to work with multiple providers. However, it is important to note that it's not a *write once, deploy anywhere* tool. Your AWS resource configurations cannot be deployed as-is on Azure, for example.

CloudFormation does not offer much in this space. Of course, you could use custom resources to consume third-party APIs, but it has a learning curve and technical challenges. Terraform has an established ecosystem where many such providers have already made solutions available for adoption by the wider community.

## Mapping a resource definition with a deployment

Unlike CloudFormation, Terraform has a one-to-one mapping between what you define in the template and what gets deployed. This means creating multiple resources from the same definition often requires duplicating code. Terraform does not have a concept similar to a *stack* in CloudFormation, which can provision multiple resources from a common definition. Stacks act as an intermediary between the definition and the actual deployment. Terraform workspaces come close to this, but having a native construct in the service is altogether a better experience.

## Support for programming constructs

Terraform has support for programming constructs, such as for-loops, string manipulation, if-else branch workflows, and so on. It is easier for software developers to have this flexibility, but overusing them can make the templates difficult to understand. CloudFormation keeps this somewhat basic with conditions and rules but does not offer a lot of flexibility in a way that it maintains the declarative aspect of the templates and does not hide a lot of details around these constructs. It's easier to mess up with this logic in Terraform and end up with an unintentional change of state.

## State management for deployed resources

CloudFormation is rock solid in this area since all states are abstracted from the end user. Change sets are reliable and give a good overview of the modifications that the stack will go through if you proceed with the deployment. This can be easily incorporated into automation workflows. When it comes to sharing state data, you have the option to use *outputs* and *exports*, which we'll cover soon in the hands-on deployment.

Terraform, on the other hand, has different options to work with state. By default, it stores everything on a local disk, which leads to all sorts of trouble when you're working within a team. Remote storage is also offered but requires other services such as S3 and DynamoDB to be provisioned first. For state dependencies, entire state files have to be exposed, which is not a secure mechanism. So, CloudFormation's opinionated approach stands out in terms of stability and security.

## Better integrations offered by cloud-native services

Working with Terraform in a highly secure cloud environment with no internet connectivity can sometimes be difficult to set up. AWS offers VPC endpoints to work around such limitations, but imagine having to set up a separate VPC endpoint for every single service you work with. On the other hand, working with CloudFormation would require the creation of a single VPC endpoint for the service itself. The provisioning requests for all other resources are then entirely taken care of by the service itself as it directly consumes the service APIs using AWS' network backbone. As you can imagine, dealing with these problems in a large-scale deployment can be a pain, and services such as CloudFormation offer a more seamless user experience.

### Modules for code reusability

Working with modules in Terraform is a better experience. First of all, a large number of publicly available modules can be used for implementing your infrastructure stacks. This reduces the development and maintenance effort and you can get started in no time. Secondly, the tooling is much better integrated with external modules as you can see all changes as part of the `terraform plan` command, which is similar to what a change set does.

To summarize, both tools have their unique strengths, which could be more or less important for your specific use case. However, if you are just getting started with hosting your workloads on AWS, and foresee large-scale deployments becoming a reality in the near future, I would recommend going ahead with AWS CloudFormation. Vendor lock-in is commonly discussed as a drawback with this service, but I'd say that applies equally to using a third-party tool from another company. It is beneficial to use the right tool for solving the right problem, even if it comes down to using different IaC frameworks for efficiently managing resources across different cloud providers. Later in this book, we will cover some enterprise-grade CloudFormation deployment frameworks that have been used by many companies already.

So far, we have covered a lot of theoretical details and I am sure it would be a great experience for you to see the CloudFormation service in action. We will use a full-fledged infrastructure rollout to host an application in the AWS account. Let's get our hands dirty.

## Hands-on deployment with CloudFormation

In the previous chapter, we deployed an AMI with Hashicorp's **Packer**, followed by EC2 instance creation. We didn't have to worry about provisioning networks, public interfaces, internet gateways, and so on. This was possible because of the default VPC resources that were made available by AWS as part of the newly vended account. In real-life implementations, this is rarely the case. You design and implement the entire infrastructure stack from scratch, and automate its management with tools. This level of customization and automation of infrastructure provisioning is going to be our focus in this section. By quickly recapping the concepts we've discussed so far, we can get our hands dirty with actual code deployment activities. I will also walk you through some networking components along the way.

We will deploy our application as part of two CloudFormation stacks:

- **Network stack**: This will include all the networking components required to host a public internet-facing application in your AWS account. We will not use any default resources, which means everything, including VPCs, subnets, route tables, internet gateways, NAT gateways, and so on, will be managed through the CloudFormation template that we develop.

- **Application stack**: Once the networking foundations are ready, we will host our application in multiple availability zones to adhere to high-availability design principles. It is a good practice to abstract the underlying compute with a load balancer at the network edge. To achieve this, we will deploy an HTTP **application load balancer** (**ALB**) in the public subnets that can then respond to incoming requests from the users.

## Network architecture design to support multi-AZ deployments

We will deploy our networking resources in `eu-central-1`, also known as the Frankfurt region. Once all the components have been deployed, we will have a final design that looks similar to what's shown in *Figure 4.3*:

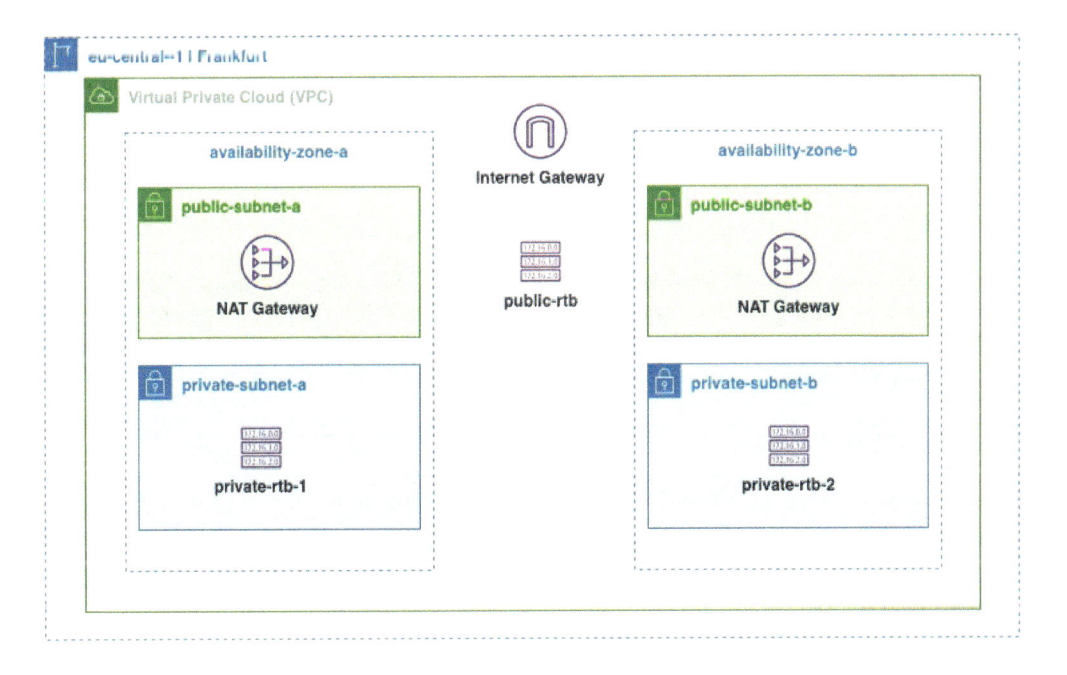

Figure 4.3: Networking resources deployed on the eu-central-1 region

Let's go through the relevant code snippets from the CloudFormation template to make deploying all these resources a reality.

### Virtual Private Cloud

These are region-scoped network entities that give you an IP address space that can be used to host your resources in the cloud. It is your private version of the data center, running in AWS. You can use a VPC to deploy application workloads that are internet-facing or completely private:

```
...
Parameters:
  VpcCIDR:
    Description: Please enter the IP range (CIDR notation) for this VPC
    Type: String
    Default: 10.192.0.0/16
...
Resources:
  VPC:
    Type: AWS::EC2::VPC
    Properties:
      CidrBlock: !Ref VpcCIDR
      EnableDnsSupport: true
      EnableDnsHostnames: true
...
```

You might notice that we haven't hardcoded any configuration values here, but instead used parameters to receive inputs at runtime. To ensure a good user experience, it's a good practice to additionally provide sensible defaults so that it becomes easy for anyone to try out these templates in their account with minimal effort.

### Internet gateway

We can use an internet gateway to allow internet traffic to flow into and out of the VPC. Internet gateways are VPC-scoped resources, which means you create them per region. It's important to note that in the absence of an internet gateway, your applications cannot receive traffic originating from the internet, even if they have public IPs attached to them. This behavior might be different from some other cloud providers. Within AWS, it helps you avoid any unplanned internet exposure, unless you set up all the required components and routing mechanisms around it:

```
...
Resources:
...
  InternetGateway:
    Type: AWS::EC2::InternetGateway
    Properties:
      Tags:
        - Key: Name
```

```
          Value: !Ref EnvironmentName

  InternetGatewayAttachment:
    Type: AWS::EC2::VPCGatewayAttachment
    Properties:
      InternetGatewayId: !Ref InternetGateway
      VpcId: !Ref VPC
...
```

In these resource definitions, we created an internet gateway and then attached it to the VPC that will host the application workloads.

### Public subnets

A VPC CIDR range is further divided into subnets that are **availability zone** (**AZ**) scoped. Since this is a multi-AZ architecture, we will deploy two public subnets. AWS does not natively support the concept of a public or private subnet. The routes that are added to these subnets define their behavior. By definition, public subnets are the ones that forward outgoing internet-bound traffic to the internet gateway. Resources hosted in a public subnet have publicly resolvable IP addresses and the subnet typically has a route for 0.0.0.0/0 pointing to the internet gateway. Let's have a look at the subnet's definition and the corresponding route table:

```
Resources:
...
  PublicSubnet1:
    Type: AWS::EC2::Subnet
    Properties:
      VpcId: !Ref VPC
      AvailabilityZone: !Select [ 0, !GetAZs '' ]
      CidrBlock: !Ref PublicSubnet1CIDR
      MapPublicIpOnLaunch: true
      Tags:
        - Key: Name
          Value: !Sub ${EnvironmentName} Public Subnet (AZ1)

  PublicRouteTable:
    Type: AWS::EC2::RouteTable
    Properties:
      VpcId: !Ref VPC
      Tags:
        - Key: Name
          Value: !Sub ${EnvironmentName} Public Routes

  DefaultPublicRoute:
```

```
      Type: AWS::EC2::Route
      DependsOn: InternetGatewayAttachment
      Properties:
        RouteTableId: !Ref PublicRouteTable
        DestinationCidrBlock: 0.0.0.0/0
        GatewayId: !Ref InternetGateway


  PublicSubnet1RouteTableAssociation:
    Type: AWS::EC2::SubnetRouteTableAssociation
    Properties:
      RouteTableId: !Ref PublicRouteTable
      SubnetId: !Ref PublicSubnet1
  ...
```

CloudFormation offers built-in functions that help you assign values that are not available until runtime. You can use these programming capabilities within your templates to construct, extract, and define different types of values. `!Select` (short form for `Fn::Select`) is one such function that can help you extract an item from a list, for a given index. Here, we get the ID of the first AZ so that we can deploy the public subnet. We also use `!Sub` to substitute the contents of the `EnvironmentName` parameter into the `Tag` value. This is an efficient approach to dynamically changing the resource tag names by modifying a single parameter in the template. You can explore other intrinsic functions supported by the service at https://docs.aws.amazon.com/AWSCloudFormation/latest/UserGuide/intrinsic-function-reference.html.

Please note that we also define similar resource blocks for the other public subnet, hosted in the second AZ, but they haven't been mentioned in this example to avoid redundancy.

We will use the public subnets to host an internet-facing load balancer that can receive requests from the end user and balance the load across multiple compute instances in the background.

### *Private subnets*

Similar to public subnets, private subnets are also carved out from the same VPC CIDR block. The key difference lies in the routes that are added to these subnets. Functionally, they are used to host resources that will not be exposed to the internet. If you recall the AMI deployment from the previous chapter, we hosted the EC2 instance directly in the public subnet of the default VPC, by allocating a public IP. In real-life implementations, it's not a good practice to expose the backend instances directly on the internet as it introduces architectural limitations around security, network ingress traffic inspection, and load balancing capabilities. So, resources such as backend servers, databases, and internal tools get deployed in these subnets:

```
  Resources:
    ...
```

```yaml
    PrivateSubnet1:
      Type: AWS::EC2::Subnet
      Properties:
        VpcId: !Ref VPC
        AvailabilityZone: !Select [ 0, !GetAZs '' ]
        CidrBlock: !Ref PrivateSubnet1CIDR
        MapPublicIpOnLaunch: false
        Tags:
          - Key: Name
            Value: !Sub ${EnvironmentName} Private Subnet (AZ1)
    PrivateRouteTable1:
      Type: AWS::EC2::RouteTable
      Properties:
        VpcId: !Ref VPC
        Tags:
          - Key: Name
            Value: !Sub ${EnvironmentName} Private Routes (AZ1)

    DefaultPrivateRoute1:
      Type: AWS::EC2::Route
      Properties:
        RouteTableId: !Ref PrivateRouteTable1
        DestinationCidrBlock: 0.0.0.0/0
        NatGatewayId: !Ref NatGateway1

    PrivateSubnet1RouteTableAssociation:
      Type: AWS::EC2::SubnetRouteTableAssociation
      Properties:
        RouteTableId: !Ref PrivateRouteTable1
        SubnetId: !Ref PrivateSubnet1
...
```

If you observe the outgoing traffic routes for the private subnet, you will see that we are leveraging another AWS service called a **NAT gateway**, which we'll cover next.

## NAT gateways

The resources that are deployed in private subnets are not exposed to the internet but still need outgoing internet connectivity to be able to download support patches, third-party hosted libraries, and so on. To support this outbound traffic flow, we must modify network routes in these subnets. Since these resources don't have a public IP attached to them, they need something to **Network Address Translation** (**NAT**) the requests when the packets go out. This is where NAT gateways come into the picture. They allow resources hosted in private subnets to have outbound internet connectivity. They are hosted in the public subnets, though, mainly because they want to route traffic to the internet via the internet gateway:

```
Resources:
...
  NatGateway1EIP:
    Type: AWS::EC2::EIP
    DependsOn: InternetGatewayAttachment
    Properties:
      Domain: vpc

  NatGateway1:
    Type: AWS::EC2::NatGateway
    Properties:
      AllocationId: !GetAtt NatGateway1EIP.AllocationId
      SubnetId: !Ref PublicSubnet1
...
```

An important CloudFormation construct that we'll cover here is `DependsOn`. This is used to mark explicit dependencies between two resources defined in the template.

We also use an **Elastic IP (EIP)** here, which is a static public IP address whose life cycle is independent of the resource it is attached to. You can move these IPs across several different AWS resources, which means you don't lose them when underlying resources are deleted. Big enterprises often follow IP whitelisting requirements with their customers. EIPs come in handy in such situations as you don't want to lose the IPs that have gone through lengthy approval processes already.

> **Tip**
> It is now possible to transfer EIPs across multiple accounts. The target account has 7 hours to accept this transfer once initiated. Organizations benefit from this transferability when they go through organizational restructuring and disaster recovery procedures.

### Stack outputs

Earlier, we discussed a best practice to keep your CloudFormation templates modular and organize them with ownership in mind. The network stack we just defined can be deployed and managed by the networking team, independent of the application teams. The application owners, however, will need to consume some resource identifiers from this stack's output (VPC ID, for example) in their own IaC stack definitions. This is where we can leverage stack *outputs* and make the outputs from this stack available for use by others:

```
...
Outputs:
```

```yaml
  VPC:
    Description: A reference to the created VPC
    Value: !Ref VPC
    Export:
      Name: !Join [ "-", [ !Ref "AWS::StackName", vpc-id ] ]
  PublicSubnet1:
    Description: A reference to the public subnet in the
1st Availability Zone
    Value: !Ref PublicSubnet1
    Export:
      Name: !Join [ "-", [ !Ref "AWS::StackName", public-subnet1 ] ]

  PublicSubnet2:
    Description: A reference to the public subnet in the
2nd Availability Zone
    Value: !Ref PublicSubnet2
    Export:
      Name: !Join [ "-", [ !Ref "AWS::StackName", public-subnet2 ] ]

  PrivateSubnet1:
    Description: A reference to the private subnet in the 1st
Availability Zone
    Value: !Ref PrivateSubnet1
    Export:
      Name: !Join [ "-", [ !Ref "AWS::StackName", private-subnet1 ] ]

  PrivateSubnet2:
    Description: A reference to the private subnet in the
2nd Availability Zone
    Value: !Ref PrivateSubnet2
    Export:
      Name: !Join [ "-", [ !Ref "AWS::StackName", private-subnet2 ] ]
```

Typically, there should only be a handful of resources that you want to share with others. For example, it does not help much if we expose the internet gateway or the NAT gateway IDs since they will always be managed by the networking team.

Now that we've covered all the CloudFormation resource definitions, it is time to roll out the network stack in our AWS account.

## Deploying the network stack

A complete version of the network stack template can be found at `https://github.com/PacktPublishing/AWS-DevOps-Simplified/blob/main/chapter-4/cfn-templates/network-stack.yml`.

From the AWS console, let's initiate a new session for our Cloud9 IDE. Once logged in, switch to the `chapter-4/` resources and trigger a stack deployment with the following command:

```
aws cloudformation deploy \
  --stack-name networking-stack \
  --region eu-central-1 \
  --parameter-overrides EnvironmentName=aws-devops-simplified \
  --template-file network-stack.yml

Waiting for changeset to be created..
Waiting for stack create/update to complete
Successfully created/updated stack - networking-stack
```

At this point, all the networking resources should be available in your AWS account, in the `eu-central-1` region, allowing us to proceed with the application deployment. Let's see what the application design and corresponding stack look like.

If you would like to see the exported data from this stack, CloudFormation offers a CLI command for this. It lists all the stack exports available in this AWS account, in the targeted region:

```
bash-5.1# aws cloudformation list-exports \
  --region eu-central-1 \

{
    "Exports": [
        {
            "ExportingStackId": "arn:aws:cloudformation:eu-central-1:643998996127:stack/networking-stack/7405c610-8540-11ed-a5cd-02aac4a6643a",
            "Name": "networking-stack-vpc-id",
            "Value": "vpc-0c522c9e7f154179e"
        }
        ...
        ...
    ]
}
```

## Hosting a sample web application with an application load balancer and Auto Scaling groups

We created our network resources across two separate availability zones in the `eu-central-1` region. For the application to benefit from this, we will deploy an **Auto Scaling group** (**ASG**) that covers both of these AZs. An ASG is an EC2 feature that offers automatic scale-in and scale-out of your application workloads, depending on some usage metrics. Due to the scope of this chapter, we will not go into a lot of the configuration details; instead; we will focus more on how the resources from the previous stack deployment will be consumed by our application. Since our backend instances will be hosted in the private subnets, we will expose them to the outside world via an internet-facing ABL, deployed in public subnets. The final application design that we will deploy can be seen in *Figure 4.4*:

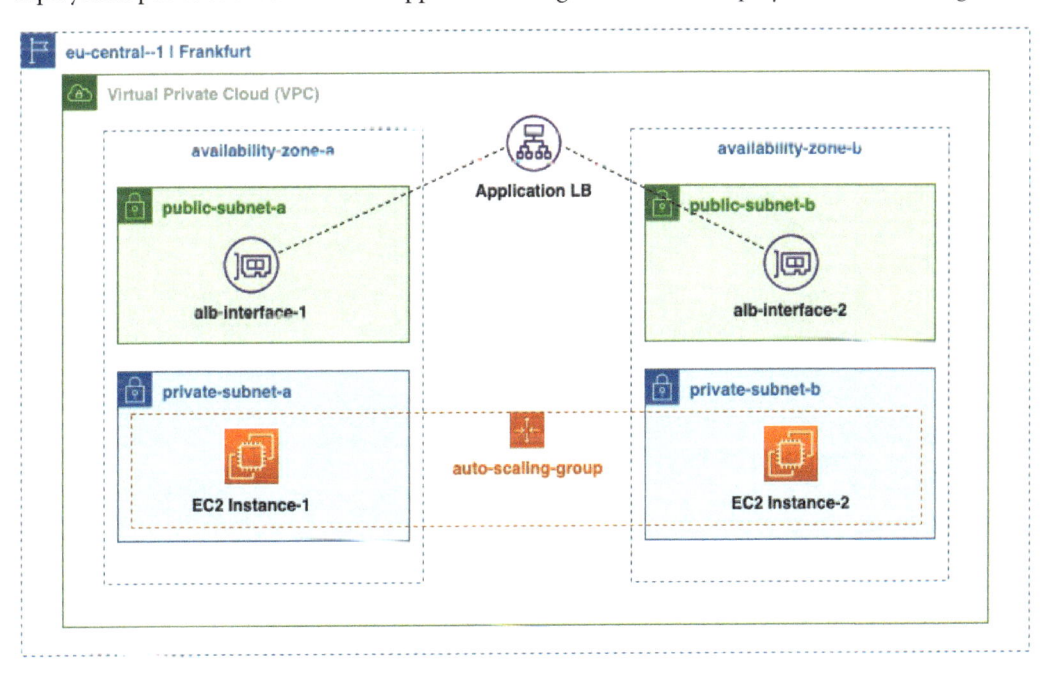

Figure 4.4: Web application with ALB and Auto Scaling groups

Let's discuss the various CloudFormation resources that come together to host the web application on top of the infrastructure components we deployed in the previous section.

### Application Load Balancer

The ALB is the component that supports both internet-facing and internal-only deployments. For our use case, we go with an internet-facing deployment scheme and host the load balancer in the public subnets. When an end user accesses the ALB domain in their browser, it resolves to the public

IP addresses of the corresponding network interfaces, and the traffic is forwarded to the backend EC2 instances:

```
Resources:
...
  AppLoadBalancer:
    Type: AWS::ElasticLoadBalancingV2::LoadBalancer
    Properties:
      Type: application
      Scheme: internet-facing
      Subnets:
        - Fn::ImportValue:
            'Fn::Sub': "${NetworkStackName}-public-subnet1"
        - Fn::ImportValue:
            'Fn::Sub': "${NetworkStackName}-public-subnet2"
      SecurityGroups:
        - !Ref AppLoadBalancerSecurityGroup
  AppLoadBalancerSecurityGroup:
    Type: AWS::EC2::SecurityGroup
    Properties:
      GroupDescription: This is the Security Group for ALB
      SecurityGroupIngress:
        - IpProtocol: tcp
          FromPort: 80
          ToPort: 80
          CidrIp: 0.0.0.0/0
      SecurityGroupEgress:
        - IpProtocol: tcp
          FromPort: 0
          ToPort: 65535
          CidrIp: 0.0.0.0/0
      VpcId:
        Fn::ImportValue:
          'Fn::Sub': "${NetworkStackName}-vpc-id"
...
```

ALB requires security group attachments, just like EC2 instances. Since this is an internet-facing application, we open the `tcp` traffic to the entire world with an ingress route for 0.0.0.0/0, over port 80,

I would like to highlight the use of two intrinsic functions that were referenced in this template:

- Importing stack outputs from a different deployment:

   `Fn::ImportValue`, as its name suggests, is used to import the outputs from another stack. We used the `aws cloudformation list-exports` command to list the exports from the network stack. The same values are referenced here, using this function. This is how CloudFormation allows you to resolve inter-stack dependencies while keeping the templates modular, and teams agile.

- Substituting data for generating configurations at runtime:

   Not all configurations can be statically defined in the templates. As seen in this example, the network stack could have been named in different ways. To keep the template definition flexible, we substituted the value of the respective parameter to form a well-defined string. Eventually, this allows us to import the required value from another stack.

### ALB listeners and target groups

To make the ALB understand the type of traffic it is handling, we can use the concept of **listeners**. They identify the protocol, port, and actions to take when packets are received. Listeners also map to a **target group**, which is where the matching traffic needs to be forwarded:

```
Parameters:
...
  NetworkStackName:
    Description: Identifies the name of the network stack.
    Type: String
...
Resources:
...
  AppLoadBalancerListener:
    Type: AWS::ElasticLoadBalancingV2::Listener
    DependsOn: AppLoadBalancer
    Properties:
      Protocol: HTTP
      Port: 80
      LoadBalancerArn: !Ref AppLoadBalancer
      DefaultActions:
        - Type: forward
          TargetGroupArn: !Ref InstanceTargetGroup

  InstanceTargetGroup:
    Type: AWS::ElasticLoadBalancingV2::TargetGroup
    Properties:
      HealthCheckEnabled: true
```

```
            TargetType: instance
            Protocol: HTTP
            Port: 8080
            VpcId:
              Fn::ImportValue:
                'Fn::Sub': "${NetworkStackName}-vpc-id"
...
```

Target groups are the entities where EC2 instances are registered by the Auto Scaling groups. We are using the !Ref keyword here to reference other resources within the same template.

All CloudFormation resources have a specific return value. It could be an ARN, ID, name, or something else. When authoring templates, you need to validate these details in the respective docs' sections. If you need to extract a value other than the default, CloudFormation offers a Fn::GetAtt function, which can help you extract a specific attribute.

### Auto Scaling groups and launch templates

These are the components that are responsible for configuring and maintaining the compute fleet at any given point. Auto Scaling groups define a minimum, maximum, and desired number of instances in the compute fleet. It also maps to a target group, where instances can be deployed.

The configurations of the instances are taken care of by launch templates. They define the AMI, instance family, instance type, and so on:

```
Resources:
...
  AppLaunchTemplate:
    Type: AWS::EC2::LaunchTemplate
    Properties:
      LaunchTemplateName: !Sub ${AWS::StackName}-launch-template
      LaunchTemplateData:
        ImageId: !Ref AMIId
        InstanceType: !Ref InstanceType
        SecurityGroupIds:
          - !Ref AppInstanceSecurityGroup

  AutoScalingGroup:
    Type: AWS::AutoScaling::AutoScalingGroup
    Properties:
      MinSize: !Ref AutoScalingGroupMinSize
      MaxSize: !Ref AutoScalingGroupMaxSize
      TargetGroupARNs:
        - !Ref InstanceTargetGroup
      VPCZoneIdentifier:
```

```
            - Fn::ImportValue:
                'Fn::Sub': "${NetworkStackName}-private
subnet1"
            - Fn::ImportValue:
                'Fn::Sub': "${NetworkStackName}-privat
-subnet2"
        LaunchTemplate:
          LaunchTemplateId: !Ref AppLaunchTemplate
          Version: !GetAtt
AppLaunchTemplate.LatestVersionNumber
```

## *Deploying the application stack*

A complete version of the application stack template can be found at https://github.com/PacktPublishing/AWS-DevOps-Simplified/blob/main/chapter-4/cfn-templates/application-stack.yml.

Similar to how we deployed the infrastructure stack, we will now use the Docker toolbox to roll out application resources. This stack expects two parameters to be injected – the AMI ID and the network stack's name:

```
aws-devops-simplified:~/environment/chapter-4/cfn-templates $ aws
cloudformation deploy \
   --stack-name application-stack \
   --region eu-central-1 \
   --parameter-overrides NetworkStackName=networking-stack AMIId=ami-0a21c185c68c76d52 \
   --template-file application-stack.yml \
   --capabilities CAPABILITY_NAMED_IAM
Waiting for changeset to be created..
Waiting for stack create/update to complete
Successfully created/updated stack - application-stack
```

After a successful deployment, we can retrieve the stack outputs, which should give us the ALB domain name where the application can be accessed:

```
aws-devops-simplified:~/environment/chapter-4/$ aws cloudformation
describe-stacks --stack-name application-stack --region eu-central-1
```

Since two EC2 instances are running in the background, you will see random instance IDs being returned in the browser, as seen in *Figure 4.5*:

Request: /

AWS DevOps Simplified - Simple HTTP Server

Response received from - i-0f96761cc3d5f4e0a

Request: /

AWS DevOps Simplified - Simple HTTP Server

Response received from - i-0a5335dd93cb28189

Figure 4.5: ALB requests randomly forwarded to both instances

## Summary

In this chapter, we discussed the benefits of using IaC. Applying the DevOps principles of software engineering to infrastructure management has a lot of benefits. This allows you to focus on the application needs and, at the same time, increases the reliability and confidence of rolling out infrastructure changes at scale.

We started by providing a basic understanding of AWS CloudFormation constructs and discussed its capabilities, and then concluded this chapter with hands-on activities around deploying infrastructure and application stacks. This should give you a strong start to managing your AWS resources with confidence. The best practices we covered were mainly aligned around organizational challenges when dealing with multiple teams and accounts. Adhering to these guidelines will improve the agility of your teams and promote reusability – which are critical pillars of the DevOps journey.

In *Chapter 5, Rolling Out a CI/CD pipeline*, we'll discuss how to automate the build, test, and deployment activities for your application stack.

# Further reading

To learn more about the topics that were covered in this chapter, take a look at the following resources:

- Sample CloudFormation templates targeting common use cases: `https://docs.aws.amazon.com/AWSCloudFormation/latest/UserGuide/cfn-sample-templates.html`
- Identify insecure infrastructure patterns with `cfn-nag`: `https://github.com/stelligent/cfn_nag`
- Validate CloudFormation templates against a resource specification: `https://github.com/aws-cloudformation/cfn-lint`

# 5
# Rolling Out a CI/CD Pipeline

For sustained growth, organizations are aiming to digitally transform their businesses. The need to deliver innovative features faster to the end consumer requires software automation, which is one of the key contributors to the **digital transformation** process. Increasing competition further results in sky-high expectations around the reliability, usability, and consistency of every new software feature that is released. So, software development practices need to adapt to meet or raise the high bar. On the other hand, at an organizational level, the need to deliver more often increases headcount. This leads to challenges around team collaboration, visibility, and confidence to roll out new features with the least effort.

**CI/CD** is a key component of the DevOps journey that solves these problems quite well. It has emerged as a time-tested approach adopted by organizations of different sizes, team models, and complex software architectures. By including automation at every stage of the software development process, it helps uncover bugs faster and promotes the idea of frequent software releases. Furthermore, it opens up the possibility to introduce several types of security checks, approvals, notifications, and code validation procedures. You can define the unique stages relevant to your use cases. Depending on your specific needs, this can grow beyond the usual *build-test-deploy* life cycle. Considering all these benefits, CI/CD is something *non-negotiable* for modern software development practices.

A quick Google search for *CI/CD tools* tells us how big the ecosystem is. There are brilliant resources on the internet that cover the "how" and "what" of these tools. Our focus in this chapter will be mainly around AWS services that help you jumpstart your CI/CD adoption with readymade integrations not just within AWS, but with external third-party ecosystems as well.

In subsequent sections, we will use services such as **CodeCommit**, **CodeBuild**, **CodeDeploy**, and **CodePipeline** to establish a software delivery process that works for our test application stack. You can use these services to work in unique ways and that's where AWS stands out. Rather than offering one central solution, the cloud provider has focused on building modular services that can be used independently, just like Lego blocks, to build the software delivery workflows you like. Like always, toward the end of this chapter, we will get hands-on by writing code and deploying the artifacts that we develop directly in our AWS accounts.

These are the topics we will cover:

- What is CI/CD?
- How to choose a CI/CD tool
- Enabling continuous integration with CodeCommit and CodeBuild
- Understanding CodeDeploy deployment workflows on different compute platforms
- Implementing end-to-end software delivery with CodePipeline

## What is CI/CD?

**CI** stands for **continuous integration** and **CD** is often used interchangeably between **continuous delivery** and **continuous deployment**. The scope of what teams end up achieving within each of these varies a lot. Some teams begin with automated testing procedures after code is merged into the `main` branch, and others might go as far as testing every single commit in the `feature` branches, while the developers push code daily. Some might deploy to test environments and wait for the QA team to give the green light, and others might deploy every single commit to production – of course, with a lot of automation baked in. Before going any further, let's detail these three concepts further.

CI is a practice that enables software teams to merge the code from all developers with the least amount of friction. This goal is achieved by running automated tests on frequently created builds. Instead of waiting for a *merge day*, or the final release, this approach promotes the idea of merging small, building frequently, running tests, locating failures, and raising them to the team before they move further away from any drift.

Continuous delivery is an extension of CI. It ensures that your code is automatically deployed to a staging environment and tested in a way that it's always available for an immediate production release. This assurance is commonly achieved by starting with acceptance tests, rolling out builds to a production-like setup, stressing them with loads similar to live environments, checking for regressions, and also carrying out integration tests. Next, these builds are marked ready for immediate deployment needs. Stakeholders are given additional visibility and control to roll them out on their own – leading to increased trust and confidence in what the software teams are delivering.

Continuous deployment is the ultimate goal of the entire CI/CD process. Here, the build is automatically deployed into productive environments once it passes all tests, and automatically rolled back, if necessary. The hardest part of continuous deployment is the automated detection of failures and quick rollbacks without any visible impact to the end user. Pushing small changes early is what defines the success of continuous deployment in practice. However, this model of software delivery is often greeted with resistance and is not adopted by organizations since the business prefers a slow rate of deployment to reduce risks.

## How does CI/CD enable faster software delivery?

Software developers check in new code in the code repository, which triggers automated test workflows usually owned by tools such as **Jenkins**, **GitLab CI/CD**, **GitHub Actions**, and others. This part ensures quick feedback for the entire team by validating the health of every single commit. In the absence of a CI system, development teams only get feedback when a bigger release is tested by a dedicated QA team. Quite often, it is already very late in the sprint cycle to identify bugs at this stage, which leads to frustration and loss of stakeholder trust. Modern software is mostly delivered as SaaS or mobile applications. Efficient CI practices further ensure that every single commit works the same on multiple browsers and operating systems. This is simply not possible to test on a developer's local machine.

Once the code passes the CI phase, it is up to the continuous delivery processes to take it further. Here, the code is promoted to production-like environments, which give real feedback about how the new features work. For a lot of teams, it makes sense to give the code promotion controls directly to the stakeholders beyond this point. As you can see, every stage in the CI/CD process builds upon the success of the previous ones. Initial tests done by the CI systems enable better adoption of continuous delivery, which then naturally evolves to a continuous deployment state.

Sometimes, teams do not progress beyond continuous delivery. Let's see why this happens.

## Why is continuous deployment hard to implement?

It mainly comes down to trust in deploying to productive environments at scale. Teams who want to adopt this model spend a lot of time thinking and developing the right (and complete) test suite before adopting this for production. What is more important is to define a minimal set of essential business features that need to work and codify the tests to give you quick feedback. Even if you start with around 95% test coverage of critical features and behaviors, it is good enough to get things rolling. Once the deployment tooling and a minimal test suite are functional, you can build from there. An immediate benefit that teams get is an understanding that this can work in practice.

However, a lot of success in this area is dictated by your branching strategy.

## An effective branching strategy is key

At the heart of a CI/CD implementation lies your code branching strategy. The main goals are to reduce the code-merge friction between several developers, make the new changes visible across the entire team, and increase the process reliability around the release of new software changes.

In continuous deployment, it is strongly recommended to work off the trunk – your `main` branch. Working with feature branches results in all sorts of issues around merge conflicts and stale code. This problem is further exaggerated with weekly or bi-weekly sprint cycles where developers work in isolation, at least until the last few days before the sprint's closure. As a side note, if you're interested in knowing why starting the sprints on Wednesdays could be a good idea, I recommend giving this post a read: `https://resources.scrumalliance.org/Article/best-day-start-sprint`

When working with trunk branches, the first question teams have is how to avoid unintentional impacts caused by new features. This is where I can recommend adopting feature toggles.

## Working with feature toggles

**Feature toggles**, also sometimes called *feature flags*, is a technique where new software features can be launched rapidly but safely. They are reflected by software design patterns where some features can be enabled or disabled remotely. This gives teams the flexibility to quickly revert to old workflows without going through the usual deployment cycles. This also allows **A/B testing** as teams can temporarily enable certain features to study the behaviors of end users and how they are consuming any new functionality.

With this, even untested and incomplete code can be safely, and silently, shipped to production as part of regular deployment cycles. However, it's important to note that feature flags come with additional complexity in the code, are harder to test, and might sometimes hide actual code running in production. So, overuse should be avoided.

As we wrap up this section, I want to offer a brief word of caution.

## Identifying what works best for you

Having noticed software teams adopting code delivery practices, tools, and procedures from the internet as-is, I recommend caution with this approach. More often than not, what works for another organization might not directly fit into your tooling landscape, long-term technology commitments, and the variety of software applications you are working with. Just like containerizing your software applications with **Docker** and **Kubernetes** cannot solve the underlying design issues, adopting the wrong tools, investing efforts in on-premises hosting, or trying to adapt your applications to how a tool expects them to work does more harm than good. So, let's look at three areas you should be considering when you're deciding on a particular offering to spearhead your CI/CD journey.

# How to choose the best CI/CD solution for your needs

The time you invest in finding out the right set of tools is worth it. It can help your business move faster in ways that were not possible before. I recommend three factors that you should consider.

## Integration with existing tools

It is not only about the software that end users would consume. Countless others might be in use already for things such as task management, paging, notifications, testing, and so on.

Ideally, the CI/CD tool should offer pre-built integrations so that you don't have to invest time in writing glue code. When readymade integrations are leveraged, it leads to easier operations and spares you time that can be used for business differentiators. Disjoint processes lead to additional overheads around switching from one tool to another and dependency on manual steps affects agility.

When operating in the cloud, you can also think of gradually replacing the other solutions with cloud-native ones as it's generally easier to integrate your CI/CD tools with them.

## On-premises hosting considerations

If you have an on-premises data center, you might consider hosting a tool on your own to save costs. A SaaS solution takes away a lot of management tasks by focusing on the core capabilities you need. Some of these CI/CD software providers also offer on-premises hosting but it has to work with your existing infrastructure type and versions.

If you need full control around customizing the solution as per your needs, you can also evaluate options to run the control plane in your data center and leverage the cloud for routine tasks such as build, test, and deployment runs.

## Open source or commercial offerings?

You can start with open source versions of the CI/CD tools, but in the long run, the overall **total cost of ownership** (**TCO**) takes a hit as it factors in the time you invest in maintaining, scaling, and operating these solutions. AWS-managed services remove this overhead and allow you to pay as you go. Economies of scale reduce the cost even further, which can be a strong proponent of adopting cloud-based solutions.

However, if you want to host an open source solution on-premises to retain full control and customize it as per your needs, look out for cloud integrations that could simplify a future move.

Having covered the basics of CI/CD, let's dive into AWS specifics and discuss the core capabilities offered by the cloud provider. Most important of all, we'll see how seamless it is to integrate them with the overall AWS ecosystem.

# Enabling continuous integration with CodeCommit and CodeBuild

AWS CodeCommit and AWS CodeBuild are two services that operate in the CI space. CodeCommit, like other **Version Control Systems** (**VCSs**), is an abstraction on top of **Git** and offers code repository management in supported AWS regions. Similar to how GitHub, GitLab, and other platforms work, it helps software teams collaborate, work with pull requests, manage branching, and so on. Speaking of the overall code management ecosystem, I wouldn't say that CodeCommit offers something that others don't, except one thing, which is integrating well with other AWS services. However, at the same time, these services offer similar integration capabilities with other platforms. So, it is very much possible for you to continue using your third-party tools of choice as the teams would already be comfortable with the code management processes offered by them.

## Key features offered by CodeCommit

In addition to generic code management capabilities, several other highlights help you establish controls to meet your organization's coding, security, or compliance requirements.

### Granular security controls with IAM

Restricting access to protected branches is as simple as applying the right IAM policies for your users or groups. You can be very specific with the criteria, such as granting permissions for specific `Git` actions (push, pull, merge, and so on), or limiting access to certain branches.

Let's see a sample IAM policy that only allows the `GitPush` action on the `dev` and `test` branches for a developer:

```
{
    "Version": "2012-10-17",
    "Statement": [
        {
            "Effect": "Deny",
            "Action": "codecommit:GitPush,
            "Resource": "arn:aws:codecommit:eu-central1:111111111111:SampleRepo",
            "Condition": {
                "StringEqualsIfExists": {
                    "codecommit:References": [
                        "refs/heads/test",
                        "refs/heads/dev"
                    ]
                }
            }
        }
    ]
}
```

It is a good practice to restrict certain Git permissions, such as `MergePullRequestByFastForward`, to individuals who are more experienced with the code base. By not allowing fast-forward merges to everyone, you avoid scenarios that could pollute the main branch if commits are not written thoughtfully. A squash merge addresses this by *squashing* all commits from the feature branch into one. Organizations usually align these permissions with the Git branching strategy that has been established for certain software or teams.

### Amazon CloudWatch event integration

You can monitor and build automations when specific events occur in your repositories. Among several others, events such as creating pull requests, adding comments, or reacting to comments could be automatically captured and forwarded to a Lambda function, which then notifies the team over Slack or email, for example.

### Data protection for meeting compliance requirements

Code is the biggest asset for software organizations as this is what differentiates them from competitors and is at the heart of their business. Protecting these resources should be a top priority and customers can use their own **KMS encryption** keys to protect data at rest. You also have in-transit protection using HTTPS, or SSH, enabled by remote endpoints for your repositories.

These days, organizations are actively adopting AWS services such as **Cloud9**, which offers a cloud-hosted **integrated development environment** (**IDE**). These instances can be hosted in your VPCs and you can further restrict the network traffic through the use of VPC endpoints. This rules out any traffic traversal over the internet when you push your code, thereby meeting the needs of highly restrictive environments.

### Automated code reviews with CodeGuru

Code reviews often become a bottleneck for software teams who want to move fast. What if your **Java** or **Python** projects can be automatically reviewed by a machine learning-enabled engine, trained on millions of lines of code? Soon after a pull request is created, **CodeGuru** adds its review comments and suggestions to the pull request. This is a great value-add for teams, who get an additional pair of eyes looking at their code and suggesting optimizations that could improve their end user experience. If you're interested, you can read more about this feature at https://docs.aws.amazon.com/codeguru/latest/reviewer-ug/how-codeguru-reviewer-works.html.

You can also control what files to exclude from this analysis by putting a service manifest file alongside your code. This reduces the costs you would incur if the entire code repository was scanned instead.

### Approval rule templates

Not all code modifications require the same level of review and analysis. To ensure the right balance between audit and agility, you can define approval templates within CodeCommit. For example, code merges into the `main` branch could require two senior developers to approve the request, while the ones on `dev` could just be approved by one.

Next, let's look into CodeBuild, which works together with CodeCommit, and others, to offload the biggest challenge teams face when working with code at scale – **build environments**.

## Automating builds and tests with CodeBuild

Ever faced issues with spiky build and test loads toward the end of a sprint? I certainly have my share of experiences. Managing build infrastructure has very similar challenges to what is observed when supporting the dynamic nature of application environments. The customers – the software developers, in this case – should be able to use these capabilities without worrying about any service limits, caring about the time of the day they are working, or facing system slowness in any regard. I have managed GitLab runners for my team in the past and had all sorts of automations and requirements covered to the best of my knowledge. But now and then, an additional edge case used to emerge, requiring more modifications around the build environment's availability and scalability, among other challenges. Striking the right balance between cost and system availability was another big task.

The cloud's pay-as-you-go model and elasticity fit very well with the needs of creating and maintaining a build/test server farm. CodeBuild adds to this by offering a lot of other features you can cherry-pick that work well with the kind of applications you are supporting. Let's dive into the basics of the service; we'll cover some interesting features later.

## How CodeBuild works

CodeBuild offers managed build environments that can be extensively customized. Whenever you're thinking of building code artifacts or testing recent code revisions, you should evaluate CodeBuild. You can choose the specifications of your build environment, what compute and memory power they should have, what runtimes they should support, and what commands or scripts need to be executed. Depending on the outcomes of these scripts, you can define follow-up workflows for your application. It uses the following constructs:

- **Build project**: This is where all the configuration sits. It defines how to run a build, where to source the code from, what commands to execute, and where to store the outputs (*artifacts*). You can be very specific with operating systems, programming language runtimes, and so on. You can choose specific build environments by targeting a `docker` image, which is what the service uses in the background, to spin up your build/test instance.

- **BuildSpec**: This is the specification of what commands to execute for validating certain aspects of your code base. It could either be defined as part of your build project or maintained separately together with your code. The latter is a common approach as it ensures visibility for all software developers and allows modifications as code. It is defined in `YAML` format and allows dynamic configuration changes. The file is parsed and evaluated at runtime when a new code revision is pushed. We will look at a `buildspec.yml` file definition as part of the hands-on exercises toward the end of this chapter.

You can leverage this service's features independently or together with CodePipeline, which we will cover in the following sections. Some of the features that make this service a great choice will be discussed next.

## Pre-configured build environments for popular programming languages

You do not need to reinvent the wheel for known programming languages and tooling dependencies. CodeBuild offers several Windows/Linux environments and programming runtimes such as Android, Golang, Dotnet, Java, Node.js, and so on. With specifications as high as 255 GB of RAM, 72 vCPUs, and 824 GB of disk space on offer, you can support complex software build and test procedures. The beauty is that you just pay for the duration your build runs. I am sure you can already imagine how different this is from traditional infrastructure provisioning.

Want to run these builds locally? You can also do this by setting up the CodeBuild agent on your local machine.

> **Tip**
> Most enterprises end up building more or less similar build and test procedures for a specific target environment or programming language. You can leverage readymade case-based samples to jumpstart your CodeBuild implementations. More than 20 templates are available at `https://docs.aws.amazon.com/codebuild/latest/userguide/use-case-based-samples.html`.

## *Amazon CloudWatch event integrations*

Similar to CodeCommit, some important metrics are passed by the service to **Amazon CloudWatch**. By doing this, you can derive interesting insights from data, such as how long it took to download your source code and run your builds, the number of times your builds failed, the resource utilization of build executions, and so on.

> **Think big**
> You can build a CloudWatch dashboard that aggregates, and highlights, sprint metrics every week to your developers. You can combine key data points from CodeCommit and CodeBuild to build a 10,000-foot view of the overall development and build/test operations. Outliers can help identify edge cases, and being data-driven leads to further optimizations. Overall transparency around this helps software teams move faster – a key goal for DevOps philosophy.

## *Test report integrations*

If your tools support reporting formats such as `JUnit XML`, `Cucumber JSON`, and others, CodeBuild can generate reports from them and show them on your project dashboard. This can help troubleshoot build execution problems.

## *Integration with existing Jenkins implementations*

A common challenge when working with Jenkins is the overall management of your build farm. CodeBuild offers seamless integration with the Jenkins control plane and all build jobs are offloaded to the AWS service, allowing the use of cloud capabilities. Such hybrid implementations abstract any changes in the existing tooling while using the cloud's scale and elasticity.

*Accessing private VPC resources*

By default, you cannot access your VPC resources when running CodeBuild projects. However, if required, the service can be configured to run the build environments within your designated VPCs and subnets. This allows it to access your private resources in the cloud or on-premises. This unlocks a lot of possibilities as you can run integration tests against resources that are privately available and not be worried about exposing anything over the internet.

# Using CodeDeploy to orchestrate deployment workflows in compute environments

Software deployments could mean different things for different technology stacks. For Python-based applications, it could mean placing the scripts at a specific location, and for Java web apps, it could mean deploying `WAR` (**web application archive**) files on **Tomcat**. Whatever the requirement, CodeDeploy can help you deploy different compute environments. You can manage your deployments on servers (EC2/on-premises), **Elastic Container Service (ECS)**, or even Lambda's serverless platform.

Like CodeBuild, CodeDeploy depends on a manifest file, known as `appspec.yml` (which can also be JSON formatted). This file contains all the steps CodeDeploy needs to manage your application deployments. On EC2 instances or on-premises servers, this task is delegated to an agent that is already running alongside your application. With ECS and Lambda, the service directly speaks to the respective control plane to roll out application changes. When it comes to deployments, DevOps methodologies advocate the adoption of different strategies such as **blue-green** or **canary** to minimize risk. These capabilities are *natively supported* by CodeDeploy, making the overall process of introducing change much safer.

To make deployments happen, CodeDeploy uses several components that describe what to deploy, where to deploy, and how to deploy. Let's see what they are and how they work.

## Key components in CodeDeploy

It is important to be clear about the major components and the role they play before you start using the service.

### Application – logical container for all configurations

An application in CodeDeploy wires all the configuration details together. As its name suggests, it identifies the application that is being deployed. When you reference an application's name in the deployment, it selects the right combination of deployment group, configuration, and type.

## Deployment group – where to deploy stuff

Deployment groups identify the targets where application artifacts are placed. In our hands-on exercise, we will be working with EC2 instances hosted in an Auto Scaling group. This group of instances is clubbed together and called a deployment group. The actions that you define in the deployment configuration are performed on these servers.

## Deployment configurations – fine-tune your deployment settings

You might want to shift all traffic to the new Lambda function in one go, or maybe you want to do it in increments. You may also want to wait for $X$ minutes before shifting the traffic to new deployments. Fine-tuning such settings is a function of deployment configurations. With health checks, you can instruct the service to only proceed further when a minimum threshold of healthy instances is ensured. These settings make rolling out and rolling back the change very reliable.

## Deployment type – a strategy for rolling out change

CodeDeploy primarily supports two different deployment types: *in-place* and *blue-green*. This controls the approach that is used to roll out application changes inside the deployment group. Depending on which approach you choose, CodeDeploy interacts with additional services on your behalf to achieve the desired deployment state.

Next, let's walk through some features that make it a valuable choice for software deployments in the cloud.

# Key features offered by CodeDeploy

In addition to regular code deployment capabilities, the service offers great flexibility around third-party integrations and adjusts quite well to your CI/CD pipeline needs. Just like CodeBuild, CodeDeploy can also operate in isolation by directly consuming build artifacts from supported sources – **S3** and **GitHub**.

## Integrations with EC2 Auto Scaling and Elastic Load Balancing

If you're working with EC2 Auto Scaling or ELBs, CodeDeploy can natively integrate with those services to roll out applications in a controlled manner. In a blue-green deployment scenario, CodeDeploy ensures that your Auto Scaling configurations are copied over to a new group, provisions the instances, deploys code, and registers them with the load balancer to serve traffic, after your deployments pass the validation tests. It can retain your previous set of instances, gradually scale them down, or immediately delete them for additional cost savings. Imagine building all the orchestration around these services on your own. You could use other agent-based configuration systems to manage similar deployments, but the native integration is something that is a big gain that comes with a low effort.

### Support for life cycle hooks that map to different phases of software change

With support for several life cycle hooks, you can pin down the actions that you want to take when you reach a particular stage of the rollout process. This could be `BeforeInstall`, `AfterInstall`, upon `ApplicationStart`, or during `ValidateService`, among several others. Depending on the chosen compute platform, you can choose and implement all the hooks that you would like to automate against. For example, `BeforeInstall` could be used to send a Slack notification to your developers, stating that they should expect a change rollout soon. We will see some of these hooks in action during the hands-on exercises.

### Monitoring events with CloudWatch

Depending on the type of event, you can build automation workflows to take some action when something expected or unexpected happens to your deployments. By creating rules for relevant **EventBridge** events, you can add triggers such as Lambda functions or forward the event payload to **Kinesis streams** for further processing. This allows you to create event-based workflows with fully managed AWS services, which makes the overall operations process very reliable.

### AWS Systems Manager support for agent installation

You can make the agent available inside your compute instances in two ways – either bake it right into your AMI image during the build process or install it with the AWS Systems Manager service. The second approach has additional benefits since you always have the most recent version of the agent installed, and secondly, you don't need to open ingress network traffic flows for your instances. With Systems Manager, it is more of a pull-based mechanism, where your instance can automatically get the agent file and deploy it. Once the agent is up and running, it's available to respond to build commands from the service control plane.

At this point, we can discuss the AWS service that brings all the others together and offers a systematic workflow mechanism to the end user – **CodePipeline**.

## Implementing end-to-end software delivery with CodePipeline

CodePipeline is a continuous software delivery service that can be used to design, operate, and automate all the stages of your software processes – that is, developing code, building and testing the artifacts, and performing the final rollout in productive environments. The entire sequence of activities is orchestrated by this service. It shares artifacts from one service to the other, checks their execution status, integrates with external tooling, and introduces a visual model around the steps you take to make the code available to the end user. However, you need to know about a few constructs when working with this service.

## Key constructs used by CodePipeline

If you have used GitLab CI/CD or Jenkins in the past, you might have come across the concept of *pipelines*. These pipelines are formed by putting together blocks of actions that you would want to perform on your code artifacts. You often isolate them to map to different phases of the application release process. Similarly, CloudPipeline offers some constructs you can use as building blocks. This allows you to form a sequence of actions using which you can not only build, test, or deploy but also invoke Lambda functions, trigger step function executions, or call an external testing service to achieve a desired outcome.

Let's see what is required to set up a pipeline.

### Stages – isolation boundaries for your environments

Think of pipelines as templates that can have multiple executions going on in parallel. Ideally, every single commit that ends up in the repository is a new change you would like to run the pipeline against. Stages are the processes you would like to avoid concurrent executions for. For example, you don't want to deploy two different commits to the dev environment in parallel. Soon after the deployment completes, you would want to run some tests against the same code. Let's say you pushed two commits, `3eedg457` and `7634hhhf`, in sequence – you would want to both deploy and test, for a single commit at a time, before proceeding to the next one. This is what qualifies as two different operations combined in a single stage, thus isolating concurrent executions from one another.

### Actions – operations you perform within a stage

Several action types are supported by CodePipeline, including `Source`, `Build`, `Deploy`, `Approval`, and others. You can combine them, run them in sequence, or parallelize them based on your needs. For each of the actions, you have some providers supporting them in the background. For example, for `Source`, the code could be coming from S3, Amazon ECR, or even CodeCommit. Similarly, for `Test`, you could be running CodeBuild, BlazeMeter, or even Jenkins jobs.

A good visual representation is provided in *Figure 5.1*:

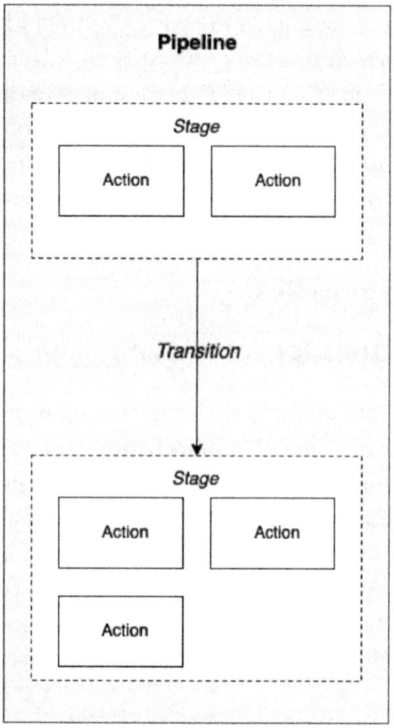

Figure 5.1 – Modeling stages and actions in a pipeline

> **Tip**
> In addition to the action providers supported by CodePipeline, you can also create your own. The service offers a framework to create and register action providers for one of the supported categories – that is, test, deploy, and so on. You can write your own Lambda function that receives such invocations from CodePipeline and leverage it to bridge any automation needs with the outside world.

Next, let's discuss how we can link several stages together to form a logical workflow, also known as a pipeline.

### Pipeline executions – releasing code changes as they happen

You can refer to each pipeline execution with a unique ID that corresponds to the respective executions in the downstream services. As discussed previously, every stage is isolated from other executions that might be happening in parallel. Apart from this, multiple pipeline executions can be in flight at the same time, covering different stages in each.

## Artifacts – data consumed and produced by actions

Artifacts are a core component of an entire pipeline's execution. This is the data that gets passed between different action providers – entirely orchestrated by the service. You don't have to manage S3 object creations, versioning, and other configurations. All of this is taken care of by CodePipeline. It uses an artifact bucket, which is more or less a message bus that offers data transmission between different operations.

We will see most of these constructs in action in the next section when we work with CloudFormation templates to roll out a pipeline in our AWS accounts. Before getting to that, though, let's discuss an underrated feature of CodePipeline – **cross-region actions**.

## Triggering actions in other regions

CodePipeline actions let you perform operations not only in the region where the pipeline is hosted but in others. The elegance of this feature is that the respective input artifacts are made available in the other region by the service itself. You just need to ensure the presence of an artifact bucket in the target region to leverage this capability.

As you can imagine, this can evolve into a deployment design, where you host your pipeline definition in one region but manage resources across multiple others. This is a functionality that is at the core of several multi-region AWS deployment frameworks.

# Rolling out a fully automated CI/CD pipeline in your AWS account

So far, we've established a conceptual understanding of how AWS services such as CodeBuild, CodeDeploy, and CodePipeline work, and how they help you automate parts of your software delivery process. The biggest advantage of these services is that you don't need to adopt a full-fledged solution. You can selectively offload specific areas of your software delivery process to one or more of these tools. Wiring them up with one another is also a seamless experience.

When a substantial number of workloads are running in the cloud, leveraging AWS native tooling for CI/CD can help a lot. Let's see these concepts in action by rolling out an end-to-end CI/CD pipeline. In the previous chapters, we used an AMI with the application code in it. To better demonstrate the capabilities of the AWS services mentioned in this chapter, we will use a slightly different AMI. The new image will differ in two aspects:

- It will no longer include the application code. We will inject the code at runtime using CodeDeploy-managed deployments.
- It will have the CodeDeploy agent installed by default. This is a prerequisite for CodeDeploy to be able to manage your EC2 instances or on-premises servers.

The overall workflow is highlighted in *Figure 5.2*:

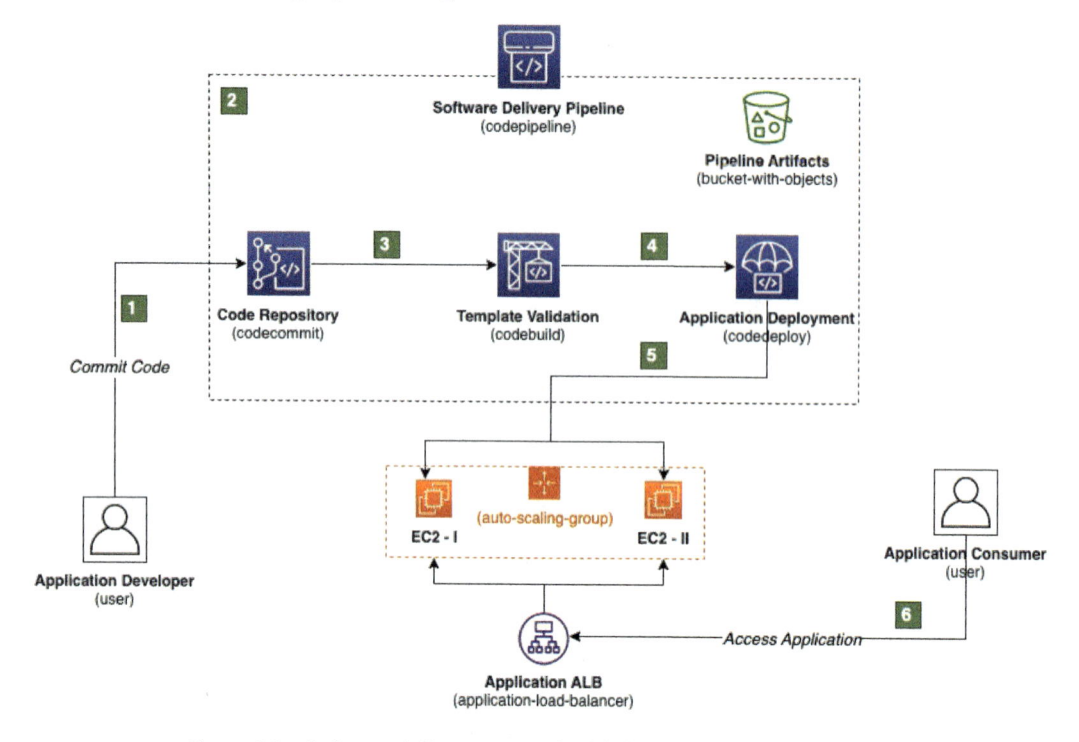

Figure 5.2 – Software delivery process highlighting the important phases

The following are the individual steps you must take, starting from writing code to deploying the changes in the production environment:

1. The application developer commits code to the CodeCommit repository. The repository contains the application code as well as the manifest files for respective services such as CodeBuild and CodeDeploy. Please note that the solution can easily adapt to other version control systems as well. Just replace CodeCommit with other providers, such as GitHub or Bitbucket, and you are good to go.

2. Completing the code check-in process triggers the pipeline's execution since CodePipeline continuously polls for new changes in the CodeCommit repository. As part of the first stage in the pipeline definition, recent code changes are pulled. The role of this stage is to pass this code (artifact) to the next stage for further processing. It is a good practice to set up CloudWatch event-based triggers for CodePipeline instead of polling for changes. For the sake of simplicity, we will restrict polling behavior in our demo.

3. CodePipeline takes the output artifact from the `source` stage and passes it further to the `build` stage as an input artifact. CodeBuild reads the `buildspec.yml` file to understand

the build instructions, runs all the validations that have been defined, and reports the outcomes (success/failure) back to the orchestrator – CodePipeline.

4. Upon receiving a successful status from the `build` stage, CodePipeline picks up the output artifacts. which in this case are the validated templates and code. It then forwards them to CodeDeploy, which serves as its input for the following steps in the process.

5. CodeDeploy makes use of the `appspec.yml` file to understand the deployment steps. Depending on the deployment configuration, it coordinates code rollout activities in the deployment group (two EC2 instances). CodePipeline tracks the output of the respective CodeDeploy deployment and upon receiving a success signal, marks the pipeline as completed.

6. Finally, the new code modifications are deployed to the underlying EC2 instances. Application consumers, or the end users, can now use the application by accessing the load balancer's URL.

> **Note**
> For a brief duration, you might notice different code versions running in parallel, across different EC2 instances. This is because we do a phased deployment rollout with CodeDeploy. This results in ALB returning different responses while the deployment is mid-way through.

Let's start with the first step of our deployment, which is to create a new AMI in the AWS account.

## Creating a base AMI for the application instances

Let's start a new session on our Cloud9 IDE before switching to the `chapter-5/` directory and using `packer` to build the AMI:

```
aws-devops-simplified:~/environment/chapter-5/packer $ packer build
ami_build.json
...
...

...
Build 'amazon-ebs' finished after 6 minutes 1 second.
==> Wait completed after 6 minutes 1 second
==> Builds finished. The artifacts of successful builds are:
--> amazon-ebs: AMIs were created:
eu-central-1: ami-09cadf1c312a9b12e
```

As discussed previously, we intentionally excluded the application source code from the AMI creation process in this chapter to demonstrate CodeDeploy's capabilities.

After the AMI build process completes, we can proceed with stack deployments using CloudFormation. We will deploy three templates in this chapter (in order):

1. **Infrastructure stack**: Deploys foundational resources such as VPCs, subnets, route tables, and so on.
2. **Application stack**: Builds on top of the infrastructure stack and deploys Auto Scaling groups, a target group, and an Application Load Balancer.
3. **Pipeline stack**: Integrates with the application resources to offer an end-to-end CI/CD pipeline for the application developer. Any code change from this point onwards will automatically be rolled out to the EC2 instances.

> **Note**
>
> You might have provisioned the first two stacks as part of the hands-on exercise in *Chapter 4, Managing Infrastructure as Code with CloudFormation*. If those resources are still available in your AWS account, you can directly proceed with deploying the pipeline stack.

Inter-stack dependencies are highlighted in *Figure 5.3*:

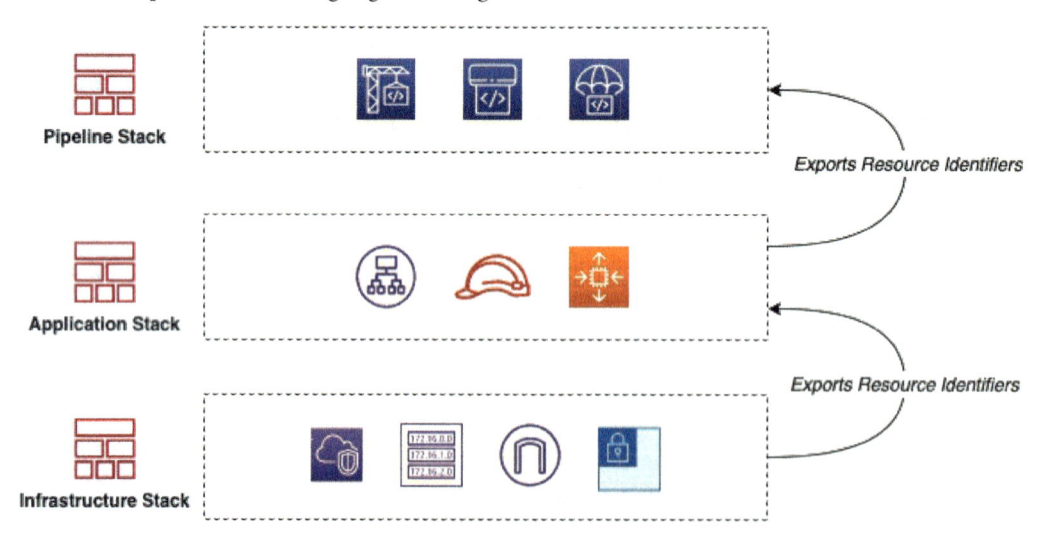

Figure 5.3 – Stacks consuming resource identifiers from each other

Let's proceed with the stack deployments, starting with the bottom layer.

## Deploying infrastructure and application stacks

Before we can deploy pipeline resources, we need to have the underlying infrastructure and application components available. This is mainly to ensure that inter-stack dependencies are met so that the pipeline stack to be deployed successfully:

1. From within the IDE, we can use the CloudFormation CLI to deploy both stacks:

    ```
    aws-devops-simplified:~/environment/chapter-5/cfn-templates $
    aws cloudformation deploy \
        --stack-name aws-devops-simplified-network-stack \
        --template-file ./network-stack.yml \
        --parameter-overrides EnvironmentName=aws-devops-simplified \
        --region eu-central-1
    Waiting for changeset to be created..
    Waiting for stack create/update to complete
    Successfully created/updated stack - aws-devops-simplified-network-stack
    ```

2. Then, we can pass the stack's name and AMI Id while deploying the application stack. Please note that certain resource identifiers, such as **Amazon Machine Image** (**AMI**) IDs, can only be referenced in a particular region. In this case, we have used ami-09cadf1c312a9b12e, which is available in the eu-central-1 region. So, you should use the same region when running these commands:

    ```
    aws-devops-simplified:~/environment/chapter-5/cfn-templates $
    aws cloudformation deploy \
        --stack-name aws-devops-simplified-application-stack \
        --template-file ./application-stack.yml \
        --parameter-overrides NetworkStackName=aws-devops-simplified-network-stack AMIId=ami-09cadf1c312a9b12e \
        --capabilities CAPABILITY_NAMED_IAM \
        --region eu-central-1
    Waiting for changeset to be created..
    Waiting for stack create/update to complete
    Successfully created/updated stack  aws-devops-simplified-application-stack
    ```

3. At this point, we have deployed the application, but if you try to access the URL for the Application Load Balancer, the request will end up with a 502 Bad Gateway error. This is expected since the application code has not been deployed to the EC2 instances yet. To do so, let's bring up the CI/CD pipeline:

    ```
    aws-devops-simplified:~/environment/chapter-5/cfn-templates $
    aws cloudformation deploy \
        --stack-name aws-devops-simplified-pipeline-stack \
    ```

```
        --template-file ./pipeline-stack.yml \
        --parameter-overrides ApplicationStackName=aws-devops-
    simplified-application-stack \
        --capabilities CAPABILITY_NAMED_IAM \
        --region eu-central-1

Waiting for changeset to be created..
Waiting for stack create/update to complete
Successfully created/updated stack - aws-devops-simplified-
pipeline-stack
```

We now have all the resources that we need in our AWS account to roll out application changes automatically. If you check the CodePipeline configurations at this point, you will notice an error in the Source stage, as shown in *Figure 5.4*:

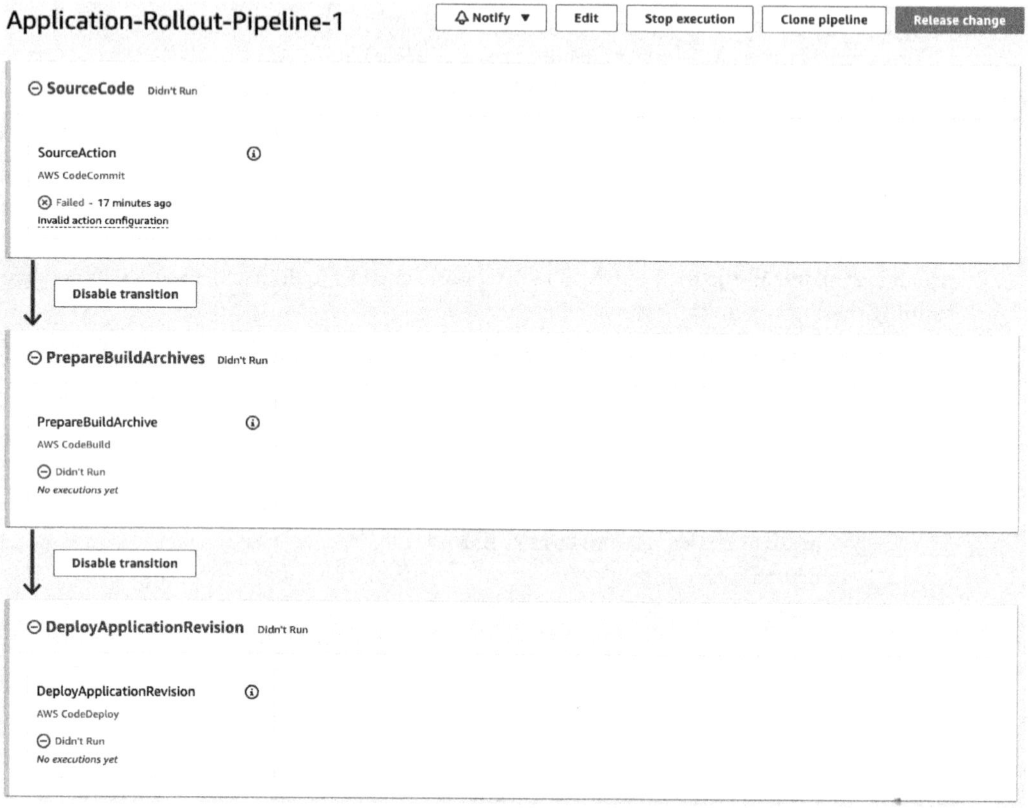

Figure 5.4 – CodePipeline snapshot immediately after CloudFormation stack deployment

As you can see, SourceAction is marked in red because the pipeline expects some code to be present in the main branch, in the configured repository. However, the repository, as expected, is empty at this point. Let's retrieve the HTTPS (GRC) URL for the repository and push some code to it for the pipeline to run. The URL can be retrieved from your AWS account's web console. Go to the **CodeCommit service** page and select the repository we created; the **Connection steps** section will lead you to the HTTPS (GRC) endpoint.

> **Note**
> To work with the CodeCommit repository, you need to create separate credentials that allow HTTPS-based access. However, we will use a mechanism to bypass this behavior by using the `git-remote-codecommit` plugin. This is already included in the Cloud9 IDE for your use. This plugin reads authentication data from your environment variables.

4. Next, we need to bootstrap our directory with some Git magic:

- Initialize a Git repository and switch to the main branch:

```
aws-devops-simplified:~/environment/chapter-5 $ git init .
hint: Using 'master' as the name for the initial branch. This default branch name
hint: is subject to change. To configure the initial branch name to use in all
hint: of your new repositories, which will suppress this warning, call:
hint:
hint:   git config --global init.defaultBranch <name>
hint: Names commonly chosen instead of 'master' are 'main', 'trunk' and
hint: 'development'. The just-created branch can be renamed via this command:
hint:
hint:   git branch -m <name>
Initialized empty Git repository in /home/ec2-user/environment/chapter-5/.git/

aws-devops-simplified:~/environment/chapter-5 (master) $ git checkout -b main
Switched to a new branch 'main'
aws-devops-simplified:~/environment/chapter-5 (main) $
```

- Configure `git remote` and add files to the staging area, followed by an initial commit:

  ```
  aws-devops-simplified:~/environment/chapter-5 (main) $ git remote add origin codecommit::eu-central-1://aws-devops-simplified-sample-application
  aws-devops-simplified:~/environment/chapter-5 (main) $ git remote -v
  origin  codecommit::eu-central-1://aws-devops-simplified-sample-application (fetch)
  origin  codecommit::eu-central-1://aws-devops-simplified-sample-application (push)
  aws-devops-simplified:~/environment/chapter-5 (main) $ git add .
  aws-devops-simplified:~/environment/chapter-5 (main) $ git commit -am "initial commit"
  ```

- Push the code:

  ```
  aws-devops-simplified:~/environment/chapter-5 (main) $ git push origin main
  Enumerating objects: 18, done.
  Counting objects: 100% (18/18), done.
  Delta compression using up to 4 threads
  Compressing objects: 100% (16/16), done.
  Writing objects: 100% (18/18), 7.26 KiB | 1.21 MiB/s, done.
  Total 18 (delta 0), reused 0 (delta 0), pack-reused 0
  remote: Validating objects: 100%
  To codecommit::eu-central-1://aws-devops-simplified-sample-application-1
   * [new branch]      main -> main
  ```

As shown in *Figure 5.5.*, soon after the code was pushed, CodePipeline picked up the change and ran the pipeline. Once the flow reaches the `Deploy` stage, CodeDeploy instructs its agents running inside the EC2 instances to pull code from the artifact repository and bring up the Python-based web server:

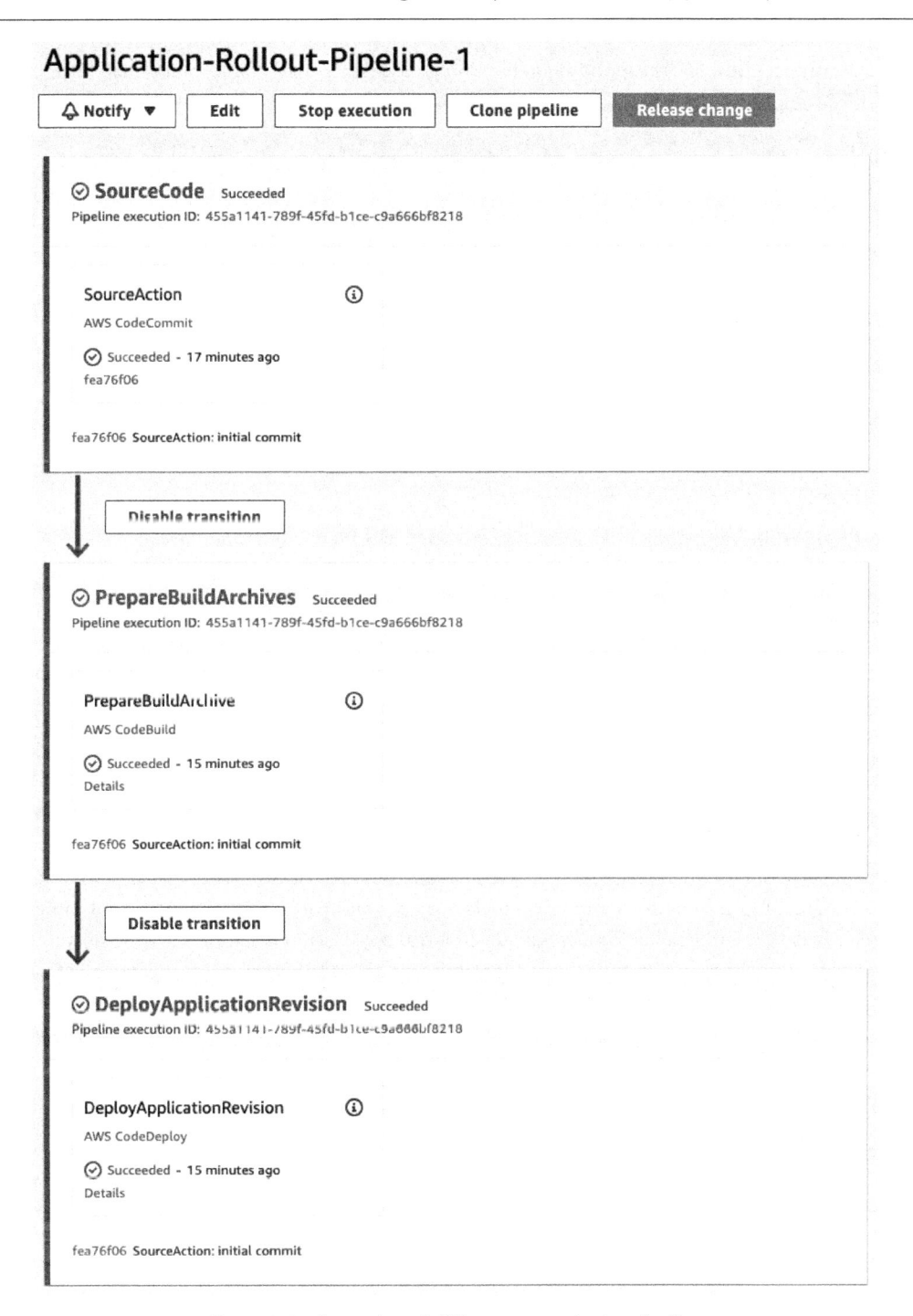

Figure 5.5 – Execution of different stages in the pipeline

The EC2 instances now start responding to incoming requests from the application load balancer, as seen in *Figure 5.6*:

```
AWS DevOps Simplified
aws-d-applo-1jsowkcdmq8sr-444693484.eu-central-1.elb.amazonaws.com

Request: /

AWS DevOps Simplified - Simple HTTP Server - V1

Response received from - i-024e0c7569a974a01
```

Figure 5.6 – Response from the Application Load Balancer after the pipeline finished execution

You can also make additional modifications in the `web_server.py` file at this point, followed by a code push to see the deployment in action.

I hope this exercise gave you good hands-on experience working with CodePipeline.

## Summary

In this chapter, we established a foundational understanding of what CI/CD is and how it supports the software delivery processes. This is key for software automation, which further drives digital innovation. Selecting a tool from countless options available these days can be a difficult task. We discussed key areas that could simplify the selection process.

Next, we learned about AWS services that offer great functionality, scale, and integration support in the CI/CD space. Starting with a basic understanding of each, we went further into the details of key differentiating features when using these services, in combination or isolation. They should always be seen as modular blocks that can stand up on their own, or work with another tool to build something customized. To see things in action, we deployed a real application stack in our AWS account and created a software change rollout pipeline using CodePipeline. This exercise was meant to expose you to how these building blocks work so that you can extend them further to cater to your specific needs. Toward the very end, we covered differentiating aspects of two commonly used tools for managing software life cycles in the cloud – Jenkins and CodePipeline.

In this chapter, all of our infrastructure code definitions have leveraged CloudFormation YAML templates. However, that's just one of the options AWS offers. In *Chapter 6, Programmatic Approach to IaC with AWS CDK*, we will use TypeScript programming constructs to create our infrastructure. This service is a game changer for organizations that are heavily invested in one of the supported programming languages and would like to build on that experience to create AWS infrastructure at scale.

## Further reading

To learn more about the topics that were covered in this chapter, take a look at the following resources:

- AWS CodePipeline integration examples: `https://docs.aws.amazon.com/codepipeline/latest/userguide/integrations-community-blogposts.html`
- Integrating CodeDeploy with a GitHub Actions-based workflow: `https://github.com/aws-samples/aws-codedeploy-github-actions-deployment`
- Practicing Continuous Integration and Continuous Delivery on AWS whitepaper: `https://docs.aws.amazon.com/whitepapers/latest/practicing-continuous-integration-continuous-delivery/welcome.html`

# 6
# Programmatic Approach to IaC with AWS CDK

Infrastructure automation is key to supporting the scale and complexities of modern software applications. How quickly and reliably you can provision infrastructure stacks for these applications has a direct impact on the overall value chain. AWS offers lots of capabilities in this domain that might be attractive for different end user personas. Organizations typically get started with the AWS web console-driven experience to get their feet wet. Once they have a good foundational understanding of how all the blocks and pieces come together, they think of hosting some development workloads on the cloud. At this point, they start looking into different options to manage and automate the infrastructure these applications will be deployed on.

AWS services are built from the ground up, exposing APIs as the primary communication interface. As an AWS user, you are either into developing CLIs and SDKs that consume these APIs as is, or you are an end user interested in building business applications and using tools that offer high-level abstractions. You likely belong to the latter group, and this is the group that is interested in the likes of the **AWS CLI, SDKs, Terraform**, and **CloudFormation**, to name a few. A good reason for not implementing the infrastructure automations from scratch, using low-level APIs, is the feature-richness and maturity of the existing ecosystem. The majority of these tools are official AWS offerings, while others have been contributed by different companies active in the DevOps space. In the previous two chapters, *Managing Infrastructure as Code with CloudFormation* and *Rolling Out a CI/CD Pipeline*, we extensively used CloudFormation, which abstracted these APIs behind YAML/JSON templates.

The abstractions these tools provide give a lot of business value as well – if you are building a three-tier web application or a data ingestion pipeline on AWS, your needs and service selection are largely going to be the same as other users. So, why reinvent the wheel by not adopting opinionated solutions that have already considered important design practices of security, operations, and reliability?

In this chapter, we will focus on the AWS **Cloud Development Kit** (**CDK**), which builds on top of the strong foundations of the AWS CloudFormation service and offers a standard programmatic approach to building infrastructure stacks at scale. This is particularly useful for programmers and DevOps professionals who have a strong programming background and comfort level with a specific language. With CDK, they can use familiar programming principles such as inheritance, composition, and loops to manage their infrastructure. CDK offers reusable blocks that speed up infrastructure deployment while keeping you away from undifferentiated heavy lifting.

We will cover the following topics in this chapter:

- Different approaches to managing infrastructure and where AWS CDK fits in
- What is AWS CDK?
- Benefits of using CDK
- Deploying a test application with AWS CDK in your AWS account

Let's start by providing a basic understanding of where CDK fits in the overall AWS infrastructure automation landscape, and also do a quick comparison with other offerings.

## Different approaches to managing infrastructure in AWS

Many years back, when I was starting with infrastructure automation on AWS, I used to bundle together some CLI commands in a Bash script and fire it off when new AWS accounts required bootstrapping. It worked like a charm for basic setups but surfaced limitations in other areas such as ongoing management, updates, stack removals, extracting resource identifiers, and so on. Every requirement would transform into more scripts being developed and managed, which of course was not a scalable solution.

Secondly, it was difficult for other team members to contribute to these scripts as they didn't have an operations or scripting background. This is where something more declarative such as AWS CloudFormation/Terraform could have helped them easily get started. There will always be a tipping point in your AWS infrastructure automation journey where you would like to switch from one approach to another as your needs outgrow the capabilities of underlying mechanisms or tools.

Luckily, when it comes to working with AWS, there are a lot of options that can be leveraged to target a specific requirement. As a cloud provider, it has always been a priority area for AWS to meet the requirements of the users, wherever they are in their cloud journey, and infrastructure automation is no different. Let's dive into the various categories of infrastructure management tools that fit the respective use cases.

### Manual infrastructure management

This is where everyone starts their AWS journey. After logging into the console, users can browse different services across 26+ regions and deploy them with the click of a button. For demonstrations and proof-of-concept development, this is still a viable approach, so long as the user takes care of the security best practices and does not expose any confidential information over the internet.

AWS offers ready-made cloud blocks such as default VPCs, which allow users to get started in their AWS account.

## Automating infrastructure rollouts with scripts

Once users are comfortable with AWS services and the idea of bundling multiple of those together to solve a business use case, they start using CLI commands and AWS SDKs to trigger some actions from their Terminal. If these follow a particular sequence, it also makes sense to tie them up with Bash scripts, for example. These scripts can then also be used in automated software delivery pipelines using tools such as Jenkins and AWS CodeBuild.

## Adopting a declarative approach

Once the needs grow beyond basic scripting solutions, organizations typically take the next steps with more advanced services such as CloudFormation and Terraform. In some cases, they might even adopt these services directly, depending on the existing experience and knowledge within the company.

These services offer a declarative approach to infrastructure definition, where the user defines a *target state* of their AWS accounts. The tools then leverage the underlying service APIs to make this declared state a reality. Reaching this target state requires a lot of magic behind the scenes in terms of state management, resolving update conflicts, dependency resolutions, and so on. All of these are abstracted from the end user.

To get started with these tools, the users need to ramp up on respective configuration languages and template structures. It's important to note that these services don't go beyond what is put in the template files. So, the user still needs to define all the components of the architecture at the most granular level and tie them up so that they work together as a solution.

The following are two configuration examples of defining an EC2 instance in a declarative way:

- With Terraform:

    ```
    resource "aws_instance" "web" {
      ami           = "ami-a1b2c3d4"
      instance_type = "t3.micro"
    }
    ```

- With CloudFormation:

    ```
    EC2Instance:
      Type: AWS::EC2::Instance
      Properties:
        ImageId: "ami-a1b2c3d4"
        InstanceType: t3.micro
    ```

Modifying any of these attributes, such as `ImageId` or `ami`, will result in an instance upgrade, but this is entirely handled by the respective tools, while the user just focuses on defining the target state of the infrastructure.

## Using infrastructure definition generators

Unlike service-native configuration languages, there is a different segment of tools that offer the flexibility to use regular programming languages, such as **Python** or **Golang**, to generate AWS CloudFormation templates. These are beneficial when organizations have a high maturity and comfort level with specific programming languages.

Tools such as **Troposphere** and **GoFormation** are well-known in this space and can dynamically generate ready-to-use CloudFormation templates based on the code written by the user.

Let's see how we could define a configuration with Troposphere:

```
>>> from troposphere import Ref, Template
>>> import troposphere.ec2 as ec2
>>> t = Template()
>>> instance = ec2.Instance("myinstance")
>>> instance.ImageId = "ami-951945d0"
>>> instance.InstanceType = "t1.micro"
>>> t.add_resource(instance)
<troposphere.ec2.Instance object at 0x101bf3390>
>>> print(t.to_json())
{
    "Resources": {
        "myinstance": {
            "Properties": {
                "ImageId": "ami-951945d0",
                "InstanceType": "t1.micro"
            },
            "Type": "AWS::EC2::Instance"
        }
    }
}
>>> print(t.to_yaml())
Resources:
    myinstance:
        Properties:
            ImageId: ami-951945d0
            InstanceType: t1.micro
        Type: AWS::EC2::Instance
```

The teams adopting such tools will still require some understanding of how services such as AWS CloudFormation function under the hood, what kind of constructs (building blocks) they expose to the end user, and so on.

## Using frameworks that offer high-level abstractions

Once users are comfortable with services such as AWS CloudFormation and have gained substantial experience debugging production-grade rollouts, they might consider adopting tools such as **AWS CDK** and **Pulumi**. AWS CDK offers an approach to managing infrastructure with general-purpose programming languages such as TypeScript, Python, Go, Java, and so on. As an official AWS offering, it has some advantages in terms of long-term commitment, support, and development from the cloud provider.

Another famous IaC platform that operates in this space is Pulumi. There are some key differences between how Pulumi and AWS CDK function, but from an end user perspective, the features are more or less the same – infrastructure resource management with commonly used programming languages. Pulumi, like AWS CDK, offers integrations with general-purpose programming languages, but this support is not limited to just AWS. It also provides more than 60+ integrations with other cloud or SaaS providers.

### *Pulumi versus CDK*

Under the hood, AWS CDK is more of a **transpiler**. Transpilers are programs that convert a piece of source code from one high-level language into another. The output from these programs has the same level of abstraction as the input. This is fundamentally different from compilers as they produce low-level code that directly interacts with the underlying machine, and is more performant.

Pulumi, on the other hand, offers deeper integrations with the programming runtime and the cloud provider by not depending on an intermediate state, such as AWS CloudFormation templates in the case of AWS CDK. Pulumi takes control of managing the life cycle of the resources that the user defined a target state for. This level of integration provides additional benefits with efficient unit and integration testing capabilities by leveraging mocked responses and other constructs.

*Figure 6.1* shows a visual mapping of the different infrastructure management approaches and the corresponding tools and frameworks:

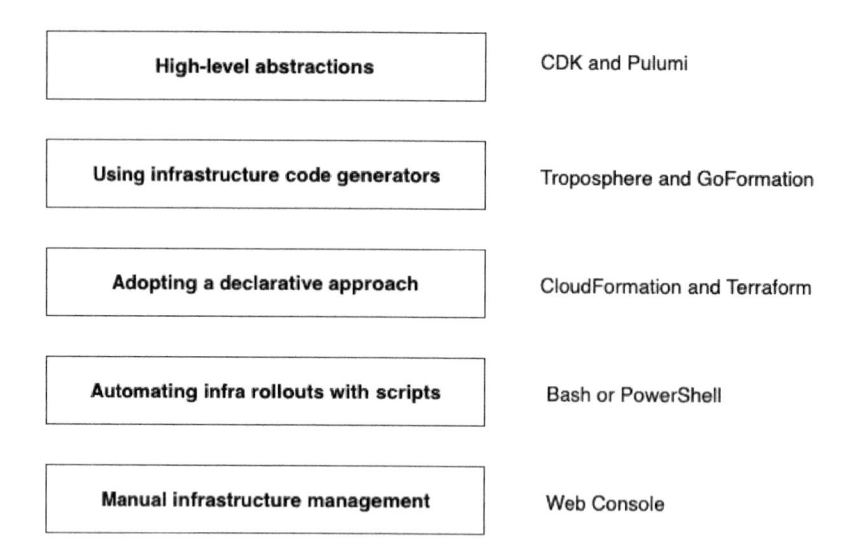

Figure 6.1 – Different approaches to managing infrastructure in AWS and the corresponding tools

|  |  |
| --- | --- |
| High-level abstractions | CDK and Pulumi |
| Using infrastructure code generators | Troposphere and GoFormation |
| Adopting a declarative approach | CloudFormation and Terraform |
| Automating infra rollouts with scripts | Bash or PowerShell |
| Manual infrastructure management | Web Console |

Having discussed all the different tools and frameworks for managing your AWS infrastructure, let's dive deeper into some CDK specifics, which is our focus for this chapter.

## What is AWS CDK?

AWS CDK enables users to leverage general-purpose programming constructs such as classes, objects, and inheritance to generate AWS CloudFormation templates, and also deploy them in the respective AWS account and region. It does not manage the deployment orchestration itself but rather offloads this responsibility to AWS CloudFormation. This means that it is also, in a way, dependent on the capabilities of AWS CloudFormation and the interfaces exposed by the service.

With familiar programming languages and integrations with commonly used IDEs, it's quite easy to start building infrastructure by leveraging the reusable classes offered by the development kit. The high-level constructs automatically use sensible defaults, which not only improves the overall security posture of your infrastructure but also empowers the users to do more with less code. When working with AWS-managed services at the application level, typically, teams combine the definition of infrastructure resources with application components, thereby deploying the whole system as a single cloud deployment. Additionally, this allows configuration reuse and efficient dependency management of both layers.

Using programming idioms such as loops, parameters, and conditionals, you can substantially reduce the overall configuration effort. Also, since the users are now working with programming languages they are already used to, it becomes easy to enforce DevOps best practices around code reviews, tests, and seamless infrastructure deployments across multiple stages of the software delivery pipeline.

CDK offers command-line tools to bootstrap project repositories and create IaC templates to manage stacks. The kit itself is developed in Typescript and the JSII framework (also developed by AWS), which enables the portability of the underlying implementation to other programming languages.

Let's discuss some key concepts that you will come across when working with CDK.

## Key concepts in CDK

The three most important CDK concepts are **constructs**, **stacks**, and **apps**. All of them are represented as classes in the respective programming languages. Let's clearly define the role of each of these concepts in realizing your infrastructure on AWS.

### Constructs

A **CDK construct** is the underlying AWS resource that you would like to manage as part of your infrastructure definitions. So, anything like an S3 bucket, Lambda function, or a DynamoDB table would be defined as a construct in your CDK code. As you might imagine, this is already available for reuse as AWS does not want you to invest time in developing low-level components that are commonly used across different use cases. Constructs are further divided into three categories:

- **L1 constructs (raw)**: These are the raw AWS resources without any bells or whistles. Every AWS CloudFormation resource has an equivalent L1 construct that you could use. They are automatically generated from the CloudFormation specification.

- **L2 constructs (curated)**: These are the AWS resources with some *intent* baked in. As an example, if you are creating an S3 bucket, then some sane defaults such as disabling public access and enabling data encryption at rest are some of the aspects that are already taken care of.

- **L3 constructs (custom abstractions)**: These represent a certain *pattern* that can be reused across a variety of business use cases. It is a collection of L1 and L2 constructs tied together to represent a specific real-world requirement. They only expose the most essential configuration parameters you would like the users to configure. The rest is designed for easy consumption; for this reason, L3 constructs can sometimes be opinionated about how they use certain resources in that pattern.

In addition to building end user-focused applications with CDK, you can use it to create reusable libraries that can then be used by other teams in your organization. This boosts agility and standardization in terms of implementing best practices.

### Stacks

**Stacks** are a collection of one or more constructs that you would like to manage as part of an independent CloudFormation template. We will cover the development workflow when working with CDK shortly, where we will further clarify how these CloudFormation templates are generated under the hood.

### Apps

An AWS CDK app refers to the entire application that you code in one of the supported programming languages. An app is composed of several stacks. This corresponds to a certain business use case the application is expected to fulfill and the scope includes all the underlying components, or AWS resources, you would like to manage as part of this application.

When using CDK for authoring your infrastructure templates, a defined workflow needs to be followed. Let's discuss what happens at which stage and how your AWS resources are deployed in an account.

### Development workflow

There are three main stages of progression when working with a CDK-based application:

1. **Create**: Create the project structure and define the source code (stacks and constructs) that represents your application environment. Let's look at the relevant commands at this stage. To *bootstrap the target* account/region pair, use the following command:

    ```
    cdk bootstrap
    ```

    To *create a new project directory* with the required prerequisites for CDK, in the programming language of your choice, use the following command:

    ```
    cdk init app --language typescript
    ```

2. **Synthesize**: Use the CDK CLI to reference the construct definitions and generate the required artifacts. An important intermediate stage used by CDK is Cloud Assembly, which involves collecting CloudFormation templates and assets. These assets are later uploaded in S3 buckets and ECR registries for services such as CloudFormation to consume.

    To create the templates and assets that represent Cloud Assembly, use the following command:

    ```
    cdk synth
    ```

3. **Deploy**: CloudFormation takes over the deployment responsibility and makes the required changes to the resources so that they match the target state defined by the user.

    To push changes to the cloud using CloudFormation deployments, use the following command:

    ```
    cdk deploy
    ```

Once the CloudFormation resources have been created, end users can use the respective AWS services or applications.

### Pros and cons of working with CDK

Like all other frameworks and services, CDK has its share of pros and cons. Ultimately, it comes down to how well the service fits with the present needs of the organization.

*Benefits of using CDK*

The main benefit of CDK is its rich ecosystem of constructed libraries. With different levels of abstraction, it empowers all types of users equally well. You can reuse the foundational constructs and also adopt higher-level opinionated abstractions with a seamless experience. Furthermore, extending the AWS CDK concepts into additional domains such as Kubernetes and Terraform makes it an interesting choice for customers who would like to reap the benefits from the time they invested in upskilling their teams with CDK.

For reference, check out the *cdk8s* and *cdktf* projects on the internet.

*Cons of using CDK*

The biggest disadvantage of using CDK is its initial learning curve. The tool is only intended for moderate to highly experienced AWS users. Its testing capabilities, on the other hand, are somewhat limited as you can only write some synthetic tests after the CloudFormation templates have been generated. Tools such as Pulumi offer a more advanced testing experience as they directly interact with the cloud provider, thereby offering capabilities to mock different types of calls, for example.

In the next section, we'll understand the test application we are going to deploy in this chapter. We will then move on to getting our hands dirty by deploying this stack into an AWS account and region of your choice.

# Deploying a test application with AWS CDK

CDK is quite mature when it comes to CLIs, its support for general-purpose programming languages, and its rich construct libraries, which provide reusable patterns for easy adoption.

So far in this book, we have mostly worked with **Amazon Machine Images** (**AMI**) and used them to deploy application code that was either baked into the image itself or deployed at runtime using services such as AWS CodeDeploy. In this chapter, we will use a different test application for demonstrating CDK capabilities – automatic image recognition and labeling. We will use the **Amazon Rekognition** service, which allows users to add image and video analysis capabilities to their applications. You can provide an image to the service and it can identify objects, people, text, and scenes. This is a very good example of how end users can leverage AWS services to build innovative applications, without having to develop a deep understanding of machine learning. The test application will also allow you to experience the ease of building supporting infrastructure services in CDK for such an application.

Let's dive straight into the specifics of how the application works.

## Understanding the different components of the image recognition application

In addition to using Amazon Rekognition under the hood, our test application also depends on a few others to offer an end-to-end workflow for the user. Here is a list of all the components and the role they play:

- **S3 bucket**: This is the end user interface that can be used for interacting with the application. Once a JPEG image has been uploaded into this bucket, it starts the application workflow for automatic labeling.

- **Event integrations**: The S3 service offers event integrations with three other services – Lambda, SQS, and SNS. In this application, we use the Lambda integration, which is automatically invoked as soon as a new object appears.

- **Lambda function**: This is the image handler that orchestrates all the activities in the application, from monitoring the object upload process to triggering Amazon Rekognition with appropriate inputs, and finally persisting the results in a DynamoDB table.

- **Amazon Rekognition**: This is a fully managed image and video analysis tool that uses machine learning models under the hood, but offers a simple HTTP-based API to the user for easier consumption.

- **DynamoDB table**: This is the persistence layer of the application and is where all the image labeling results are finally stored.

The entire workflow is depicted in *Figure 6.2*:

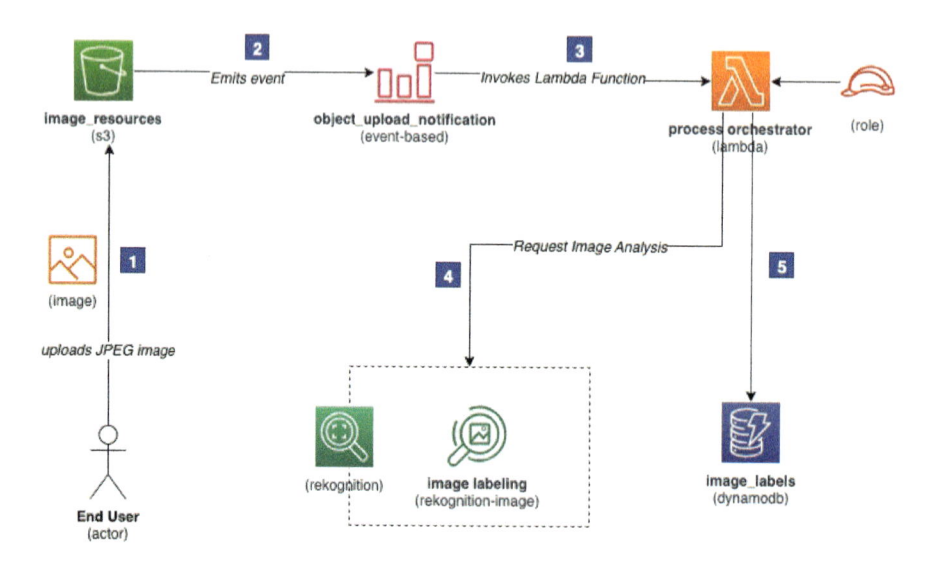

Figure 6.2 – Automatic image labeling with Amazon Rekognition

The advantage of working with toolkits such as AWS CDK is that lot of plumbing and glue code is automatically done for the user, with the least effort, as opposed to the code you would end up writing when working with services such as AWS CloudFormation. We will see a synthesized version of our template that will better explain this point shortly.

From a functional standpoint, the following stages are happening in the workflow depicted in *Figure 6.2*:

1. The end user uploads a file into an S3 bucket. I have tried to keep several aspects of this test application simple to demonstrate the capabilities of CDK. As an alternative approach, you could abstract this piece with a web-based UI, where a user drags and drops an image into a defined section of the page, thereby initiating the analysis process.

2. Once the image has been uploaded, the S3 service generates a notification; this is frequently leveraged in event-driven architectures. You can forward these events to several destinations, such as an SNS topic, SQS queue, or Lambda function.

3. The Lambda integration is used to invoke a function that would have been deployed already as part of our CDK stack.

4. The Lambda function delegates the image labeling task to Amazon Rekognition. Rekognition utilizes the underlying machine learning models to come up with a visual analysis categorization and confidence score and returns the response to the Lambda function.

5. To persist the results of the analysis, the Lambda function stores the information in a DynamoDB table for future use.

Next, let's start with some hands-on deployment activities for provisioning the previously discussed stack using CDK.

> **Note**
> For the sake of simplicity, some of the steps (commands or code) from the following sections have already been completed for you, inside the `chapter-6/` directory, inside your Cloud9 IDE. You will find a note, just like the one that you are reading now, in the relevant sections asking you to skip the command execution or the code definitions.

## Bootstrapping a new CDK project

The very first step before we can work with AWS CDK is to bootstrap an empty directory with one of the supported programming languages. To make this task easier for users, CDK offers a command-line interface utility that is pre-installed for you in the Cloud9 IDE that we have been using throughout this book.

> **Note**
> The steps in this section have already been executed for you, inside the `chapter-6/` directory, so you may just skim through them for understanding.

Let's start a new session on our Cloud9 IDE and switch to the `chapter-6/` directory in the terminal, before starting the CDK project initialization process:

```
aws-devops-simplified:~/environment/chapter-6 $ npx aws-cdk init
--language typescript
npx: installed 1 in 8.495s
Applying project template app for typescript
# Welcome to your CDK TypeScript project
This is a blank project for CDK development with TypeScript.
The `cdk.json` file tells the CDK Toolkit how to execute your app.
## Useful commands
* `npm run build`   compile typescript to js
* `npm run watch`   watch for changes and compile
* `npm run test`    perform the jest unit tests
* `cdk deploy`      deploy this stack to your default AWS account/
region
* `cdk diff`        compare deployed stack with current state
* `cdk synth`       emits the synthesized CloudFormation template
Initializing a new git repository...
...
...
```

`cdk init` uses the name of the directory to generate dynamic prefixes, or suffixes, for most things – classes, subfolders, and so on.

> **Tip**
> You might have noticed that instead of using the `cdk` command line directly, we used `npx aws-cdk` instead. This practice allows you to pin these components to specific versions and ensure that every developer uses the same versions. Generally speaking, new releases of these components are always backward compatible, so the chance of something breaking is rare.

Once the bootstrapping is complete, you will observe the following hierarchy of folders and files in your project directory. I have added some descriptions highlighting the significance of each of these:

```
aws-devops-simplified:~/environment/chapter-6 $ tree -L 1 .
.
├── README.md
├── bin              >> (Application entry point)
├── cdk.json         >> (CDK project configurations)
```

```
├── jest.config.js    >> (Configs for JEST tests go here)
├── lib               >> (Definition of stack resources)
├── node_modules
├── package-lock.json
├── package.json
├── test              >> (Test definitions)
└── tsconfig.json
```

Having bootstrapped the code directory that will host our application code, let's move on to preparing our AWS account so that CDK can use it to deploy resources.

## Bootstrapping the AWS account to enable CDK deployments

AWS CDK deployments are targeted in a specific region of an account. Before you go ahead and deploy some resources, you need to *bootstrap* the target environment. As part of the bootstrapping process, CDK creates resources such as S3 buckets, IAM roles/policies, ECR repositories, and SSM parameters. These resources are later used by the CDK toolkit to orchestrate deployment activities in your account. Before proceeding with the `cdk bootstrap` command, we need to run `npm install` as a prerequisite so that all Node.js modules can be fetched. Bootstrapping is as simple as running the following commands:

```
aws-devops-simplified:~/environment/chapter-6 $ npm install
npm WARN old lockfile
npm WARN old lockfile This is a one-time fix-up, please be
patient...
npm WARN old lockfile

added 312 packages, and audited 331 packages in 20s
...
...
aws-devops-simplified:~/environment/chapter-6 $ cdk bootstrap
```

At this point, both the AWS account and local code repository have been prepared for deployment. Now is a good time to add concrete resources that will make up our application.

## Defining CDK constructs for application components

> **Note**
> The steps in this section have already been completed for you, inside the `chapter-6/` directory, so you may just skim through them for your understanding.

In its current state, the project directory provides a bare-bones structure that does not deploy any resources as such. Let's go ahead and add relevant construct definitions referenced in the workflow diagram. All the changes we will make here are supposed to be added to `lib/chapter-6-stack.ts`, which hosts our stack definition.

All stable constructs are currently mapped to the `aws-cdk-lib` module, which is version 2 of the AWS CDK library.

> **Note**
> Version 1 of the AWS CDK library reached end-of-support in June 2023. Given that there are a lot of resources on the internet that still refer to the v1 code, please exercise extra caution when using them.

For our requirements, we will add three AWS resource types – a Lambda function handler, an S3 bucket to host the images, and a DynamoDB table for persisting the results from Amazon Rekognition. Before we can use these constructs, we will have to import the respective libraries that expose the required TypeScript classes:

```
import * as lambda from 'aws-cdk-lib/aws-lambda';
import * as s3 from 'aws-cdk-lib/aws-s3';
import * as iam from 'aws-cdk-lib/aws-iam';
import * as s3_notifications from 'aws-cdk-lib/aws-s3-notifications';
import { AttributeType, Table, TableClass} from 'aws-cdk-lib/aws-dynamodb';
```

If you've worked with object-oriented programming languages in the past, the structure in this file might look similar. You'll notice that CDK has added a class definition that extends `cdk.Stack` and exposes a constructor to initialize all the resources within this stack. We can extend this constructor definition to add constructs that we need:

```
const dynamodbTable = new Table(this, 'image_labels',
  partitionKey: {
    name: "object_key",
    type: AttributeType.STRING
  }
})

const bucket = new s3.Bucket(this, 'image_bucket',
  removalPolicy: cdk.RemovalPolicy.DESTROY
})

const imageHandler = new lambda.Function(this,
"image_handler", {
```

```
  runtime: lambda.Runtime.PYTHON_3_7,
  code: lambda.Code.fromAsset('resources/lambda'),
  environment: {
    'IMAGE_LABELS_TABLE': dynamodbTable.tableName
  },
  handler: 'image.lambda_handler'
})
```

The three objects that we initialize in the code will correspond to CloudFormation resources in the stack. We will see this in action soon after we synthesize our CDK stack.

Of course, there are a few other aspects of this solution that are still pending. As you might have noticed, we didn't assign any permissions to our application orchestrator – the Lambda function. Furthermore, we need to add event notifications for the S3 bucket so that all subsequent image uploads are automatically sent to the Lambda image handler function:

```
// Add appropriate permissions for Lambda to work with S3, Rekognition
and DynamoDB
const rekognitionPermissionsForLambda = new iam.PolicyStatement();
rekognitionPermissionsForLambda.addActions("rekognition:*");
rekognitionPermissionsForLambda.addResources("*");

const s3PermissionsForLambda = new iam.PolicyStatement();
s3PermissionsForLambda.addActions("s3:*");
s3PermissionsForLambda.addResources(bucket.bucketArn);
s3PermissionsForLambda.addResources(bucket.bucketArn + "/*");

const dynamodbPermissionsForLambda = new iam.PolicyStatement();
dynamodbPermissionsForLambda.addActions("dynamodb:*");
dynamodbPermissionsForLambda.addResources(dynamodbTable.tableArn);

const kmsPermissionsForLambda = new iam.PolicyStatement();
kmsPermissionsForLambda.addActions("kms:*");
kmsPermissionsForLambda.addResources("*");

const createLogsPermissionsForLambda = new iam.PolicyStatement();
createLogsPermissionsForLambda.addActions("logs:CreateLogGroup");
var logGroupResource = `arn:aws:logs:${process.env.CDK_DEFAULT_
REGION}:${process.env.CDK_DEFAULT_ACCOUNT}:*`
createLogsPermissionsForLambda.addResources(logGroupResource);

const putLogEventsPermissionsForLambda = new iam.PolicyStatement();
putLogEventsPermissionsForLambda.addActions("logs:CreateLogStream");
putLogEventsPermissionsForLambda.addActions("logs:PutLogEvents");
```

```
var logGroupArnResource = `arn:aws:logs:${process.env.CDK_DEFAULT_
REGION}:${process.env.CDK_DEFAULT_ACCOUNT}:log-group:/aws/lambda/*:*`
putLogEventsPermissionsForLambda.addResources(logGroupResource);
imageHandler.addToRolePolicy(rekognitionPermissionsForLambda);
imageHandler.addToRolePolicy(s3PermissionsForLambda);
imageHandler.addToRolePolicy(dynamodbPermissionsForLambda);
imageHandler.addToRolePolicy(kmsPermissionsForLambda);

// Trigger lambda function when S3 object is added
bucket.addEventNotification(s3.EventType.OBJECT_CREATED, new s3_
notifications.LambdaDestination(imageHandler));
```

This completes our construct definitions. Before we move ahead with synthesizing our template, let's add the code for our Lambda function. The `imageHandler` construct definition has a mandatory argument called `code :`, where we define the location of our Lambda function code. The `lambda.Code.fromAsset('resources/lambda')` value requires this function to be present in a subfolder called `resources/lambda`. So, let's go ahead and create it.

## Defining Lambda code for orchestrating the application workflow

> **Note**
> The steps in this section have already been completed for you, inside the `chapter-6/` directory, so you may just skim through them for your understanding.

Let's create a new file called `image.py` that will host our Python code for the Lambda function:

```
aws-devops-simplified:~/environment/chapter-6 $ mkdir -p resources/
lambda
aws-devops-simplified:~/environment/chapter-6 $ cd resources/lambda
aws-devops-simplified:~/environment/chapter-6 $ touch image.py
```

If you remember the workflow diagram that we discussed a while back, the two main responsibilities of the Lambda image handler are as follows:

- Extract the S3 `bucket` and `key` information from the event payload and pass it on to the Amazon Rekognition service
- Persist the results of the image labeling process in the DynamoDB table

We'll use the `boto3` AWS library to interact with both services and add the following code to `image.py`:

```
import boto3
import logging
import os

def lambda_handler(event, context):
    logger = logging.getLogger()
    logger.setLevel(logging.INFO)

    logger.info("Received an event from S3:" + str(event))
    rekognition_client = boto3.client('rekognition', region_name = 'eu-central-1')

    logger.info("Passing S3 object file reference to Amazon Rekognition")
    try:
        label_detection_response = rekognition_client.detect_labels(
            Image = {
              "S3Object": {
                  "Bucket": event["Records"][0]["s3"]["bucket"]["name"],
                  "Name": event["Records"][0]["s3"]["object"]["key"]
                }
            }, MaxLabels=5,  MinConfidence=70)
    except:
        logger.exception("Unexpected exception raised by Rekognition. Please check CloudWatch Logs")
        raise

    logger.info("Put identified labels into DynamoDB table")
    ddb_client = boto3.client('dynamodb', region_name = 'eu-central-1')
    ddb_client.put_item(TableName=os.environ['IMAGE_LABELS_TABLE'],
    Item={'object_key': {'S': event["Records"][0]["s3"]["object"]["key"]},
    'object_labels': {'S': str(label_detection_response['Labels'])}})
```

Before proceeding with the deployment, we can *synthesize* the CloudFormation template, which includes all the resources we defined previously. Template synthesis is an activity that should ideally be included in your CI/CD pipelines as a review/approval mechanism before any real changes are deployed in the cloud.

## Synthesizing the template

The synthesizing process generates a valid CloudFormation YAML template. At this point, you could also deploy it directly within your AWS environment, or instruct CDK to do so. For now, let's trigger template synthetization with the `cdk synth` command:

```
aws-devops-simplified:~/environment/chapter-6 $ cdk synth
Resources:
  imagelabelsD31B94E7:
    Type: AWS::DynamoDB::Table
    Properties:
      KeySchema:
        - AttributeName: object_key
          KeyType: HASH
      AttributeDefinitions:
        - AttributeName: object_key
          AttributeType: S
      ProvisionedThroughput:
        ReadCapacityUnits: 5
        WriteCapacityUnits: 5
    UpdateReplacePolicy: Retain
    DeletionPolicy: Retain
    Metadata:
      aws:cdk:path: Chapter6Stack/image_labels/Resource
  imagebucket0CAF3977:
    Type: AWS::S3::Bucket
    UpdateReplacePolicy: Delete
    DeletionPolicy: Delete
    Metadata:
      aws:cdk:path: Chapter6Stack/image_bucket/Resource
  imagebucketNotifications2F6EEDF9:
    Type: Custom::S3BucketNotifications
    Properties:
      ServiceToken:
        Fn::GetAtt:
          - BucketNotificationsHandler050a0587b7544547bf3
          - Arn
      BucketName:
        Ref: imagebucket0CAF3977
      NotificationConfiguration:
...
...
```

The 40-odd lines of code we added to the `lib/chapter-6-stack.ts` file resulted in a template 10 times its initial size. That's the power of abstraction that AWS CDK offers you. As you may have noticed, several things are happening behind the scenes that would otherwise require the user to code all of this manually in CloudFormation. Starting from defining resource dependencies, and creating IAM roles, to uploading the Lambda functions in a CDK-managed S3 bucket, CDK took a lot of plumbing tasks away from us. In addition to displaying the YAML formatted template over STDOUT, you can also check the JSON output in the `cdk.out/Chapter6Stack.template.json` file.

## Deploying the CDK stack into an AWS account

As the final step of our hands-on exercise, let's go ahead and deploy the application in an AWS account using the `cdk deploy` command:

```
aws-devops-simplified:~/environment/chapter-6 $ cdk deploy
✨  Synthesis time: 9.92s
Chapter6Stack: building assets...
[0%] start: Building
ce2a824fd1c4ca5e141f6fe8e8de52a282e9e2ba283f:current_account-current_region
[0%] start: Building
bf157b5e94348d9175ab2f11a2c2f9ec5792c303783:current_account-current_region
[50%] success: Built
ce2a824fd1c4ca5e141f6fe8e8de52a282e9e2ba283:current_account-current_region
[100%] success: Built
bf157b5e94348d9175ab2f11a2c2f9ec5792c303783:current_account-current_region
Chapter6Stack: assets built
Chapter6Stack: deploying... [1/1]
[0%] start: Publishing
ce2a824fd1c4ca5e141f6fe8e8de52a282e9e2ba283f584f2f9a03280462e418:current_account-current_region
[0%] start: Publishing
bf157b5e94348d9175ab2f11a2c2f9ec5792c30378379f76cf190328386a1822:current_account-current_region
...
...
```

Once the deployment completes, we can check the relevant resources that were created as part of the CloudFormation deployment. The most important ones for us are the S3 bucket and the DynamoDB table. If you go to the CloudFormation service in your account, you will find a stack called `Chapter6Stack`.

After clicking on the stack's name, you can check the resources, as shown in *Figure 6.3*:

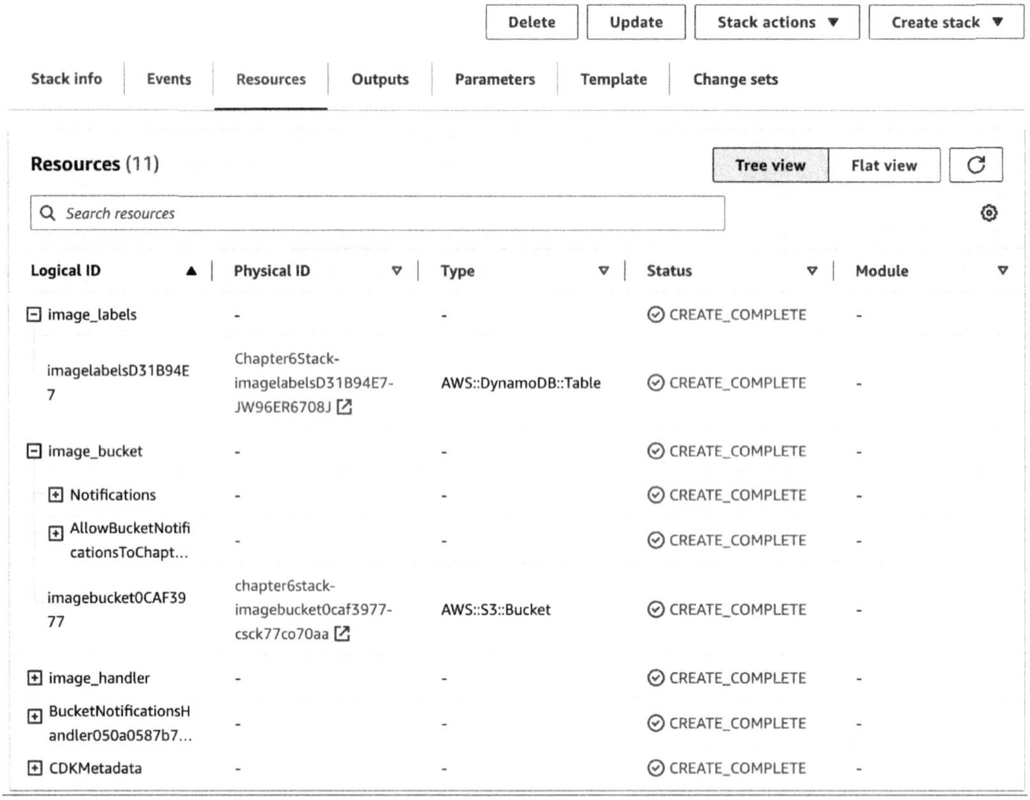

| Logical ID | Physical ID | Type | Status | Module |
|---|---|---|---|---|
| image_labels | - | - | CREATE_COMPLETE | - |
| imagelabelsD31B94E7 | Chapter6Stack-imagelabelsD31B94E7-JW96ER6708J | AWS::DynamoDB::Table | CREATE_COMPLETE | - |
| image_bucket | - | - | CREATE_COMPLETE | - |
| Notifications | - | - | CREATE_COMPLETE | - |
| AllowBucketNotificationsToChapt… | - | - | CREATE_COMPLETE | - |
| imagebucket0CAF3977 | chapter6stack-imagebucket0caf3977-csck77co70aa | AWS::S3::Bucket | CREATE_COMPLETE | - |
| image_handler | - | - | CREATE_COMPLETE | - |
| BucketNotificationsHandler050a0587b7… | - | - | CREATE_COMPLETE | - |
| CDKMetadata | - | - | CREATE_COMPLETE | - |

Figure 6.3 – Stack resources deployed as part of the CDK deployment

Having completed the deployment, let's go ahead and test the end-to-end workflow.

## Testing the image analysis workflow

The test application we've deployed in the AWS account expects an image to be uploaded in the S3 bucket, which then triggers the Lambda function that interacts with the Amazon Rekognition service. The image I used for testing the workflow can be found at `https://tinyurl.com/3z9ecjpb`. You might want to upload it or use a different one.

Once the upload completes, the S3 event notification will fire off the Lambda function. The image label analysis results will be available in the DynamoDB table, as shown in *Figure 6.4*:

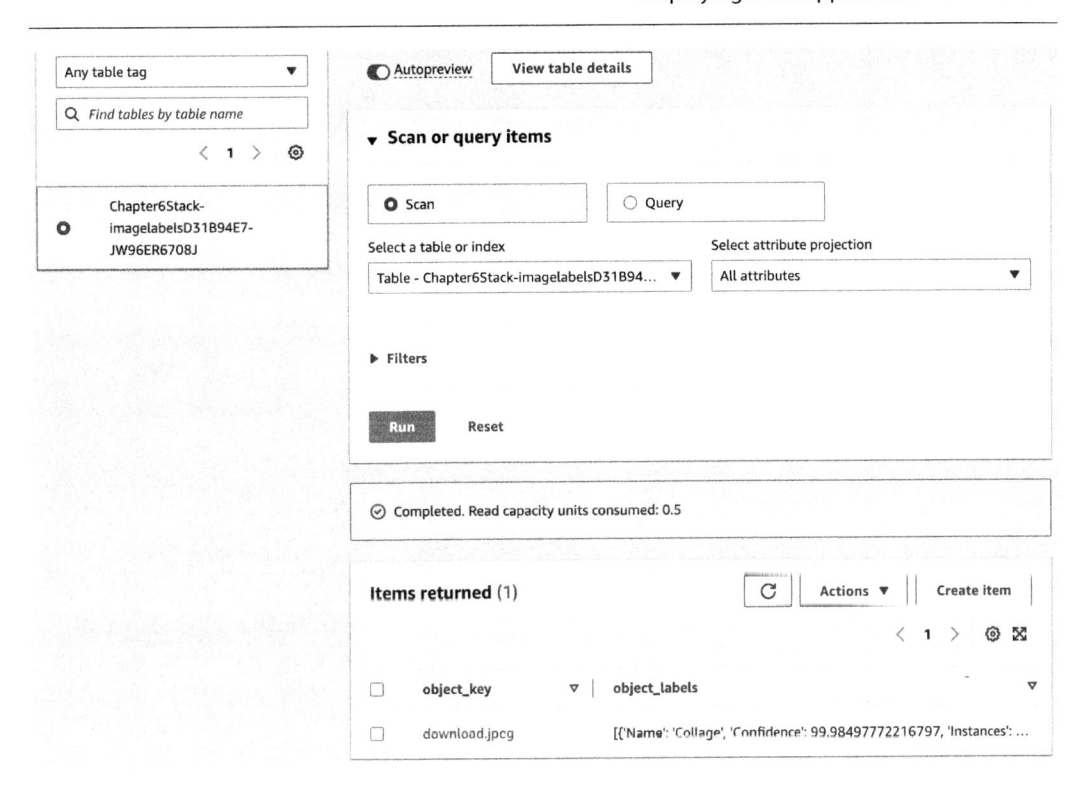

Figure 6.4 – Image labeling results persisted in DynamoDB

The response from Rekognition includes a JSON payload that defines the matched categories and respective confidence scores:

```
[
    {
        "Name":"Cityscape",
        "Confidence":99.99959564208984,
        "Instances":[
        ],
        "Parents":[
            {
                "Name":"Architecture"
            },
            {
                "Name":"Building"
            },
            {
                "Name":"Urban"
            }
```

```
            ]
        },
        {
            "Name":"Urban",
            "Confidence":99.99959564208984,
            "Instances":[
            ],
            "Parents":[
            ]
        },
...
...
```

This completes our test for the image labeling automation that we built using CDK.

> **Note**
> If you face any issues with the workflow, or the labeling results are not available in DynamoDB, you might want to check CloudWatch Logs. If you remember, we gave permissions to our Lambda function to be able to create a CloudWatch log group and publish the logging events into the log group for every invocation. It's a good place to start debugging any unexpected scenarios.

## Summary

In this chapter, we learned about the basics of working with AWS CDK to create infrastructure resources using general-purpose programming languages. This approach to managing cloud infrastructure is particularly useful for teams who are used to working with CloudFormation, have experience using the service in an enterprise-grade environment, and would now like to take the next steps by utilizing different forms of abstraction.

We started this chapter by discussing various segments of AWS IaC tools and compared them with AWS CDK. Toward the end of this chapter, we deployed an automated image labeling system using Amazon Rekognition. This not only allowed us to learn a new service but at the same time recognize the benefits offered by high-level constructs that make infrastructure management much easier than working with raw YAML/JSON templates in CloudFormation.

In *Chapter 7, Running Containers in AWS*, we will delve into the relevance of containers in modern software development, and the services provided by AWS in this space.

## Further reading

To learn more about the topics that were covered in this chapter, take a look at the following resources:

- AWS CDK examples in different programming languages: `https://github.com/aws-samples/aws-cdk-examples`
- The AWS jsii framework, which powers AWS CDK: `https://github.com/aws/jsii`
- AWS CDK patterns: `https://cdkpatterns.com/patterns/`

# Part 3
# Security and Observability of Containerized Workloads

In this part, you will learn about the three main pillars of modern software development: containers, observability, and DevSecOps. In addition to building a solid foundational understanding of Amazon ECS, an AWS-managed container platform, the chapters focus on integrations with external, mature open source tools and platforms. By the end, you will have multiple solution patterns deployed in your AWS account, which can be customized to meet your organization's security and observability needs.

This part has the following chapters:

- *Chapter 7, Running Containers in AWS*
- *Chapter 8, Enabling the Observability of Your Workloads*
- *Chapter 9, Implementing DevSecOps with AWS*

# 7
# Running Containers in AWS

It's a well-known fact that traditional monolithic software architectures hosted on-premises slow down teams who want to deliver business outcomes to their customers by leveraging cloud capabilities. So far in this book, we have discussed quite a lot of technical and organizational impacts such applications can have. To overcome these blockers, software teams prefer breaking down the monoliths into smaller manageable components, also known as microservices. These services commonly communicate with each other over HTTP(S), or asynchronous messaging protocols, while offering a unified interface to the end user, as if everything is being managed as a single application. When the right services are used, they are comparatively easy to scale and operate in the cloud. If you are into designing software applications, I would highly recommend going through *Characteristics of Modern Microservices Architecture*, by Martin Fowler (`https://martinfowler.com/articles/microservices.html`).

To simplify the adoption of microservice architectures and building applications that are optimized for cloud computing, software teams also use the **twelve-factor** design pattern (`https://12factor.net/`). These are time-tested best practices for building modern **Software-as-a-Service** (**SaaS**) applications. The 12 factors mainly drive the idea of the following:

- Using *declarative formats* to set up automation
- Having a clean contract with the underlying operating system, offering *maximum portability across environments*
- Building apps that are *suited for deployment on cloud platforms*
- *Scaling up without significant changes* to tooling
- Having *minimum divergence between environments* such as development and production

If I had to call out a single technology that powers all of these areas, it would be **containers**. Microservices and containers go incredibly well together. They empower users to pass on the benefits of the strong application foundations to the end users in the form of frequent and stable business features. In the modern era, containers are the de facto standard for software deployment in the cloud or on-premises. By offering benefits such as low compute and memory footprint, isolation boundaries, and build-once-deploy anywhere possibilities, containers have emerged as a strong candidate for any greenfield or brownfield application effort. You used the Docker toolbox image to execute all the hands-on exercises in the previous chapters and presumably agree that the consistent experience these containers offer is unmatched. Irrespective of the underlying system configurations, operating systems, or libraries, the hands-on experience for you will be similar. Isn't this great? These days, it's unusual for software applications to not have a container-based deployment model. It simplifies a lot of areas that otherwise would have been a pain to manage.

In this chapter, we will further grow our knowledge of containers in AWS by covering the following topics:

- A quick introduction to the container ecosystem
- AWS services that support running containers in the cloud
- Using AWS ECS to deploy a test application stack

## A quick introduction to the container ecosystem

If you've not been exposed to containers in your software landscape yet, then this is the introduction for you. I will try to keep it short since there are great resources on the internet if you wish to dive deep into the technology.

### What are containers and why do we need them?

*Containers* are not a new idea. They have been around for many years in the *Solaris*, *FreeBSD*, and *Unix* operating systems as *Solaris Zones*, *Jails*, and *Chroot*, respectively. In the compute space, we have already experienced a lot of innovations that raise the technical maturity bar while abstracting the underlying complexity. We started with bare-metal servers, moved onto virtual machines for hardware-level virtualization, started using containers for software virtualization, and now have serverless technologies that abstract all of it away from the end user. However, in comparison to serverless technologies, containers are still heavily used due to the balance of maturity and control that they offer. This is often an important requirement for enterprise-scale adoption and usage.

Just like how **Java** and **Python** prevent us from having to write assembly-level code, containers abstract a lot of operating system internals to offer benefits such as resource isolation and security boundaries, which ultimately lead to improved agility. Unlike virtual machines, containers are a form of operating system virtualization. They are standard units of software that encapsulate the code, and all of its dependencies, so that the application can be executed reliably, and quickly, on multiple environments.

**Docker** is an open source container platform that has revolutionized the concept of containers. It offers yet another layer of abstraction and constructs that have now shaped the industry norms when it comes to containerized tooling, applications, and platforms. Let's discuss the key benefits you get with Docker and the underlying constructs it uses.

## Docker as a container platform

Docker is a portable runtime application environment that allows us to run an application bundled together with its dependencies, on several platforms, with the same end user experience.

The key reason for Docker's success and industry-wide adoption are the benefits that it helps realize – that is, portability, immutability, faster developments and deployments, and efficient resource utilization. It's important to reinforce that all these benefits trace back to the *microservices architecture* and *twelve-factor* design methodologies that we discussed at the beginning of this chapter.

### *Key concepts used by Docker*

To offer a consistent experience to the application developers, some key concepts are used in Docker's architecture that are worth discussing.

#### Docker images

A Docker image is a reusable *read-only template* that includes code, dependencies, runtime, and tools that can be replicated by one or more containers. It is usually based on another parent image and adds some customization delta on top of it. For example, using Ubuntu as a base image, you could add Nginx on top to build an image that offers web server capabilities.

You can create your own `Dockerfile` – a blueprint that contains all instructions for creating Docker images. It specifies the base image to use, the dependencies to install, and the commands to run during the image creation process. Once the Docker image has been built, it can be used to spawn multiple containers.

#### Filesystem layers

This is what powers the creation of images and container executions. Every single instruction in your `Dockerfile` results in a new read-only layer being added on top of previous instructions. When a container is spun off from this image, Docker adds an ephemeral thin read-write layer for the specific container instance that can be used by processes running inside that container.

#### Docker containers

Containers are the *running instances* of an image. The thin write-only layer they get lasts for the lifetime of the container and can be used by the contained processes for any *transient needs*. The `docker run` command we have used in the book creates a container by pulling the `akskap/awsdevopssimplified-toolbox` image onto your local system (if it doesn't exist already) and then running a container from the packaged artifact.

We can see how containers, images, and the surrounding tools work together in *Figure 7.1*:

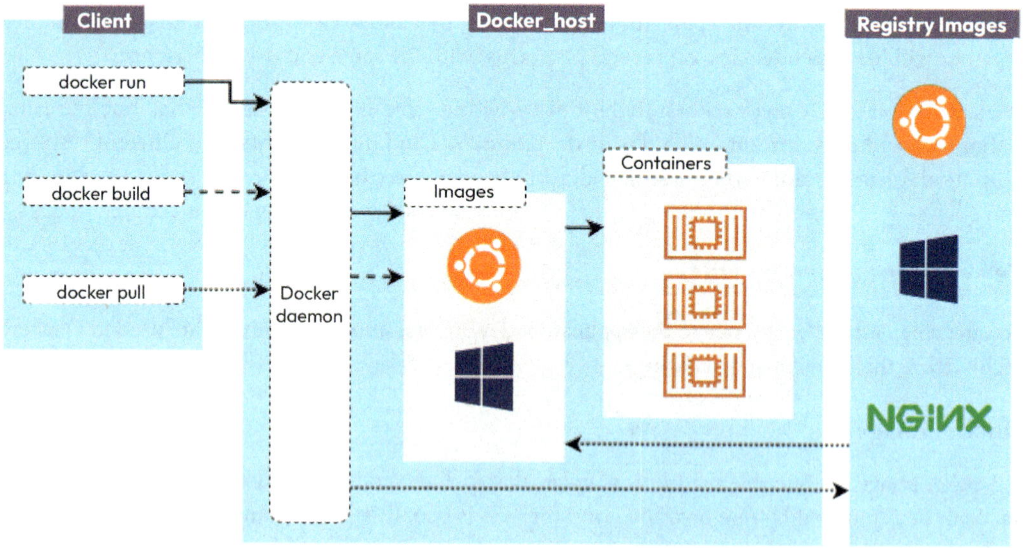

Figure 7.1 – Docker ecosystem and the relationship between containers and images

Next, let's briefly discuss what registries are and how they work.

### Docker registries

Registries host Docker images. They can be public or private, depending on how you would like to distribute those artifacts to the end user. Common examples are **Docker Hub** and **Amazon ECR**. Organizations that need to host private registries and encrypt the data at rest can use managed KMS keys and IAM. Under the hood, ECR stores the images in Amazon S3.

By leveraging these capabilities, it's not very difficult to get started with basic container deployments. However, some areas need more attention.

## Scaling containerized deployments beyond simple use cases

Running one or two container instances on your local system is easy. For CI/CD use cases, teams often run multiple in parallel. This does require some additional development effort on top of the interfaces exposed by respective tools (for example, **GitLab CI/CD** pipeline templates), but it is still manageable. The real challenge, however, comes up when you want to run hundreds and thousands of containers for a production workload. How do you figure out which compute node to place the container on? How do you monitor whether they are still running? How can they securely consume other services such as databases and in-memory caches from the underlying cloud provider? These are the areas that justify the need for a full-fledged container management platform so that you can offload these tasks. These platforms are engineered to solve such problems at scale so that you can focus on writing application code.

There are some key responsibilities and characteristics of such platforms, as we'll discuss next.

## Key responsibilities of container platforms

A container platform should allow the developers to build, deploy, and manage container services at scale. In addition to providing capabilities around the life cycle management of these containers, there are several other areas these platforms typically support.

### *Orchestrating the placement of containers*

Scheduling containers over multiple compute nodes is not an easy feat. This requires the platform to interact at both the infrastructure and application levels. The container platform consumes key metrics based on the current consumption of the underlying servers and matches them to the resource needs of the application. Some platforms allow the end user to implement advanced placement logic that matches their application needs.

### *Integrations with other services*

In addition to running applications, these platforms offer a host of integration capabilities. As you can imagine, running containers on AWS will, at some point, require collaborating with underlying networking (VPC, subnet addressing, and so on), persistent storage (EBS or EFS), and monitoring and logging services. These integrations remove a lot of plumbing efforts that the developers would otherwise have to invest time in.

### *Monitoring containerized workloads*

Running multiple containers in parallel requires a holistic view of how your applications are performing. Creating a dependency graph, monitoring key utilization metrics, deriving insights from the logs, or offering ready-to-use integrations with third-party solutions are some of the differentiating capabilities these platforms offer. In *Chapter 8, Enabling the Observability of Your Workloads*, we will dive deeper into some of the AWS offerings in this segment.

### *Enforcing security guardrails for containerized applications*

Being an operating-system-level virtualization technology, there could be scenarios where you would run multiple applications on the same host. Container platforms should offer strong security boundaries that do not allow compromised applications to gain unprivileged access to the host kernel. We will cover some of the security best practices later in this chapter in the *Ensuring a good security posture with ECS* section.

Lastly, when deciding on a container platform, it's important to always keep the complexities of managing the control plane itself in mind. Be it the requirements around automatically rolling out security patches or dynamically scaling the underlying components used by Kubernetes, you will always benefit from offloading these un-differentiated tasks to the platform.

## AWS services that support running containers in the cloud

It mainly comes down to the trade-offs between the level of control and ease of operations. Depending on the needs of your workloads and your teams' comfort with containerization, you might decide to choose one of the three AWS offerings discussed in this section.

### AWS Elastic Compute Cloud (EC2)

Organizations that prefer to have maximum control and visibility of the container workloads may decide to run the entire stack on their own, in the compute instances provided by AWS. Technically speaking, nothing stops them from using tools such as **Docker Compose**, **Docker Swarm**, or even standard Docker clients to manage multiple containers within an EC2 instance. However, the broader question they should answer is whether they want to invest in developing orchestration at this level for productive use cases that quickly expand beyond the scope of what a single EC2 instance can manage. More often than not, the answer is no.

Secondly, when it comes to integrations with other AWS services for logging, monitoring, and operational needs, it can become quite a challenge to scale and operate the overall tooling that glues the application with the AWS platform. AWS-managed services do a lot of heavy lifting in this area, requiring your efforts for application-specific implementation only. Integrating with such services is just a matter of defining relevant properties in the respective manifest files.

### AWS Elastic Kubernetes Service (EKS)

**EKS** is a managed Kubernetes service that can be used to run Kubernetes not just in the cloud but also on-premises. With the recent announcements in the hybrid environment space, AWS has extended the EKS experience to run clusters on-premises (**EKS Anywhere**), with the same tooling interface that users are used to. Users can still use the cloud-based EKS dashboard to manage containerized apps on-premises. These offerings are relevant for customers that have regulatory or compliance needs to fulfill.

Furthermore, EKS is also interesting for organizations that want to avoid vendor lock-in. Using AWS services that are built on top of open source frameworks allows them to easily port their applications to a different provider anytime in the future, if required.

If you are interested in learning more about EKS offerings in the hybrid space, I recommend looking into Amazon EKS on AWS Outposts or Amazon EKS Anywhere.

### AWS Elastic Container Service (ECS)

The highest form of abstraction and opinionated tooling usually comes with a lot of best practices baked in that you can trust and adopt from the very beginning. **Amazon ECS** is one such service that is very easy to start with and offers deep integrations with not only other AWS services but also third-party partner ecosystems. Users don't need to manage any control plane nodes, and just like EKS, you can also expand your application footprint to on-premises servers if needed.

The service allows you to declaratively define your application manifests, which contain the resource requirements along with other dependencies. Furthermore, you can offload the underlying infrastructure provisioning (EC2 nodes) tasks to AWS and benefit from high-security standards of isolation and access management. ECS leverages the Docker runtime under the hood to manage your applications. We will see the service in action in the hands-on exercise.

For the remainder of this chapter, we will dive deeper into ECS and the related features the service comes with.

## ECS constructs and security features

Being an opinionated container management service from AWS, some constructs are unique to the ECS service. Since they are not commonly used across other tools or platforms in the container ecosystem, let's briefly discuss them.

### Important constructs used by ECS

Similar to how we declaratively define the state of our resources in a CloudFormation template, we use JSON-based manifests to outline the needs of our containers, how they are related to each other, as well as their integration with other services. The next step is to pass them over to ECS to manage.

#### Container definitions – the most basic level of container configuration

This is the lowest level of configuration detail expected from the user. Within a container definition, you can define properties such as Docker images, CPU and memory allocation, networking, security, Linux parameters, volume mounts, port mappings, and so on.

A container definition includes all the information required by the orchestrator to host this application on a specific node and configure all the settings needed to have the application up and running. This construct maps one to one to the containers you would run to manage your application.

#### Task definitions – logically encapsulating related containers

After you have the container definitions chalked out, you can logically club them together into what is known as a task definition. This is an ECS-specific construct that can be used to define (and manage) your application components individually. Let's say you have a web application within which the backend application container always communicates with the database container. So, these two can naturally fit into a single task definition as you won't be exposing the database to the outside world anyways.

You can also define resources such as CPU and memory at the task definition level, which will then be further distributed among all the containers. For granular access control, task definitions can be attached to specific IAM roles, which then grant permissions to the containers for carrying out specific actions on a related AWS service.

### *Tasks – an instance of a task definition*

A **task** is an instance of a task definition. You can run multiple tasks from the same task definition and ECS will ensure the desired count of instances, and other configurations, are met. Do keep in mind that all containers that are part of the task definition will be scaled up or down together. So, this is the unit of deployment in the ECS world.

### *Exposing long-running tasks with ECS*

Often, you will want to have long-running versions of your tasks. This is a common use case for web applications. ECS has a scheduler component that monitors your running tasks and reschedules them automatically when they fail.

ECS also allows you to configure *placement strategies and constraints* if you like to customize how the scheduler places and terminates a task.

### *ECS launch types to support different ownership models*

Depending on the level of control that you want on the underlying infrastructure that hosts your application containers, you can configure specific launch types with ECS. They come in two flavors:

- **ECS on EC2**: The user is responsible for managing and patching the EC2 instances on which the tasks run. ECS offers official AMIs that contain the ECS agent, which communicates with the ECS control plane and orchestrates activities within your instance.

- **ECS on Fargate**: This is a very interesting option for customers who are not bound by any regulatory or specific compliance requirements. AWS manages the infrastructure on your behalf and offers a strong isolated environment (lightweight VMs) where your containers are hosted. Each task gets a dedicated execution environment. The beauty of this solution is that it supports using interfaces from your existing VPCs and subnets, thereby giving you the firewalling and security control that you would expect from regular EC2 instances.

> **Tip**
> From a security standpoint, it's important to keep your EC2 nodes updated (when not using the Fargate launch type) with recent patch upgrades. AWS makes this information available as an SSM parameter in your account:
> ```
> aws ssm get-parameters --names /aws/service/ecs/optimized-ami/amazon-linux-2/recommended --region eu-central-1
> ```

## ECS constructs and security features

Having covered the primary constructs in ECS, let's also discuss some security best practices that will help you ensure a good cloud posture for your organization.

## Ensuring a good security posture with ECS

Security guardrails can have multiple dimensions. AWS offers services that cater to most of these needs – be they Route53 DNS, firewall, network packet inspection through a network firewall, network access control lists for subnets, or security groups for managing traffic at the interface level. In the context of ECS (and containers in general), let's discuss some low-hanging fruits that can provide big security benefits.

### Locking down permissions with IAM roles

IAM is what defines everything around authentication and authorization in AWS. ECS is no different. The service allows you to define and map IAM roles at the ECS agent level, as well as the application task level. They are known as **ECS Task Execution Role** and **ECS Task Role**. The ECS task agent will typically require access to the ECR registry, SSM parameters, and CloudWatch logs. In addition to this, you can restrict the permissions for the application running inside the ECS container. When the application container bootstraps, ECS ensures that dynamic credentials are injected into it. This helps you avoid having to manage long-term static security credentials, which can be a security risk.

### Ensuring security patch readiness when CVEs are identified

With ECS on Fargate, you can offload the security patching work to AWS and the cloud provider takes responsibility for dynamically patching your instances for any newly identified **Common Vulnerabilities and Exposures** (**CVEs**). However, if you are running ECS on EC2, you have to be aware of the Shared Responsibility Model from AWS (https://aws.amazon.com/compliance/shared-responsibility-model/). The most important thing to remember is that AWS is responsible for the security *of the cloud*, and the customer is responsible for security *in the cloud*. This applies not only to containers but also the entire AWS ecosystem in general. So, regularly patching the EC2 instances is the customer's responsibility and can be easily managed by dynamically updating the affected libraries or adopting the idea of infrastructure immutability, as discussed in *Chapter 3, Leveraging Immutable Infrastructure in the Cloud*. This essentially means that you can replace the whole AMI with a new official artifact from ECS as soon as it is available. However, this requires a solid software delivery and test process that is automated.

### Network isolation using the task-level ENI

ECS is quite flexible when it comes to networking the properties of the tasks in your cluster. There are three modes: *host*, *vpc*, and *bridge*. From a security standpoint, this capability allows you to manage the network traffic for this container, just like you would do it for an EC2 instance. Depending on what networking mode you use, you can either isolate the container within the boundaries of the underlying host with a *bridge* network, use the VPC constructs to assign ENIs directly to the containers, or completely abstract the containers behind the host IP using the *host* mode.

Tasks that solely focus on some sort of batch processing can be run in isolation by leveraging the Docker-managed bridge network. For others, where you would like to expose the workloads outside the host, you could use the other two modes.

### Container secrets and kernel capabilities

Injecting secrets into the container environment can be achieved by defining the relevant keys, and respective values, in your container definitions. However, when dealing with secure parameters, you can make use of the Secrets Manager integration to avoid leaking any confidential data as part of the code, or related configurations.

All applications running inside containers need system call capabilities to perform some functions. ECS makes it possible to granularly assign the exact system calls that should be allowed by the particular task. Unless you are running container workloads that need to make some changes directly on the underlying host, you should try and avoid *privileged* mode. This essentially makes the container behave like a root user on the underlying host.

## Deploying a test application on ECS

It's always fun to see what we've learned in action. Based on what we have explored so far, let's get our hands dirty by deploying a test application on Amazon ECS. This time, we'll create a new application that you can also use and customize beyond the scope of this chapter, as per your personal preferences – a **To-Do List Manager**.

We will sprinkle some data persistence elements into the application architecture to make it as close as possible to real-life usage patterns, where you would like to add new tasks and delete a few others daily. Let's outline the main components of the application, as highlighted in *Figure 7.2*.

### Understanding the test application architecture

To-Do List Manager is an application that allows you to manage all the tasks that you accomplish in your day-to-day routine. In this exercise, we will develop and host two features: creating new tasks and deleting the ones that are complete. You can also further extend the scope of the application and personalize it to your taste. Several application- and infrastructure-level components communicate with each other to expose task management capabilities to the end user. They can be broadly categorized into two segments – **infrastructure components** and **application components**.

## Infrastructure components

These are the services that support the underlying infrastructure foundations on top of which the application runs. As always, you need a VPC, subnet, and corresponding route tables for traffic flow management. Once the user requests hit an Application Load Balancer hosted on the edge, it forwards the packets to an ECS cluster, which then returns a HTTP response, based on the type of request that was sent. As we've already discussed in this chapter, ECS is further composed of services, tasks, and task definitions. We will make use of all of them to host our Python-based web application in an AWS account.

As we saw in the previous chapter, *A Programmatic Approach to IaC with AWS CDK*, it's very efficient to leverage existing CDK constructs to build and deploy AWS infrastructures at scale. This enables us to avoid investing a lot of time in writing CloudFormation templates from scratch. Therefore, we will define the entire infrastructure required in this chapter using AWS CDK.

The following are the three layers under the infrastructure segment:

- **Network infrastructure** (**VPCs, subnets, and route tables**): We will create a standard `10.0.0.0/16` VPC CIDR block for this exercise and carve out two public and two private subnets, each with a `/24` mask. We will offload all the tasks around route table creation, route entries, NAT gateways, and internet gateways to CDK using the `aws-cdk-lib/aws-ec2` library.

- **Container platform** (**ECS**): Within the scope of ECS, we will create *task definitions* that allocate compute and memory resources, and further define two containers for the application and the database. To have an always running application instance, we will wrap it into an ECS service that integrates with the Application Load Balancer. As we don't want to manage any EC2 instances, we will use the Fargate launch type, thereby offloading this responsibility to the ECS service.

- **Traffic controller** (**Application Load Balancer**): To receive requests from the end user, we will create a public-facing Application Load Balancer and drop its interfaces into the public subnets of the VPC. ECS automatically registers the running containers with the respective target group, thereby abstracting the container port, `5000` (used by Flask), behind the regular `HTTP 80`.

Take a look at *Figure 7.2* for a visual understanding of what the overall communication flow looks like:

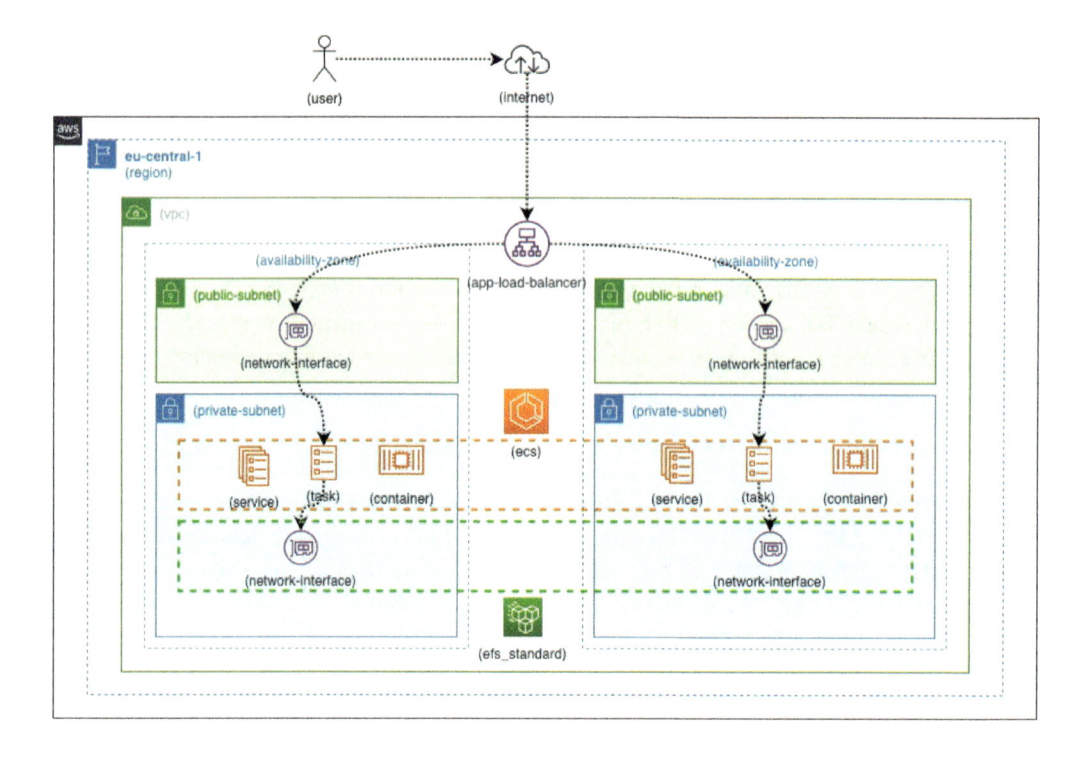

Figure 7.2 – Infrastructure components of the To-Do List Manager application hosted on ECS

The infrastructure elements by themselves don't support any real-life usage patterns. So, let's dive into the application components that will breathe life into these foundational elements.

## Application components

This is supposed to be a long-running application that will primarily consist of two containers – a web application and a database. We can define them in their respective container definitions, which can then both be mapped to a single task definition. ECS offers the *service* construct to manage such long-running applications, so we will use it to expose the application container to the outside world on port 5000. As a best practice, we will front the application with an Application Load Balancer and the ECS service will take care of registering/de-registering the containers as part of their life cycle.

To build the core of our application, we will use the Python-based Flask framework. Among many other features the web application framework offers, we are mainly interested in static file support, template rendering, and HTTP request/response management. We will see these code snippets in action in the following sections. The application frontend will be rendered using HTML and Bootstrap. All the user interactions (creation or deletion of tasks) will be mapped to the corresponding APIs in Flask:

- **Frontend** (**HTML** and **Bootstrap**): Using standard HTML elements such as tables and forms, we allow the users to interact with the application with an easy-to-use interface where they can create, categorize, and delete tasks. Each action on the web page is mapped to backend APIs that we manage with Flask.

- **Backend** (**Flask framework**): Flask offers easy-to-implement HTTP routing mechanisms using the `@app.route` function decorators. We will use them to handle the `GET` and `POST` requests originating from our application. As you can imagine, these APIs will further interact with the database layer since we want to persist all the tasks and avoid any data loss.

- **Data persistence** (**MongoDB** and **EFS**): MongoDB is a NoSQL database program that simplifies the process of storing, retrieving, and manipulating JSON-based documents. We will use the official MongoDB Docker image to run a container in ECS. Since container storage is ephemeral, we will mount an external EFS volume using ECS task definition capabilities so that no data is lost, should a container require a restart for any reason. Managed services such as ECS make this very easy for the user by automatically mapping such volumes in the container instances. Otherwise, doing something similar in an EC2 instance manually requires some scripting effort.

Similar to what we have used for the command-line utilities required in all exercises so far, I have published the bundled application code for the test application in a Docker image, in the public *DockerHub* registry. This should save you some hassle around building and hosting this image on your own. Refer to *Figure 7.3* for a visual understanding of how the application containers hosted in ECS interact with other infrastructure elements:

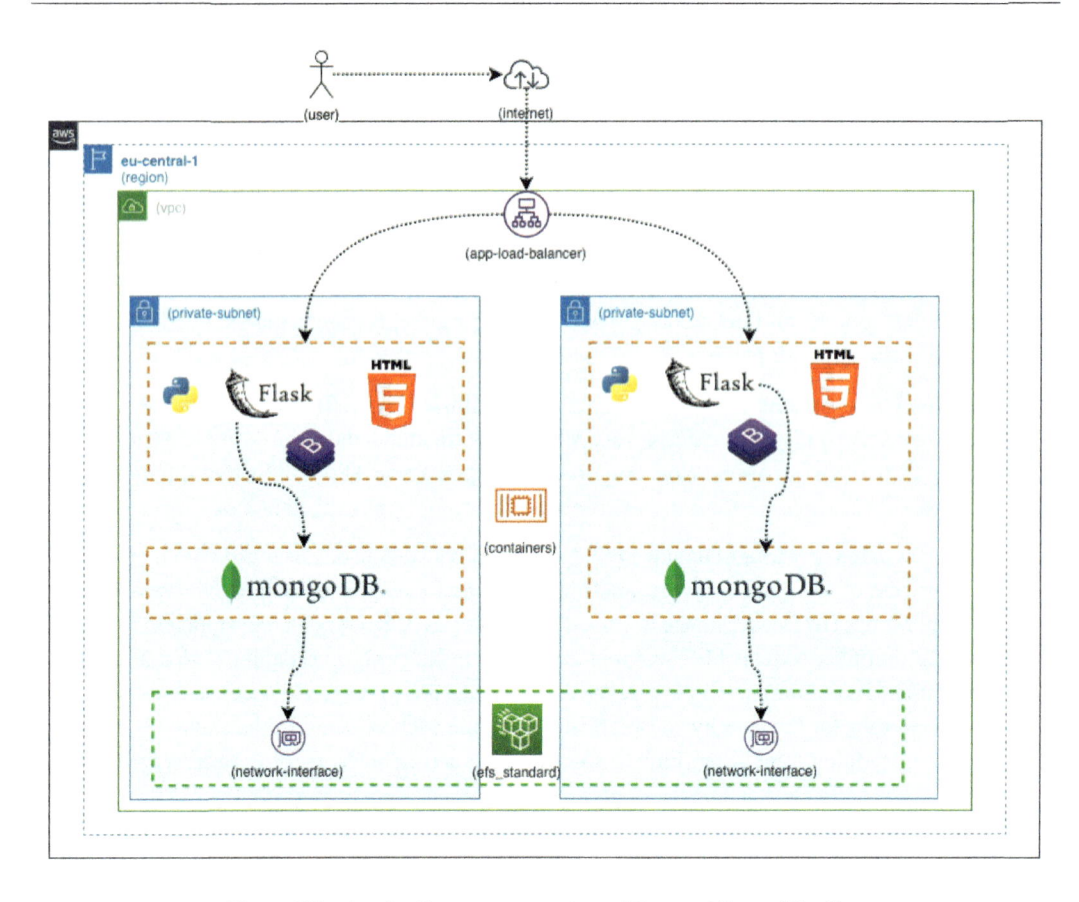

Figure 7.3 – Application components and the workflow of the To-Do List Manager application hosted on ECS

We intend to use CDK to deploy our infrastructure and application elements. So, let's discuss the stack components we will require.

## Defining the CDK stack constructs

We will define the previously discussed infrastructure components inside a CDK stack. The complete CDK project is available in your Cloud9 IDE, in the `chapter-7/chapter-7-cdk/` directory. We will not go through the CDK project initiation steps in detail as these were already covered in the previous chapter, *A Programmatic Approach to IaC with AWS CDK*. Let's dive into the code-level constructs and gain some understanding of what is needed to get the application up and running. As usual, all the CDK construct definitions can be found inside the `lib/` folder of the project directory – in this case, `chapter-7/chapter-7-cdk/`. Let's dive into each infrastructure component in detail.

### Networking foundations and the ECS cluster

A common starting point for all infrastructure stack definitions is to create a VPC, subnets, and corresponding route tables. You will also need to set up an internet gateway for the VPC and a NAT gateway in each of the public subnets to enable packet traversals over the internet:

```
import { Vpc, SubnetType} from 'aws-cdk-lib/aws-ec2';
...
const customVPC = new Vpc(this, 'CustomVPC', {
  cidr: '10.0.0.0/16',
  maxAzs: 2,
  subnetConfiguration: [
    {
      subnetType: SubnetType.PRIVATE_WITH_EGRESS,
      name: 'privateSubnet',
      cidrMask: 24,
    },
    {
      subnetType: SubnetType.PUBLIC,
      name: 'publicSubnet',
      cidrMask: 24,
    }
  ],
  natGateways: 2
})
```

After adding the VPC resources, we are all set to define our ECS cluster and link it to this custom VPC:

```
import * as ecs from 'aws-cdk-lib/aws-ecs';
...
const ecsCluster = new ecs.Cluster(this, 'ECSCluster', {
  vpc: customVPC,
  clusterName: "aws-devops-simplified",
})
...
```

These simple constructs abstract a lot of complexity from the user. If you perform cdk synth at this point, you will appreciate the heavy lifting that goes on behind the scenes in generating the CloudFormation template for this stack.

Now that the cluster is ready, it's time to define the *task definition* that will host both of our containers.

### Adding a task definition for our ECS cluster

As part of this configuration, we will also create the IAM policies that can be attached to the *task role* and the *execution role*. These permissions give these constructs access rights to the relevant AWS services:

```
import * as iam from 'aws-cdk-lib/aws-iam';
...
const execRolePolicy =  new iam.PolicyStatement({
  effect: iam.Effect.ALLOW,
  resources: ['*'],
  actions: [
          "ecr:GetAuthorizationToken",
          "ecr:BatchCheckLayerAvailability",
          "ecr:GetDownloadUrlForLayer",
          "ecr:BatchGetImage",
          "logs:*",
          "elasticfilesystem:*"
        ]
});
const fargateTaskDefn = new ecs.FargateTaskDefinition(this,
"FargateTaskDefn", {
  cpu: 4096,
  memoryLimitMiB: 8192,
});
fargateTaskDefn.addToExecutionRolePolicy(execRolePolicy);
fargateTaskDefn.addToTaskRolePolicy(execRolePolicy);
```

You might notice that we have also added IAM permissions for the ECR service. This is to support the consumption of Docker images from the ECR repository, in case you decide to not use the existing image from DockerHub.

Task definitions help us configure the parameters, resources, and mount points that will eventually be used by containers provisioned as part of this task – the application and database container in our case. Now, let's proceed with defining the containers and their respective settings.

### Configuring the application and database containers

Think of all the configurations that would be needed for an application to run inside a container and respond to traffic originating from the internet. On the other hand, we don't want to expose our database to the outside world and it's just going to be available for the application over `localhost`. We will start by allocating a chunk of CPU and memory resources to both containers from the bigger *task* pool. By default, the Flask application runs on port `5000`. This is something we want to expose to the outside world:

```
...
const appContainer = new ecs.ContainerDefinition(this,
"AppContainerDefn", {
  image: ecs.ContainerImage.fromRegistry("akskap/flask-todo-list-
app"),
  taskDefinition: fargateTaskDefn,
  cpu: 512,
  memoryLimitMiB: 1024,
  logging: ecs.LogDrivers.awsLogs({streamPrefix: "aws-devops-
simplified-app-container"})
})
appContainer.addPortMappings({
  containerPort: 5000
})
...
const dbContainer = new ecs.ContainerDefinition(this,
"DBContainerDefn", {
  image: ecs.ContainerImage.fromRegistry("mongo"),
  taskDefinition: fargateTaskDefn,
  cpu: 512,
  memoryLimitMiB: 1024,
  logging: ecs.LogDrivers.awsLogs({streamPrefix: "aws-devops-
simplified-db-container"})
})

dbContainer.addMountPoints({
  containerPath: mountPath,
  sourceVolume: volumeName,
  readOnly: false,
})
...
```

As you can see, we are using separate image identifiers for both containers. One points to our Flask application code image, while the other points to an official MongoDB image, but both are hosted in DockerHub. You might also remember that we discussed mounting an EFS filesystem to the MongoDB container to persist all changes to the underlying data. This can be achieved with `dbContainer.addMountPoints`, as seen in the code. We also added a host port mapping for the application container using the `appContainer.addPortMappings` function.

At this point, however, ECS will complain that the mount point is not recognized. This is understandable because we haven't provisioned an EFS filesystem yet, and secondly, we didn't map it to the task definition before using it in the container definition. So, let's ensure that these prerequisites are covered.

### Adding an EFS filesystem and mapping it to the task definition

Considering the scope of our test application, we will keep the EFS configurations simple and just declare `fileSystemId`, which is mandatory. Since EFS is accessed over the network, we also need to ensure that appropriate security group configurations are in place before this filesystem can be mounted inside the database container:

```
import { SecurityGroup, Port, Peer } from 'aws-cdk-lib/aws-ec2';
import * as efs from 'aws-cdk-lib/aws-efs';
...
const efsSecurityGroup = new SecurityGroup(this, "EFSSecurityGroup", {
  allowAllOutbound: true,
  vpc: customVPC,
  description: "Security Group for the EFS File System"
})

efsSecurityGroup.addIngressRule(Peer.anyIpv4(), Port.tcp(2049));

const fileSystem = new efs.FileSystem(this, "FileSystem", {
  vpc: customVPC,
  securityGroup: efsSecurityGroup,
})

const efsVolume = {
  name: volumeName,
  efsVolumeConfiguration: {
    fileSystemId: fileSystem.fileSystemId
  }
}

fargateTaskDefn.addVolume(efsVolume);
...
```

We allow incoming traffic on port 2049 from any private IPv4 address, which in this case can only be the application container in the same Docker network.

### Adding the Fargate service with Application Load Balancer integration

The last piece remaining in the infrastructure stack is the ECS service, which acts as the glue between the Flask container and the Application Load Balancer. It takes responsibility for registering the task IP and port in the load balancer's target group:

```
import * as ecs_patterns from 'aws-cdk-lib/aws-ecs-patterns';
...
```

```
const fargateService = new ecs_patterns.
ApplicationLoadBalancedFargateService(this, "FargateService", {
  cluster: ecsCluster,
  taskDefinition: fargateTaskDefn,
})
...
```

In this case, we're leveraging an existing ECS pattern in CDK constructs, which simplifies the process of creating a Fargate service that's exposed over the internet with an Application Load Balancer. This saves us quite a lot of implementation effort.

At this point, we are done with all the infrastructure components that will be required to provision the application in our AWS accounts on an ECS cluster.

Before proceeding with the CDK deployment, let's discuss what makes up our Flask application code and the resulting Docker image. Discussing Flask's capabilities in detail is outside this chapter's scope, but I will try and give you a brief walkthrough of the most important capabilities we are leveraging.

## Preparing the web application code

We are using the Flask web framework to build the user-facing browser interface, as well as the backend APIs that the frontend will communicate with. Flask uses the concept of `@app.route` annotations, better known as *decorators*. They convert a Python function into a `view` function, which returns HTML code that can be rendered by the browser, or any other client for that matter. So, if you can prepare a function to return HTML content such as `<h1> hello world! </h1>`, then Flask can help you map this functionality with a URL endpoint such as `/hello`. As a user, you can just focus on writing these Python functions; then, Flask glues them together with specific URL endpoints that applications can leverage.

In our case, the primary functions of our application are to create and remove tasks. So, we can think of three HTTP endpoints to support these scenarios.

- `GET /` to retrieve all the tasks from the database
- `POST /` to add a new task to the database
- `POST /<id>/delete` to delete a task from the database

With the increasing scale of the applications, it might not be easy to directly work on HTML syntax, so Flask offers additional capabilities around rendering HTML templates with dynamic data, using Python constructs such as *for loops*. We will see this being used in our HTML web page when we return the database objects for user interaction. Now that we've put everything together, let's have a first look at our application endpoints.

> **Note**
>
> All application code discussed here onward is available inside your Cloud9 IDE at the `chapter-7/chapter-7-flask-app` path or can be referenced in this book's GitHub repository: https://github.com/PacktPublishing/AWS-DevOps-Simplified/tree/main/chapter-7/chapter-7-flask-app.

### *Initializing the Flask application and MongoDB connection*

We can use existing Python modules to interact with Flask and MongoDB. These dependencies have been defined in the `requirements.txt` file inside the application directory:

```
from flask import Flask, render_template, request, url_for, redirect
from pymongo import MongoClient
from markupsafe import escape
from bson.objectid import ObjectId

# Initialize global variables for MongoDB connection

app = Flask(__name__)
mongodb_client = MongoClient('localhost', 27017)
todos_db = mongodb_client.flask_db
todos_collection = todos_db["todos"]
...
```

After importing the necessary modules, we initialize a DB client, database, and corresponding collection that will host our JSON documents in MongoDB.

Now, we can move on to defining the `view` functions and the related HTTP methods using Flask decorators:

```
...
@app.route("/", methods = ('GET', 'POST'))
def todos():
    if (request.method == "POST"):
        todo_item = request.form["todo"]
        todo_type = request.form["tasktype"]
        todos_collection.insert_one({"todo": todo_item,"tasktype": todo_type})
        return redirect(url_for('todos'))
    all_todos = todos_collection.find()
    return render_template('index.html', all_todos = all_todos)

@app.post("/<id>/delete")
def delete(id):
```

```
    if (request.method == "POST"):
        todos_collection.delete_one({"_id": ObjectId(id)})
        return redirect(url_for('todos'))
...
```

The three HTTP endpoints we discussed previously can be seen in this code snippet. `@app.post` is just a shorthand syntax for `@app.route("/", methods = ('POST'))`, which was added in newer versions of Flask.

> **Tip**
> HTML does not support the `DELETE` method type in form submissions yet, only `POST` and `GET`. That's the reason we could not use the `DELETE` method type in the second use case – *deletion of a task*.

## Preparing the static HTML template

Browsers only understand HTML, so that's what we need to return from the Python `view` functions, but sprinkled with dynamic data. This can be done using the `render_template('index.html', all_todos = all_todos)` call, where we pass the `all_todos` object data to the HTML template. But the important question is, what helps Flask identify the placeholders in the static HTML template where this data needs to be injected? The answer is Jinja templating.

Jinja templates allow us to use regular Python constructs in a static template. Upon expansion, you get raw data injected into the template, which makes it look like any other regular HTML data.

The relevant lines in our HTML template that leverage this functionality can be seen in the following code snippet:

```
...
<tbody>
{% for todo in all_todos %}
<tr>
    <td>{{todo['todo']}}</td>
    <td>{{todo['tasktype']}}</td>
    <td>
        <form method="POST" action = "{{ url_for('delete', id=todo['_id']) }}">
            <button type="submit" class="btn btn-sm btn-outline-danger" value="Delete Task" onclick="return confirm('Are you sure you want to remove this task?')">Delete Task</button>
        </form>
    </td>
</tr>
{% endfor %}
```

```
</tbody>
...
```

Up next, lets look at the steps needed to deploy the static website within an ECS container.

## Bundling all application dependencies together for deployment on ECS

ECS requires a Docker image that can be referenced in your task definitions. You could host them in DockerHub or ECR, which is Amazon's offering for hosting your Docker image artifacts. For simplicity, we will use the image hosted in DockerHub in this exercise, which can be found at `akskap/flask-todo-list-app`. However, if you wish to build your own image, you can reference the Dockerfile available at `https://github.com/PacktPublishing/AWS-DevOps-Simplified/blob/main/chapter-7/chapter-7-flask-app/Dockerfile`.

## Deploying our CDK stack in an AWS account

Finally, let's trigger a deployment of the CDK stack in one of our AWS accounts to see the application in action. We will start by securing a new session for our Cloud9 IDE. Once we are inside the CDK project folder, `chapter-7/chapter-7-cdk/`, we can trigger an installation of NPM modules, followed by the `cdk synth` command, which will give us a summary of the rendered CloudFormation template file:

```
aws-devops-simplified:~/environment/chapter-7/chapter-7-cdk $ npm
install [ ................] | fetchMetadata: sill pacote version
manifest for bser@2.1.1 fetched in 346ms
...
...
```

Completion of the `npm install` command will place all the module dependencies in the `node_modules` folder. At this point, we are all set to trigger the template synthesization process:

```
aws-devops-simplified:~/environment/chapter-7/chapter-7-cdk $ npm
install

Resources:
  CustomVPC616E3387:
    Type: AWS::EC2::VPC
    Properties:
      CidrBlock: 10.0.0.0/16
      EnableDnsHostnames: true
      EnableDnsSupport: true
      InstanceTenancy: default
      Tags:
```

```
        - Key: Name
          Value: Chapter7Stack/CustomVPC
    Metadata:
      aws:cdk:path: Chapter7Stack/CustomVPC/Resource
  CustomVPCprivateSubnetSubnet1Subnet6940697D:
...
...
```

You might notice that the 100-odd lines of code we added to our CDK stack have resulted in about 800 lines of a rendered CloudFormation template. A quick way to check this could be to run `cdk synth | wc -l`.

Now, let's provision the resources in our AWS account:

```
aws-devops-simplified:~/environment/chapter-7/chapter-7-cdk $ cdk
deploy -y

✨  Synthesis time: 12.83s
Chapter7Stack: building assets...
...
...
Do you wish to deploy these changes (y/n)? y
...
[100%] success: Published 35b80399fc491dc502df8e5f40f2587918b2d7045bc2
2bc0e3ba0eea19d30595:current_account-current_region
Chapter7Stack: creating CloudFormation changeset...
...
...
 ✅  Chapter7Stack
✨  Deployment time: 261.46s

Outputs:
Chapter7Stack.FargateServiceLoadBalancerDNS9433D5F6 = Chapt-Farga-
GEIPMTTLTGLY-2055706317.eu-central-1.elb.amazonaws.com
Chapter7Stack.FargateServiceServiceURL47701F45 = http://Chapt-Farga-
GEIPMTTLTGLY-2055706317.eu-central-1.elb.amazonaws.com
Stack ARN:
arn:aws:cloudformation:eu-central-1:852467203672:stack/
Chapter7Stack/659a4770-b4ea-11ed-bdbc-0a3cfb4cfe00
✨  Total time: 274.3s
```

Post-deployment, we get an Application Load Balancer URL that can be accessed in the browser to launch our To-Do List Manager application. Once you copy that link over, you will see the application, as shown in *Figure 7.4*:

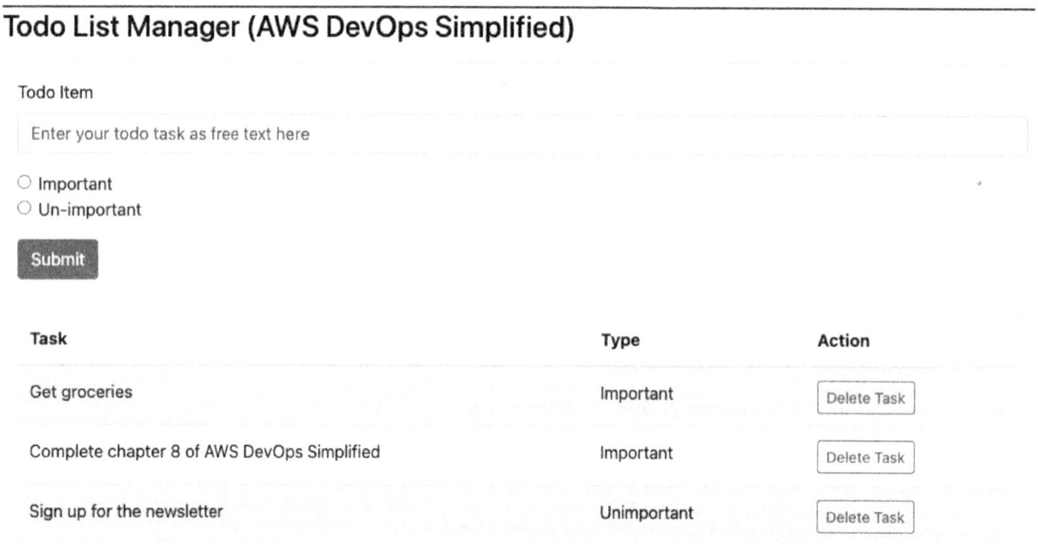

Figure 7.4 – The To-Do List Manager application running on ECS

The application gives you a blueprint that can easily be extended, and customized, based on your preferences for and desired functions from any To-Do List Manager application.

## Summary

We started this chapter by understanding the relevance that containers have in modern software applications. They not only speed up the development velocity but also adhere to the microservices patterns and twelve-factor design principles, which are an inherent part of your software artifacts. In case you had not been exposed to containers yet, we started with a basic understanding of how they work and then moved on to outlining the constructs of Docker, a container runtime environment.

With the foundations covered, we discussed the need for a container orchestrator system when running production workloads in the cloud. AWS ECS is an opinionated offering from AWS that simplifies operating containers in an enterprise-grade environment. Next, we dived deeper into Amazon ECS and the native constructs used by the service to define logical components in your application stack. Of course, security is paramount when deploying resources in the cloud. So, we discussed some best practices to ensure least privileged access patterns for your container applications, as well as integrations with other AWS services. To give you a practical hands-on experience of everything that was discussed around ECS, we worked on deploying a To-Do List Manager application from scratch. Building on what we had learned in previous chapters, we used CDK to manage the infrastructure components that were needed.

In *Chapter 8*, *Enabling the Observability of Your Workloads*, we will outline the need for software observability and the tools that AWS offers for reactive and proactive alerting. As always, we will go through some hands-on deployment exercises and how AWS integrates with well-known tools from the open source community.

## Further reading

To learn more about the topics that were covered in this chapter, take a look at the following resources:

- *Running Containerized Microservices on AWS* whitepaper: `https://docs.aws.amazon.com/whitepapers/latest/running-containerized-microservices/welcome.html?did=wp_card&trk=wp_card`
- *Security Overview of AWS Fargate* whitepaper: `https://d1.awsstatic.com/whitepapers/AWS_Fargate_Security_Overview_Whitepaper.pdf`
- ECS workshop covering blue/green deployments, stateful workloads, and networking: `https://www.ecsworkshop.com/`

# 8
# Enabling the Observability of Your Workloads

The ever-increasing complexities of our software applications demand insights at a level of detail that was not common before. Breaking down monoliths into a set of microservices comes with well-established benefits but we certainly need to do more to have the same or, in some cases, even better understanding of how our systems are performing under the hood.

When something is wrong with an application, it affects the user experience and ultimately the business. If such occurrences happen frequently, they can even lead to a loss of customer trust due to unreliable software systems. Therefore, it's very important to detect problems as soon as possible, and then understand why it's happening and how the problem can be fixed.

**Monitoring** is what deals with the *reactive* part, and **observability** is what deals with the *proactive* part. With monitoring, you already have a good idea about the factors that will negatively influence software availability – for example, a storage disk that is soon going to be full. Observability, on the other hand, is mostly about anticipating the problems that could happen, and simplifying the analysis of root causes, when they happen. For the same storage disk, an observability solution could analyze disk usage logs and correlate them to increased latency or errors during software release cycles, for example. The administrators could leverage these findings to optimize the storage configurations before they result in an outage. In the ideal case, the software patterns that have the potential to cause customer impact should surface much earlier than a metric alarm being triggered, or even before customers start to experience service degradation. This should be the *North Star* of all observability efforts by a team that manages software applications at scale.

Having worked with several software teams in my career, a common approach I've noticed is that observability and monitoring are always seen just in the light of technical metrics. Sometimes, software professionals are a bit disconnected from understanding the business impact their code has, and how exactly the end users consume the applications they develop daily. Observability, from my perspective, is all about *empathizing with the customer* and feeling what they feel, seeing what they see, and measuring what matters to them the most. It is only then that we can improve their experience, every single time they use our application. Of course, this in a way depends on the underlying technical metrics, but the approach should always be to work backward from the business goals that drive customer experience, and then derive relevant metrics that influence those goals. Building a technical strategy that is disconnected from your business requirements will result in an ineffective solution.

As a concrete example of an e-commerce platform, customers are least concerned about rising CPU and memory usage on the backend servers. However, if they are unable to complete an order in a reasonable time, they are going to be unhappy about it. So, it might be valuable to focus on the *order completion time* as a metric and work back from there to figure out if an increase in CPU utilization causes it.

In this chapter, we will cover the following topics to learn a few things about enabling the observability of your workloads running in AWS:

- What is observability?
- Key AWS offerings for monitoring and observability
- Best practices for building a solid observability strategy
- How to go about defining your observability strategy for workloads hosted in AWS
- Deploying a basic observability stack for our test application hosted in ECS

Let's begin by understanding the core idea behind observability.

## What is observability?

Simply put, it's all about understanding the current state a running system is in, from the work it is doing and the data that it is emitting. Developing a solid observability strategy is not a one-time thing and it will always have scope for optimizations as your business needs evolve. But, before you can even understand what is going on, it's important to ensure that the system at least emits some data for us to be able to derive some reasoning out of it. But what kind of data?

Observability has three foundational pillars that allow you to convert data into information, and derive insights from that information, which ultimately leads to the actions that need to be taken:

- **Logs**: These are the *discrete events* that have occurred across several components in your systems while serving a customer request. It's invaluable to store these logs in a centralized data store so that information can be securely extracted, and analyzed, as and when needed.

Logs are particularly helpful in situations where some components stop pushing metrics to an event store due to an unhandled exception. This could be caused by third-party dependencies, network issues, or other unforeseen circumstances. Logs are the ultimate source of truth for the events that are happening in a system. Therefore, it's important to enforce appropriate security guardrails to prevent any modifications after they have been created. In AWS, it's a good practice to encrypt these logs at rest using services such as **Amazon Key Management Service** (**KMS**).

- **Metrics**: These are the *raw data points* that reflect the performance of your systems over time and are particularly useful in alarming, trend analysis, and scenario forecasting. For on-premises deployments, organizations typically leverage third-party tools and **application performance monitoring** (**APM**) solutions that gather underlying infrastructure and application metrics. However, in AWS, most of the services automatically publish key metrics without any additional configurations or cost to the user. This information, which is available free of charge, can be used to define alarms for threshold breaches or mathematical analysis – for example, maximum IOPS for a disk in any 5-minute interval.

- **Traces**: When working with multiple microservices, a holistic view is often necessary to understand the request flow and identify bottlenecks. This allows the software teams to zoom in on how the information *traversed multiple systems* for a particular request, and identify if something didn't go as expected. These traces are also valuable input for service maps as they can be used to visually depict the dependencies each service has and some problematic areas.

AWS's Swiss-army knife solution for all observability needs is **Amazon CloudWatch**. CloudWatch can be used for a variety of customer needs to continuously monitor the applications and underlying infrastructure.

Having understood the three main pillars of observability, let's see the main benefits they help achieve.

## Benefits of observability

There are multiple benefits that teams get when they make their systems observable:

- **Enhanced customer experience**: There is no doubt that the better you understand your system behaviors, the easier it is to maximize customer benefits from your software applications. Product managers can leverage this data to understand how a particular software application is used and carve out a future strategy for new features and enhancements that would delight their customers.

- **Efficient troubleshooting**: A good observability strategy leads to reduced investigation time around operational issues and outages. This allows the team to have more time for building differentiating features instead of being pulled into long-lasting investigations.

- **Visibility**: Observability is not only about fire-fighting operational issues but there are sometimes questions you would like to ask yourself to better understand the consumption patterns of your software application. *Where are the majority of my users coming from? How much time do they* *typically spend on filling up a particular form? How many clicks does it take for a user to order an item on my website? How many users are passing wrong parameters to my APIs, and so on?*

Having established a foundational understanding of what observability is and why it matters, let's discuss some AWS offerings in this space.

## Key AWS offerings for monitoring and observability

AWS offers a variety of native services that enable customers to implement end-to-end observability solutions for their application workloads. All three pillars of observability are well covered. CloudWatch is AWS's primary observability platform, which is a suite of different solutions that address customer needs around logs and metrics collection. For **traces**, AWS offers the **X-Ray** service, which makes it very easy to trace individual requests or workflows in your applications.

Interestingly, there are also quite a lot of customers in the observability space that have been working with open source solutions and would like to extend their existing implementations in the cloud. AWS offers managed solutions for **Prometheus** and **Grafana**, which we will cover in a lot more detail during the hands-on exercise, later in this chapter. Furthermore, AWS has been quite active in the **Cloud Native Computing Foundation's (CNCF's) OpenTelemetry** project, also known as **Otel** for short. It is a vendor-neutral framework for managing telemetry data. OpenTelemetry introduces the concept of a *distribution*, which is a customized version of a specific OpenTelemetry component. **AWS Distro for OpenTelemetry (ADOT)** is an AWS distribution based on the OpenTelemetry project. It provides out-of-the-box capabilities to instrument your applications once and send the metrics and data to multiple AWS services, including Amazon CloudWatch, X-Ray, and Amazon Managed Service for Prometheus.

Before diving into the best practices for a good observability strategy, let's understand various components of AWS's observability platform – Amazon CloudWatch.

### Amazon CloudWatch

CloudWatch is a centralized platform that allows customers to collect, monitor, and visualize their application logs, metrics, and X-Ray traces, all in a single dashboard. It is invaluable in providing a unified view of operational health for all the workloads the customer is managing.

There are three main areas of features that CloudWatch offers.

#### *Infrastructure monitoring*

Infrastructure monitoring covers the foundational aspects of metrics, alarms, and related insights.

## CloudWatch metrics

Most AWS services emit free metrics by default that can be used to understand the performance of your systems and enable search and visualization capabilities. Customers can either use basic monitoring of metrics (free) or the detailed version (paid), which is only offered by some services. Depending on the time granularity of these metrics, the users could use them to understand trends and patterns of how certain parts of the system are working. Users can also leverage **CloudWatch Metrics Insights**, which is a SQL query engine that allows real-time analysis of metrics.

## CloudWatch alarms

A **CloudWatch alarm** can be configured to monitor a certain metric or the result of a math expression that covers multiple metrics. For example, if an AWS service emits read IOPS and write IOPS independently, you can use metric addition to derive the total IOPS and configure an alarm whenever the total IOPS threshold is breached.

Alarms can be configured to send **Amazon Simple Notification Service (SNS)** notifications and start/stop EC2 instances as a target action, for example.

### Application monitoring

With **application monitoring**, CloudWatch offers additional insights into how your applications are working under the hood. Several services are offered in this category.

## Synthetic monitoring

CloudWatch allows you to simulate an end user's interaction with your application from multiple locations in the world – just as real users would use your application.

## Service lens

**Service lens** aggregates all data from traces, metrics, logs, and alarms onto a single dashboard. This gives the user a unified view of not only the service map, which highlights the different components involved in the application workflow but also brings the bottlenecks and metrics for important data to the surface, such as requests per minute and average response times. This visibility allows you to easily pinpoint the needle in a haystack of data, and you can work back from this analysis to uncover the underlying problem.

## CloudWatch real user monitoring

CloudWatch **real user monitoring (RUM)** can offer real user insights that give visibility into what the end user is experiencing. It's a JavaScript code snippet that you can add to your application and start measuring key metrics immediately. The data that's captured by the RUM agent and injected into your web page can extract page load times and client-side errors, among many other use cases.

*Insights and operational visibility*

This category of offerings is a huge differentiator when it comes to providing ready-made solutions that extract data from multiple sources and deriving insights out of those to provide actionable next steps to the user.

**Container insights**

When working with AWS services in the container landscape, you can use **CloudWatch container insights** to summarize metrics and logs from your containerized applications. It offers deep insights into problems such as continuous container restarts, for example.

**Lambda Insights**

When running serverless workloads on **AWS Lambda**, Lambda Insights can offer a deep understanding of system-level metrics and events from your Lambda invocations. For supported runtimes, you can add an extension that starts gathering useful data and helps the users identify problems such as cold starts.

> **Did you know?**
> At the time of writing, Amazon CloudWatch is used to monitor more than 9 quadrillion metric observations and ingests more than 5 exabytes of logs per month. Comparing this with over 8 billion people on Earth would mean that the service manages roughly 1 million events per person on the planet, per month. That's the scale CloudWatch operates at.

There is so much that users can do by leveraging the right solutions from the CloudWatch observability platform. However, there are some best practices that I would like to discuss next so that you can maximize your benefits when using these tools.

# Best practices for a solid observability strategy

In this section, we will be covering some fundamentals of how to best represent your observability data while maintaining the right balance of information you need to process.

## Build a hierarchy of dashboards

A key measure of success for your observability strategy is the **Mean Time to Recover** (**MTTR**). This defines how soon an engineer working on operational issues can understand and recover from the underlying problem. To begin with, it's important to have dashboards that provide just the right amount of detail. Reducing unwanted noise is crucial in reducing the overall MTTR. A common problem software teams run into is creating a data-heavy dashboard that covers many different aspects of their application, all on one screen. This often leads to false negatives consuming a lot of investigation time.

As outlined at the beginning of this chapter, you must build your observability strategy while keeping your customer in mind and empathizing with them. To have a feel of what they are experiencing as an end user, you can build a hierarchy of dashboards that starts with the top-level global view and has links to other child dashboards as you dive deeper into each component. Each of these child dashboards caters to a specific design domain of your application. As an example, let's consider a typical web application architecture that's implemented with several microservices. After starting with a high-level dashboard that provides latency for important APIs, service map health, and distributed tracing data, you can narrow down your investigation scope to specific dashboards that provide more detail about the frontend, application, or data tier. This allows you to focus on just enough information and move further into the investigation, one step at a time. Additionally, you could implement a global dashboard that highlights resource capacity issues for all the components and corresponding resources. *Figure 8.1* highlights the specific areas of your architectures these dashboards could focus on:

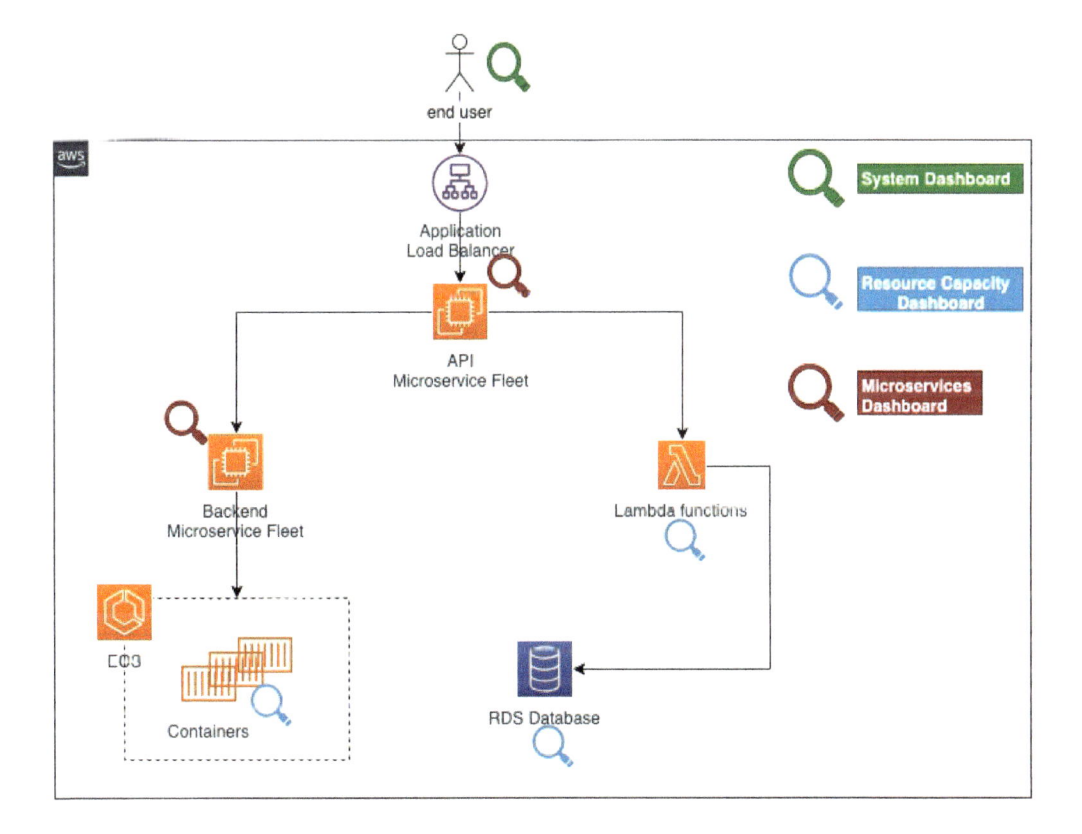

Figure 8.1 – Building the right hierarchy of dashboards to reduce MTTR

A lot of practices can further simplify or enhance the data represented by dashboards. Let's go through some of them.

*Adopt time series pattern analysis*

For some metrics, it is more relevant to observe the time series pattern instead of scalar values. This can boost proactive analysis when your operation team notices that the API error count spikes up every 10 minutes, but never crosses the threshold your alarms are set at.

You can also plot related time series data on the same graph to draw a relative understanding of how certain parameters have been evolving over time and if there is a correlation you need to have a deeper look into.

*Annotate graphs with good and bad thresholds*

Different applications could have different thresholds of what good or bad looks like. It might be ok to have CPU utilization for a compute-intensive batch workload consistently reported at 80%, but on the other hand, this might not fall into the expected utilization bands for another type of application. Furthermore, teams keep evolving, new members might get onboarded, and a few others might be offboarded at some point. When such threshold ranges are embedded and plotted together with underlying metrics, you can effortlessly identify outliers and what is not OK.

*Plot the right dimensions*

CloudWatch metrics work on the concept of dimensionality. Plain metrics are just data, but when we add a particular number of related dimensions, they get converted into information. How you utilize these dimensions can play an important role in bringing the most relevant information to the surface on your operational dashboards.

As an example, one dimension could be the total number of API errors occurring in a defined time window. But this could also mean that a single customer is consistently hitting an API endpoint with the wrong payload. Of course, this is not something you want to be paged on, so a better dimension to look at could be API errors occurring per customer. This can help with ruling out false positives, thereby saving precious investigation time.

## Use consistent time zones across all systems

Almost every outage investigation starts with the time of event occurrence. This then serves as the key to searching related information across other dashboards, systems, and logs. As a rule of thumb, always opt for UTC references so that you are comparing data and investigations against the same time standard. This is particularly useful when you're plotting different metrics on the same dashboard and writing logs with timestamps that are later pushed to a centralized logging platform.

## Propagate trace identifiers

Adopting distributed architectures can mean that a single request flows through multiple systems or microservices before any response can be sent back to the user. Debugging such requests in the absence of related context can be painful. Therefore, it's a good idea to attach a unique request identifier to the payload as it passes through multiple components. The respective logs of each microservice can then utilize the same trace identifier, along with additional metadata, such as the time it took to process the request.

This simplifies the debugging activities to a great extent as you could filter a particular request identifier and instantly gain visibility into how a particular request traversed the system. This is highlighted in *Figure 8.2*:

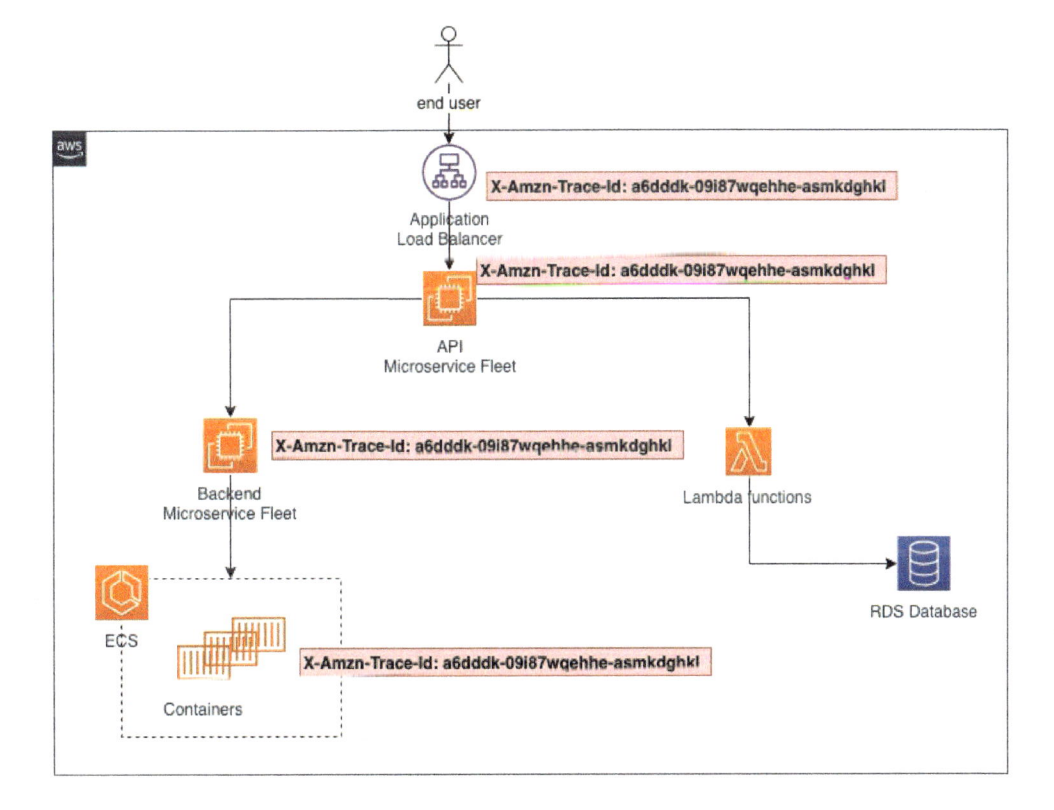

Figure 8.2 – Injecting trace identifiers in each request

In addition to trace identifiers propagating request metadata, it's also important that all the components of the system make the user aware of their health.

## Ensure that all components of your system emit events

Be it logs, metrics, or traces, in the ideal case, there should be no component in your system that acts like a black box. Every service, be it managed or unmanaged, should log events in your central observability platform. This is also an important criterion when selecting a particular service from cloud providers. It always helps to validate what kind of logs are offered out of the box, what metrics are made available, how these events can be aggregated into your tool of choice, and so on.

It's important to note that often, some components are indeed a black box as they were inherited from some other team, code is no longer available, or some form of technical debt does not allow you to add instrumentation at the code level. In such cases, you can explore *sidecar patterns*, where a minimum level of instrumentation comes from another software or tool. These tools are deployed alongside such components and can trace calls made to the underlying kernel or other libraries without causing any performance issues.

Next, we'll dive into the test application. This will help us gain hands-on experience with some services from AWS and the open source community.

# Defining your observability strategy for workloads hosted in AWS

There is never a perfect observability strategy that can give you the most granular view of your systems at scale. Rather, it's an *ongoing journey* that keeps evolving as you release new features and updates to your software application. You continue to adapt the observability stack by ensuring that it highlights the adherence to key business goals at any point in time. To kick off your observability journey on AWS, you could consider the following aspects.

## Deploying an observability stack for a test application hosted in ECS

In *Chapter 7, Running Containers in AWS*, we saw how easy it was to run containerized workloads on AWS. We developed a **To-Do List Manager** application using the Python **Flask** framework and deployed it on **Amazon ECS**, with infrastructure components rolled out with **CDK**. By leveraging ECS's **Fargate** deployment model, we were able to offload the management of underlying container nodes to AWS while we focused on just the application logic and the security guardrails around it. Taking the same example further, we will learn how to go about adding observability constructs for such an application. As a best practice, this is something you should start focusing on when you're writing the first few lines of code. Where would you process the logs, how would you visualize the metrics, what are the key thresholds you should be alerted for, and so on?

This section of this book will specifically focus on a hands-on implementation to help you experience the key areas of observability we have been discussing throughout this chapter. We will learn how to forward logs to CloudWatch, process metrics in Prometheus, and finally visualize everything on a Grafana dashboard. We will be extending our code base from the previous chapter, *Running Containers in AWS*, and integrating it with other tools that take the observability of our application to the next level. Let's start with an overview of the changes we plan to implement.

## Overview of the target architecture

Before we dive into the code-level changes, let's get a visual understanding of the components we plan to add around our test application stack, and how they communicate with each other. We will focus on capabilities that help us monitor the application logs and metrics on tools of our choice.

We will extend our existing application architecture with the following components to capture and display observability data:

- **CloudWatch Logs**: Amazon ECS offers integrations with several logging platforms, with CloudWatch being one of them. We can make use of CloudWatch Logs to ingest all data written on `STDOUT` of our application containers running in ECS.

- **Amazon Managed Prometheus**: The biggest challenge with Prometheus installations is data retention and dynamically scaling the storage infrastructure as the rate of metrics ingestion increases. Similar to the benefits offered by other AWS services, we would like to offload the maintenance of the Prometheus server and related storage to the cloud provider. AWS simply offers us a data ingestion endpoint that can be used by applications to push metrics data to the platform.

- **Amazon Managed Grafana**: To visualize the metrics captured by Prometheus, we will use Grafana as our dashboarding solution. AWS offers us the same experience we would get by running a Grafana open source solution. The additional benefits are the readymade integrations around AWS data sources and configurations that come out of the box when using the service offered by AWS.

- **OpenTelemetry Collector**: A common deployment pattern for using third-party tools in containerized environments is to deploy them as a *sidecar*. In our case, we will be deploying an OpenTelemetry collector from AWS, in the same ECS task definition that hosts the web application and MongoDB container. This will allow the collector agent to scrape metrics information from the application container on the `/metrics` endpoint.

All these components and the corresponding information flows are highlighted in *Figure 8.3*. In this case, the Flask-based web application forwards logs to the CloudWatch Logs service. The application metrics are scraped by the OpenTelemetry sidecar container and then forwarded to the **Amazon Managed Prometheus** (**AMP**) service. Finally, we configure **Amazon Managed Grafana** to query data from both these sources and display it in a centralized dashboard:

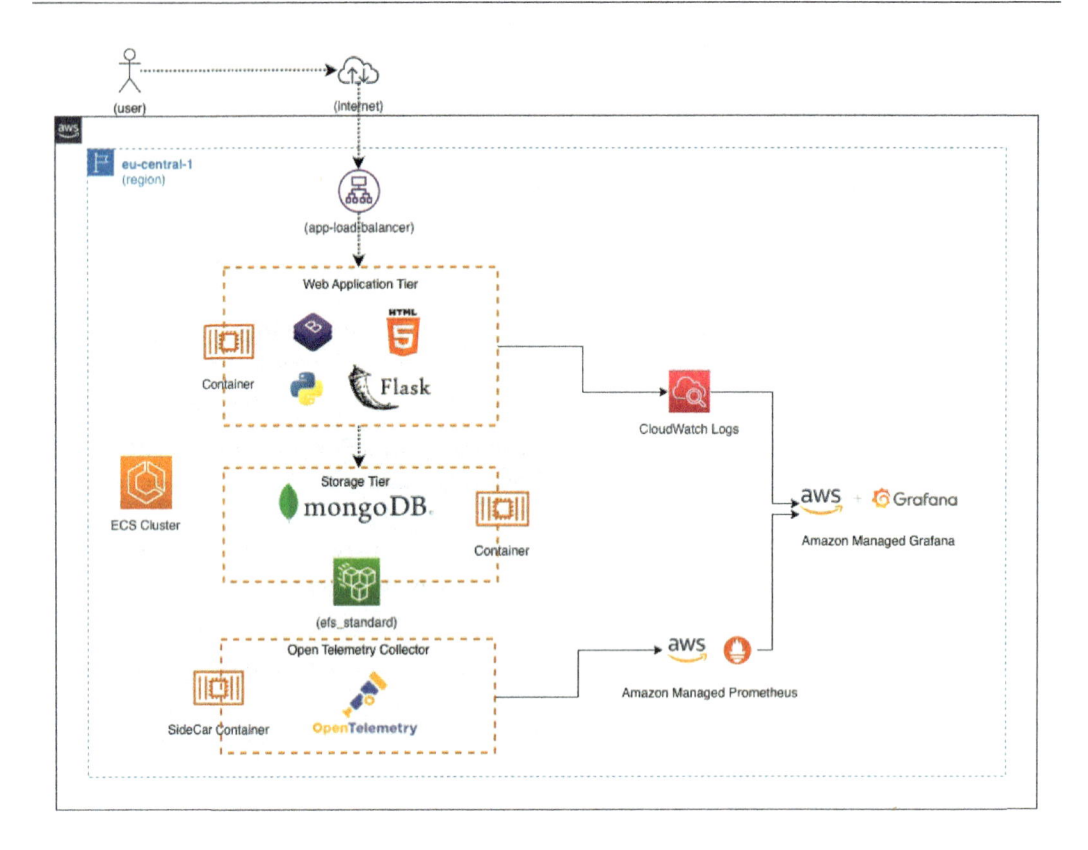

Figure 8.3 – Observability stack for the To-Do List Manager test application

> **Note**
> If you have been exposed to Prometheus tooling in the past, you would have typically experienced a pull-based approach where the Prometheus server fetches the metrics directly from the relevant targets and stores them. In this case, however, we are using the OTEL collector sidecar pattern from AWS, which pushes the metrics to the Amazon Managed Prometheus workspace after scraping the application endpoints.

As a next step, let's get our hands dirty with some code-level modifications to realize the architecture we just discussed.

## Extending the code base for better observability

As you can imagine, in addition to adding CDK constructs to our stack, we also need to make a few changes to our Flask-based web application so that it starts offering metrics and insights to tools such as Prometheus. Let's start with the application-level changes first.

## Modifying the Flask application code

There are two main changes that we need. First, we must add logging capabilities to the code base, and second, we must allow the code to publish Prometheus metrics that can be consumed by the OpenTelemetry collector that we will deploy later.

Just like other reusable Python modules, Prometheus offers a variety of ready-to-use integrations for commonly used application frameworks. Flask is no different. The two libraries that are relevant for our use case are prometheus-client and prometheus-flask-exporter. It is very simple to expose Prometheus metrics by simply importing these libraries into our code, as we will see shortly. For logging requirements, we will use the standard logging library.

### Enabling Prometheus metrics in your application

The Flask application code sits in the app.py file. The complete file is available for your reference at https://github.com/PacktPublishing/AWS-DevOps-Simplified/blob/main/chapter-8/chapter-8-flask-app/app.py. Soon after we create an instance of the PrometheusMetrics class, it hooks onto the Flask framework under the hood, thereby directly capturing all the relevant metrics. Whenever a GET or POST request comes in, Prometheus gets to know about it. This avoids any extra effort from the developer's side unless they want to define and export additional custom metrics based on the application's business use case:

```
...
from prometheus_flask_exporter import PrometheusMetrics
...
...
app = Flask(__name__)
metrics = PrometheusMetrics(app)
...
```

To include these modules in our build workflow, we should also add them to the requirements.txt file so that they are picked up when a Docker image is created. As a best practice, we should lock them down with exact version identifiers:

```
...
...
Werkzeug==2.2.3
zipp==3.14.0
prometheus-client==0.16.0
prometheus-flask-exporter==0.22.3
```

Deploying the application at this point will automatically enable the /metrics endpoint, which exports Prometheus metrics extracted from the Flask application.

## Logging important events in the application

We will use the Python standard `logging` library to add logs for relevant events occurring in our application. Before using it, we need to instantiate an object with default configurations that apply to the following log statements:

```
...
import logging
import sys
...
...
root = logging.getLogger()
root.setLevel(logging.DEBUG)
handler = logging.StreamHandler(sys.stdout)
handler.setLevel(logging.DEBUG)
formatter = logging.Formatter('%(asctime)s - %(name)s - %(levelname)s - %(message)s')
handler.setFormatter(formatter)
root.addHandler(handler)
...
```

The next step is to use the logging module in our Flask decorator function, which receives the task creation or retrieval request:

```
@app.route("/", methods = ('GET', 'POST'))
def todos():
    if (request.method == "POST"):
        logging.info('Received a %s request for %s ', request.method, request.url)
        todo_item = request.form["todo"]
        todo_type = request.form["tasktype"]
        try:
            logging.info('Submitting \'%s\' task: \'%s\' to persistent storage ',request.form["tasktype"], request.form["todo"])
            todos_collection.insert_one({"todo": todo_item, "tasktype": todo_type})
            return redirect(url_for('todos'))
        except Exception as e:
            logging.error("Exception occurred while submitting data to MongoDB", exc_info=True)
    all_todos = todos_collection.find()
    return render_template('index.html', all_todos = all_todos)
```

Similarly, we can add corresponding log statements to the function. These are responsible for task deletion:

```
@app.post("/<id>/delete")
def delete(id):
    if (request.method == "POST"):
        logging.info('Deleting task represented by ID: \'%s\'
',ObjectId(id))
        todos_collection.delete_one({"_id": ObjectId(id)})
        return redirect(url_for('todos'))
```

This completes all the changes we require in the application code. You can build your own Docker image at this point, or use the DockerHub version, available at `akskap/flask-todo-list-app-with-metrics`, which includes all the changes already.

### Extending the CDK stack with new constructs

Now that we have made the code changes for our Python application, let's define the additional infrastructure elements we need in the CDK stack.

> **Note**
> All the code definitions are available for your reference at `https://github.com/PacktPublishing/AWS-DevOps-Simplified/blob/main/chapter-8/chapter-8-cdk/lib/chapter-8-cdk-stack.ts`.

As usual, all the CDK construct definitions can be found inside the `lib/` folder of the project directory, `chapter-8/chapter-8-cdk/`, hosted in your Cloud9 IDE.

#### Creating a workspace in Amazon Managed Service for Prometheus

Amazon Managed Service for Prometheus is a serverless Prometheus-compatible service that is highly resilient and scales automatically to changing storage or performance needs. It is well integrated with AWS's container ecosystem.

For our use case, we need a workspace that offers dedicated storage and querying capability for Prometheus metrics. At the time of writing, there are no `L2-level` or `L3-level` CDK constructs available for the service, so we will use an `L1 CloudFormation` construct in our CDK stack:

```
...
import { aws_aps as aps } from 'aws-cdk-lib';
...
...
const apsWorkspace = new aps.CfnWorkspace(this, 'APSWorkspace', {
  alias: 'aws-devops-simplified-aps-workspace'
});
```

```
...
...
```

The CloudFormation resource simply creates a Prometheus workspace for us, but we still need something that publishes the relevant metrics into this workspace. Let's cover this next.

**Injecting a sidecar OpenTelemetry container in the ECS task definition**

With Prometheus created, we can now add a sidecar container to the same ECS task definition that hosts our Flask application and MongoDB database containers. This will allow the OTEL collector to scrape metrics from our application and push them over to the managed Prometheus workspace that we created in the previous section:

```
const otelCollector = new ecs.ContainerDefinition(this,
"OtelCollectorDefn", {
  image: ecs.ContainerImage.fromRegistry("public.ecr.aws/aws-
observability/aws-otel-collector:v0.26.1"),
  taskDefinition: fargateTaskDefn,
  command: ["--config=/etc/ecs/ecs-amp-prometheus.yaml"],
  logging: ecs.LogDrivers.awsLogs({streamPrefix: "aws-devops-
simplified-otel-collector"}),
  environment: {
    "AWS_PROMETHEUS_ENDPOINT": `${apsWorkspace.attrPrometheusEndpoint}
api/v1/remote_write`,
    "AWS_PROMETHEUS_SCRAPING_ENDPOINT": "0.0.0.0:5000"
  }
})
```

As you can see, we are referencing the workspace endpoint in the `apsWorkspace` CDK resource and passing it further, as the value of the `AWS_PROMETHEUS_ENDPOINT` environment variable, into the OTEL container. With this, the OTEL collector knows where to push the collected metrics to. Secondly, we define `AWS_PROMETHEUS_SCRAPING_ENDPOINT`, which tells the collector where to scrape the metrics from. All these configurations are governed by the type of config file that we are using for the OTEL collector. The AWS OTEL collector supports several platforms where it can consume data from or send data to. In our case, we are mostly interested in Prometheus metrics, so we used the `/etc/ecs/ecs-amp-prometheus.yaml` file from the OTEL Docker container.

> **Note**
> If you are interested in exploring the contents of this file and all the configuration options it offers, you can go to this link: https://github.com/aws-observability/aws-otel-collector/blob/main/config/ecs/ecs-amp-prometheus.yaml.

Having made all the required code changes for the application and infrastructure, we can now proceed to the most exciting part – deploying the solution in our AWS account.

## Deploying the stack in an AWS account

At this point, we can deploy our CDK stack in the AWS account. Alongside core infrastructure elements such as VPCs, subnets, and gateways, it will provision the ECS cluster, which contains three containers – the application, the database, and the OpenTelemetry collector. We will also deploy an independent workspace for Amazon-managed Prometheus. Toward the end, we will deploy Grafana manually since it is not supported for deployment via CDK at the time of writing.

### Rolling out the CDK stack

First and foremost, let's start a new session for the Cloud9 IDE and switch to the directory that contains the resources for this chapter.

Once we are inside the CDK project folder for this chapter, we can use the `npm install` command to download all the node modules. After the installation completes, we can trigger `cdk synth` to get a high-level understanding of the CloudFormation template that is going to be deployed in our AWS account:

```
aws-devops-simplified:~/environment/chapter-8/chapter-8-cdk $ cdk synth
Resources:
  CustomVPC616E3387:
    Type: AWS::EC2::VPC
    Properties:
      CidrBlock: 10.0.0.0/16
      EnableDnsHostnames: true
      EnableDnsSupport: true
      InstanceTenancy: default
      Tags:
        - Key: Name
          Value: Chapter8CdkStack/CustomVPC
    Metadata:
...
...
```

Once you have taken a quick look at the template and understood the resources that are being provisioned, you can proceed with the final stack deployment:

```
aws-devops-simplified:~/environment/chapter-8/chapter-8-cdk $ cdk deploy
✨  Synthesis time: 11.93s
Chapter8CdkStack: building assets...
...
...
```

```
Do you wish to deploy these changes (y/n)? y
...
Chapter8CdkStack: creating CloudFormation changeset...
...
...
 ✓  Chapter8CdkStack
 ✦  Deployment time: 245.97s

Outputs:
Chapter8CdkStack.FargateServiceLoadBalancerDNS9433D5F6 = Chapt-Farga-
65SZA285PPO1-1511829492.eu-central-1.elb.amazonaws.com
 ✦  Total time: 257.9s
```

After the CDK stack deployment completes, we will get the load balancer URL as an output on the screen. This can be used to access the application in a browser. We will use the same URL to generate some load so that we see some metrics and data being pushed to different components of our observability stack. But before that, let's configure the Grafana dashboard so that it's ready to consume metrics from Prometheus.

### Creating a workspace for Amazon Managed Grafana

AWS's official documentation outlines all the steps you need to perform to set up a personal Grafana workspace in your account, using the web console. To ensure that you are following the up-to-date instructions, I suggest going through the official link at https://docs.aws.amazon.com/grafana/latest/userguide/AMG-create-workspace.html. Please ensure that you are using the same AWS region where you deployed your CDK stack. Grafana configures user access via SSO or SAML. If you are new to both these concepts, I recommend setting up an AWS SSO user in your account. It's free of cost and at the same time gives you a secure mechanism to govern access to multiple AWS accounts in your organization, from one central panel.

For data sources, we need to select **Amazon Managed Service for Prometheus**.

After the installation is complete, you can proceed to the user administration section for the Grafana workspace. You can follow the steps shown in *Figure 8.4* and assign the SSO/SAML user you have configured as the admin for this Grafana installation:

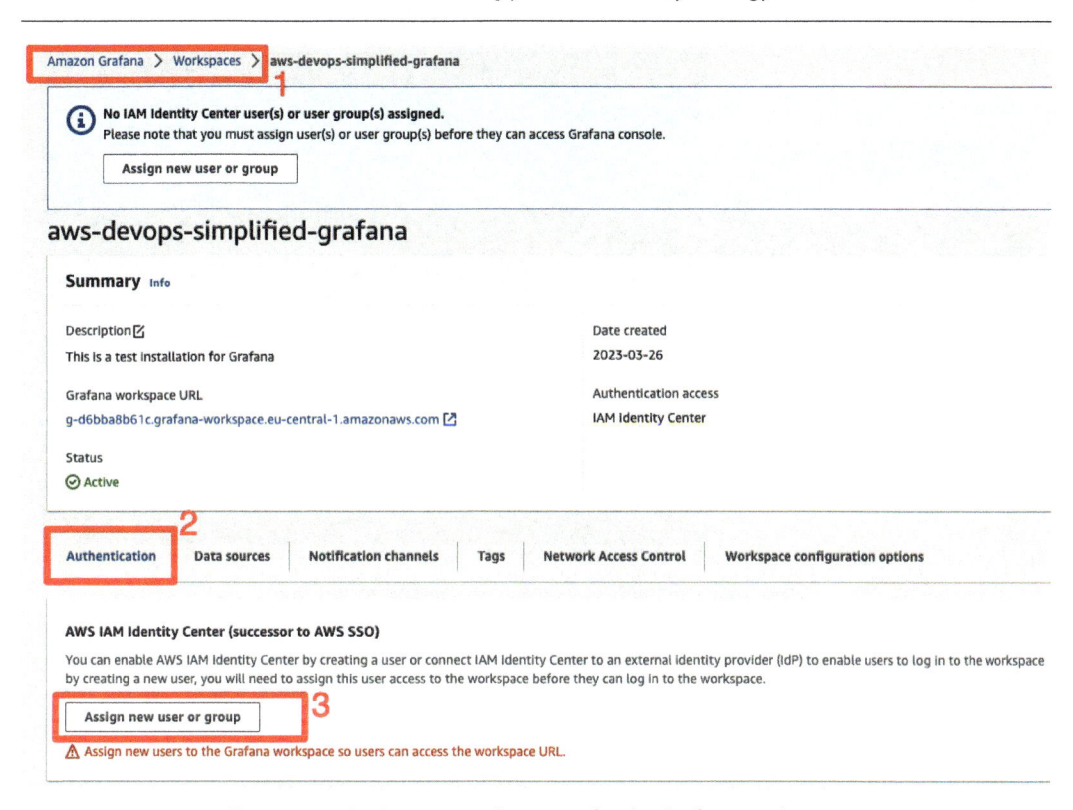

Figure 8.4 – Assigning an admin user for the Grafana workspace

Once you've added an admin user for your new Grafana workspace, you can proceed to the login page, enter the necessary credentials, and follow the data source configurations, as shown in *Figure 8.5*. This will allow Grafana to query metrics from the Prometheus workspace that was created as part of the CDK deployment:

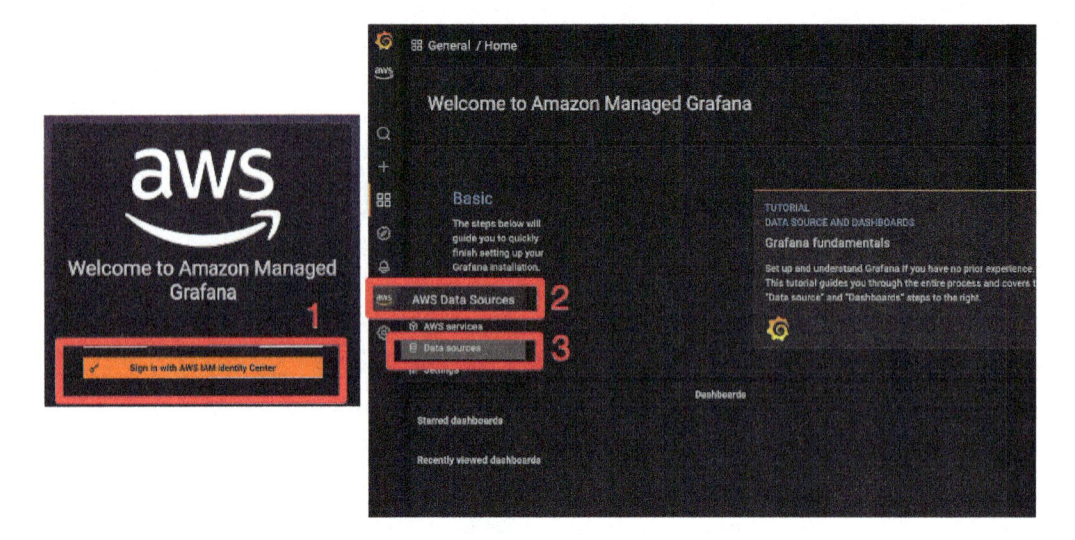

Figure 8.5 – Grafana login and data source configuration

This option leads to the data source configuration page, where you can add additional details of the Prometheus workspace you want to integrate with. Assuming that you haven't created any other workspace in the same account, you will find the one that was provisioned by the CDK stack, after you select the appropriate AWS region, which in our case is always `eu-central-1`, or Frankfurt.

If you see multiple workspaces, please reference the identifier for the one that was created as part of the CDK deployment. This should be available on the recently deployed CloudFormation stack details page.

Once you've filled in all the data source configuration fields for Prometheus, you should see something similar to the following:

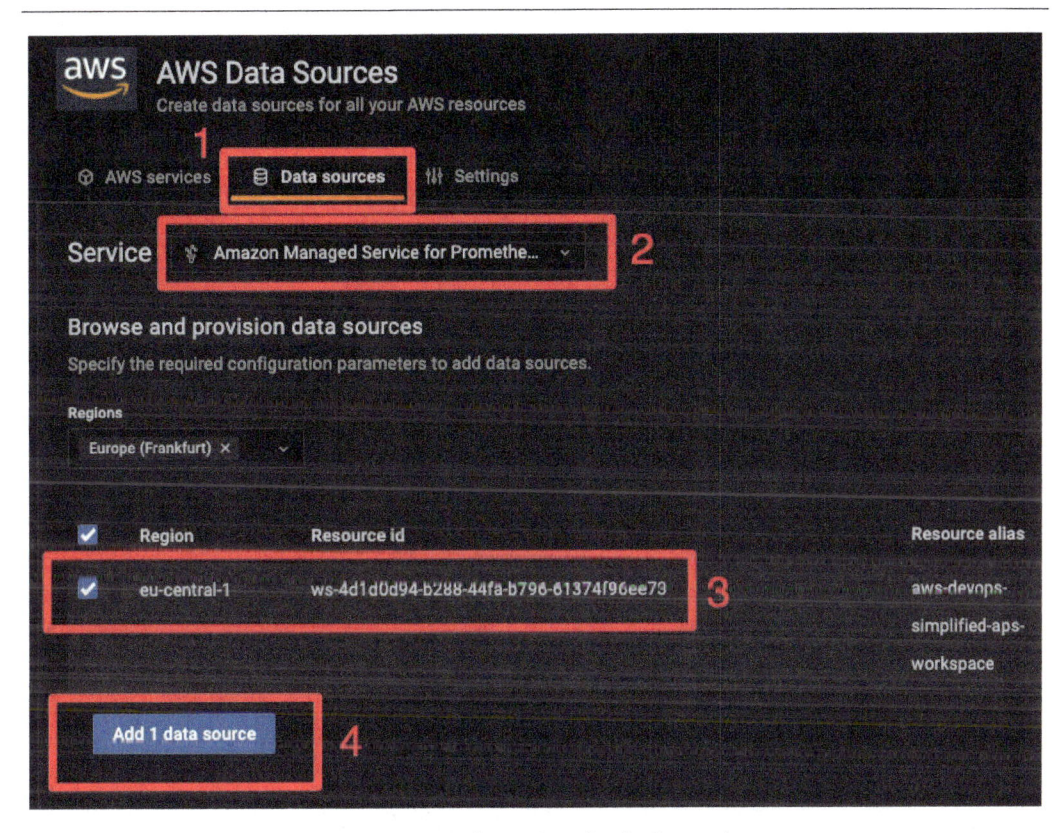

Defining your observability strategy for workloads hosted in AWS    187

Figure 8.6 – Data source configurations for the Prometheus connector

At this point, Grafana will start pulling metrics from the Prometheus server and make it available to you as a visualization in the dashboard.

As shown in *Figure 8.7*, you will see the following categories of metrics for selection:

- `ecs_*`: These are added automatically by the AWS OTEL collector, which includes some interesting metrics from the ECS control plane. Through these metrics, you can derive insights such as the reservation and utilization of key resources, including network, CPU, memory, and storage.
- `flask_*`: These metrics come from the instrumentation that we added inside our Flask application code using the `prometheus-flask-exporter` library.
- `python_*`: The Python runtime provides some interesting data around file descriptors, garbage collection, and so on, which gets picked up by the OTEL collector and pushed to Prometheus and, eventually, Grafana.

188    Enabling the Observability of Your Workloads

- `scrape_*`: Scraping metrics reflect the duration and samples that have been collected through OTEL as part of the configuration (`/etc/ecs/ecs-amp-prometheus.yaml`) we selected in the ECS task definition:

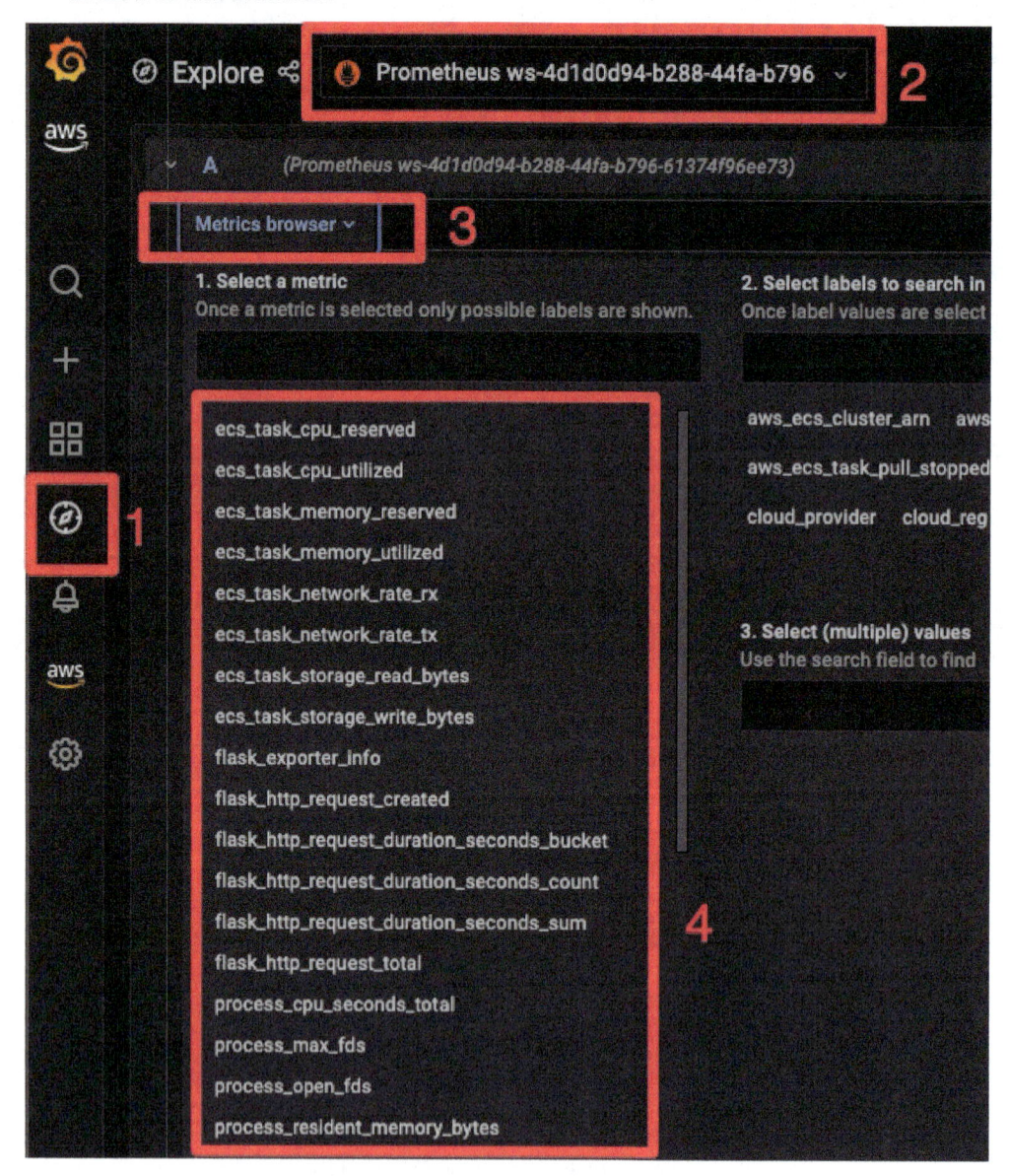

Figure 8.7 – Prometheus selectors for different categories of metrics

Once you've selected the metrics as per your choice, you need to induce load on our web application so that you can start seeing relevant telemetry data across different platforms and tools.

## Load testing your application to generate data

A simple way to load test your To-Do List Manager application could be to run a `curl` query that targets the application load balancer URL, from within your Cloud9 IDE's terminal.

For hash generation, we can leverage the RANDOM variable and derive a md5 checksum value from it, using the following command:

```
echo $RANDOM | md5sum | head -c 20
```

We can utilize the hash generation inside a `curl` command that triggers a POST request on the application endpoint:

```
curl --location --request POST 'http://chapt-farga-
65sza285ppo1-1511829492.eu-central-1.elb.amazonaws.com/' \
    --form "todo=`echo $RANDOM | md5sum | head -c 20`" \
    --form 'tasktype="Un-important"'
```

To prepare this for infinite execution (until it's manually interrupted), we can wrap up the command with a `while` loop:

```
while true; do curl --location --request POST 'http://chapt-farga-
65sza285ppo1-1511829492.eu-central-1.elb.amazonaws.com/' --form
"todo=`echo $RANDOM | md5sum | head -c 20`" --form 'tasktype="Un-
important"'; done
```

Leave this code snippet running for some time so that enough data is generated in our observability tools.

## Observing data to understand application behavior

Debugging operational incidents often requires correlating information across several metrics and deriving insights from the underlying data. Our test application stack publishes different types of data in different tools. We have infrastructure metrics and logs available in CloudWatch, and additionally, we are publishing metrics in Prometheus. Let's take a look in CloudWatch to see if we got some logs as part of the logging that we enabled in the Flask decorator functions.

### Monitoring logs with Amazon CloudWatch Logs

To check CloudWatch Logs, you can go to the CloudWatch service console and click on the relevant log group. This seamless log ingestion is provided by the integration between ECS and CloudWatch. As a best practice, you should always emit the log stream on STDOUT so that the data can be easily ingested into other platforms.

As you may recall, we had a logging configuration in each CDK construct that represented one of the ECS containers. For the application container, the configuration looked something like this:

```
logging: ecs.LogDrivers.awsLogs({streamPrefix: "aws-devops-simplified-
app-container"})
```

This single line of config ingests data from the app container and forwards it to the CloudWatch service, on the predefined stream prefix. Checking the logs for this log stream on CloudWatch shows some interesting insights, as highlighted in *Figure 8.8*:

```
2023-03-27 17:15:28,947 - werkzeug - INFO - 127.0.0.1 - - [27/Mar/2023 17:15:28] "GET /metrics HTTP/1.1" 200 -   1
2023-03-27 17:15:29,266 - werkzeug - INFO - 10.0.3.223 - - [27/Mar/2023 17:15:29] "GET / HTTP/1.1" 200 -  2
2023-03-27 17:15:32,239 - werkzeug - INFO - 10.0.2.30 - - [27/Mar/2023 17:15:32] "GET / HTTP/1.1" 200 -   2
2023-03-27 17:15:34,852 - root - INFO - Received a POST request for http://chapt-farga-65sza285ppo1-1511829492.eu-central-1.elb.amazonaws.com/
2023-03-27 17:15:34,873 - root - INFO - Submitting 'Un-important' task: 'b5777d9e5ff1361d3f6f' to persistent storage  3
```

Figure 8.8 – Application logs captured in CloudWatch Logs

Let's take a closer look:

1. `GET /metrics`: HTTP invocations from the OpenTelemetry collector scrape application metrics at a predefined interval and publish them on the Prometheus server. As we can see, the source of the request is `127.0.0.1`, which is expected because the collector runs inside the same task definition as the application.

2. `GET /`: These are invocations on the application root that seem to originate from two IP addresses, `10.0.3.223` and `10.0.2.30`. These are the application load balancer interfaces and trigger regular health check requests against the application.

3. `POST`: This is a request on the application domain that is a result of the `curl` command that we triggered from our local Terminal to generate some load. You will see many of these, depending on how long you keep the command running.

CloudWatch also allows you to create metrics from these logs based on some patterns. So, a user could track the number of `POST` calls coming in a time window of 1 minute and raise an alarm if it crosses the expected threshold. Furthermore, you could also track the source IP addresses from such requests and figure out the highest contributors to application load in a certain time frame. As you can see, the possibilities are endless, and it all depends on how deep you want to go with such insights.

Next, let's have a look at our Prometheus metrics.

### *Instrumenting application metrics with Amazon Managed Prometheus*

As discussed previously, instantiating the Prometheus client inside our Flask application additionally enabled a `/metrics` endpoint that exposed application metrics to scrapers – in our case, the OTEL collector.

You can also look at these raw metrics by hitting the application load balancer URL, with the `/metrics` suffix at the end.

In my case, accessing the `http://chapt-farga-65sza285ppo1-1511829492.eu-central-1.elb.amazonaws.com/metrics` URL gave me the following output:

```
...
# HELP flask_exporter_info Information about the Prometheus Flask exporter
# TYPE flask_exporter_info gauge
flask_exporter_info{version="0.22.3"} 1.0
...
# HELP flask_http_request_duration_seconds Flask HTTP request duration in seconds
# TYPE flask_http_request_duration_seconds histogram
flask_http_request_duration_seconds_bucket{le="0.005",method="GET",path="/",status="200"} 309.0
...
```

The lines starting with `# HELP` describe some information about the following lines and how to interpret them, while the ones starting with `# TYPE` show the type of metric (histogram/gauge) and the related values that can then be visualized by tools such as Grafana.

### *Visualizing data with Amazon Grafana*

So far, we have validated that the application is exposing metrics data on the `/metrics` endpoint and that the OTEL collector is scraping this endpoint and further publishing it in the Prometheus workspace we provisioned in our CDK stack. The final tool in our architecture was Grafana. As described in *Figure 8.7*, you can select certain metrics to be shown on the Grafana dashboard. I selected a few of those and got the following screenshot (*Figure 8.9*), which highlights the network request spikes that lasted for some time while the `curl` command was running in the background:

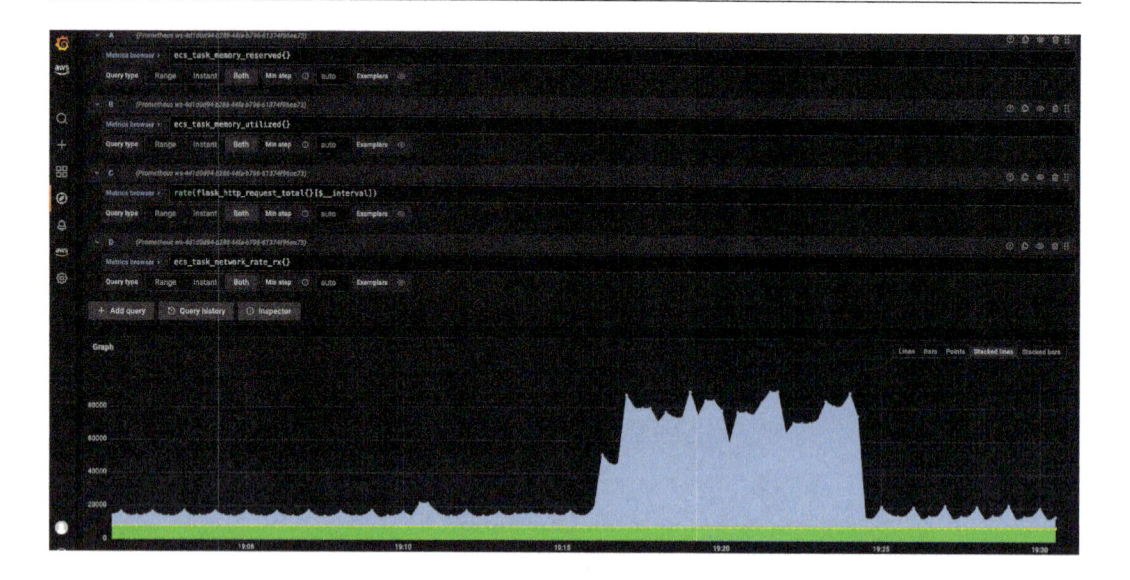

Figure 8.9 – Visualizing metrics on the Amazon Grafana dashboard

Ideally, you would customize the field selectors based on the key metrics that define your system behavior and also pin them to a dashboard that can be continuously monitored.

## Summary

Developing software applications is only one part of the challenge. Maintaining them in a productive environment (at an enterprise scale) requires equal commitment and engineering effort. This can only be achieved with a solid observability strategy that allows you to not only react faster to operational issues but also gather meaningful insights that allow you to continue delivering differentiated business outcomes to your users.

We started this chapter with a basic understanding of what observability is and why it matters. Equipped with that knowledge, we then moved on to discussing the AWS observability platform – CloudWatch – and the solutions or integrations it offers for each of the observability pillars – metrics, logs, and traces. In addition to that, we discussed AWS's efforts in the CNCF's Open Telemetry project and the ADOT collector, which allows you to seamlessly collect, process, and export metrics, logs, and traces to other AWS services.

Outside AWS, solutions such as Prometheus and Grafana are widely adopted by companies due to their maturity, ease of use, and scalability. To ensure a hands-on experience that covers all these solutions, we went ahead with deploying an observability stack for the To-Do List Manager, our test application from the previous chapter. This allowed us to have a holistic view of how we can integrate all these tools and adapt them to our specific needs.

In the next chapter, *Implementing DevSecOps with AWS*, we will focus on an approach that enables us to integrate security throughout the entire IT life cycle.

## Further reading

To learn more about the topics that were covered in this chapter, take a look at the following resources:

- How British Telecom handles CloudWatch to monitor millions of devices: `https://aws.amazon.com/blogs/mt/how-bt-uses-amazon-cloudwatch-to-monitor-millions-of-devices/`
- Building dashboards for operational visibility: `https://aws.amazon.com/builders-library/building-dashboards-for-operational-visibility/`

# 9
# Implementing DevSecOps with AWS

**Equifax**, a credit reporting agency, reported unauthorized access to the personal records of 143 million US citizens in a data breach in 2017 that went unnoticed for 76 days (https://www.csoonline.com/article/3444488/equifax-data-breach-faq-what-happened-who-was-affected-what-was-the-impact.html). What started as **Common Vulnerabilities and Exposures** (**CVE**) in **Apache Struts**, a well known framework used by Java applications, resulted in financial and reputational damage for the company. Even after corrective measures, a few servers remained unfixed due to the dependency on manual processes. These gaps, combined with teams' lack of awareness of security breaches in general, were exploited by malicious actors to gain access to one of the servers, and then several others. Security incidents like these harm business health and, most importantly, result in loss of customer trust, along with reputational damage.

The evolution of software practices and rapid cloud adoption has further contributed to the surge in security risks that modern applications are exposed to. This is mainly caused by increasing dependencies on third-party software modules, frequent changes, and multiple levels of abstraction that are now part and parcel of every software artifact that gets deployed. Security these days is no longer about a monolith Java application deployed on-premises, for example. The same application might have now transformed into a set of microservices, each exposing an API, and deployed as a container image, onto a Kubernetes cluster running in the public cloud. In addition to the application code itself, we have several other layers to secure. What if there are vulnerabilities in the base container image or the custom libraries that we add on top? How do we manage secure HTTPS communication interfaces for all microservices at scale? Securing other components such as the Kubernetes control plane and cloud networking configurations, which are more of a black box to the developers, is a different challenge altogether. Furthermore, how is all of this going to be handled on an *ongoing basis*, ensuring that every new line of code that is written still adheres to the security standards we have set?

As you can see, the new software patterns have introduced risk dimensions that, in most cases, are not easy to fix, or even identify, as the software teams often don't have the required depth and visibility into these layers themselves. However, with a focused effort in three areas – let's call it the *AEA framework* – they can ensure good security coverage for their workloads in the cloud:

- *Awareness* of the existence of security risks in your systems, and the corresponding criticality
- *Enablement* of people so that they can comprehend and act on any information or alert that comes up
- *Automation* to detect these security risks as early as possible in the delivery chain

These three aspects are going to be the theme of this chapter and we will learn about them in the light of an important concept called **DevSecOps**. Similar to how DevOps enables software teams to culturally transform and deliver software faster, DevSecOps introduces new ideas and practices that focus on security. DevSecOps should be seen as an iteration of your DevOps practices in the sense that it wraps an additional security layer to your existing development and operational processes. This is fundamentally different from traditional software development approaches, where security was seen as an afterthought.

At a broader level, we will cover the following topics in this chapter:

- Trade-offs and challenges of security
- What is DevSecOps?
- Securing your workloads in AWS
- Rolling out a test CI/CD workflow for DevSecOps

> **Tip**
> If you are curious about the different types of security risks in the cloud and how they could impact you, I recommend reading this blog: `https://appinventiv.com/blog/cloud-security-risks-and-solutions/`.

The key requirements for consistently rolling out software artifacts with a high degree of success are *automation* and *effective feedback cycles*. Driven by this idea, a DevOps strategy aims to optimize every single step of the software delivery life cycle. A developer writes code on their local machine and commits the changes to a version control system. At this point, the delivery pipelines take over, testing the changes and creating a new version of the software artifact, providing feedback at every stage. If all test cases are green, it promotes the artifacts to subsequent environments in the delivery chain, eventually taking the changes to pre-production or production. However, in practical scenarios, this is easier said than done, especially when releasing software artifacts at a rapid scale. While several factors can slow you down, the most critical one to accommodate is security. Let's see why that is the case.

# Trade-offs and challenges of security

Every software team can have its own unique set of challenges to solve, be it technical or cultural. Before we dive into the specifics of DevSecOps, let's try to understand what led to the need for an iteration of existing DevOps methodologies. Along the way, we will discuss why security can sometimes be seen as a resistive effort, instead of a positive push to continuous application delivery. In my experience working with different teams, there are four main patterns that I have commonly observed to be the root cause of this slow-down:

- Lack of ownership
- Last step in software delivery
- The rapid evolution of application architectures
- Outdated security tools

Let's look at each of these in detail.

## Lack of ownership

Often, developers and operation team members *don't feel responsible* for the security posture of their applications. Being on the other side of the spectrum, which involves building new features and rolling them out on production, they see security as something that hinders growth. The security adherence is left to a professional that sits in another room.

Unless this becomes a shared responsibility and the team members start contributing to identifying and fixing issues collaboratively, security will continue to be a show-stopper. The entire software delivery process is going to be *as fast as the weakest link* in the chain – and we don't want security to be there. Furthermore, it's important to highlight that adopting DevOps comes with security as a recurring theme in everything that you do, to give you immediate benefit.

## Last step in software delivery

In the previous chapters, we discussed quite a few things around infrastructure automation, application delivery, and how we can optimize most of these tasks by adopting DevOps methodologies. However, a critical step in the software release cycles that we haven't discussed enough is security. The problem is not with the *criticality* that slows down the teams – it's more to do with it being the *last step*.

Traditionally, software teams developed features with a waterfall model approach and pushed them over the fence to the security team, close to the go-live date. These mammoth releases make it very difficult to accurately identify all the security risks that the new code opens up the application to. Manual testing takes time and eventually, all of this leads to a divergence between the pace at which software is developed, and the pace at which it is released. As a DevSecOps practitioner, you should always keep an eye on such bottlenecks as they can slow down your team, resulting in frustration, delays, and reduced confidence. But what exactly makes security audits slow?

### The rapid evolution of application architectures

An important dimension that we cannot overlook is the evolution of application architectures over the past years, which, in a way, has added an additional burden to security investigations and sign-offs.

These days, monolith applications are broken down into microservices, resulting in hundreds or thousands of APIs. Previously, you just needed to safeguard countable entry points, but now, you have a dynamic scale to manage. Highly secure environments further enforce communications over **mutual TLS (mTLS)** between these microservices. This results in the need to manage a lot of certificates. From an operational and scalability standpoint, a common next step is to look into containerization options. Since running these containers reliably at scale is not an easy feat, the orchestration provided by a managed container platform becomes the ideal next step. Of course, who doesn't want to simplify the management of these platforms so that a good chunk of these applications makes cloud providers such as AWS their new home?

If you take a brief pause at this point and look at this gigantic shift from a security perspective, you will notice that all of this has greatly contributed to an increase in the attack surface and introduced new risks that the teams now need to safeguard themselves against. Things are no longer constrained to the application itself, but also the abstraction layers that are built on top – that is, APIs, container abstractions, and cloud platforms – each having their share to contribute.

### Outdated security tools

Security professionals, on the other hand, have since long been used to a specific set of tools that might not have evolved as fast as the fancy innovations in software development. As a result, security not only needs to keep up with the new tools that the developers adopt but also be on the constant lookout for new attack surfaces. In some cases, this might warrant the need for finding new security tools, adopting third-party cloud security software, or even developing bespoke solutions.

All of this leads to one important point – security is never done. *It's an ongoing cycle of improvement.* This makes it very difficult for security professionals working in modern software teams to keep up with the pace of delivery. Potential risk surfaces have increased manifold and this cannot be tackled with manual testing anymore, and at the same time, we cannot wait until the very end of the software delivery process. Therefore, injecting security scans at every single step of the delivery life cycle is key, and this is what DevSecOps is all about.

## What is DevSecOps?

Simply put, DevSecOps is the practice of integrating security tests into every stage of the software delivery life cycle. It is an *extension* of the DevOps approach that we have discussed so far in this book. Using tools and processes, it promotes collaboration between development, operations, and security teams. This results in software artifacts that are not only operationally efficient to produce but also safe to be released in production, at any point in time. Similar to DevOps, DevSecOps also brings in a cultural shift around how we approach security in conventional software delivery processes. Security teams should no longer be seen as some form of resistance, but more as enablers of the adoption of security best practices in the organization.

Before we move further, I would like to clarify one point that you might be thinking of at this stage – the difference between DevOps and DevSecOps.

## How is it different from DevOps?

The core idea behind DevOps is to get the application into the hands of the end user as fast as possible. While this revolves a lot around cultural transformations, automation tools, and processes, security can sometimes be left behind. Software teams often see security as an isolated process, or team, that comes into the picture only before a deployment. In some cases, these security clearances and processes might as well be completely overlooked, which is an even more critical situation to be in.

DevSecOps, on the other hand, aims to address this gap by ensuring a seamless integration of security practices into day-to-day development activities. Developers and operations team members work together with security professionals to *share the responsibility of releasing secure artifacts* to the end user every single time. This collaboration often results in the adoption of automations and tools that extend the current CI/CD processes used by these teams.

One important thing I would like to highlight here is that your DevSecOps success will be largely defined by how stable your DevOps foundations are. It can only be built on top of existing implementations of DevOps practices, such as continuous integration, operational procedures, and team culture. It is an approach to further amplify the returns of your DevOps investments and gain from the benefits offered by continuous security enforcement and validations.

To justify the need of adopting certain practices or ways of working, it's important to analyze the benefits that come with it. We'll discuss this next.

## Key benefits of DevSecOps

There are a lot of areas that are positively influenced by the adoption of DevSecOps practices in the **software development life cycle** (**SDLC**). While every team's mileage would vary, certain benefits apply to most teams. Let's take a look.

### Reduced time to market

Lack of security awareness and automated code validations can hamper the benefits you might achieve with the adoption of just DevOps. Along with releasing frequent code changes multiple times a day, DevSecOps ensures that software developers are safeguarded from unknown security risks that can result in a degraded end user experience and loss of trust. Reduction of time in security assessments automatically increases the software deployment rate.

### Improved security awareness of team members

Developers and operation team members often find themselves in situations where they could easily adopt an existing open source tool or third-party library to implement functionality. While it is always a good practice to approach these decisions with a *build versus buy* mindset and not reinvent the wheel, usage of such external code bases can lead to unknown risk exposures. It might as well be the case that a library that is safe to use now might not be safe enough with future release iterations. In the *Rolling out a test CI/CD workflow for DevSecOps* section, we will cover some security tools that scan the code against public vulnerability databases (such as **National Vulnerability Database (NVD)**) that are continuously updated. This drastically improves the awareness of everyone involved in the delivery of code. In addition to *identifying* risks, most of these tools also help the developers with suggestions on how to immediately fix the vulnerability.

Being *aware* of such problems is a great benefit that comes with the adoption of integrated security practices advocated by DevSecOps.

> **Note**
> A good example that fits here is the zero-day Log4j vulnerability from 2021, which exposed security loopholes in the Log4j logging utility, commonly used in Java programs. If you were not exposed to this news, I recommend reading more about it at `https://builtin.com/cybersecurity/log4j-vulnerability-explained`.

### Develop new features with confidence

While security is an ongoing process, the feedback that's received via automated validations and code checks helps fix problems sooner, resulting in increased confidence in software developers. They can trust the scans performed by multiple tools in the delivery chain and be at least confident about a minimum baseline of security posture being met.

### Improved compliance in regulated environments

Regulated industries such as pharmaceuticals, defense, and aerospace follow traditional development practices that involve a lot of manual testing procedures. To comply with multiple regulations and standards, it becomes difficult for them to release code changes at a scale similar to how other non-regulated companies, with fewer things to worry about, would do. This has a direct impact on the release velocity and productivity of the software teams.

Additionally, they need to maintain software applications for a much longer time, and the changes in the underlying platform and infrastructure warrant the need for continuous evaluation procedures that can be repeated even for the smallest of code changes.

## Early identification of issues

DevSecOps tooling automations can kick off as early as when the developer commits code to their local git repositories. By leveraging git's `pre-commit` hooks, they can benefit from the feedback of these code scans even before they push the changes to a remote repository.

> **Tip**
> **Trufflehog** is one such tool that stops you from accidentally committing secrets into your source code. You can read more about this tool and how you can configure it as a pre-commit hook at `https://github.com/trufflesecurity/trufflehog`.

This controls any risk exposures that are introduced by recent code changes. The problems are easier to fix as the developers have a full context of what they were trying to do and the modifications are still fresh in their mind.

A *defense-in-depth* strategy also ensures that similar guardrails are applied and evaluated at multiple stages of the code development process. So, even if the local configurations on a developer's machine are not functional, such risks can be mitigated at the next level, which could be a server-side hook configured in the remote repository management system, such as **GitHub** or **GitLab**.

An important aspect of DevSecOps that we have been discussing a lot is the cultural shift and change in roles and responsibilities. Next, we'll discuss what this means for the different personas in a software team.

## What it means for security professionals

Security colleagues have always been seen as some sort of gatekeepers and are ultimately responsible for any security risks that come up. As per DevSecOps methodology, this needs to change. Instead of resisting frequent code modifications and releases, they should act as enablers. The mantra for success for these professionals should be *guardrails but not blockers*. They need to continuously learn how DevOps works across the organization and evolve security processes by embedding the controls right into the DevOps methodologies.

### Define security policies for both application and infrastructure

Security risks are now multi-dimensional. They apply to anything that is managed as code – so both infrastructure and applications. Security professionals should focus on defining the policies around what these code bases should and should not be allowed to do. Rather than dictating granular policies for each application or team, they should invest effort in establishing guardrails that protect the company and individual teams.

*Introduce automated guardrails for policy enforcement*

Manual assessments are a thing of the past. The policies should automatically apply to any workload that is deployed in the environment. AWS offers a lot of capabilities in this area where you can enforce *detective*, *preventive*, and *proactive* controls with the use of **AWS Config**, **Service Control Policies (SCPs)**, and **CloudFormation hooks**, respectively.

*Enable developers to identify and fix security issues*

The shared responsibility approach means that developers and operators should feel equally responsible and capable of identifying and fixing security issues. This can only happen when the security professionals invest time and effort in making other team members aware of the security risks, identifying the right solutions, and enabling them to leverage those solutions. Automation goes a long way, so being on the constant lookout for pockets of optimization is going to help a lot. This also points back to the *Awareness* and *Automation* pillars we discussed previously.

## What it means for developers

Previously, developers always focused on just application code. Security-focused feedback received from tools and automations should allow them to proactively look into new risks that are being introduced into the system. Also known as *shift-left*, this methodology aims to identify every security risk, ideally during the development phase itself. Automation plays a big role in defining its success; we will look at a hands-on example of this, toward the end of this chapter.

## What it means for the operations team

Security is never done. After the code deployments are completed, the operations team should always keep an eye on any unexpected application patterns, logs, or behaviors. In a way, this is also linked to the observability strategy of the organization, but the core idea here is to *shift right* and make security an inherent part of day-to-day operational efforts.

Let's shift gears and discuss what these security assessments look like in practice. We'll discuss these in the context of AWS specifically.

## Securing your workloads in AWS

Running workloads in self-managed on-premises data centers requires safeguarding against a variety of attack vectors, such as applications, platforms, and infrastructure. With providers such as AWS entering the game, your risk postures need to be re-evaluated. The moment you move your applications to the cloud, you *transfer* some of those risks to the cloud provider, and in other cases, *mitigate* or *introduce* new ones. The focus of this section will be to walk you through some practical scenarios and approaches around security in AWS. We will center our discussions around an internet-facing web application, as an example. Let's start with the common problems software teams face at the onset of their cloud journey.

# Security challenges for operating workloads in the cloud

There are two common blockers that software teams adopting AWS face, or any other cloud provider for that matter, when it comes to security.

## *Understanding the security responsibilities in the cloud*

The first thing we need to understand is where exactly the cloud provider's responsibilities end, and yours, as a customer, begin. These responsibilities can further vary depending on the type of cloud service tier (**IaaS**, **PaaS**, or **SaaS**) you are using. We discussed all three tiers in detail in *Chapter 2, Choosing the Right Cloud Service*. For example, when running your applications in EC2, patching the security vulnerabilities or upgrading the AMIs is your responsibility. But the same is not true if your code is deployed on Lambda, in which case the security of the underlying compute infrastructure sits with AWS. The cloud provider is responsible for the security *of the cloud*, and the customer is responsible for security *in the cloud*. To explain this further, if a hypervisor vulnerability allows another AWS user to gain unauthorized access to your EC2 instance, then this is a lapse of AWS' security. On the other hand, misconfigured security groups allowing unrestricted SSH access to an EC2 instance in AWS are the customer's fault. I would recommend going through the AWS shared responsibility resource to dig deeper into the details: `https://aws.amazon.com/compliance/shared-responsibility-model/`.

For software applications, the risks are more or less the same if you are running your workload on-premises or in the cloud. However, something that does change is the processes and solutions to address those risks. AWS offers several services that can help you secure the network, data, and identity and access management. Considering our example of an internet-facing web application, you could transfer your risks of managing a self-hosted load balancer to AWS Elastic Load Balancer with web application firewall integrations. Extracting the frontend API logic from the code base and migrating to API Gateway transfers your risks to the cloud provider, and modernizing a traditional static website and hosting it on CloudFront with no servers to manage eliminates your risks. So, it's important to understand what exactly needs to be secured.

Once the responsibilities have been clarified, the second problem teams run into is how to manage their risks.

## *Identifying and prioritizing the risks*

Software teams often begin by securing parts of the application architecture that they are most familiar with. This can sometimes hide other risks, potentially with a higher probability of occurrence. A good way to understand (or raise *Awareness*, as defined in the AEA framework) your risk exposures is to begin with a **threat modeling** process.

Threat modeling is an assessment that outlines the risks that currently deployed resources are exposed to, and what their priorities are based on respective criticalities. With the evolution of application architecture, these risks will also keep on changing, and so should the mitigations. Threat modeling is sometimes seen as a one-time activity that's conducted in the later stages of the software delivery process, before a go-live. This should be avoided as per DevSecOps methodologies, which promote the idea of building security practices right into the development life cycle. So, it makes a lot of sense to involve security team members during the design phase of the application so that the risks are surfaced as soon as possible. In the early stages of development, it is also less costly for the developers to fix an architectural approach that has security implications.

For an internet-facing web application, here are some examples of potential risks:

- **Distributed Denial of Service (DDoS)** attacks
- A user breaching the multi-tenant boundaries of the application to extract data belonging to other users
- SQL injection and cross-site scripting attacks

A threat modeling exercise in this case should consider the probability of each of these risks' occurrence and suggest steps for mitigation. Organizations with mature DevSecOps practices further ensure that their threat modeling process is a *recurring* activity. This ensures that a good security posture is verified not only during the first production release, but constantly evaluated, and optimized, against new risks and exposures.

> **Tip**
> OWASP Top 10 is a good resource for understanding different types of web application security issues your applications could run into. As part of your threat modeling activities, you can consider evaluating your workloads against these risks as a starting point: `https://owasp.org/www-project-top-ten/`.

Not all risks stem from the proprietary code written by software developers. A large number of the vulnerabilities come from the dependencies and open source libraries consumed by these projects. The 2022 State of Open Source Security report from **Snyk** and **Linux Foundation** states the following:

> *"The average application development project has 49 vulnerabilities and 80 direct dependencies, and the time it takes to fix vulnerabilities in open source projects has steadily increased, more than doubling from 49 days in 2018 to 110 days in 2021."*

Even though these numbers reflect the state of open source projects, they speak a lot about the need for continuously scanning any untrusted code and surfacing the vulnerabilities as soon as possible. Let's discuss some test strategies you could consider.

## Test strategies for your AWS workloads

Code is no longer restricted to the business application that your end users consume. Your infrastructure, CI/CD pipelines, and all the automations that you build to support your application's delivery are equally good candidates for risking your security posture. Assuming most (if not all) components of your architecture are deployed via pipelines, there are two main aspects to consider:

- Security *of* the pipeline
- Security *in* the pipeline

Let's take a look.

### Security of the pipeline

A high degree of automation built into your pipelines also means that any unintended code changes can go very far in your delivery life cycle, eventually reaching production. Good security practices restrict any form of human access in productive environments, which, on the other hand, requires CI/CD pipelines to have highly privileged access permissions. Therefore, it is important to ensure that your pipelines are also *treated as code*, continuously checked, and monitored for security breaches. Five main areas that require safeguarding will be discussed next.

#### Identity and Access Management for your pipelines

**AWS Identity and Access Management (IAM)** helps manage the identities and their access to AWS services, for both human and non-human access patterns. For example, the **CodePipeline** pipelines we deployed in previous chapters used a *service role*, where we define what the service can or cannot do in the AWS account on the user's behalf. Depending on the actions a pipeline needs to carry out, you should always aim to give minimum permissions based on the principle of least privilege.

Companies with highly mature DevSecOps practices can also consider building pipeline factories, which can emit the least privileged reusable templates for pipelines targeting common application patterns.

#### Detecting unusual behaviors

You should capture all the execution logs of your pipelines in AWS, just like you would do for an application. Furthermore, services such as CodePipeline and CodeBuild offer log and metric integration capabilities with CloudWatch Logs and CloudWatch Metrics. Enabling these settings is a matter of adding a few configuration lines in your infrastructure code.

Maintaining the confidentiality and integrity of these logs is an important security measure and a good organizational strategy additionally captures all the IAM action events in CloudTrail. This facilitates seamless audit procedures when needed. For example, a sudden surge in denial of IAM access requests could hint at compromised systems and can be tracked using the `Error code` property of the respective CloudTrail events. Furthermore, defining thresholds for metrics of interest and forwarding these events to your alerting tools can bring the outliers to the surface. An unusually high number of build executions or timeouts, for example, can point to other issues, which might otherwise go unnoticed.

**Protecting data processing in the pipelines**

Who can change, commit, and approve code? Consider protecting direct commits to branches that are linked to deployment in specific environments. Preventing production data from being introduced into non-production environments can be enforced by strict isolation between the pipelines and the data plane layer in the form of network policies.

**Leverage incident detection and monitoring**

**Amazon Macie** is a threat detection service that uses machine learning and pattern-matching capabilities to identify sensitive data being stored in S3. Customers can also define custom patterns that are used by the service to identify risks and raise security findings in **AWS Security Hub**, a threat detection, aggregation, and remediation service. All your pipeline logs can be fed into such services for continuous automatic analysis.

Similarly, for artifacts such as container images produced by CI/CD pipelines, **Amazon Inspector** can be used. It integrates with Amazon ECR and creates a finding for software vulnerabilities as soon as new container images are pushed.

Next, we'll investigate ways of enforcing security in the pipeline, which covers the steps to protect the code and dependencies in the application.

## Security in the pipeline

After securing the pipeline itself, the next step is to secure the application code. It's a daunting task to come up with a list of all security risks introduced by the code and the associated dependencies. Secondly, even if developers are made aware of the risks, it's not practical for them to manually scan their code on every single commit. Therefore, in this section, we will focus on the *Automation* pillar of the AEA framework, as introduced at the beginning of this chapter. These automations are largely covered by different types of security scans that are embedded into different stages of the CI/CD pipelines. Additionally, I will highlight some open source tools that are commonly leveraged for continuous security feedback.

As shown in *Figure 9.1*, the idea is to make these scans an inherent part of your *code, build, test*, and *deploy* phases. This ensures that we are not waiting for security clearance until the very end and the problems are much easier to fix if the feedback is shared in small iterations, as and when new code is added:

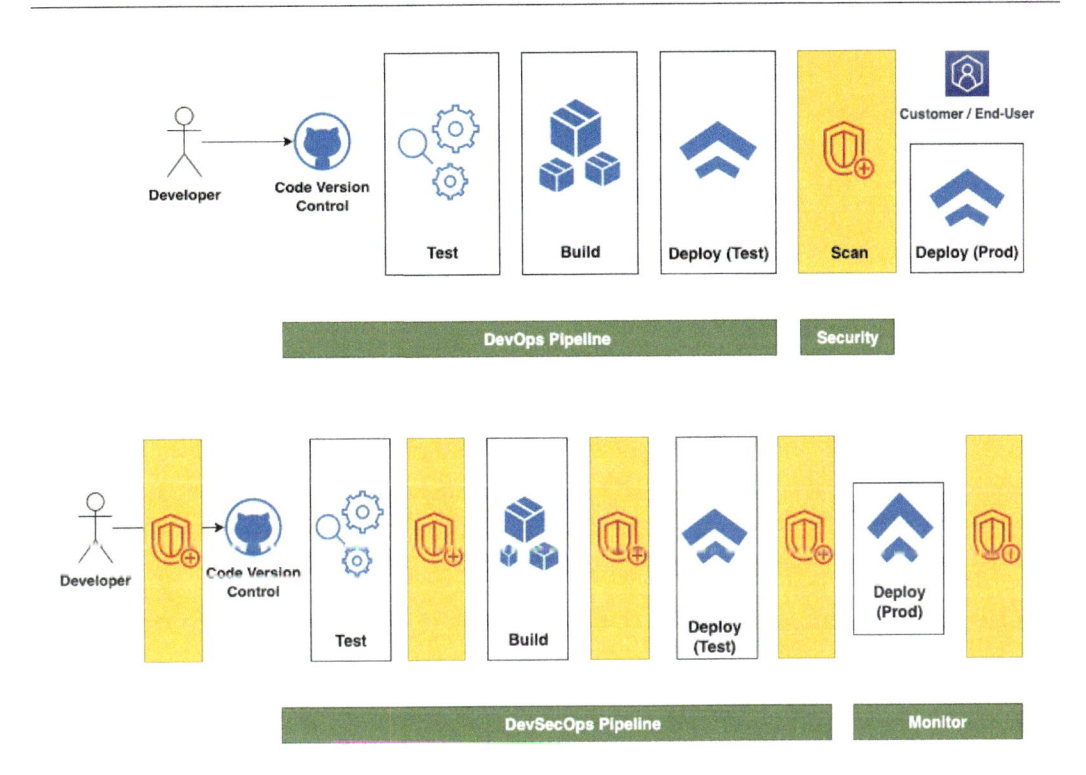

Figure 9.1 – Embedding security in all stages of CI/CD

In line with the *shift left* strategy we discussed previously, DevSecOps aims to enable developers to secure their code themselves. To facilitate this cultural transition, different types of code testing methods can be used to provide feedback to the developers.

## Software Composition Analysis

A lot of modern applications these days are composed of open source code, and this is a big challenge for organizations. They need to scan all these dependencies, along with their code, to effectively manage risk. **Software Composition Analysis** (**SCA**) can track all software licenses and dependencies that have reported vulnerabilities and potential exploits. Additionally, these tools generate a **software bill of materials** (**SBOM**) that can be used to track all the assets the software depends on. These tools should be integrated early in the SDLC, as and when new dependencies are brought in, or versions are upgraded.

### Static Application Security Testing

**Static Application Security Testing (SAST)** tools scan the code that is proprietary to the organization. They evaluate the code against known programming patterns that introduce security risks. As part of the analysis, they also provide some improvement feedback on how to make the code more secure. Both SCA and SAST methods don't require your code to be deployed for testing. It's appropriate to run these scans early in the SDLC before the code is deployed into a test environment.

### Dynamic Application Security Testing

As the name suggests, these tests are dynamic. They try to penetrate the security of an application and bring vulnerabilities to the surface. Commonly used in production environments, the feedback that's received from such tools is valuable for continuous compliance of security policies and standards.

**Dynamic Application Security Testing (DAST)** tools are mostly used for web applications as they are frequently exposed to untrusted networks and users over the internet. As the application code evolves, these tools continue to scan them before the newly identified risks turn serious.

### Securing infrastructure defined as code

**Infrastructure as Code (IaC)** is an approach to defining and managing your infrastructure components on-premises, or in the cloud, through configuration files. Commonly used tools and services in this space are **Pulumi**, **CloudFormation**, **Terraform**, and **AWS CDK**. Securing them requires the security team to define a set of rules that can then be codified and used for evaluating any change in these configurations. **Open Policy Agent (OPA)** is one such tool that allows you to validate your infrastructure code against custom-defined policies.

The tooling landscape is quite vast when it comes to all these security test mechanisms. Before we dive into the hands-on exercise, let's have a quick overview of some tools that you can consider adopting, depending on the use case at hand.

## Important tools for security assessments

The following table provides a list of some open source scanners that help mitigate a variety of security risks:

| Secrets Scanner ||
| --- | --- |
| `git-secrets` | This utility prevents you from accidentally committing secrets and credentials into git repositories. Ideally, it should be invoked as part of a `pre-commit` hook. |

| Vulnerability Scanners for Third-Party Libraries ||
|---|---|
| `Grype` | Grype scans the container images and filesystems for vulnerabilities from third-party dependencies. It supports Docker, Ruby, Java, and Python, among others. |
| `OWASP dependency-check` | This utility scans the dependencies against the vulnerabilities registered in the NVD database. It supports Java, JavaScript, and Ruby. |
| `Trivy` | Trivy scans container images, git repos, and dependency frameworks such as `maven`, `npm`, and `yarn`. |
| **Security Scanners for CloudFormation, CDK, and Terraform Code** ||
| `cfn_nag` | It searches the CloudFormation templates for indicators of insecure infrastructure, which includes overly permissive IAM rules, security groups, missing access logs, and so on. |
| `cfn_guard` | Technically, `cfn_guard` is similar to the OPA. You can use it to define declarative policies, which can then be used for evaluating CloudFormation templates. |
| `cdk_nag` | Searches for security compliance issues in CDK applications. It also supports a list of rules that can be used for HIPAA, NIST, and PCI compliance. |
| `checkov` | `checkov` is a static code analysis tool that scans IaC templates and looks for vulnerabilities in open source packages. |
| `tfsec` | `tfsec` is a code scanner from AquaSec. It reports misconfigurations in infrastructure configurations. |

In the next section, we will get hands-on and deploy a test CI/CD workflow that summarizes all our learnings so far.

## Rolling out a test CI/CD workflow for DevSecOps

To put things into practice, we'll deploy a test pipeline in an AWS account to demonstrate the usage of various tools (**AWS** and **open source**) from a security perspective. More concretely, let's consider a requirement that almost every modern software development team needs to address – securely delivering Docker images at scale. In real-life scenarios, you should consider deploying the output artifacts (Docker images) from such workflows to dedicated test environments where DAST investigations can be performed. This is particularly useful before deploying the image into subsequent environments (pre prod, prod, and so on).

To have a visual mind map of what we are going to build, let's dive into the details with an architecture diagram that highlights the end-to-end flow.

## Understanding the target architecture of the DevSecOps pipeline

A pipeline definition in AWS CodePipeline consists of at least two stages, and corresponding actions within each stage. We covered the constructs of AWS CodePipeline in detail in *Chapter 5, Rolling Out a CI/CD Pipeline*. Typical stages that come to our mind when we think of the entire life cycle of software delivery are *source*, *build*, *test*, and *deploy*. In the exercise that follows, we will mainly focus on the first two stages and understand how DevSecOps practices could be introduced in a Docker image delivery workflow, as an example.

We developed and deployed a Python-based **To-Do list manager application** in the previous chapters. We will reuse the application code and respective *Docker manifest* file. Our main focus will be on introducing security assessments that can be integrated into the build phase of this application, leading to the creation of a secure Docker image. *Figure 9.2* highlights the different types of security scans we will run:

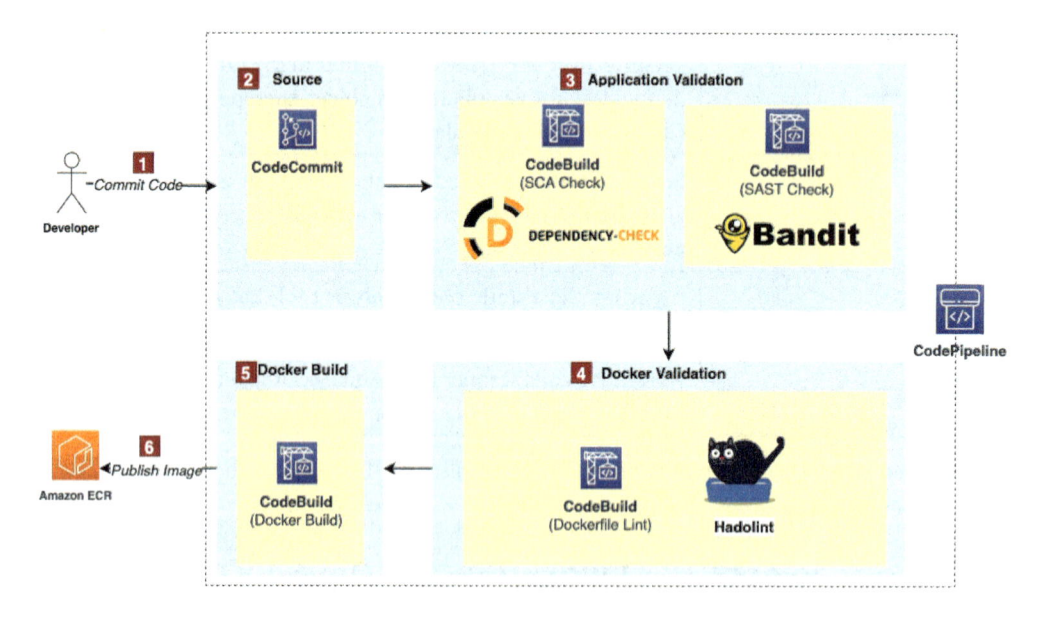

Figure 9.2 – Different stages of the DevSecOps pipeline

Let's begin by outlining the steps that are executed in each stage of the pipeline:

1. **New code changes**: Almost every CI/CD pipeline has an automated trigger for an event of interest. In this case, we are interested in new commits being pushed by a developer into the CodeCommit repository that contains the application code.

2. **CodePipeline execution**: Soon after a git commit is registered in the CodeCommit repository, the pipeline execution begins. As shown in the preceding diagram, **Source** is the first stage, and this is where CodePipeline pulls the most recent version of the code changes and makes them available in subsequent stages and actions.

3. **Application validation**: The second stage in the pipeline defines the actions that assess the code and its dependencies against security vulnerabilities. This stage further consists of two *actions* that execute in parallel:

   I. **Software Composition Analysis (SCA)**: This is a CodePipeline action within the application validation stage. We leverage CodeBuild to provide a temporary compute environment that can be used to install the **Dependency-Check** utility from **OWASP**. Post installation, we validate the Python code dependencies defined in the `requirements.txt` file. If you have not worked with Python before, the `requirements.txt` file lists all the dependencies – that is, the libraries and packages used by a Python project.

   Dependency-check is an SCA tool that works with various programming languages and detects publicly disclosed vulnerabilities of the project dependencies. This is achieved by assessing the presence of a **Common Platform Enumeration** (CPE) identifier for a specified dependency. In the event of discovery, a comprehensive report will be generated, containing links to the corresponding CVE entries.

   II. **Static Application Security Testing (SAST)**: In this CodePipeline action, we use the **Bandit** utility, which scans Python code to bring security issues to the surface. Bandit creates an **abstract syntax tree** (AST) from all the Python code files it scans and then runs security validation plugins against this AST. The output is a report that highlights security issues, along with the suggested actions for the developers.

4. **Dockerfile validation**: This is the third stage of the pipeline and is triggered after the application code scans are green. As you might notice, we are following the principle of *inside-out*, by first scanning the application itself, and then tackling the abstractions on top of it, one level at a time. This also helps with optimized usage of pipeline resources since there is no point in testing the Docker image before ensuring a good security posture for the code that will be added to it.

   For Dockerfile linting and security analysis, we make use of **hadolint**. In addition to providing basic linting capabilities, hadolint also allows security professionals to enforce certain things. For example, you can define the trusted registries these Dockerfiles can be based on or suppress false positives. All validations from hadolint can be accessed at `https://github.com/hadolint/hadolint#rules`.

5. **Dockerfile build**: This is the last and final stage of the pipeline where a Docker image is built and then published to an **Elastic Container Registry** (ECR) repository for use in deployment activities.

The workflow we are deploying can be easily extended with specific deployment actions for any other software. In the ideal scenario, you would have additional stages that consume the artifacts (Docker images) from this pipeline and deploy them onto an environment that supports running Docker containers, such as **Elastic Container Service (ECS)** or **Elastic Kubernetes Service (EKS)**.

Having understood the overall flow and what we are trying to achieve with the DevSecOps pipeline, let's outline the two components of the code base that we will be working with.

## Understanding the code base

Similar to other chapters, the code for the exercise that follows can be found in the project directory, `chapter-9/`, inside your Cloud9 IDE. Two subfolders contain the code for both the Python application and the infrastructure for rolling out a DevSecOps CI/CD pipeline. Let's walk through the contents of both:

- **Python Flask application**: This folder includes the code required to run a Python-based **To-Do list manager** application in the form of a Docker container. In addition to the `app.py` file, a `Dockerfile` manifest lists all the instructions you will need to create a Docker image.

- **DevSecOps CI/CD pipeline constructs**: We will be leveraging **AWS CDK** constructs to deploy the components of our CI/CD pipeline and see what a typical DevSecOps workflow looks like. All the resource constructs we use in the CDK stack are AWS-managed services, so that avoids the need for any foundational infrastructure elements such as VPCs, subnets, internet gateways, and so on.

Before we can commit the code for the Python application and assess it for any security risks, we need to deploy the CDK stack and provision the pipeline components.

## Deploying the CDK stack in an AWS account

To deploy the stack resources, we first need to fire the `npm install` command so that all the project dependencies can be downloaded. After the installation completes, you can use the `cdk synth` command to check the CloudFormation template, if you like.

At this point, we are all set to deploy the stack in the AWS account, which will set up all the stages and corresponding actions of the pipeline using the **AWS CodePipeline** service:

```
aws-devops-simplified:~/environment/chapter-9/devsecops-cicd-pipeline
$ cdk deploy
...
...
✨  Synthesis time: 12.65s
DeliveryPipelineStack:  start: Building 46e40c3e0f5b985e8b4b1bbc5c4eb-
24cacee4d46e40c3e0f5b985e8b4b1bbc5c4eb24cacee4d04d15ecbcbecbc4839d8f-
9d1cf:current_account-current_region
...
Do you wish to deploy these changes (y/n)? yF
DeliveryPipelineStack: deploying... [1/1]
...
DeliveryPipelineStack: creating CloudFormation changeset...
```

✓ `DeliveryPipelineStack`
✦ `Deployment time: 202.82s`

After the CDK application has been successfully deployed, you can access the CodePipeline service to see all the stages and corresponding actions that have been provisioned. You will see something similar to *Figure 9.3*:

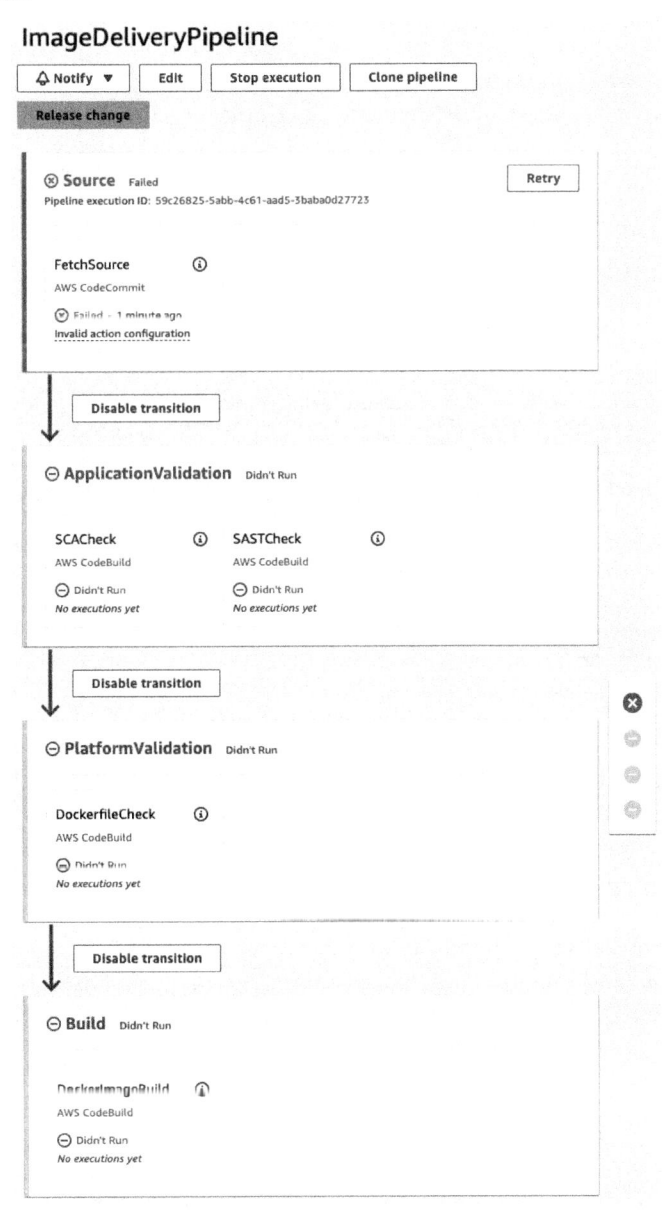

Figure 9.3 – Different stages of the CI/CD pipeline

As you can notice, the first stage reports a failure, which is expected since there is no code in the freshly provisioned CodeCommit repository. So, let's go ahead and commit the application code into the repository. CodeCommit recommends using the `git-remote-codecommit` plugin for authenticating against the HTTPS (GRC) endpoint. This GRC endpoint can be retrieved from the CodeCommit service page for your repository, in the AWS web console. The `git-remote-codecommit` plugin is already included in the Cloud9 IDE that you've installed in your AWS account.

One last step before we can see the pipeline in execution is to initialize a local git repository and set up the git remote so that it points to our CodeCommit repository in the AWS account. We just need to push the application code, so let's switch the working directory as well:

```
aws-devops-simplified:~/environment/chapter-9 $ cd chapter-9-flask-app/
aws-devops-simplified:~/environment/chapter-9/chapter-9-flask-app $ git init .
aws-devops-simplified:~/environment/chapter-9/chapter-9-flask-app $ git checkout -b master
aws-devops-simplified:~/environment/chapter-9/chapter-9-flask-app $ git add .
aws-devops-simplified:~/environment/chapter-9/chapter-9-flask-app $ git commit -m "Sample application for DevSecOps pipeline"
```

After files have been added to Git's staging area, we can push them to the CodeCommit repository:

```
aws-devops-simplified:~/environment/chapter-9/chapter-9-flask-app $ git remote add origin codecommit::eu-central-1://image-delivery-pipeline
aws-devops-simplified:~/environment/chapter-9/chapter-9-flask-app $ git push origin master
...
```

As soon as the commits are registered in CodeCommit, the pipeline execution begins. CodePipeline can now source the code from the CodeCommit repository on the configured branch (`master`). Let's dive into the result of security assessments that are configured in the pipeline.

## Checking the result of security assessments

Every stage of the pipeline validates some or the other aspect of the application against security risks. We follow the same *inside-out* principle and start from the application itself, before moving on to Docker validations.

### Software Composition Analysis with dependency-check

If you observe the output of the pipeline execution, you will notice that the first stage, `ApplicationValidation`, reports an error in the SCACheck CodeBuild action. Checking the CodeBuild build execution log reveals a finding in the Flask framework and since the criticality exceeds the threshold value of 7 (as configured in the `buildspec.yml` file), an error has been raised. Such security validations flag any new dependency that your developers might introduce into the application. The criticality of these findings can vary, and not all would be relevant, but having some false positives is still better than no reporting at all.

In this case, the OWASP `dependency-check` utility, in addition to flagging a potential risk, gives us a URL that contains more information about the specific CVE that has been reported.

```
"vulnerabilities": [
  {
    "source": "OSSINDEX",
    "name": "CVE-2023-30861",
    "severity": "HIGH",
    "cvssv2": {
      "score": 7.5,
...
...
    "cwes": [
      "CWE-539"
    ],
...
    "description": "Flask is a lightweight WSGI web application framework. When all of the following conditions are met, a response containing data intended for one client may be cached ... https://ossindex.sonatype.org/vulnerability/CVE-2023-30861
...
```

As shown in *Figure 9.4*, visiting the CVE URL in your web browser further explains how certain configurations in the Python Flask framework can be exploited. `dependency-check` parsed the `requirements.txt` file to figure out the third-party dependency names and their version. It then verified these dependencies against the publicly available vulnerabilities database – in this case, NVD. Since the version we are using in the application is flagged as a potential risk, it was called out by the `dependency-check` utility. However, in this case, we are not working with cookies or headers, so we can safely suppress the finding:

216  Implementing DevSecOps with AWS

**Vulnerability**
CVE-2023-30861

🗨 Report advisory or correction

**CVSS Score**
**7.5**
HIGH

**CVSS Vector**
CVSS:3.1/AV:N/AC:L/PR:N/UI:N/S:U/C:H/I:N/A:N

**CWE**

[CVE-2023-30861] CWE-539: Information Exposure Through Persistent Cookies

**Description**

Flask is a lightweight WSGI web application framework. When all of the following conditions are met, a response containing data intended for one client may be cached and subsequently sent by the proxy to other clients. If the proxy also caches `Set-Cookie` See More

**Deviation Notice:**
Sonatype's research suggests that this CVE's details differ from those defined at NVD or other reporting sources; **sign in for details.**

Figure 9.4 – CVE finding reported by the dependency-check utility

> **Tip**
> On every run, utilities such as `dependency-check` download all the CVEs from public databases and store them locally for evaluation. As CodeBuild environments are ephemeral, it leads to a loss of information every time the build completes. This results in really high execution times (>5 minutes) for each run. This can be optimized by leveraging CodeBuild build caches that allow you to mark a directory that needs to be saved and reused in subsequent build runs. You can read more about this feature at https://docs.aws.amazon.com/codebuild/latest/userguide/build-caching.html.

For simplicity's sake, let's say we are not interested in any vulnerability findings where the CVSS score is below 8. We can adapt the respective `buildspec` file for the CodeBuild action and commit the changes. To do this, we can modify the CVSS threshold to 8 in the `buildspecs/sca.yml` file:

```
...
  build:
    on-failure: ABORT
    commands:
      - dependency-check --scan "${PWD}" --enableExperimental --failOnCVSS 8 --format JSON
...
...
```

By default, this utility dumps a report file after the command's execution is complete. In addition to JSON, there is support for several other formats, which can be automatically parsed for any additional automation you want to build on top of it. After making these changes, you can push the new updates to the repository hosted on AWS:

```
aws-devops-simplified:~/environment/chapter-9/chapter-9-flask-app $
git commit -am "Increased threshold for CVSS score in SCA check"
[master 73db6e9] Increased threshold for CVSS score in SCA check
 1 file changed, 1 insertion(+), 1 deletion(-)

aws-devops-simplified:~/environment/chapter-9/chapter-9-flask-app $
git push origin master
Enumerating objects: 7, done.
...
...
   0032123..73db6e9  master -> master
```

Next, we can move on to the outputs of the SAST stage.

### Static Application Security Testing with Bandit

**Bandit** is a famous **SAST** utility for testing security issues in Python code. This is the second action in the ApplicationValidation stage of our pipeline that executes in parallel to SCA, which we discussed previously.

We also have an error that has been reported here. It seems to point to incorrect usage of exception handling in Python:

```
>> Issue: [B110:try_except_pass] Try, Except, Pass detected.
   Severity: Low   Confidence: High
   CWE: CWE-703
   More Info: https://bandit.readthedocs.io/en/1.7.5/plugins/b110_try_
except_pass.html
   Location: app.py:35:8
34              return redirect(url_for('todos'))
35          except Exception as e:
36              pass
```

The problem with this code is that we are catching all exceptions and silently ignoring them. This represents a potential security risk as a large number of errors from a service can hint at attempts to interfere with the application. Even if we don't want to handle the exception in a particular way, we should at least log the failure message and not just suppress it with `pass`.

Let's replace the problematic line of code in app.py with a logger statement and commit the changes again:

```
...
    return redirect(url_for('todos'))
except Exception as e:
    logging.error("Exception occurred while submitting data to MongoDB", exc_info=True)
...
```

Now that we've fixed this security risk, the last validation check that must be configured in the pipeline involves bringing potential risks, or issues, with the Dockerfile to the surface.

## *Validating the Dockerfile manifest with hadolint*

In addition to linting Docker files, **hadolint** also performs bash code validations through the shellcheck utility. If you are into writing bash scripts for day-to-day operational procedures, I highly recommend using **shellcheck**, if you don't use it already.

There are a few errors you will notice in the CodePipeline execution under the PlatformValidation stage that require fixing. Let's have a look:

```
...
...
Dockerfile:10 DL3018 warning: Pin versions in apk add. Instead of `apk add <package>` use `apk add <package>=<version>`
Dockerfile:22 DL3059 info: Multiple consecutive `RUN` instructions. Consider consolidation.
Dockerfile:24 DL3020 error: Use COPY instead of ADD for files and folders
Dockerfile:29 DL3042 warning: Avoid use of cache directory with pip. Use `pip install --no-cache-dir <package>`
Dockerfile:29 DL3013 warning: Pin versions in pip. Instead of `pip install <package>` use `pip install <package>==<version>` or `pip install --requirement <requirements file>`
...
...
```

While some of these are opportunities to optimize the Dockerfile layer's structure, the others that ask for specific versions of the libraries to be pinned have some security benefits.

It is always good practice to avoid cached directories for installation and use the latest versions of the libraries. This also goes against the idea of immutability because when new versions of those libraries are released, you might unknowingly end up with a different library version than the one you tested. This can introduce potential security risks if new vulnerabilities were introduced in the latest packages.

To fix the reported errors, we can make the following modifications in the Dockerfile:

```
# Install packages
RUN apk update && apk add --update --no-cache \
    bash=5.2.15-r0 \
    python3=3.10.11-r0 \
    py3-pip=22.3.1-r1 \
    py3-cryptography=38.0.3-r1 \
    vim=9.0.0999-r0 \
    wget=1.21.4-r0 \
    curl=8.1.1-r0 \
    tree=2.0.4-r0

RUN apk --no-cache add --virtual \\
    builds-deps=20230523.220926 \
    build-base=0.5-r3 && \
    mkdir /opt/aws-devops-simplified
...
...
```

With the library versions pinned down and the RUN commands consolidated, we now follow the best practices recommended by the hadolint utility.

Once all these changes have been committed back into the CodeCommit repository, we should have a successful run of CodePipeline, which builds a Docker image and pushes it to the ECR registry that we created as part of the CDK stack.

## Summary

In today's software landscape, security is crucial not only for the financial, social media, and e-commerce sectors but for all industries. With evolving software practices and cloud adoption, the complexity and risks associated with modern applications have increased significantly. These risks, often beyond the control of development teams, can have severe consequences, including reputational damage, information loss, and loss of customer trust. An important concept that helps us address these requirements while ensuring more collaboration among developers, operations, and security team members is DevSecOps.

We started this chapter by introducing what DevSecOps is and the benefits it offers. Similar to DevOps, it is not just about technical optimizations but also promotes the idea of shared responsibility between developers, operations, and security. This ensures that any new risks that the applications might be exposed to are mitigated as soon as possible. After learning about some practical approaches to different test methodologies, we also did a hands-on deployment to experience DevSecOps tools in a CI/CD pipeline. We mostly worked with open source tools as they are already very mature in this space and it's easy to find the right mix of tools without committing to a broader-scoped service or solution.

In the next chapter, *Setting Up Teams for Success*, we will cover some ideas that foster collaboration, learning, and growth. We will also focus on the benefits of a no-blame feedback culture.

## Further reading

To learn more about the topics that were covered in this chapter, take a look at the following resources:

- Common cloud security issues and threats: `https://www.strongdm.com/blog/cloud-security-issues-risks`
- Workshop for threat modeling for builders: `https://catalog.workshops.aws/threatmodel/en-US`

# Part 4
# Taking the Next Steps

This part focuses on setting up your teams for success, both from a cultural and technology standpoint. It dives into the typical problems enterprises face with the increasing adoption of AWS and offers practical tips to address them, while increasing team collaboration and streamlining developer processes. You will learn about some strategies for continuous improvement and adherence to the AWS Well-Architected Framework. Through the concept of landing zones, we will additionally introduce you to some open source solutions and frameworks. These frameworks can be combined with AWS services such as Control Tower for improved compliance and security of your multi-account, multi-Region environments.

This part has the following chapters

- *Chapter 10, Setting Up Teams for Success*
- *Chapter 11, Ensuring a Strong AWS Foundation for Multi-Account and Multi-Region Environments*
- *Chapter 12, Adhering to AWS Well-Architected Principles*

# 10
# Setting Up Teams for Success

In the DevOps realm, the success and effectiveness of all initiatives depend on the coordinated integration of both people and technology. Focusing on just one is not going to reap many benefits. By recognizing the importance of both, organizations can unlock the full potential of DevOps, resulting in faster software delivery life cycles with increased quality and reliability.

**People** drive the cultural and collaborative aspects of DevOps. They bring their skills and expertise to drive a mindset of shared responsibility, continuous improvement, and effective communication. **Technology**, on the other hand, provides the necessary tooling, automation, and infrastructure management to support this mindset. Software delivery approaches such as CI, CI/CD pipelines, and **Infrastructure as Code** (**IaC**) empower teams to improve the overall efficiency of delivering code to the customers.

With DevOps, people reach for tooling too quickly. Before they do that, they need to ensure the right foundations of – culture and working model. Once people are aligned with the value and benefits of both, they will be motivated to adopt the required technology changes and ways of working by themselves. In this chapter, we will focus on the two pillars – people and technology – and what you can do in the AWS world to set up your teams for success. Additionally, I will introduce you to some resources that you can leverage for continuous learning and enablement of your DevOps teams. Adoption of AWS often opens up new opportunities to innovate and sometimes even leads to role transitions within the company. Toward the end of this chapter, we will cover a basic learning path that you could consider for yourself or other team members who would like to get more involved in DevOps on AWS.

Our agenda for this chapter is as follows:

- Building a collaborative and agile team setup and culture
- Technology best practices and considerations for success
- Resources to support AWS learning and development
- Learning path for transitioning into DevOps roles

## Building a collaborative team setup and culture

Adopting DevOps practices is easier said than done. A fundamental problem that most organizations struggle with is looking at tools and automation as the golden solution to all their problems – or even worse, hiring DevOps engineers from the market and embedding them into existing teams, hoping that they will introduce automations and cloud services that will magically address all gaps. Before going this route, they first need to ensure *people readiness*. In this section, we will discuss the various aspects of building an effective team structure that supports successful DevOps implementation across your organization. We will focus on the importance of fostering a culture of collaboration and effective communication that, in turn, drives value creation for customers.

### Enable your teams to create more value

The first challenge you need to tackle is your company's operating model. How are the teams structured, what are their responsibilities, how do they communicate, and how well does this structure align with the business goals? Does it allow them to independently deliver business outcomes to the customer? Is there a need for frequent hand-offs to other teams for routine day-to-day work? Do they lack expertise in areas that are critical to the functioning of their software, and so on?

Four foundational team structures can be adopted by organizations operating at any scale. Before we dive into the details, it's important to highlight that these team setups might take slightly different forms, depending on the size and DevOps maturity of the organization. So, instead of applying them as a static template, consider them as inspirations from which new teams could be formed, or existing teams could transition into. Focus more on what value these structures bring and how they could help your teams focus on what they do best.

#### *Value-stream aligned teams*

These teams are laser-focused on a well-defined unique stream of work. They are your front-line warriors, always having well-established communication interfaces with the end customers, external or internal. The north star for this team should be providing business value to the end user. Depending on the company size and product offering, this single stream could be scoped to a complete product or service, a collection of features within a product, or something more granular if needed. What is important is that they take complete responsibility, starting from gathering inputs from the customers, understanding their pain points, developing software to address the gaps, and operating it in production. Companies such as **AWS**, for example, might want to align these team structures with different services that the cloud provider offers. So, a dedicated team might take care of **AWS CodeBuild**, and another could own **AWS CodePipeline**, for example. These teams have possess cross-functional skills that allow them to understand the business needs of the customers and translate those needs into software features. They should also have all the skills in-house for operating these workloads at a global scale. From a DevOps perspective, this checks all boxes, such as you-build-it-you-run-it, operating with autonomy, building with the end customer in mind, and so on.

Taking a different example of, let's say, **eBay**, might warrant the need to scope the streams a bit differently. So, there could be a team responsible for *checkout*, one for *product catalog listing*, another for *fraud management*, and so on. However, the core principles remain the same. These teams should be able to deliver value almost independently of any other team in the company.

Another challenge organizations frequently face is how big these teams should be. To ensure effective collaboration, shared responsibility, and team dynamics, it's a good rule of thumb to keep the headcount below 10-12. This is what Amazon also calls the *2-Pizza team*, a team that can be fed with two pizzas and has the full authority to make decisions in the best interest of their stream.

The other teams we are going to discuss are more *enablers* for the core value streams in your organization. They are the ones coming into the picture to offer support in areas that slow down the value streams in providing value to the end users.

## *Platform teams*

The platform teams are focused on developing and maintaining reusable services for their customers – the individuals in the different value streams, across the organization. The sole success criteria for the platform teams should be the ease of adoption, usage, and documentation of the services they provide. The more compelling and easier to use these services are, the wider the adoption.

In *Chapter 1, Accelerating Your DevOps Journey with AWS*, we discussed the idea of reducing cognitive load for customers. The concept of a platform team strongly relates to this idea. They should enable the value stream members to be able to focus on differentiating business outcomes. This is only possible by offloading other undifferentiated tasks from them. The outcomes from the platform team address the common needs of all other value streams. For example, if all the software artifacts depend on containerized workloads running **Amazon Elastic Kubernetes Service** (**Amazon EKS**), then the right focus area for the platform team should be ready-made templates for deploying, monitoring, and operating services in these EKS environments. They could offer centralized dashboards and out-of-the-box logging integrations for the value streams to easily adopt and benefit from.

However, it is important to note that ownership of the production environments of software developed by respective value streams still sits with them.

In *Chapter 11, Ensuring a Strong AWS Foundation for Multi-Account and Multi-Region Environments*, we will discuss the concept of a **Landing Zone**. This maps well to the scope of work that a platform team would ideally deal with, in the context of AWS environments. This enables the application teams to focus on what they do best while leaving the complexities around the foundational aspects of a multi-account, multi-region environment with the central platform team.

### Specialist teams

Depending on an organization's domain of business, there might be certain specialized areas that are overarching across most, if not all value streams. These areas require special skills that are not commonly found in the industry, or within the company. This could be deep expertise in media encoding, financial risk analysis algorithms, high data compression techniques, and so on.

In all likelihood, this knowledge is core to the artifacts that the value streams provide. It is essential to continue providing value to the end customers. In such cases, the organizations can consider establishing these specialist teams who *consult* the value streams on best practices around the niche skillset. Highly mature DevOps companies also invest in offering these specialized skills *as a service*, often abstracting the underlying details with easy-to-understand interfaces, thereby reducing the cognitive load of the value streams.

### Enablement teams

The ever-increasing pressure to deliver more features sometimes derails the value streams from focusing on their core differentiated offering. They might get pulled into tasks that are temporary but require a deep skillset, or experience, which they don't necessarily have the time to learn.

This pattern frequently surfaces in organizations that, for example, are migrating their applications from one technology stack such as OpenShift (RedHat's Kubernetes offering) to EKS in AWS. Not all value streams might be aware of the peculiarities of such a migration and the dependencies in their application stack that they should consider evaluating. To spearhead the progress of such migrations, it often helps to set up enablement teams, a temporary structure that is formed of individuals who have been involved in similar migrations, for many other workloads in the company. The experience they have had in the past can be a big value add for the teams who want to do something similar.

*Figure 10.1* highlights the flow of change in software and the respective interactions within different teams – all with a common goal – providing value to their customers:

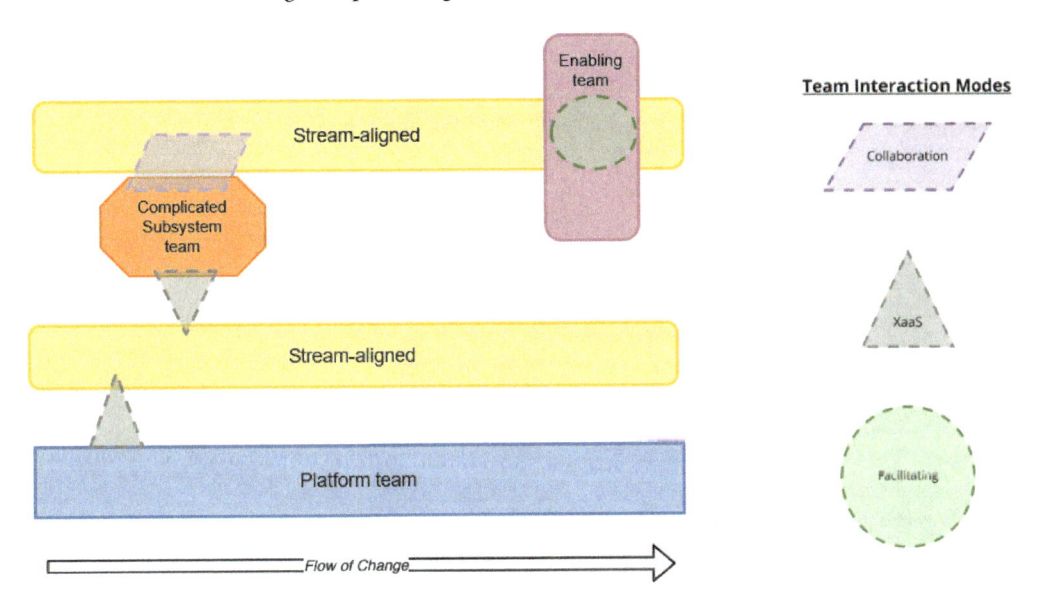

Figure 10.1 – Collaboration between different team structures
(Source: https://github.com/TeamTopologies)

You might have somewhat similar or largely different team structures within your organization. If you are just establishing your teams from scratch, you could consider these structures as a guiding force. If you already have an established working model, you might want to align that with the principles that these teams live by. Doing this will allow the right balance of autonomy, growth, and ownership. Defining the boundaries of responsibilities is essential for effective communication within and across the teams.

## Establishing a culture of collaboration and learning

Breaking down the teams into smaller focused groups has its advantages, such as complete autonomy, team cohesion, end-to-end responsibility, and clear alignment with customer expectations. Sometimes, this can also mean that there are pockets of innovation happening within these teams that might be valuable, but unknown to other parts of the organization. Or, there could be recurring patterns of problems that each of the value streams faces, which might hint at underlying gaps in the offerings from the platform team. This is where establishing **Communities of Practice (CoP)** plays a very important role.

A CoP is a group of people within the organization that share a concern or passion for something. They meet regularly to collaborate and learn from each other. These communities might have multiple dimensions of purpose; sometimes, helping other communities with everyday work needs, sharing best practices and guidelines for the organization, or fostering breakthrough innovations and new practices. As shown in *Figure 10.2*, a CoP is an overlapping structure that spawns multiple teams in the company and gets everyone with similar interests together in a room:

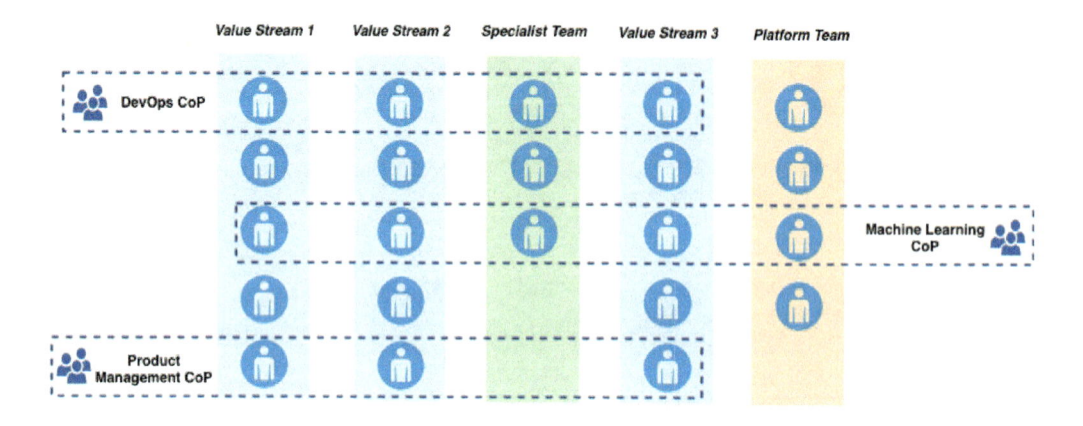

Figure 10.2 – Establishing a CoP for shared interests and passions

Organizations typically plan these collaborative working sessions at least once a week, when undergoing major transformations. In later stages, they might want to revisit the cadence by further reducing or increasing it, depending on the value that the teams are driving from the setup.

## Measuring the DevOps maturity of your teams

An important prerequisite to improving something is to start measuring it. The same applies to the DevOps maturity of your teams. It is essential to identify the areas of improvement, understand progress, and track the effectiveness of any process or change rolled out as part of DevOps practices in your organization. But what exactly needs to be measured, you may ask?

**Accelerate 2022 State of DevOps Report** (Ref: `https://services.google.com/fh/files/misc/2022_state_of_devops_report.pdf`) mentions two clusters of analysis, one targeted toward *software delivery performance*, and the other toward *operational performance*. These reports are based on inputs from more than 33k respondents from different organizations. *Figure 10.3* highlights the four key metrics in the software delivery performance category that will help you quantify your team's current performance and measure it against the industry benchmark:

| Software delivery performance metric | Low | Medium | High |
|---|---|---|---|
| **Deployment frequency**<br>For the primary application or service you work on, how often does your organization deploy code to production or release it to end users? | Between once per month and once every 6 months | Between once per week and once per month | On-demand (multiple deploys per day) |
| **Lead time for changes**<br>For the primary application or service you work on, what is your lead time for changes (i.e., how long does it take to go from code committed to code successfully running in production)? | Between one month and six months | Between one week and one month | Between one day and one week |
| **Time to restore service**<br>For the primary application or service you work on, how long does it generally take to restore service when a service incident or a defect that impacts users occurs (e.g., unplanned outage or service impairment)? | Between one week and one month | Between one day and one week | Less than one day |
| **Change failure rate**<br>For the primary application or service you work on, what percentage of changes to production or released to users result in degraded service (e.g., lead to service impairment or service outage) and subsequently require remediation (e.g., require a hotfix, rollback, fix forward, patch)? | 46%-60% | 16%-30% | 0%-15% |

Figure 10.3 – Four metrics to measure software delivery performance
(source: Accelerate 2022 State of DevOps report)

It gives you an idea of how other companies are doing and if you'd like to aim higher by improving your current standings in any way.

However, all of this needs to be discussed and planned against the real needs of your application and the expectations of the end customers. So, context matters. Not all teams and applications require 10 deployments per day, but if they do, it's necessary to make sure that your release processes support it.

The same report further describes a second clustering approach that accumulates the metrics from software delivery performance and sprinkles the reliability aspect on top of it. A holistic view of all these areas gives a representation of the current state of the workloads that you are managing, resulting in four different categorizations:

- Starting
- Flowing
- Slowing
- Retiring

As a DevOps practitioner, your goal should be to ensure that the result of this analysis matches the expectation from the workload or the value stream. These categorizations are highlighted in *Figure 10.4*:

| Cluster | Stability | | Operational Performance | Throughput | | % respondents |
| --- | --- | --- | --- | --- | --- | --- |
| | Time to restore service | Change failure rate | Reliability | Lead time | Deployment frequency | |
| Starting | Between one day and one week | 31%-45% | Sometimes meet expectations | Between one week and one month | Between once per week and once per month | 28% |
| Flowing | Less than one hour | 0%-15% | Usually meet expectations | Less than one day | On demand (multiple deploys per day) | 17% |
| Slowing | Less than one day | 0%-15% | Usually meet expectations | Between one week and one month | Between once per week and once per month | 34% |
| Retiring | Between one month and six months | 46%-60% | Usually meet expectations | Between one month and six months | Between once per month and once every 6 months | 21% |

Figure 10.4 – Clustering software delivery and operational performance metrics to identify the current state of the workloads (source: Accelerate 2022 State of DevOps report)

## De-silo Dev and Ops

Many organizations might divide their teams into separate functional areas, leading to groups consisting of developers, operations, QAs, and so on. This model keeps you away from the benefits that shared responsibility, ownership, and team cohesion can bring on your DevOps journey. The whole idea of the DevOps methodology is to break down these silos, ensure teams speak more often, are aligned on what the end customer needs, and collaborate on achieving this goal. The wall that exists between these teams creates resistance to change that is detrimental to reliably releasing software more often. Developers who have had some system administration background in the past should actively involve themselves in improving the operations of the software. Operators, on the other hand, might be well versed in some application programming languages, so they could leverage those capabilities to assist the developers in reliably rolling out changes at scale.

However, introducing this change in organizations that have since long been using these siloed models might face some resistance. A strategy that I've seen work quite well in such teams is to temporarily *embed* DevOps practitioners into the teams who can act as agents of change. By introducing new practices around development, operations, and communications backed by automation and tooling, they can motivate the team members to think beyond their preset boundaries and focus on driving customer value.

## Blameless post-mortems and RCAs

Failure is the only constant. Software fails all the time and the best we can do is to architect for reliability and learn from those failures so that a re-occurrence can be avoided. Aptly put by *Devin Carraway, Member of Technical Staff at Google*:

*"The cost of failure is education"*

A good mechanism to learn from these failures is **Root Cause Analysis** (**RCA**) sessions. The main goal behind them is to document the incident and ensure that all causes are identified and the preventive actions are noted. Most importantly, all of this needs to happen in a blameless way without pointing out any individual or team. It should be seen as a learning opportunity in terms of what could be better next time. The tone of the documentation should also reflect the fact that what everyone did was in the best interest of keeping the service available for use.

However, not all incidents require post-mortems. The criteria that should lead to a deep investigation should be defined upfront by the stakeholders, depending on what is critical to the business. This could mean a resolution time beyond $X$ hours, data loss, or a monitoring failure.

Having discussed some people initiatives that could set up your teams for success, let's delve into some technical bits.

# Technology best practices and considerations for success

Technology plays an important role in complementing the cultural and working model practices that we discussed previously. They make the team more efficient with their work, leading to increased efficiency. Let's discuss some ideas that you could consider adopting.

## Right-size the teams based on the technology cognitive load they can handle

**Cognitive load** is the amount of working memory your brain uses to accomplish a task. Just like how heavy memory usage in the computer slows it down, teams' performance can take a hit when they are burdened with a lot more than they can handle.

You might have also heard questions about how big a microservice should be. Where exactly should you draw the line when it comes to defining the responsibilities of a software team in a huge monolith or microservices-based application? These decisions should be driven by the cognitive load a team can efficiently handle. However, at the same time, the structure needs to be flexible to change. As a DevOps practitioner, it's important to always be on the lookout for team burnouts and rapid expansion of technical landscapes. Operating a monolith in the early days might be manageable work, but it might not be when the application has been launched in multiple geographies around the world. At this point, specific areas of the monolith might have to be carved out as a separate service, owned by a dedicated team. What is essential is that a single team should own the entire life cycle of the service they manage, from ideation to production operations, and they should perform this role quite well, with full autonomy and ownership.

## Invest in building abstractions that promote best practices

Creating Amazon RDS databases is not a differentiated task. Using these databases to extract value from data and demonstrating engineering excellence is.

If you leave the infrastructure life cycle management of such services to respective teams, there's a high chance that every team in your organization might implement it a bit differently. Some might not enable encryption at rest, and others might not enforce SSL connection parameters. It could also be the case that organizations just getting started with AWS might want to ensure a minimum security posture in the cloud while the teams gain a better understanding of best practices. Services such as **AWS Service Catalog** can be very beneficial here. The platform teams could offer a ready-made *catalog* of packaged products to the end users by implementing and abstracting the implementation details in Service Catalog. The product in this case could be implemented with **CloudFormation** or **Terraform** scripts under the hood, two famous IaC solutions. The value streams need not bother about the configuration specifics of these offerings from the platform team, but just use them as a service, just like they would do with any other SaaS product out there. These products could also adapt to the software environment they are being provisioned for. In production, they could enable backup retention and prevent accidental deletion, while in dev, they could enforce low-cost configurations.

## Making injection of failure scenarios a routine practice

For critical business applications with a very high uptime requirement, organizations might implement **disaster recovery** (**DR**) processes and architectures to survive regional outages. The rarity of such scenarios occurring means that the disaster recovery procedures are hardly tested before a real event happens. AWS services such as **Fault Injection Simulator** and **Resilience Hub** allow users to intentionally introduce certain failure scenarios, such as the unavailability of an **Availability Zone** (**AZ**) – a collection of data centers in AWS, sudden CPU usage spikes on a container, and so on. In addition to giving the teams confidence around how gracefully their workloads survive these situations, these procedures also help uncover aspects that developers might not have thought of. DR procedures that haven't been triggered in the last 2 years are as risky as not having any at all.

Organizations with highly mature operational practices regularly operate their critical workloads from a standby site multiple times a year.

## Aligning technology decisions with business expectations

As they say, working with AWS services is like being a kid in a candy shop. There's so much around you that you want to have it all. It's important to balance the consumption of these services with the real needs of your workload. Multi-region availability, for example, might not always be a must-have for applications. Containerizing an existing monolith might not always lead to happy outcomes. Aiming for an additional 0.01% of application uptime time can lead to an increase in costs and architectural complexities that do not justify the minuscule increase in availability. Therefore, it's necessary to weigh all decisions against the actual business needs and keep your architectures as lean as possible.

If you remember the metrics highlighted in the *Accelerate DevOps* report that we discussed previously, application reliability was called out as an important DevOps maturity indicator, just like software delivery.

Therefore, defining realistic thresholds and availabilities for your workloads is a very important input for an efficient cloud architecture that meets your needs. But how do you go about measuring the reliability of your systems and communicating them to your customers? Two important metrics here are **service-level objectives** (**SLOs**) and **service-level indicators** (**SLIs**). An SLO is the promise that a company makes to its users regarding the availability of a system. As a service provider, you could promise an SLO for 99.99% monthly availability. An SLI, on the other hand, is a key metric that identifies if the SLO is being met or not. It is the actual measured value for the metric described in the SLO.

Based on the SLO committed by a service, the providers then create a **service-level agreement** (**SLA**). The SLA states the action that the company will take in case it is not able to meet the committed SLO. Typically, these actions translate into service credits or billing discounts.

> **Did you know?**
>
> Google implements periodic planned downtime of some services to prevent a service from being *overly available*. They tried this initially with some frontend servers in an internal system. This downtime uncovered some other services that were using these servers inappropriately. With that information, they were able to move workloads to somewhere more suitable while maintaining the servers at the right availability level.

The adoption of new ways of working by DevOps methodologies combined with innovative use of AWS services often leads to new roles and roadmaps being identified within organizations. Out of personal interest, some of the existing employees might as well feel motivated to transition their careers and develop breadth and depth in cloud skills. In the next section, I'll introduce you to some learning resources that can set up your teams for success.

## Resources for continuous learning and enablement

These are time-tested practices that have been adopted by Amazon either for its use or for building innovative solutions for their customers. Let's dive into the key focus areas for each:

- **Amazon Builders' Library**

  The Amazon Builders' Library is a collection of articles that explain how Amazon creates, designs, launches, and manages technology. These articles are written by experienced technical leaders and engineers from Amazon. They cover various topics related to architecture, software delivery, and operations. For instance, you can learn about Amazon's methods for automating software delivery, which allows them to make more than 150 million deployments in a year. You can also explore how Amazon's engineers use principles such as shuffle sharding to build strong and reliable systems that can handle errors and stay accessible even during failures. The Builders' Library collection of articles is available at https://aws.amazon.com/builders-library.

- **Solutions Library and its patterns**

  Today, organizations are looking for trusted solutions and helpful advice to quickly solve their business problems. The AWS Solutions Library provides a variety of solutions created by AWS and its partners. These solutions can be used as they are or customized to meet specific needs. They cover a wide range of industries and technology use cases, giving customers options that fit their requirements. You can access all these patterns at https://aws.amazon.com/solutions/.

- **Workshops on AWS**

  What better than to try out hands-on tutorials that introduce you to practical skills, concepts, and techniques that allow you to solve business problems? You can make use of the curated content developed by the AWS teams available at https://awsworkshop.io/.

- **Local communities and user groups**

  Another source of great knowledge exchange can be participating in local communities and user groups where people share their experiences with a particular technology stack in AWS to solve a problem. You can search for these communities in portals such as Meetup: https://www.meetup.com/.

After acquiring all the skills and knowledge, a common problem still faced by many DevOps individual contributors is the ability to drive change within their organization. Let's discuss some tips to help you succeed.

# Driving change from the bottom up

There are multiple levels of influence within a company, starting from the CEO and coming down to the engineer writing code that delivers value to the customer. As a DevOps practitioner, it can sometimes become a challenge to *sell* ideas or benefits behind adopting a tool or automation that can help the wider team in delivering more value to the customers. This section covers some tips that you could consider to demonstrate the real value of what you are proposing. This is not easy because your level of influence as an individual contributor might not offer you a position to push ideas downwards. But the good part is that you're in a unique position to actually *implement* a change at the ground level and quickly *validate* the idea to demonstrate tangible value. Within this scope, you can easily take the first steps around breathing life into your proposal and see if it works for you. Once it does, it's time to push it forward. Let's discuss a few things that will help you sell your DevOps ideas higher up in the organizational chain.

## Structure your ideas well

Don't start with the deepest technical implementation details when describing your ideas. Focus on the value it provides and how that leads to success. If you've built a tool that injects failures into various components of the architecture stack to test their resiliency, make sure you highlight the value all your customers get by adopting this approach. While this certainly helps the software developers test the resiliency of their application stack and how the code behaves during disasters, it ultimately benefits the end customers as well since the application they use will be more reliable and sustain the unexpected scenarios quite well.

## Demonstrate commitment

Develop a **proof of concept** (**PoC**) that works end-to-end and demonstrates the benefits of using it. This shows that you are committed to the idea and will not leave it unfinished. Furthermore, by doing this, you either reduce or completely remove the potential risk of something resulting in a wasted effort for the stakeholder. It makes it a lot easier to get buy-in and experience the idea in a working form.

## Find collaborators and share good practices

Once the initial PoC has been validated, you might want to look for additional collaborators within and outside your team and share the benefits of adopting the tool, or automation, with a larger group. In addition to getting feedback on the current state of implementation, this also helps you gather ideas and problems from other team members. Demonstrating these PoCs in CoP sessions, for example, could be a good way to take things forward.

## Summary

We started this chapter by highlighting the importance of integrating both people and technology in the DevOps realm for successful initiatives. While people drive the cultural and collaborative aspects of DevOps, technology provides the necessary tools and infrastructure. The most important takeaway should be to focus on establishing the right foundations of team culture and the working model before adopting technology.

We then moved on to discussing some team working models that provide the right balance of ownership, ease of management, and autonomy. Even if they do not fit as-is into your organization, they can act as a target model that you would eventually want to transition into. By doing this, you will already start reaping the benefits they provide. Next, we discussed technical best practices that can help your teams adopt the AWS services in the best way possible. Making technology decisions while considering business needs, building the right abstractions, and developing reusable workflows can help everyone on your team perform better.

Of course, doing all of this can sometimes lead to role transitions within the company. To make this transition as smooth as possible, we discussed some strategies for continuous learning and development, and how to drive change from the bottom up – a common challenge that individual contributors face. In the next chapter, *Ensuring a Strong AWS Foundation for Multi-Account and Multi-Region Environments*, we will look at best practices for operating multi-account environments in AWS. Additionally, we will look into some AWS services and open source solutions that can help orchestrate such an environment as code.

## Further reading

To learn more about the topics that were covered in this chapter, take a look at the following resources:

- Hands-on AWS tutorials for team enablement: `https://aws.amazon.com/getting-started/hands-on/`

- Accelerating cloud adoption by creating a cloud enablement engine: `https://aws.amazon.com/blogs/training-and-certification/accelerate-cloud-adoption-by-creating-a-cloud-enablement-engine/`

# 11
# Ensuring a Strong AWS Foundation for Multi-Account and Multi-Region Environments

An AWS account is a *logical container* for the AWS resources that you create. It provides a structure that can be used to easily manage the access, billing, and isolation needs of a group of related resources.

All organizations start their AWS journey by creating an account and hosting some **proof of concept** (**PoC**) workloads on it. As they gain more experience and know-how, their confidence and comfort with cloud services increases. At a certain point, the organizations might decide on migrating their on-premises production workloads to the cloud. Or, even better, they might directly start developing cloud-native applications by leveraging AWS services for maximized innovation.

There is often a pivoting point where they must decide if all their workloads should be hosted in one or multiple AWS accounts. Key drivers behind these discussions are the problems associated with a single account. These problems surface when the AWS platform's usage outgrows its initial intent of hosting PoC workloads and transitions into a full-grown environment that now requires enterprise-grade security, governance controls, cost management, granular access policies, and so on.

However, the nature of these problems could vary across different organizations operating at different scales. Some might find it difficult to manage granular security policies for multiple users in a single account, while others might struggle with boundary enforcement between development and production workloads, for example. In addition to the application challenges, there are also service limits and quotas that are set by the cloud provider, which could limit the usage of a single AWS account beyond certain thresholds. Whatever the reason for the initial conversations, all organizations face these challenges once their AWS usage matures and will have to adopt a multi-account strategy.

Enabling software developers to seamlessly onboard their workloads into a dedicated AWS account, while *automatically* providing a minimum-security baseline, network connectivity, and operations, are some of the key responsibilities of the *platform team*, who manages the entire cloud landscape for the organization. These teams play a significant role in providing a solid multi-account, multi-region cloud foundation – also known as the **Landing Zone**. Why do we even need a strategy for this, you may ask? Think of a scenario where multiple AWS accounts must be created to address all the problems we discussed previously. Individually managing a handful of accounts is not a problem, but as soon as the count increases to 10s and 100s – which is typical for a mid-sized enterprise – you immediately face scaling problems. Furthermore, how do you ensure workload compliance within all accounts? How can global resources be provisioned (as code) in every account in one go? Is there a way for the CISO team to easily validate the security posture of the entire AWS landscape? How does the platform team provide telemetry capabilities across the entire AWS landscape? How can workloads communicate over the network with each other, and on-premises data centers? How can you enforce an organization-wide policy that blocks the usage of certain AWS regions and high-cost GPU instances?

These are a few examples of the challenges that platform teams typically face, and how to solve them is going to be the theme of this chapter. We will look at the capabilities that AWS offers to simplify the management of these multi-account environments via some services and ready-made solutions. Also, the Landing Zone is also *managed as code*, just like any other software application. So, all DevOps and DevSecOps principles that we have discussed previously, such as IaC, continuous testing, and shifting left with regard to security, are equally applicable to this concept as well.

As a DevOps practitioner, whenever you notice organizational complexities associated with the usage of a single, or very few, AWS accounts, it might be the right time to brainstorm and promote the idea of a well-defined, automation-driven, multi-account environment – a Landing Zone. These complexities, if left unaddressed, will directly impact the agility of the software teams in seamlessly adopting the AWS offerings. Furthermore, it is important to highlight that these concepts are not limited to big enterprise companies but are equally relevant for others that are taking the first steps toward solidifying their AWS accounts posture for increased agility, governance, and control in the cloud.

We will cover the following topics in the sections that follow:

- What is a Landing Zone?
- Key considerations in a Landing Zone
- Best practices for operating multi-account architectures
- Orchestrating multi-account deployments with Control Tower and CfCT

## What is a Landing Zone?

A Landing Zone is the concept of a pre-defined multi-account environment that allows you to securely onboard application workloads onto the cloud in an *automated* way. A good multi-account foundation reduces the cognitive load of different teams and allows the developers to move faster. It either blocks any misconfigurations by default or recovers from an issue without much effort. These foundations typically unlock two main use cases – migrating workloads from on-premises environments or net new development in the cloud. Therefore, the main goals here are as follows:

- Secure and compliant
- Scalable and resilient
- Flexible to future change

A good KPI to measure a Landing Zone's maturity is – how long it takes to create a new AWS account and make it ready for hosting production workloads. There's a lot that goes on in between, starting with account requests, approvals, provisioning, and actual usage, highlighting various challenges ranging from humans to technology and automation.

The term **Landing Zone** is often used, or misused, in different contexts, which can be confusing for users. Let's go through four common patterns I've observed over the last few years:

- **Landing Zone as a concept**: This is the idea of a multi-account cloud foundation, as well as the tangible outcome that gets deployed in your AWS environment. It helps the organizations reap benefits from the cost segregation, security and access management, and reduced blast radius offered by AWS account boundaries. It promotes the idea of managing all infrastructure automation with code that is repeatable, easy to test, and automate.

    Throughout the chapter, we will be using the term landing zone for both the concept and the tangible foundational structure that represents this concept.

- **Landing Zone as a solution**: A solution is a pre-baked, ready-to-deploy implementation that fulfills a particular need – in this case, a multi-account architecture – by leveraging a variety of AWS services. A few years back, AWS offered a publicly available gigantic CloudFormation template known as **AWS Landing Zone (ALZ)** that could be used by customers to deploy multiple services, accounts, and policies into their AWS organization. It gave them a solid enterprise-grade foundation to begin their AWS journey. It is no longer supported and deprecated in favor of a managed service called **AWS Control Tower**, which we will cover in more detail later in this chapter. Some examples of other solutions that are offered by AWS are **Customizations for Control Tower (CfCT)** and **Account Factory for Terraform (AFT)**.

- **Landing Zone as an AWS service**: Solutions such as ALZ required a lot of customization to adapt to the unique needs of an organization. As it was completely managed with a CloudFormation template, it was not easy to maintain and operate, not to forget the missing AWS support that you would generally get with AWS services. To fill these gaps, and reduce the complexities involved with the use of ALZ, AWS launched a service – AWS Control Tower – that was based on the field experiences gathered from multiple enterprise customers and how they used the ALZ solution to architect a solid foundation that applications could be hosted on. Control Tower offers automation to create new accounts, baseline them with basic security resources, enforce governance controls, and much more. A lot of times, when using the term Landing

Zone, the users tend to refer to services such as Control Tower instead. Landing Zone is a broader concept that the service *implements* (to some extent).

- **Landing Zone as a reference to deployment orchestration frameworks**: At its core, Landing Zone is a multi-account concept. Applying this concept to your AWS Organizations organization in practice requires deploying resources in multiple AWS accounts. Some organizations end up developing home-grown solutions using CloudFormation, CDK, or Terraform. Some orchestration frameworks are available as open source code on GitHub. Users might start referring to these as Landing Zones, but they are nothing more than deployment frameworks that can be leveraged to roll out resources in multiple accounts. They have their relevance, even when not used in the context of a Landing Zone.

Two commonly used open source frameworks are **AWS Deployment Framework (ADF)** and **Service Catalog Tools**.

*Figure 11.1* highlights all the different entities and their relationship with the Landing Zone concept:

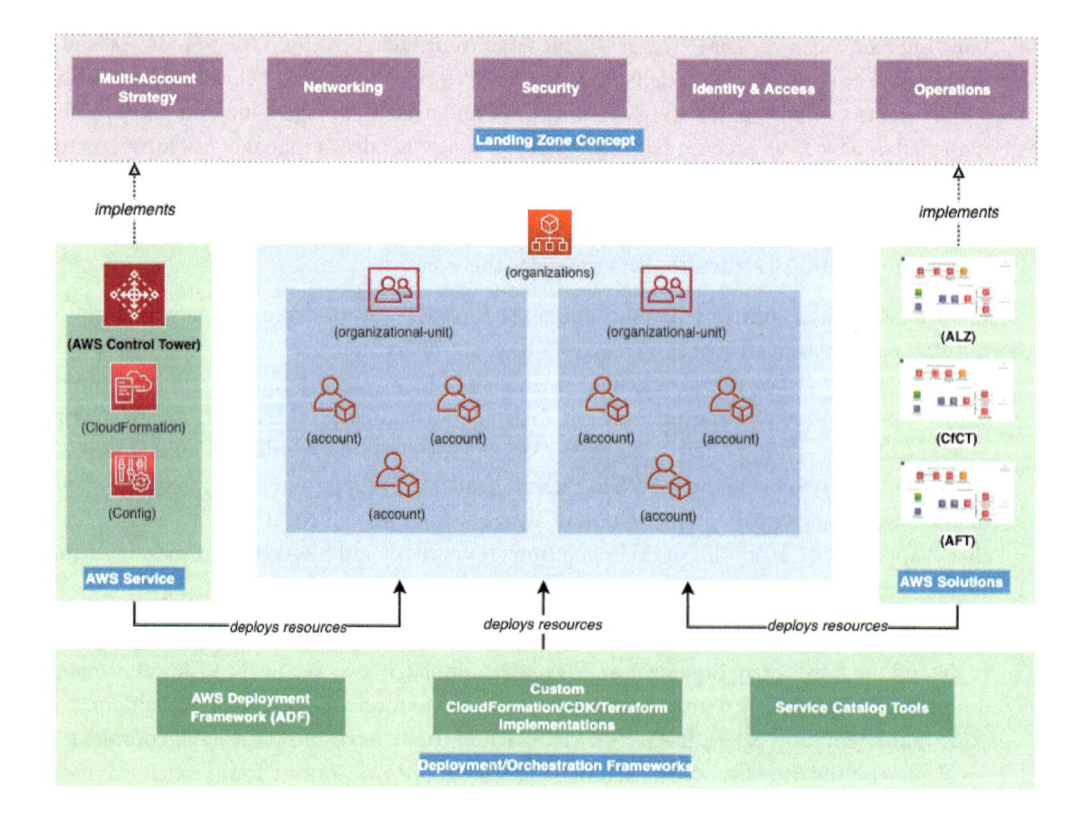

Figure 11.1 – Relationship between different entities and the Landing Zone concept

> **Note**
> Even though some frameworks such as ADF have "AWS" in their name, they are not officially supported by the cloud provider as part of the enterprise support plans. This can be one of the criteria that companies might want to consider, or at least be aware of. On the other hand, the two solutions – AFT and CfCT – do come with official AWS support, just like other services. These solutions are maintained by the Control Tower service team.

We could dedicate an entire book to the development of a Landing Zone. An important callout is that this is an *evolving* thing. The ever-changing requirements of the organization will dictate new criteria and goals that have to be met by the Landing Zone design. To achieve this, services, solutions, and deployment frameworks will have to adapt. How you use these services and solutions is going to be largely driven by the unique needs and implementations within your organization. This is a reason why you will never come across an end-to-end implementation that can be adopted as-is. The services and solutions will always focus on the *lowest common denominator* that applies to the majority of enterprise use cases. Almost always, there is a customization layer that comes on top, to make it a complete solution that addresses your needs.

Therefore, the main priorities of this chapter are to introduce you to the key considerations of a Landing Zone, relevant AWS services, solutions, and frameworks. This will help you identify the areas that you should look into, as well as introduce you to deployment orchestration frameworks, for rolling out resources across multiple AWS accounts and regions. Equipped with this knowledge, you can come up with custom implementations or designs that work for you.

# Key considerations in a Landing Zone

Creating a Landing Zone concept from scratch that will cater to all current and future organizational needs can be intimidating. Five areas are essential for all organizations, big or small, to build an AWS foundation that scales. We will discuss them in this section, starting with the multi-account structure.

## Defining a structure for organizational units and accounts

At the core of your Landing Zone design is an account structure that enables an organization to move fast, enforce granular controls, establish isolation boundaries, and reduce blast radius, while remaining flexible to future changes. So far in this chapter, we have discussed quite a few areas that benefit from a multi-account structure. All of this aligns well with the **AWS Organizations** service offerings, which help you manage your entire AWS landscape under the same umbrella. It gives you organizational controls that are otherwise difficult to establish, and maintain, across many discrete AWS accounts that act as independent entities. So, enabling AWS Organizations is essential if you don't leverage it already. Available at no charge, it gives you immediate benefits around consolidated billing, service integrations, policies to centralize service usage control, and grouping your accounts for budgetary and compliance needs. Let's discuss them in more detail and highlight some best practices as we progress.

## Grouping accounts for compliance and regulatory needs

**Organizational units (OUs)** are an AWS Organizations feature that allows you to amalgamate multiple AWS accounts into one logical entity. It's a soft structure that can be used to group certain accounts that exhibit the need for similar governance and control. For example, there might be a subset of enterprise applications that are regulated by the **Health Insurance Portability and Accountability Act (HIPAA)**, and as a result, might not allow usage of certain AWS services. It's easy to group these accounts, form an OU, and enforce policies at the OU level, which are then inherited by all accounts. Furthermore, any other AWS account that gets placed in this OU, even in the future, automatically follows the same rules, thereby ensuring continuous compliance. As another example, some companies might want to group all their dev workload accounts together so that they can apply certain policies that block the usage of high-cost compute. Keeping custom requirements aside for a moment, certain OUs apply to the majority of organizations, as covered here:

- **Shared services OU**: This OU contains the platform services' accounts that would be consumed by all other AWS accounts, basically a shared resource. It is common to host systems such as **Active Directory**, network appliances, or proxy services in this OU (in dedicated accounts) that can only be accessed by authorized personnel.

- **Security OU**: This is where you group your **Audit** and **LogArchive** accounts, which external auditors and in-house security teams will have access to. All platform logs coming from **CloudTrail** and **Config** should be pushed into the central LogArchive account, as a best practice, so that they can be independently analyzed by **Security Information and Event Management (SIEM)** systems for threat detection purposes.

- **Automation OU**: A while ago, we slightly touched upon the need for deployment frameworks that make the Landing Zone concept a reality. It's a good practice to host an independent Automation account in this OU, which contains the frameworks responsible for rolling out resources across all other accounts, in an automated fashion. Since this account has privileged access to almost every other account in the organization, access is generally limited to the tools that manage the entire AWS landscape. Human access, if any, should be actively monitored.

- **Maintenance OU**: Once the security and regulatory policies have been applied to an OU, it's difficult to sometimes carry out maintenance procedures on the accounts contained therein. Therefore, it's recommended to create a maintenance OU that temporarily hosts all the AWS accounts that need to be prepared for a specific need or operated upon. A common use case is to enable AWS opt-in regions by placing the AWS account in this OU. Normally, this would be a restricted action across all OUs and accounts as users could enable regions that might break the compliance posture of the company. Once the regions are enabled, accounts are placed back into their original OU. Think of this OU as a *pit stop*, used in racing competitions for minor servicing and refueling.

  As a security measure, it's also important to revoke permissions from all other AWS users that allow them to manually move any account into this OU, as that would immediately lift all the restrictions by which the accounts were otherwise blocked.

- **Suspended OU**: All suspended AWS accounts remain in the same state for 90 days, as a cool-off period, before they are removed. As a security measure, this OU restricts all actions in these accounts to prevent any additional billing or unauthorized usage.

- **Development OU**: Striking the right balance between security controls and agility is key to innovation. Organizations often enforce a standard set of policies and controls across all AWS accounts, which holds back developers from testing new ideas and innovating in the cloud. As AWS puts it, a good Landing Zone design follows the *Guardrails, but not blockers* principle. Therefore, it is important to create a dedicated OU where individual developers or team accounts can be hosted acting as the innovation space. You can still apply certain budgetary constraints on these OUs and block IAM actions that could hinder the security posture of the organization.

Having covered the most important OUs in any Landing Zone, let's see what an OU setup would look like for a huge organization that has dedicated teams specializing in different areas of the technology stack, and application workloads that need to adhere to regulated standards such as HIPAA.

## Sample OU design for a regulated organization

Large enterprises typically have dedicated teams handling security, network operations, audit, software development, and so on. These teams are often grouped by cost centers, require customized access controls, and are governed by security controls and governance policies. Software development teams, on the other hand, are grouped by business domains or value streams and have several environments, such as development, staging, and production, where they host their application workloads. The boundaries provided by an AWS account in terms of billing, access, and isolation needs map well to such scenarios. OUs can provide a logical structure that these accounts can be further grouped under, for access control and policy enforcement. A sample OU structure is given in *Figure 11.2*:

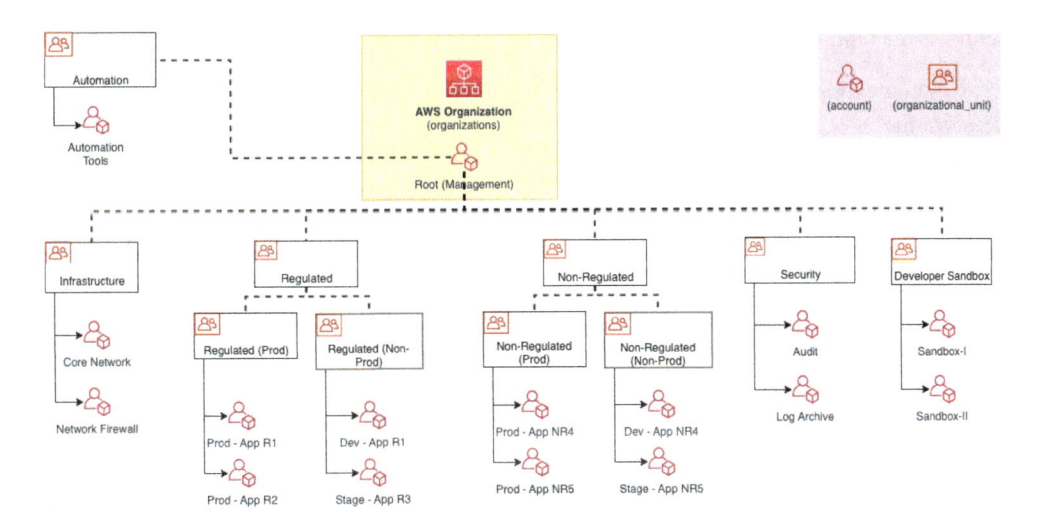

Figure 11.2 – Sample OU hierarchy for an organization hosting regulated workloads

Grouping the AWS accounts under specific OUs simplifies the definition, and mapping of policies. Let's discuss this in the following section.

### Enforcing policies to control service usage and tag assignments

Three types of policies are supported by AWS Organizations – **Service Control Policies** (**SCPs**), **Tagging Policies**, and **Backup Policies**.

SCPs can restrict certain IAM actions to all OUs, or accounts they are mapped to. It is important to not overuse them as there are restrictions around policy size (5,120 bytes) and the total number of policies that can be directly applied to an AWS account or OU (currently 5). Think of them as *global controls* that deny all actions that you do not want your users to perform. For example, denying all other AWS regions except the ones you want to operate in is a common SCP control. Another could be denying the configurations to make an S3 bucket public or restricting certain EC2 instance types that can have cost repercussions or be misused in a certain way. AWS IAM inherently denies all actions that are not explicitly added to a policy, but SCPs are a type of global administrative mechanism that takes the highest precedence, even in scenarios where a certain IAM action has been mistakenly allowed on a user or resource.

Tagging policies, in combination with SCPs, are used to enforce the existence of certain tag keys and the corresponding values. Almost all AWS resources support tags, which are key-value pairs that are used to provide additional context to a particular resource. This is particularly useful for tracking down the owners and application teams for support, operations, or cost analysis needs. A common mistake that organizations make is investing too much time and effort in coming up with a tagging strategy that will fulfill all their future needs. It's highly recommended to start backward – that is, identify the problem that you want to solve with tags and then arrive at a tagging policy that helps you enforce it. For example, if an organization is struggling with identifying the resource owners in the aggregated cost and usage reports, it might help to enforce the tag keys that map teams and individuals.

Backup policies are used to automatically apply backup plans to supported resources, across all your AWS accounts.

### Leverage service integrations with AWS Organizations

AWS services such as **AWS Security Hub**, **AWS CloudFormation**, and **AWS Config**, among many others, can leverage an AWS Organizations feature known as **Trusted Access** to piggyback on organization service capabilities and automatically manage multiple accounts throughout the organization. This greatly simplifies administrating certain tasks such as enabling compliance recording of all AWS resources in an account as soon as it is created, for example. Similarly, Security Hub can auto-enroll any new account in the organization and start scanning it for security risks. To find a list of all AWS services that integrate with AWS Organizations, you can refer to this page: `https://docs.aws.amazon.com/organizations/latest/userguide/orgs_integrate_services_list.html`.

## Focus on cross-account and hybrid networking needs

Whether you are planning to use AWS to migrate on-premises workloads or develop new applications in the cloud, network connectivity is going to be a fundamental requirement. Applications will need to communicate with shared services hosted in another account and talk to other counterparts on-premises. From a security and compliance standpoint, you might want to implement packet-level inspection for internet ingress and egress or cross-account communication. The network flow can be customized to a great extent to address organization-specific needs. AWS offerings in the networking space have increased exponentially over the past years, but that does not mean you need to adopt and use the fanciest of services from the very beginning. A Landing Zone evolves over time and this applies equally well to networking needs.

As an example, I have often observed teams leveraging **AWS Transit Gateway** from the very beginning. If you are just managing a handful of accounts, the majority of the use cases can be simply solved by sharing subnets across multiple accounts and implementing VPC peering connections, even for cross-region data transfer needs. You should be conscious of the design tradeoffs and cost, or complexity implications, that can come up with a premature adoption of such services. Furthermore, a mesh network is oftentimes not needed, so it's invaluable to start by understanding the different network flows that the platform needs to support and build an architecture that does what's necessary in a cost-optimized and secure manner.

The same goes for on-premises connectivity, where high bandwidth, low latency **Direct Connect** connections might not be needed unless there are concrete requirements from the applications depending on it. Grouping multiple site-to-site VPN connections over a single Transit Gateway can often solve the bandwidth and high availability requirements for a hybrid setup.

However, there are scenarios where enterprises do need a more complex setup to support the compliance, packet inspection, or needs of performance-sensitive applications. In these cases, several networking constructs, such as ingress VPCs, egress VPCs, and centralized packet inspection architectures, can support the needs of any new AWS account that gets onboarded onto the Landing Zone. Diving deeper into the architectural details is beyond the scope of this chapter, but if you're interested in learning more, I recommend the following blog: https://aws.amazon.com/blogs/networking-and-content-delivery/tag/hybrid-connectivity/.

## Securing the Landing Zone with IAM and security services

The Landing Zone's design needs to consider who would access the AWS accounts, and what kind of permissions they will have. The principle of least privilege helps as a guide for defining the bare minimum permissions the developers or the tools need to perform some activity in the AWS accounts.

Auditing all activities with AWS CloudTrail, which is the security auditing and troubleshooting service, allows the platform owners or security professionals to alert and investigate any unexpected usage across all AWS accounts. We discussed the service integrations with AWS Organizations, and this is something that CloudTrail can also benefit from. As a best practice, enabling an organization wide trail allows centralized aggregation of audit data in an S3 bucket that sits in the LogArchive account. This automatically injects trail configurations into the new accounts as and when they are created, or an existing account joins the organization. As part of enterprise security measures, you should enforce an SCP that blocks any IAM action that could result in tampering with the data contained in this S3 bucket, or modification of any encryption keys used by the CloudTrail service.

Secondly, for user access needs, I would highly recommend using **AWS IAM Identity Center**, which allows you to create and connect all workforce users centrally and manage their access across all other AWS accounts. With Identity Center, you can leverage existing **identity providers** (**IdPs**) such as Azure Active Directory to federate users into the AWS accounts.

> **Note**
> The IAM Identity Center control plane is only available in the AWS region where the service is instantiated. It's good practice to prepare for scenarios where the same region is impacted by a disaster. Identity Center not being available could mean that all your users' access to AWS accounts would be locked out. To mitigate this, it's recommended to have a set of *break-glass* IAM users that can be used in exceptional circumstances for emergency access. These credentials should be safeguarded with MFA; the access key ID and secret access key should remain with different people to avoid misuse. Of course, all the activities should be audited and credentials rotated at regular intervals.

Third, it's difficult to ensure awareness and preventive measures of all possible security incidents that can happen in the AWS accounts. **Amazon GuardDuty** is a low-hanging fruit that leverages machine learning to identify unusual network traffic, DNS logs, CloudTrail events, and potential scenarios of privilege escalation. It can also alert about unusual EC2 behaviors that are representative of malware and Bitcoin mining. By leveraging integration with AWS Organizations, GuardDuty can automatically scan all your AWS accounts across the organization and feed the findings into AWS Security Hub, which is an aggregator of security checks from multiple other services.

## DevOps and config management

Your Landing Zone implementation is going to be managed as code, just like any other software application. It's highly recommended to start this off with well-defined practices such as IaC, CI, and automated code validations. Any CloudFormation templates you author should pass the security check gates and policies that define what you can and cannot do in your AWS landscape.

Most of the AWS solutions trigger off of a source code repository, often managed in **AWS CodeCommit**. We will see what this looks like in practice when we cover the **CfCT** solution later in this chapter.

As the deployments tools have permission to deploy resources into almost any other account in your organization, it's invaluable to enforce the right access controls on these pipelines so that they are not misused in any way. Access to the accounts that host the deployment tools and frameworks should be highly restricted as well. If you'd like to use other CI/CD systems, such as **GitLab**, you might be interested in looking at **Open ID Connect** (**OIDC**) integrations with AWS IAM, which removes the need for provisioning any temporary IAM users, or credentials, for use in your CI/CD pipelines.

## Operations

Your Landing Zone strategy needs to factor in requirements such as the observability of your platform and applications, infrastructure monitoring, application monitoring, incident management, change management, and so on.

Notifications, alerting, and reporting should integrate with existing paging tools. This should allow the on-call operation teams to support the landing zone, or any outage, with the same priority they would give to a productive application that no longer works. AWS offers additional services such as **Personal Health Dashboards** (**PHD**) and **Service Limits** alerting, which are quintessential to surface any ongoing issues with the services in a particular region, as well as the planned maintenance activities of your resources.

Having covered the key considerations of a good Landing Zone concept, let's dive into some best practices that will set you up for success.

## Best practices for managing multi-account architectures

The best practices that follow touch upon a lot of areas that we covered in the previous section. Based on my experience developing Landing Zones for multiple enterprise customers, I would like to share some insights into the best practices that you could consider adopting for your organization.

### Limiting access to the management account

The AWS account where you bootstrap the AWS Organizations organization is known as the **management account**, or the master payer. This is a highly privileged account that gives access to policy management, centralized billing and cost reports, and account management. It should only be accessed by selected personnel, under exceptional circumstances.

SCPs do not apply to the management account, which makes it difficult to enforce any policies or governance control at this level. Secondly, by default, AWS Organizations injects an IAM role into all AWS accounts in the organization, with AdministratorAccess privileges, and a trust policy that allows the management account unrestricted access. This implies that anyone who has access to the management account can assume this role and gain escalated privileges into any other account in the organization unless some additional measures have been taken to not allow this. Furthermore, since all policies are managed and enforced from the management account, you can lift all restrictions and expose the entire organization to security risks.

As part of the Landing Zone automation process, certain use cases cannot be avoided where tools need access to the management account to carry out some operations that can only be executed from within the management account. For example, enabling an opt-in region, or moving an account to a different OU, can only be performed from within the management account. A good security practice is to create fine-grained IAM roles in the management account that give permissions to the Landing Zone automation tools to only execute the IAM actions that are permitted.

AWS Organizations also has an interesting feature known as **Delegated Admin**, support for which is now being expanded to many AWS services. This allows the *delegation* of the administrative capabilities of a specific service to another account in the organization. Delegated Admin further limits the need to log into the management account and allows the service owners to administer a certain service from the delegated account itself.

## Adopting solutions that offer the right balance of ease and control

It's worth repeating – no AWS solution, service, or framework is going to fulfill all your Landing Zone needs as-is. Every customer is different, and every use case requires in-depth analysis, leading to custom implementations. The good part of all the services and frameworks is that they might be limited in what they do, but they do it well. So, it will always help to think of them as complementing technologies that can be wired together to build up your Landing Zone. To take a concrete example, the AWS Control Tower service will help you build the initial 30-40% of what every company needs in less than an hour. You then need to focus on coupling this service with another framework that helps you build the remaining 60-70%.

Ideally, the only code that you should be developing yourself is an orchestrator across all these services and frameworks while leveraging the best of what they can offer.

On the other side of the spectrum, some organizations are heavily invested in technologies such as **CloudFormation** and **Terraform**. Depending on their expertise and comfort level, they might also decide on building the entire Landing Zone from scratch, which is also fine, so long as they are clear on the tradeoffs between maintaining those frameworks on their own and more control that they will benefit from in the long run.

## Invest in building an Account Vending Machine

When it comes to managing the Landing Zone as code, most organizations focus on building the IaC layer, which directly interacts with the cloud provider APIs and deploys resources into the AWS accounts. They miss two key things as part of the overall foundation they are building:

- First is the over-arching layer that integrates this framework with existing tools and processes within the company
- Secondly, overlooking the fact that there is a life cycle associated with the entire IaC layer, it's never a one-step thing

Even before IaC deploys something into the account, certain prerequisites must be met. After the accounts are provisioned, you might need some post-installation procedures to be carried out, which might deal with notifications, ticket closures, or anything else. This is where the concept of an **Account Vending Machine** (**AVM**) comes in. It takes care of these two requirements and acts as a glue between the organization processes, actual IaC itself, and the stages in the life cycle of AWS account management. Its core responsibility is to *vend accounts* as if they are coming out of a factory and immediately ready to host production-grade workloads. Let's see an example.

Enterprises typically have ticketing processes or some other mechanisms using which AWS accounts are requested and approved. Some examples are **ServiceNow**, **Jira**, or a home-grown custom solution. Once the requests are in, you will want an event-driven invocation of the AVM, which you can do by passing a payload that reflects the input from the ticketing system. The AVM then manages the life cycle of the account creation process, starting with ensuring that prerequisites are in place, deploying resources via the IaC stack, and finally carrying out post-deployment procedures.

## Maintain a separate AWS Organizations organization for platform development

Similar to software development life cycles, it's important to test new Landing Zone features and changes in an isolated environment first, and then roll them out in the production AWS organization. Small changes such as SCP modifications, network route configurations, and security policy upgrades can have a big impact with multiple accounts being affected all at once. Misconfiguring CloudTrail S3 buckets, for example, can result in log and audit data not being aggregated as expected, resulting in the loss of valuable information.

Developing the overall platform in the same AWS organization that hosts production workloads increases the blast radius by a great deal. AWS accounts are free resources, so there isn't a huge cost impact for replicating a similar structure to what you have in production. To further limit any additional spending in the development environment, it's a good practice to set up billing alerts and remove all the resources across the entire organization using IaC automation when not needed, after office hours or during weekends. It's a common practice to empty all the accounts using tools such as **aws-nuke** (https://github.com/rebuy-de/aws-nuke). This validates the functionality and repeatability of the IaC framework so that it can spin up the entire platform from scratch, should the need arise, such as in the event of a disaster.

## Avoid provisioning any IAM users

The single most frequent source of credential leaks is AWS IAM access keys, which can be accidentally committed into source code or left in an EC2 instance that is no longer used. You should always aim to leverage IAM roles for any access requirements in the AWS Landing Zone. It's a security best practice to deny the creation of IAM users in all AWS accounts in your Landing Zone. Technically, all AWS identities, be it users, services, or resources themselves, can assume an IAM role and *request temporary credentials* at the time of use, from the IAM control plane. EC2 instances have the concept of an instance profile, and services such as Lambda and RDS use service roles, which gives them access to the allowed resources.

The majority of enterprises already have some form of IdP solution in use in the organization. AWS IAM supports out-of-the-box integration with such providers through **OIDC** or **Security Assertion Markup Language (SAML)**, which removes the need to provision and manage any users throughout the organization. IAM federation further prevents credential sprawl and any employees that are offboarded from the authoritative identity source, such as Active Directory, automatically lose access to all AWS accounts, which is a good security win.

### Prefer no-code or low-code solutions

A lot of integrations that previously had to be built out manually are now natively supported by many AWS services. While this greatly improves the development velocity, it also leads to less maintenance of code and an increase in efficiency. Landing Zone implementations heavily depend on services such as **AWS Step Functions**, **AWS Organizations**, **Lambda**, and **IAM**, to name a few. In recent times, AWS Step Functions, a workflow management service, has launched native integrations with AWS Organizations, Lambda, and many other services. So, an action such as moving an account to a different OU, which previously required a Lambda function to assume a role in the management account, can now directly be executed by AWS Step Functions, without you having to write any code.

Sending out platform notifications is another example where the developers had to leverage a combination of services such as Lambda, events, SNS, or SES. With **AWS User Notifications**, you can leverage automatic notifications for selected **EventBridge** events, and the entire responsibility of event capturing, payload parsing, and notification triggers are offloaded to the service. It sends out notifications on multiple channels, such as **Microsoft Teams**, **Slack**, and **Email**.

Having discussed a few best practices when building out your Landing Zone foundations, let's discuss what this looks like in practice when combining a service such as AWS Control Tower with CfCT, an AWS-offered solution for deploying resources across multiple accounts.

## Building a Landing Zone with Control Tower and CfCT

AWS Control Tower gives users a jumpstart in establishing their Landing Zone foundations, in contrast to building everything from scratch. Starting from a basic OU structure to host the security and workload accounts, it offers an *account factory* – an abstraction on top of **Service Catalog** that is used to create new accounts and provision resources in them. From a logging and security standpoint, it automatically rolls out organizational trails with AWS CloudTrail and also aggregates the compliance status by leveraging AWS Config's features. At its core, it *orchestrates* account-related activities across several other AWS services to realize the benefits of a multi-account structure. Furthermore, it defines a security and compliance baseline that is composed of AWS Config rules, IAM policies, and SCPs. These sane defaults block actions such as making an S3 bucket public, disabling CloudTrail logs, or switching off Config recorder logs, thereby ensuring a good security posture out of the box.

For enterprises that are just getting started with building their AWS foundations, AWS Control Tower does a lot of heavy lifting for them and reduces the implementation effort and time. Others, who are more hands-on and well-versed with the AWS technology stack, might still decide to go ahead and build a customized version of the Landing Zone as it gives them more control and choice of tooling. This is because, as a service, Control Tower on its own doesn't do much. It's based on the best practices that most customers follow when establishing a cloud structure that can be safely used to launch applications with the least resistance and delays. For account management, it depends on AWS Organizations, for policies, it depends on SCPs, and for compliance, it depends on AWS Config; deploying resources in target accounts is entirely offloaded to CloudFormation. To benefit from the readymade prescriptive foundation that it offers, it is still a good idea to use it for that and fill the gaps with another deployment solution or framework that complements it.

At the time of writing this book, there are also some areas where the service doesn't shine as much. Due to its lack of API support, I would suggest exercising caution before building any hard dependencies on the service for features that require frequent invocations. Carrying out actions over the web console simply does not scale, and you need to give someone access to the management account (the service can only be deployed there), which is not desirable. It's important to highlight that the service operations are single-threaded, which means they can only work on one thing at a time. This limit does not exist for some features, such as account requests, where you can go up to a maximum of five, but these limitations can be a blocker for some organizations that are going to provision and manage accounts at scale.

Therefore, my advice for companies who are just getting started with their AWS foundation would be to leverage the service for what it offers, and let it play its role in the bigger Landing Zone arena. You will need a complementing solution or framework to implement other functionalities that are not bundled as part of the service. For companies that have an existing Landing Zone, or framework that works with IaC, I see less value in switching over to Control Tower. The latter is more specific to companies that are comfortable getting hands-on and maintaining such solutions at scale on their own. Due to the variety of implementation options here, it's out of this chapter's scope to cover all possible implementation scenarios. In the following sections, we will focus more on using Control Tower alongside another framework of your choice to build an end-to-end Landing Zone platform.

Before we get to the topic of integrating a deployment solution or framework, let's ensure we have a good understanding of the Control Tower service by looking at a diagram:

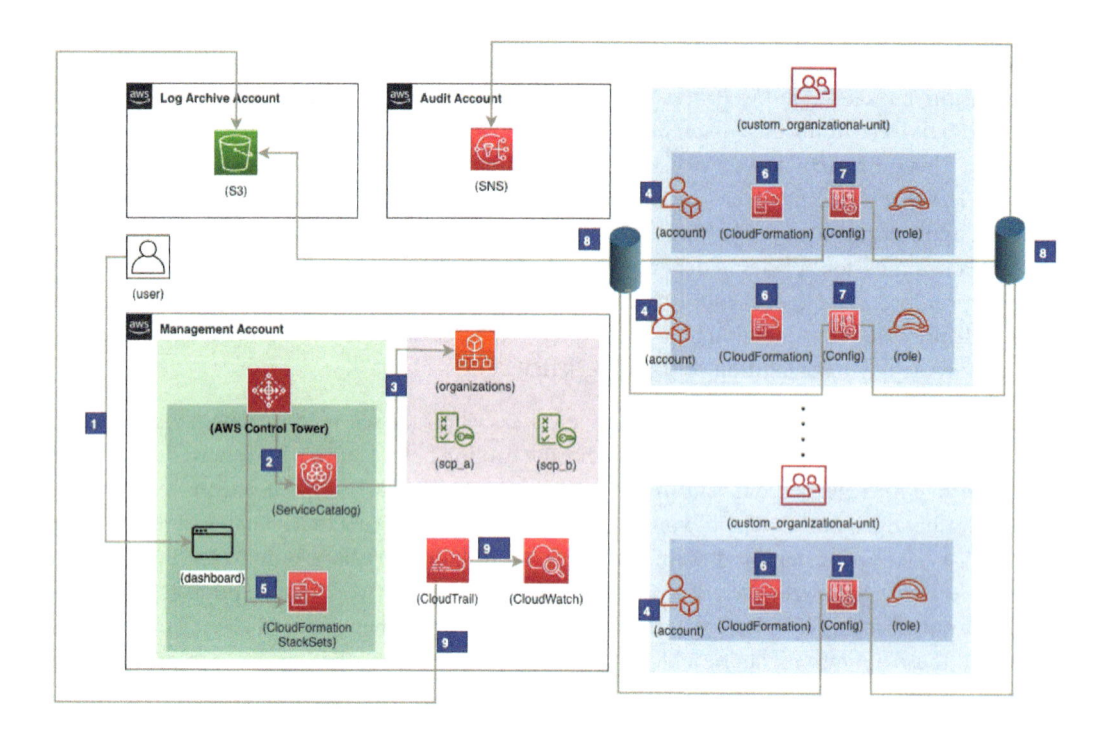

Figure 11.3 – Orchestration of different AWS services by AWS Control Tower

This diagram is not an extensive representation of every single function that AWS Control Tower takes care of under the hood. Rather, it aims to highlight the different steps involved in an account creation workflow, followed by deploying resources into it. Let's take a look at this diagram in more detail:

1. The platform developer uses the AWS Control Tower console UI to register a new account creation request, as well as the target OU the account should be part of.

2. AWS Control Tower passes on the request to Account Factory (a Service Catalog product), which initiates the account provisioning workflow.

3. Under the hood, the request results in the AWS Organizations API being invoked to create a new account.

4. An AWS account gets created and placed in the target OU, which defines what kind of policy controls and governance will apply to the workloads hosted in this account.

5. **AWS CloudFormation StackSets**, a service feature that automatically deploys stacks into an account-region combination, already has some reusable templates defined by the AWS Control Tower service. A new stack instance for the StackSet definition is created by AWS Control Tower, which initiates the provisioning of an AWS CloudFormation template in the target account, in

the respective region. As an example, if you are governing three regions in the target account, you get three stack instances.

6. AWS CloudFormation stack provisioning starts inside the target account, in a particular AWS region, and deploys resources such as the AWS Config recorder, IAM roles, and other things that are needed to manage this account in a compliant manner.

7. AWS Config sets up a *recorder* that monitors changes to all resources in the accounts and sets up a delivery channel

8. The configuration recorder is a mechanism that registers any resource configuration changes and sends the data to a centralized S3 bucket for auditing needs; notifications are sent to an SNS topic in parallel. The SNS notifications are aggregated per region and can be used for advanced analysis and automated alerts by the security teams when unexpected resource changes happen.

9. When you first install AWS Control Tower, it creates an organization-wide AWS CloudTrail trail that automatically picks up new accounts in the organization and aggregates trail data into the central S3 bucket in the LogArchive account. It also pushes logs to the CloudWatch log group in the management account. This provides audit and investigation possibilities to a central security team without the need to access all the accounts in the Landing Zone.

All of these features are available out of the box with Control Tower, which takes roughly 1 hour to install. As you might have noticed, there is no application or organization-specific deployment need that the service covers. So far, it's a prescriptive setup of good practices that will be rolled out as soon as an account is created. To roll out other AWS services and resources, you would need a deployment solution or framework that fills the gaps needed to get to a complete Landing Zone platform.

Next, let's have a look at CfCT. This is an AWS-supported solution that integrates with the AWS Control Tower service to roll out custom resources defined by AWS CloudFormation templates. Say you require a particular IAM role for your security scanning third-party platform that should be automatically deployed in all AWS accounts as soon as they are provisioned. CfCT can help with this. Alternatively, you might want to deploy certain Config rules into all AWS accounts contained in the production OU, but not others.

## Deploying resources with CfCT

CfCT is a deployment framework that integrates with your Control Tower service deployment. It needs to be installed in the management account, in the same region where Control Tower was initially set up. It hooks onto the service events and runs a workflow that provisions SCP policies or AWS CloudFormation resources across account targets in your organization.

The framework is used to deploy two types of resources: SCP policies and CloudFormation StackSets. Each has a dedicated deployment workflow that is implemented through AWS Step Functions. User interaction with the framework happens through a manifest file that has a well-defined YAML format. Whenever the file is committed to version control, the framework picks up the changes and executes the pipeline.

We can look at *Figure 11.4* to understand the different components involved in the deployment framework:

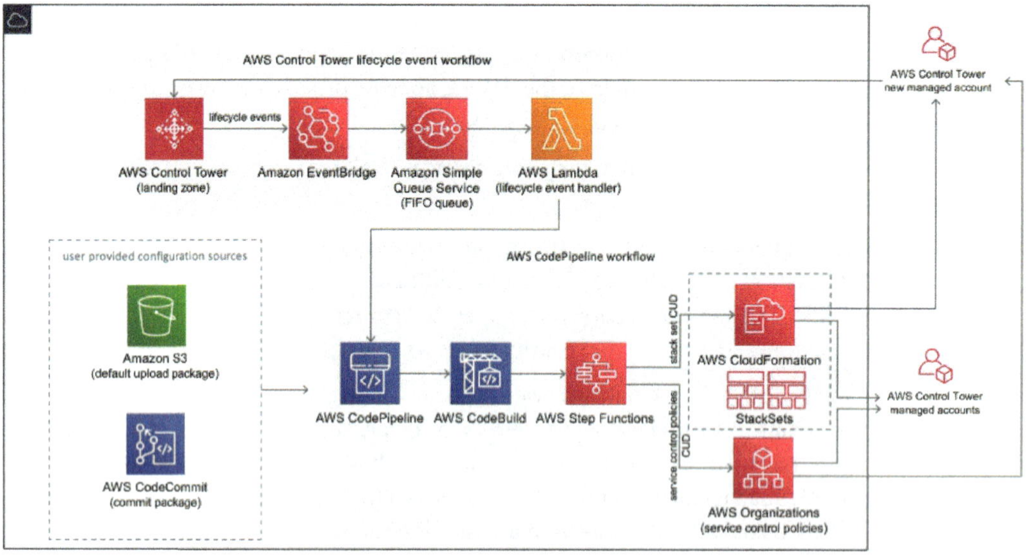

Figure 11.4 – Components of the CfCT framework (source: https://docs.aws.amazon.com)

The entire solution can be deployed as a CloudFormation template in your AWS management account. As you can see, there is a CodePipeline pipeline that pulls the most recent changes from the version control (S3 or CodeCommit) and triggers a CodeBuild project that validates the manifest file initially. If all looks good, the framework proceeds with an invocation for both the SCP Step Functions state machine and the CloudFormation Step Functions state machine. If you haven't been exposed to the AWS Step Functions service before, it is a workflow orchestrator that helps you build programmable flows that invoke various AWS services to get a job done. Let's look at an example of the manifest file that's used by the framework to deploy resources in your Landing Zone:

```
---
region: us-east-1  # Control Tower Home Region
version: 2021-03-15
resources:
  - name: test-preventive-guardrails
    description: Prevent deleting or disabling resources
    resource_file: s3://marketplace-sa-resources-ct-us-east-1/ctlabs/preventive-guardrails.json
    deploy_method: scp
    deployment_targets:
      organizational_units:
        - Security
        - Sandbox
...
```

```
...
  - name: create-iam-role
    resource_file: s3://marketplace-sa-resources-ct-us-east-1/ctlabs/
describe-regions-iam-role.template
    deploy_method: stack_set
    deployment_targets:
      organizational_units:
        - Security
        - Sandbox
      regions:
        - us-east-1
```

The manifest file answers three questions, represented by keys in the YAML structure:

- `Resource_file`: Where is the code that needs to be deployed?
- `deploy method`: What needs to be deployed? This can have two values – `scp` or `stack set`.
- `deployment_targets`: Where should the resource be deployed? Here, you can use individual accounts or OUs that represent a collection of accounts.

As soon as this file is committed into the Git repository tracked by the solution, the pipeline triggers, resulting in the SCP and the CloudFormation template being deployed in the target destinations – in this case, the security and sandbox OUs.

One benefit of using AWS-offered solutions is that you are covered by AWS Support, should the need arise. This is not the case with other custom implementations that you might develop.

## Summary

We started this chapter by identifying the need for a multi-account structure and the benefits it provides when hosting multiple workloads in AWS. Multiple services, solutions, and deployment frameworks fulfill a certain need, but it's important to understand that they are not going to help you just on their own. Some level of customization is always needed for organizations to implement their specific needs. With the needs and benefits clarified, we moved on to key considerations that you should have when designing a Landing Zone concept. We also looked at some best practices in the areas of multi-account structure, security and IAM, DevOps and Config management, and operations.

Toward the second half of this chapter, we took a deeper look into how AWS Control Tower works under the hood, and out-of-the-box integrations with the CfCT solution. One of the key benefits that customers get from these solutions is that they are supported by AWS, just as they would support any other service.

In the next chapter, *Adhering to AWS Well-Architected Principles*, we will investigate the key pillars of a solid foundation that you can consider for your application workloads.

## Further reading

To learn more about the topics that were covered in this chapter, take a look at the following resources:

- AWS Deployment Framework (ADF): https://github.com/awslabs/aws-deployment-framework
- Account Factory for Terraform: https://docs.aws.amazon.com/controltower/latest/userguide/aft-getting-started.html
- Best practices for OUs with AWS Organizations: https://aws.amazon.com/blogs/mt/best-practices-for-organizational-units-with-aws-organizations/

# 12
# Adhering to AWS Well-Architected Principles

Back in 2012, one of the famous **Amazon Web Services** (**AWS**) services—Amazon **Elastic Block Store** (**EBS**)—had an outage that affected the workloads of many customers. Interestingly, though, the impact was negligible, or not seen at all by a few customers. This clearly meant that in addition to the capabilities provided by the cloud provider, the *usage pattern* of those services played an important role in the stability of customers' workloads. Deeper investigations surfaced some architectural patterns that a few AWS customers had been following. This, combined with the data and analysis from AWS, led to the formation of **AWS Well-Architected**. Since then, this has been used to educate customers on how to architect their cloud workloads in a reliable and efficient manner. What started as a set of best practices then transformed into some whitepapers and architectural guides for hosting applications on AWS. These practices will never cater to 100% of the architectural patterns that your workloads will have but will serve the need for strong foundational practices and guidance that help you identify, measure, and optimize your architectures over time, leading to business success.

AWS Well-Architected has since then evolved quite a lot. As of today, it offers much more than just generic architectural best practices. It can be used by application teams to benchmark their workloads against technical and business-vertical best practices. In addition to identifying their areas of strength, they also get to know about the opportunities for future optimization. Some organizations might consider AWS Well-Architected as a mechanism to *audit* their workloads, which is *not* correct. As a DevOps professional, you should advocate for these practices as a constructive discussion that promotes better architectural decisions, rather than using them as a mechanism to point out individuals or teams responsible for building those architectures in the cloud. IT architecture is always a trade-off—you win something, and you lose something else. The same applies to your applications hosted in AWS. Ensuring a higher availability of your applications might result in a cost increase, and implementing cross-region **disaster recovery** (**DR**) procedures, on the other hand, could complicate operational procedures and stress the design of your application code. Being aware of these trade-offs will help you align your technical decisions with your business needs and assist your decision-making when architecting for the long term.

In this chapter, we will discuss the different components of AWS Well-Architected, and how you can leverage them to host your mission-critical applications with confidence. Starting with a brief understanding of AWS Well-Architected, we will then dive into sample implementation use cases, covering common problems that apply to most enterprises. Considering the scope of the chapter, we will not be able to cover code-level details of these implementation examples, but the idea is to give you a basic understanding of how the workflows look and which AWS services you could leverage to roll these out. It's expected that you might have to do some self-explorations to build and deploy these solutions in your AWS organization.

We will cover the following topics in this chapter:

- Understanding different components of AWS Well-Architected
- Aligning your architecture with the six focus pillars of the framework
- Sample practical implementations to adhere to these well-architected best practices

As mentioned before, AWS Well-Architected is much more than just architectural practices. Let's start with a basic understanding of the different offerings under this umbrella that come together to help you with a consistent approach to architecture evaluation and scalable design implementation.

## Understanding different components of AWS Well-Architected

**Well-Architected** is an AWS offering that grants customers access to the wealth of knowledge acquired through numerous architectural reviews with other customers, over the years. This ensures that customers are well informed about the most effective practices and can mitigate architectural risks their applications might be exposed to. With Well-Architected, organizations can identify areas within their architecture that need enhancement, thereby allowing them to address and overcome ongoing challenges that divert their focus from value-adding activities.

In essence, it serves as a mechanism for organizations to achieve the following:

- Acquire insights into effective strategies and best practices for cloud-based architecture
- Assess their architecture against established best practices
- Enhance their architecture by resolving any identified issues

There are three main components of AWS Well-Architected—the **framework** itself, **Well-Architected Lenses**, and the **Well-Architected Tool**. Let's discuss them in detail.

## The AWS Well-Architected Framework

The Well-Architected Framework offers a collection of questions for customers to assess their architecture and its alignment with AWS best practices. Learning from what has worked well for other AWS customers in the past avoids the need to reinvent the wheel and provides a consistent approach that can be leveraged to architect modern cloud-based systems that are secure, cost-effective, efficient, reliable, and sustainable. As new application patterns evolve, this framework is going to continuously adapt to them. Therefore, it is necessary to look at this as an *ongoing activity* where you can continuously measure progress and ensure that you are moving in the right direction.

To categorize these learnings into well-defined focus areas, AWS Well-Architected uses six key pillars, which we will cover in the upcoming sections.

## AWS Well-Architected lenses

To evaluate your architectures against a well-defined technical or business scope and context, there are dedicated *lenses* that can be leveraged. AWS Well-Architected Lenses expand on the advice provided by the AWS Well-Architected Framework and cater to distinct industry verticals and technology domains. Depending on the nature of your applications, you can assess them against business verticals such as **financial services**, **media streaming**, or **healthcare**, or you could also assess technical maturity around topics such as **hybrid networking**, **high-performance computing**, **containers**, or **SaaS (Software as a Service)** capabilities.

As a DevOps professional, you can leverage these lenses and align application design, deployment, and operational activities to ensure that your applications will meet the business needs when deployed on AWS. The lenses *add a new dimension* to each of the six pillars covered in the framework.

Let's take an example of the *SaaS lens* for the AWS Well-Architected Framework. It is targeted toward customers that host SaaS applications on the cloud. Diving into common areas of concerns that multi-tenant SaaS applications have, such as data isolation, noisy neighbor problems, tenant onboarding, and tenant consumption, the lens provides best practices around how to solve these problems by leveraging AWS services and mechanisms. These lenses provide prescriptive guidance that can help you solidify your workloads' security, resiliency, and availability while reducing the overall cost.

In the previous chapter, *Chapter 11, Ensuring a Strong AWS Foundation for Multi-Account and Multi-Region Environments*, we covered the concept of a **landing zone**. To identify best practices for the management and governance of your multi-account environment, there is a dedicated guide in the AWS Well-Architected Framework that outlines various aspects of networking, security, identity management, and monitoring that you should consider. Refer to the following link for more details: `https://docs.aws.amazon.com/wellarchitected/latest/management-and-governance-guide/management-and-governance-cloud-environment-guide.html`.

### The AWS Well-Architected Tool

The **AWS Well-Architected Tool**, also known as the **WA Tool**, is a free-to-use service to review your workloads hosted in AWS. It is a cloud-based solution that presents a uniform approach to evaluating your architecture against the AWS Well-Architected Framework. By using the AWS Well-Architected Tool, you will receive valuable suggestions to enhance the security, cost-effectiveness, and efficiency of your workloads. It not only helps you identify opportunities for improvement but also to track progress over time. It's a *living database* of your workloads' current and future target state.

By documenting the decisions that you make (in the tool), you can ensure that future team members will have a good understanding of the technology decisions that were made to meet a specific business goal.

Having discussed the key components of AWS Well-Architected, let's now dive into the details of the six pillars of the framework. Most importantly, we will be discussing some practical implementation scenarios, under each pillar, that can address common challenges faced by organizations when operating in the cloud.

# Aligning your architecture with the six focus pillars of the framework

The AWS Well-Architected Framework categorizes all practices under six main pillars, which are **Cost Optimization**, **Reliability**, **Operational Excellence**, **Performance Efficiency**, **Sustainability**, and—most importantly—**Security**. Let's start with **Operational Excellence**, which focuses on best practices for operating your workloads at scale and evolving them over time to ensure a great customer experience.

## Operating your workloads with confidence

The **Operational Excellence** pillar aims to optimize the delivery cycle of new features and bug fixes in customer environments, in a reliable and repeatable manner. Developers can only focus on building new capabilities when they are not frequently pulled into operational issues that distract them. To ensure this, Operational Excellence promotes the idea of automating changes and responses to events, continuously monitoring running systems, and improving processes or procedures when necessary. In the initial chapters of this book, we discussed software delivery concepts such as **Continuous Integration and Continuous Delivery** (**CI/CD**), which are essential for achieving the operational excellence of your workloads in AWS. Let's discuss some best practices that you can consider adopting in this area.

### *Best practices for efficiently operating workloads in the cloud*

Irrespective of the business vertical or technical domain your application corresponds to, you can use these practices to enhance operations on AWS.

### Releasing small and releasing early

Your infrastructure design should allow for *frequent and incremental updates*, enabling a steady stream of changes to be rolled out into your environment. Implementing changes in small, reversible steps allows for easy identification and resolution of any issues that may arise without causing major disruptions to the operations of your workloads.

### Managing infrastructure as code

In the cloud, you should apply similar engineering principles to your entire infrastructure as you do to your application code. By representing your entire technology stack (applications, infrastructure, and so on) as code, you can easily update and manage it programmatically. Automation allows you to script operational procedures and trigger them in response to events, minimizing the chance of human errors while ensuring consistent responses to various situations.

### Leveraging operational failures for learning and improvement

Embrace a culture of learning from all operational events and failures. If there's anything that operational outages can help you with, it's knowledge and experience. Use them as *opportunities* for improvements and knowledge sharing throughout the organization.

### Frequently updating and enhancing operations methods

Just as your applications keep evolving over time, your operational procedures need to keep up with the changes as well. It's not a one-time activity, and you should continuously seek opportunities to refine and enhance these procedures so that new operational risks are managed effectively. To validate your existing procedures, you can organize **operational game days** that allow your teams to inject failures into a test environment and collaborate on solving them quickly while validating that your existing operational procedures, runbooks, scripts, and automation still work as expected.

Let's go through an implementation workflow that is often needed by enterprises that work with multiple AWS accounts and regions—automatic enablement of opt-in regions for new AWS accounts. Activities such as these, if not automated, can lead to a lot of operational overhead for the teams managing the AWS platform for the entire organization.

### *Automatic enablement of opt-in AWS regions for new accounts*

As discussed before, we will not go into code-level details of the implementation but describe the implementation workflow in sufficient detail so that you can leverage these understandings to build the same, or similar, automations in the future and optimize your operational practices. Have a look at the following diagram:

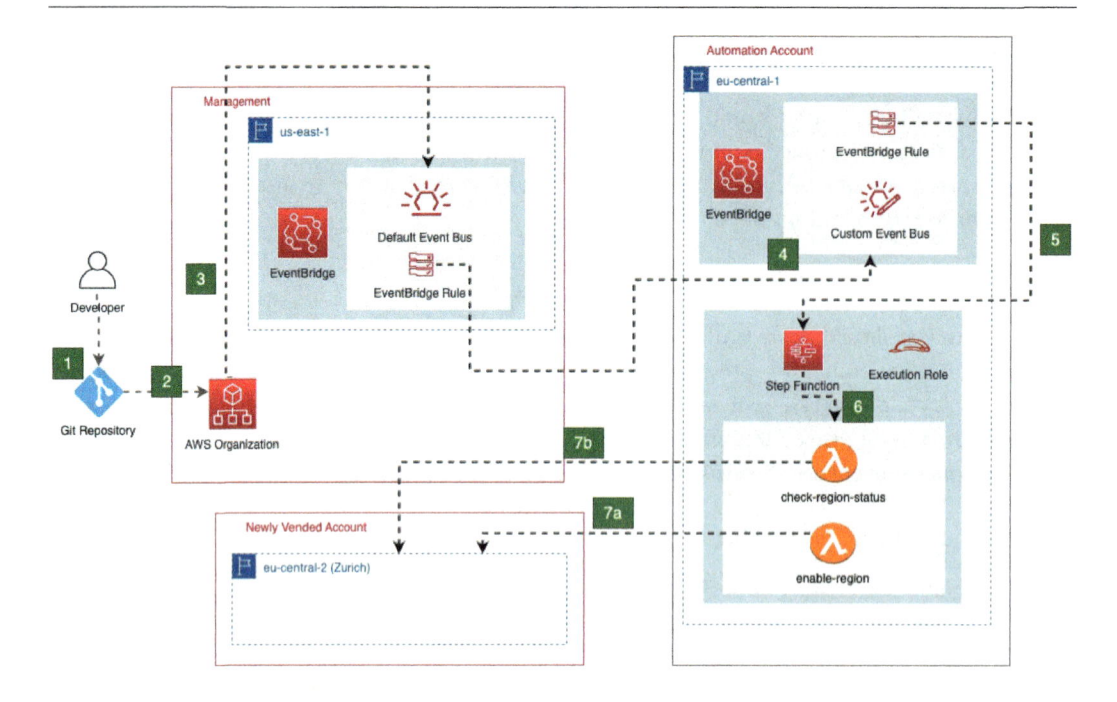

Figure 12.1: Automatic enablement of opt-in AWS regions for new accounts

Not all AWS regions are enabled by default when a new account is created. All AWS regions where you plan to host your workloads need to be *opted in* first before you can deploy any resources into them. This also means that basic security guardrails, automations, network baselines, and so on cannot work until the new region is configured for use. To handle this use case, one can implement an automated workflow design, as shown in *Figure 12.1*. The sequential steps for this workflow are described next:

1. Platform developers leverage **infrastructure as code** (**IaC**) practices to add a new account configuration, using tools such as CloudFormation, Terraform, or **Cloud Development Kit** (**CDK**).
2. The CI/CD pipeline kicks off and provisions a new account in the AWS Organizations organization.
3. The AWS Organizations service emits an event in `us-east-1`, which is the default region where events from global services are generated.
4. To limit access to the organization's management account, it is a good security practice to forward respective events to a designated *automation* or *tooling account* and host all the automation there. In this architecture, we follow the same practice and forward the event to a custom event bus, in another account, in a different region.
5. Once the event is received in the target account, an EventBridge rule invokes the **AWS Step Functions** state machine, which is an AWS service for orchestrating workflows.
6. The AWS Step Functions state machine can further trigger several other AWS services and orchestrate their execution. In this example, we use the state machine to invoke two Lambda

functions: one that enables the opt-in region (`eu-central-2`, or Zurich in this case) and another that checks whether the region is ready for use. This operation can take anywhere between 15 and 60 minutes, which is a strong indicator of why such operations should be automated.

7. The two Lambda functions invoke respective API calls on the new AWS account to achieve the desired target state, which is the enablement of the new AWS region so that workloads can be hosted in the new account.

Having learned about the best practices to achieve operational excellence, let's discuss some ways to secure your workloads and infrastructure on AWS.

## Enhancing the security posture of infrastructure and workloads

The **Security** pillar of the Well-Architected Framework focuses on improving the security posture of your infrastructure and application workloads. In previous chapters, we discussed the concept of the AWS Shared Responsibility Model, which emphasizes the point that AWS, as a cloud provider, is responsible for the security *of* the cloud, and the customers are responsible for security *in* the cloud. The Security pillar identifies steps that can be taken by customers to improve the security of users and workloads *in the cloud*. Let's go through some of those.

### Best practices for enhancing your cloud security posture

Starting from how your users gain access to AWS accounts and applications, to protecting data in transit and at rest, there are quite a few areas that need to be addressed to ensure a good security posture on AWS.

### Centralizing identity and access management

Avoid creating static **identity and access management** (**IAM**) credentials in any AWS account and federate all human access through a centralized **identity provider** (**IdP**) that you might already be using in your organization. It's a common practice to use solutions such as **Azure AD**, **OneLogin**, and others for centrally authenticating and authorizing human users. AWS services such as **IAM Identity Center** make it easy to leverage the same IdP to federate users into AWS accounts with different levels of access rights. For technical use cases, where applications or automation tools need access to AWS services, always leverage IAM roles without any static provisioning of user credentials. IAM roles give you dynamically generated temporary credentials, which greatly improves your security posture.

However, there are exceptions where you might have to create a pair of IAM credentials in the management account, as per the best practices for *break-glass access patterns*. These patterns advocate the creation of a limited number of static credentials in the management account to handle scenarios such as outages of the IdP or security incidents that require manual intervention procedures to be invoked. However, it's important to note that there should be adequate monitoring around the usage of these credentials, and all activity should be audited. Toward the end of this section, we will discuss an implementation using the **AWS User Notifications** service, which can be used to send out notifications through commonly used communication platforms and channels.

### Implementing security-in-depth principles

Security should be applied at multiple layers, starting from the edge of the network to the perimeter of VPCs and subnets, and moving down to the instance level, securing the application and operating system itself. It's a good practice to implement security controls, both preventive and detective, to allow healthy communication patterns.

With a combination of AWS **service control policies** (**SCPs**), AWS Config Rules, and networking controls such as subnet **network access control lists** (**NACLs**), security groups, and so on, appropriate measures can be taken to implement security in depth.

### Protecting data in transit and at rest

Many AWS services offer out-of-the-box data encryption at rest. At the bare minimum, this provides security coverage for your data, but the ownership and management of the encryption key resides with AWS. Customers operating in more sensitive domains such as financial services might use their own encryption keys that can be managed using AWS **Key Management Service** (**KMS**).

### Automating security measures as code

Utilize automated software-based security mechanisms to enhance scalability while ensuring cost-effectiveness. Develop secure architectures with version-controlled templates defining and managing security controls as code.

### Reducing direct human data access patterns

Utilize mechanisms and tools that minimize or eliminate the need for direct access or manual handling of data, reducing the risk of mishandling and human errors involving sensitive data.

### Preparing for security incidents

Every organization operates in the cloud in a slightly different way when it comes to incident management. It is therefore necessary to have a well-defined incident management procedure that is tested and tailored to your unique needs and team structures.

Up next, let's look into a common security monitoring requirement for break-glass user access, which we discussed a while ago.

#### *Security monitoring for break-glass user access*

In order to trigger alerts when credentials of break-glass users are used, organizations can implement a solution that is detailed in *Figure 12.2*:

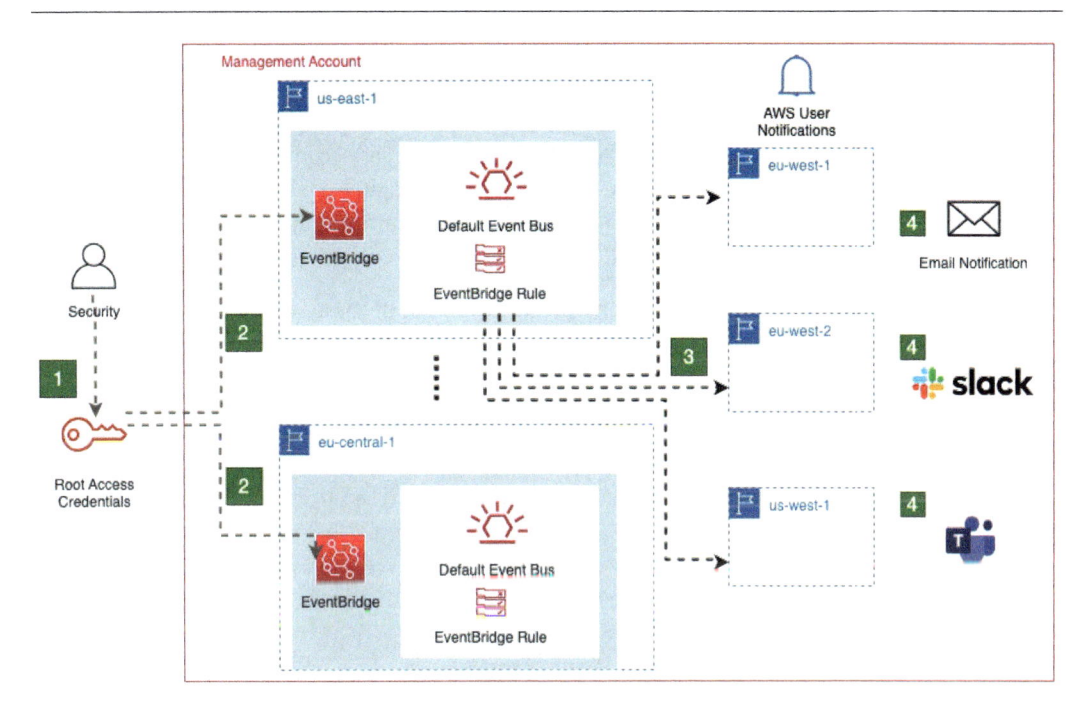

Aligning your architecture with the six focus pillars of the framework     265

Figure 12.2: Monitoring usage of security break-glass users

Let's look at this in a bit more detail, as follows:

1.  During events of security breaches involving the IdP or outages of the service itself, security team members might have to invoke the break-glass process by using the IAM user credentials configured in the AWS management account.

2.  The user login results in the creation of an event in the EventBridge service, in the region where the user logged in.

3.  To track these events, one can leverage the **AWS User Notifications** service, which handles the lifecycle management of event tracking and forwarding in the target regions of the management account.

    To track the event that defines console login for the break-glass user, one can configure the IAM user **Amazon Resource Name (ARN)** in the User Notifications service. For example, to track a user named `break-glass-1`, one can use the following ARN in the service: `arn:aws:iam::<management_account_id>:user/break-glass-1`.

    The event is then forwarded to one of the three *aggregator* regions that are also managed and configured by the service.

4.  A notification is sent out on the configured destination platform, which as of writing this chapter can be MS Teams, Slack, or email.

## Building resilient and highly available systems

The main focus of the **Reliability** pillar within the AWS Well-Architected Framework is to create systems capable of automatically recovering from infrastructure or service interruptions and seamlessly adjusting to evolving conditions. The ultimate objective is to guarantee applications' **high availability** (**HA**), resilience, and maintainability, by keeping downtime at a minimum and delivering a reliable and uninterrupted experience for end users.

Let's discuss some best practices that simplify the achievement of these objectives when deploying workloads on AWS.

### Best practices for building reliable applications on AWS

Through the implementation of automated recovery processes, rigorous testing, horizontal scaling, and efficient change management, organizations can ensure their applications remain resilient and provide a consistent experience for users. It's important to remember that every single component in your AWS architecture can fail; therefore, you need to at least have a plan in place that outlines the course of action when unforeseen events happen.

#### Automatically recovering workloads from failures

A good monitoring and alerting strategy depends on business KPIs instead of technical thresholds. Depending on the nature of your application, you can start with what good looks like, and derive business KPIs from that, which can then be monitored. For example, an e-commerce shop could watch for delays in shopping cart processing time instead of blindly looking at the CPU crossing 90% usage thresholds, as the latter does not help you measure the business outcome.

#### Scaling your workloads by leveraging AWS availability constructs

All AWS regions are composed of three or more **Availability Zones** (**AZs**), which by themselves are a collection of multiple data centers. When architecting systems in the cloud, it's important to spread your resources throughout these discrete locations and horizontally scale your systems. Also, resource constraints are usually scoped to a particular AZ. So, distributing your applications across multiple AZs offers additional benefits of higher availability and uniform resource spread, eventually improving your application uptime and reliability.

#### Dynamically adapting to changing capacity demands

Static provisioning of resources in AWS will not offer you the elasticity to automatically scale up or scale down based on changing demands. With features such as **Elastic Compute Cloud** (**EC2**) Auto Scaling or serverless capabilities of AWS services, you can ensure that reasonable demand needs are met automatically, without any manual intervention or interruptions to the application's availability.

An e-commerce shop might have demand spikes during specific times of the year that can be easily met with such practices, for example. On the other hand, there should also be controls that *block* automatic scale-up beyond certain thresholds, which might instead be representative of service availability attacks such as **Distributed Denial-of-Service** (**DDoS**) attacks. These measures avoid any unexpected cost burden and misuse of services.

**Leveraging automation for any changes to the infrastructure or application**

Completely avoiding manual interventions for any changes to be rolled out in the application or infrastructure is an important step in the direction of building reliable systems. When operating in AWS, you might be deploying resources across multiple accounts, regions, and AZs. This necessitates the need for automation even further as the chances of configuration drift increase when these changes are rolled out manually. Secondly, any modern application these days is composed of several services that can only be efficiently managed when modifications are coordinated and rolled out using code that has been tested in another environment beforehand.

Such approaches make the process of rolling out changes at an infrastructure or application level more reliable, visible, and trackable, additionally allowing you to focus on differentiated value creation.

Most companies architect their cloud applications for failure handling but rarely test these scenarios in practice, which results in a lack of understanding of how these applications actually behave when unforeseen situations happen. Let's look at a test setup demonstrating how one could simulate outages across different components of a typical web application stack.

### *Injecting failures with AWS Fault Injection Simulator*

Simulating failures across different application components can be carried out with manual actions in the console, automated test scripts, or by leveraging services such as **AWS Fault Injection Simulator** (**FIS**). FIS provides out-of-the-box integrations with services such as EC2, **Relational Database Service** (**RDS**), **Elastic Kubernetes Service** (**EKS**), and so on to simulate operational events. These simulations surface software behaviors that are otherwise only experienced during real outage events.

Have a look at the following diagram:

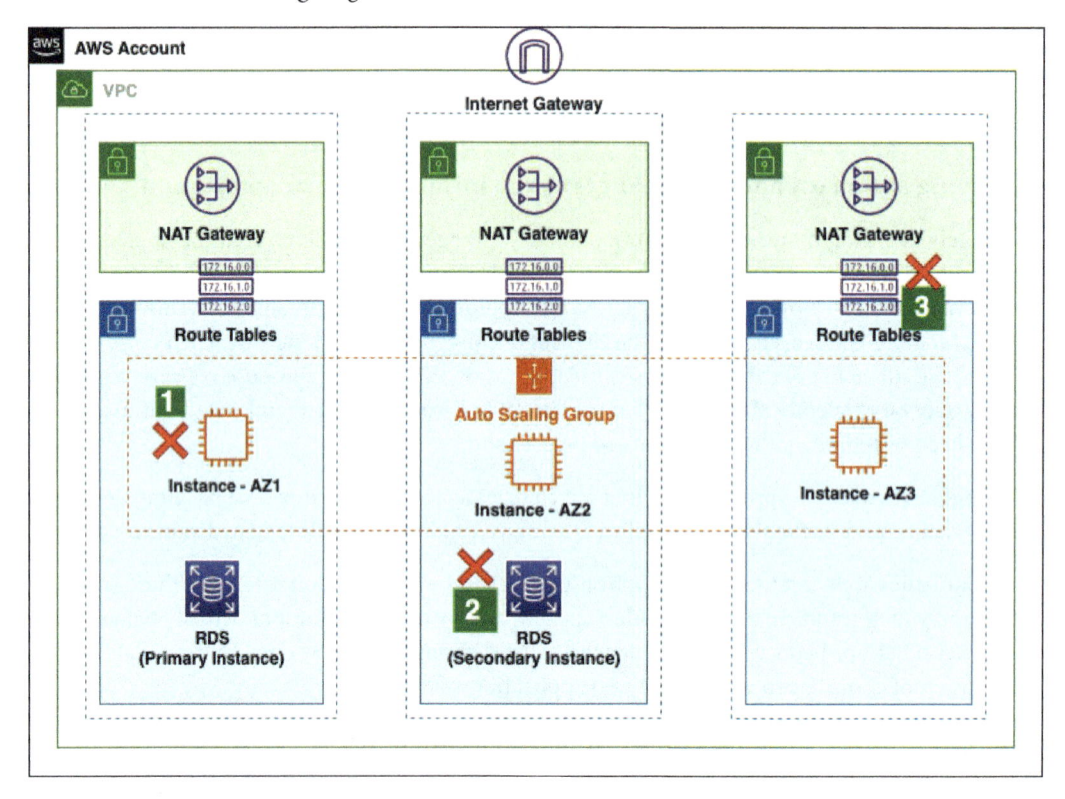

Figure 12.3: Simulating failures with AWS Fault Injection Simulator

For a typical web application fronted by a load balancer and application code deployed in EC2 instances that persist data in a Multi-AZ RDS database, one could follow these steps for failure injection, using the FIS service:

1. Random EC2 instances in the architecture are shut down, and the application, as a whole, is still expected to work fine as incoming requests should be distributed to the remaining EC2 instances by the load balancer. During these resiliency tests, one starts with a *hypothesis* on what they expect to happen when a failure occurs and confirms that hypothesis by actually carrying out the corresponding action. To continuously check the response of an application API during this time, one could leverage the **AWS CloudWatch Synthetics** service, which repeatedly tests an endpoint, generating traffic just like a regular end user.

2. After the compute instances' failure simulations are validated, one can move ahead with database-level resiliency tests. The FIS service supports restarting the active database instance from an RDS cluster, in a Multi-AZ setup. This should mimic the scenario where a particular AZ is affected, resulting in a trigger of the database failover process.

3. Finally, after the failures of individual resources and their corresponding impacts have been analyzed, one can proceed with an AZ-wide outage. This is commonly achieved by detaching NACLs from the subnets in the second or third AZ, as shown by *point 3* in *Figure 12.3*. This will make all resources in that AZ unreachable, and the tests can validate how the application responds to this situation.

Using these resiliency test procedures gives software teams confidence by increasing awareness of unknown limitations of the software application architecture, or the expectation from AWS cloud services. It's advisable to execute these tests regularly so that operational runbooks and procedures can also evolve over time, leading to a more reliable cloud presence.

## Improving the performance efficiency of your workloads

The core idea of the **Performance Efficiency** pillar revolves around optimal utilization of computing resources, to meet specific business requirements in the most effective manner. Furthermore, it delves into strategies for sustaining this efficiency amid fluctuating demands and ever-evolving technologies.

### Best practices for extracting the most out of your workloads on AWS

These practices are focused on achieving optimal utilization of computing resources while fulfilling specific performance requirements. With this, organizations can maximize the value of their cloud-based systems and enhance overall cost-effectiveness.

#### Avoiding reinventing the wheel and delegating repeatable tasks

With AWS, you can let the cloud vendor handle repeatable tasks that don't provide any differentiated value for your software teams. For example, maintaining a database running in EC2 or hosting a self-managed load balancer is not going to help you in the long run, unless there are strong business reasons to demand that. So, whenever possible, it's recommended to adopt AWS-managed services, which reduce the time and effort you would have otherwise invested in maintaining this stack. This effort-saving directly impacts your **total cost of ownership** (**TCO**) when operating in the cloud.

#### Adopting serverless technologies to reduce cost and operations

Serverless technologies such as **AWS Lambda**, **DynamoDB**, and **Step Functions** abstract a lot of intricate details under the hood, which removes a lot of overhead around the maintenance and development of complicated technology stacks. While spearheading the development of actual applications, they shorten the time-to-business-value realization, which is very beneficial for software teams that are just getting started or already very mature with their cloud strategy.

### Deploying applications closer to end users for increased performance and reliability

By leveraging AWS services such as **CloudFront edge locations** and **AWS Global Accelerator**, application teams can host their applications closer to end users, which reduces response latency, increases performance, and allows you to extract more value out of the same set of compute resources.

### Experimenting with different service configurations

Be it running applications' business logic in **AWS Lambda** functions or running CI/CD build jobs using **AWS CodeBuild**, it's important to right-size your compute configurations to address the use case at hand. For example, increasing the memory size of your Lambda function might allow you to process the same request in reduced time, eventually leading to lower costs as the billed-duration metric decreases substantially.

Before starting with any optimizations in the application code or the AWS components used in the technology stack, it's important to measure important metrics to surface the bottlenecks and identify areas of optimization. To support this, the **Amazon CloudWatch** observability platform offers a *cross-account observability* feature that can be used to analyze metrics throughout your organization, in one central AWS account. Let's look at an example implementation of how this works in practice.

#### *Aggregating cross-account observability data to identify performance bottlenecks*

When operating workloads on AWS, most organizations do not invest in building a centralized observability platform that can help correlate performance metrics in a central place. Using Amazon CloudWatch, one can leverage the embedded **Observability Access Manager (OAM)** feature to link multiple *source accounts* with a central *monitoring account*. Without incurring any costs, important indicators of performance bottlenecks, such as logs, metrics, and traces, can be sourced from multiple accounts into one central location.

Using the AWS Organizations service, one can automatically configure the collection of observability data using **CloudFormation StackSets** or a similar deployment framework. Let's see how these steps look in practice, in *Figure 12.4*:

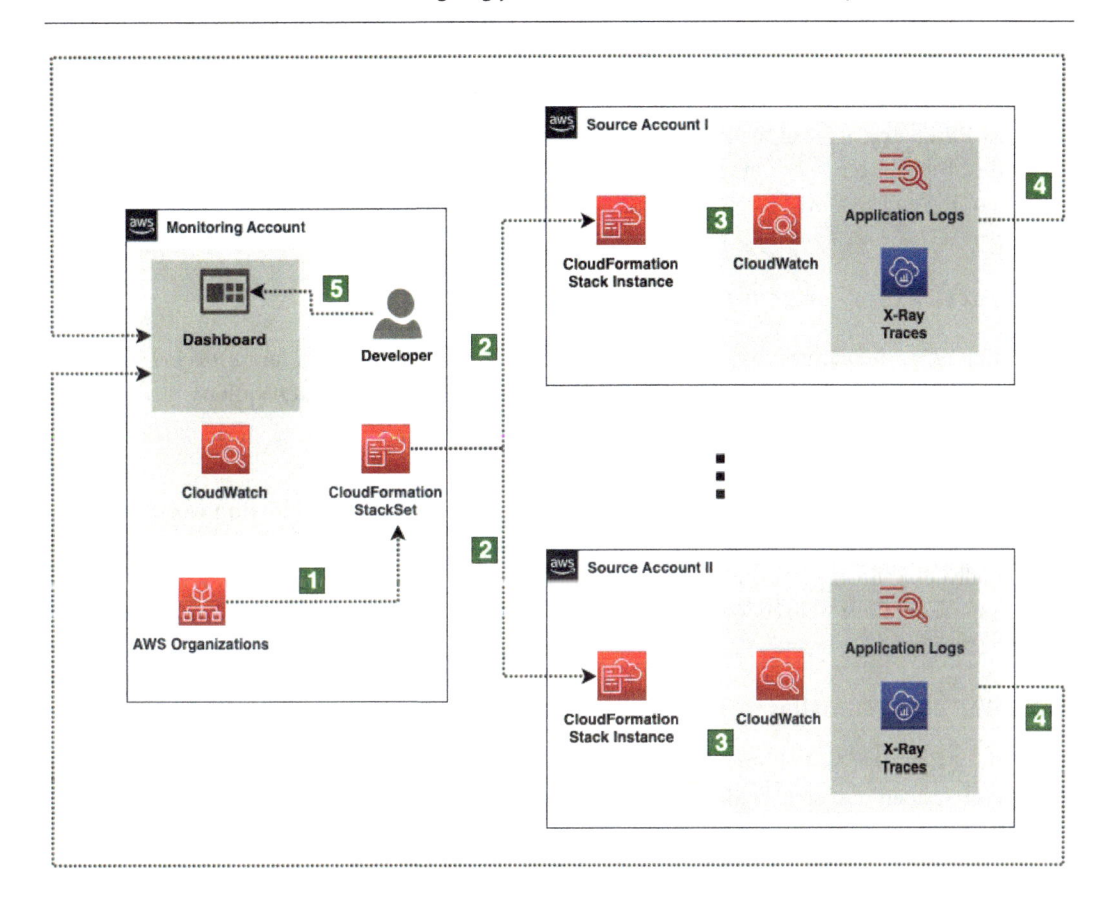

Figure 12.4: Cross-account observability to observe metrics and identify performance bottlenecks

Let's look at this in a bit more detail, as follows:

1. **CloudFormation StackSets**, under the hood, hooks into AWS Organizations events that notify the service of any new accounts that are created in the organization.
2. **CloudFormation OAM** requires data sharing to be configured from the *source accounts*. This can be easily accomplished using StackSet instances, which set up the required configuration.
3. After the stack instance deployment is complete, observability data, such as logs, metrics, and X-Ray traces are automatically shared with the central monitoring account.
4. Software developers, or members of the operations team, can view the aggregated metrics in the central account to understand system behaviors and identify performance bottlenecks. Once they are identified, additional measures can be taken to improve performance or right-size resources for better efficiency.

## Minimizing cloud costs while maximizing business value creation

The **Cost Efficiency** pillar of the AWS Well-Architected Framework focuses on optimizing the use of cloud resources to achieve maximum value and thereby reduce expenses. With resource usage understanding and cost management practices, users can make informed decisions to optimize their cloud spend. There are some best practices recommended in this area, which we'll look at next.

### Best practices for reducing your cloud spend

Depending on particular use cases and application needs, certain measures can result in substantial cloud spend reduction. Let's discuss a few practices that can benefit most applications.

#### Aligning consumption with business needs

Not all compute resources have to be running all the time. Except for production workloads, it is generally possible to stop development and test environments completely outside working hours. Additionally, configuring low-cost resource types for these non-critical environments can result in cost savings that can be utilized for experimental or research and development work, leading to room for innovation.

#### Analyzing cost anomalies

Regularly review cost and billing reports to identify unexpected cost increases and investigate the reasons for sudden cost spikes. Making software teams aware of the cost impact their architectural decisions have is a good first step to begin with.

#### Opting for cost-effective alternatives when possible

Services such as AWS Lambda allow you to match your specific requirements and financial constraints with serverless computing resources, with a *pay-as-you-go* model. By billing you only for the actual usage, they eliminate the need to manage and bear the cost of dedicated server resources that might remain idle for a substantial period of time.

To optimize cloud costs, it is important to set up automated reporting and analysis of resource consumption. A common enterprise pattern to implement this is by utilizing AWS **Cost and Usage Reports (CUR)**. *Figure 12.5* describes how one could approach collection, automated analysis, or reporting with such a solution.

### Automated analysis of cost and usage of your AWS resources

AWS services that are relevant for implementing this functionality are Amazon CloudWatch, AWS CUR, AWS Lambda, and Amazon **Simple Storage Service (S3)**. The cost analysis logic can be customized based on specific requirements, and the solution can also be extended to send out automated notifications, or emails, if necessary:

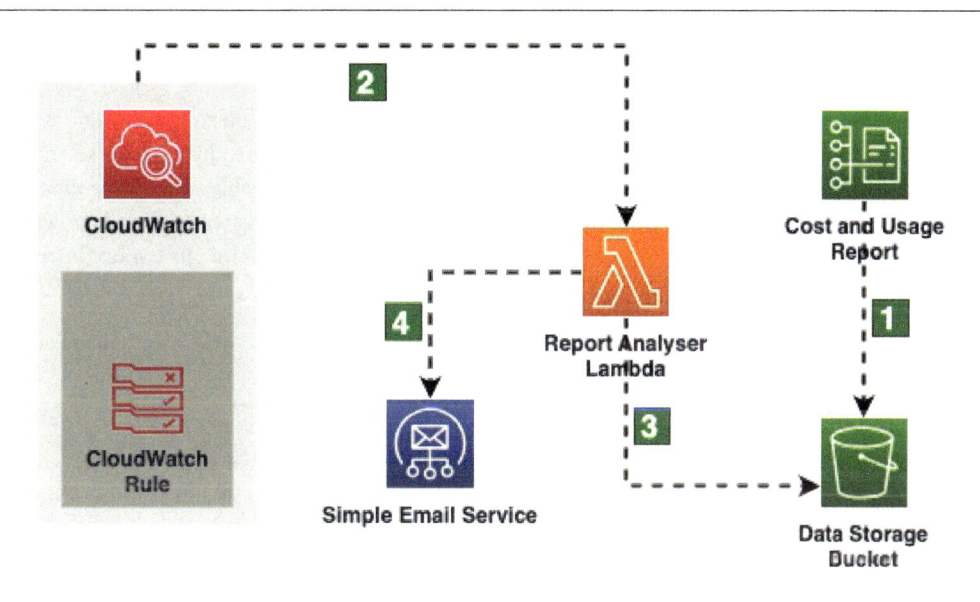

Figure 12.5: Automated analysis of cost and usage reports in AWS

Let's look at this in a bit more detail, as follows:

1. AWS CUR provides a comprehensive report collecting the cost and usage data across several accounts. These reports can be automatically published up to three times a day into a destination such as an Amazon S3 bucket.

2. Amazon CloudWatch rules can be configured to trigger at a pre-defined time of day, depending on your use case. You might want to process these records daily, or maybe on a weekly or monthly basis. Alternatively, one could also define S3 event notifications to automatically trigger a Lambda function as soon as an object is uploaded. These CloudWatch rule triggers are usually configured to invoke a pre-deployed Lambda function that has the necessary permissions to pull and process data from the S3 storage bucket in question.

3. The Lambda function pulls the recent reports, parses the CSV records, and derives additional insights from the raw data, converting it into actionable information. This processed information might support the creation of visuals, graphs, or any other form of insight that can then help your teams understand the cost impact of the decisions they are making.

4. After the insights are prepared, they can be shared with the relevant teams over email or other forms of notifications.

## Building sustainable workloads in the cloud

The **Sustainability** pillar of the AWS Well-Architected Framework focuses on controlling and reducing the environmental effects of cloud resources that your applications consume. Just as with security, this is also a *shared responsibility* model where AWS focuses on using renewable sources for data center energy requirements, and users are expected to do their part, by avoiding wastage and carrying out architectural improvements when possible. From the users' perspective, it mostly comes down to the reduction of resources and maximum utilization of what is available.

As with the other pillars, there are also a few sustainability best practices, which we will cover next.

### Best practices for making cloud environments sustainable

These practices focus on the *indirect emissions* that users can help reduce since AWS has little control over how you manage your workloads and the kind of resource consumption it results in. The actual consumption depends on the type of AWS services that the customers use, the energy requirements of those services, and finally the energy requirements of the data center to continue running those workloads.

#### Deriving actionable KPIs from your usage patterns

First and foremost, users need to understand and measure the impact of their cloud workloads by including all forms of impact, including how the end customers use their products and what the entire lifecycle leading to resource decommissioning looks like. Once the measurements are in place, it becomes easy to derive the energy requirements per unit of work and then work toward reducing that requirement through efficient architectural design and usage of AWS cloud resources.

#### Maximizing utilization of provisioned resources

Eliminating resource wastage is a low-hanging fruit that contributes the most to your sustainability goals. A subsequent step is to maximize the utilization of provisioned resources by optimizing software design and architecture, which leads to lower energy consumption. Idling resources in CI/CD pipeline execution environments are good candidates for first-level optimizations, after which teams can focus on individual applications.

#### Leveraging a shared pool of managed service resources

Resource sharing by multiple customers results in optimal usage of data center infrastructure and thereby allows AWS to reduce the sustainability impact by making decisions that benefit a large group of customers. For example, when migrating applications to managed services such as **AWS Fargate serverless**, customers benefit from shared data center resources such as power and networking, efficiently handled by AWS on a large scale.

## Summary

In this chapter, we delved into the fundamental principles and significance of AWS Well-Architected, which serves as a comprehensive guide for designing and operating reliable, performant, cost-effective, secure, and sustainable cloud systems.

We started with a discussion of different components of AWS Well-Architected—the framework, the lenses, and the Well-Architected Tool. An important takeaway from all these learnings is that it is an evolving concept. The cloud provider will keep on extending the framework and the suggestions under each of the pillars as the cloud capabilities evolve and by looking at how different customers use these capabilities to solve their unique business problems. The lenses additionally provide focused attention on a particular business or technical domain that customer workloads map to. Documenting workload evaluations and learnings based on Well-Architected suggestions is an important activity that is fulfilled by the use of the Well-Architected Tool. Only then can you continually measure progress and identify the drivers of certain architectural decisions for your future team members.

In the last section of the chapter, we focused on the six pillars of the framework and covered organizational best practices under each of them. These practices serve as a guiding path toward the most important aspects an enterprise should consider on its AWS cloud journey. For each of these pillars, we also covered an example implementation workflow that highlighted common use cases that apply to most enterprises.

As a DevOps practitioner, it's important that you advocate the adoption of these practices and continuous evaluation of workloads against the Well-Architected Framework. At the same time, it is equally important to discourage the use of Well-Architected as an audit or blame mechanism.

I hope these learnings will help you create a strong AWS foundation on which you can base your processes and technical architectures. Establishing a continuous improvement culture based on learnings from how other customers have used AWS services will additionally enable you to solve organizational needs of reliable, cost-effective, secure, and sustainable cloud systems.

## Further reading

Here are some case studies outlining the benefits that three companies realized, with the adoption of the AWS Well-Architected Framework and practices:

- https://aws.amazon.com/solutions/case-studies/moots-technology-wa-case-study/
- https://aws.amazon.com/solutions/case-studies/well-architected-natura-case-study-en/
- https://aws.amazon.com/solutions/case-studies/bmc-software-wa/

# Index

## A

abstraction level  22
  business requirements  23
  cloud skills and resources  23
  security considerations  23
  simplicity versus control  22
abstract syntax tree (AST)  211
A/B testing  92
Account Factory for Terraform (AFT)  239
Account Vending Machine (AVM)
  building  248
Amazon Builders' Library  234
Amazon Chime  32
Amazon CloudWatch  12, 97, 169, 170, 270
Amazon CloudWatch, application monitoring  171
  real user monitoring (RUM)  171
  service lens  171
  synthetic monitoring  171
Amazon CloudWatch, infrastructure monitoring
  CloudWatch alarm  171
  CloudWatch metrics  171
Amazon CloudWatch, insights and operational visibility  172
  container insights  172
  Lambda Insights  172

Amazon CloudWatch Logs
  used, for monitoring logs  189, 190
Amazon EC2
  Amazon VPC  31
  Elastic Block Store  31
  Elastic File Storage  31
Amazon ECR  144
Amazon ECS  176
Amazon Elastic Kubernetes Service (Amazon EKS)  225
Amazon Grafana
  used, for visualizing data  191, 192
Amazon GuardDuty  246
Amazon Inspector  206
Amazon Key Management Service (KMS)  169
Amazon Machine Image (AMI)  61, 62, 107
  building, with Packer  49-52
Amazon Macie  206
Amazon Managed Grafana  177
  workspace, creating  184-188
Amazon Managed Prometheus (AMP)  177
  used, for instrumenting application metrics  190, 191
Amazon Managed Service, for Prometheus
  workspace, creating  181
Amazon Rekognition  123

278    Index

Amazon Resource Name (ARN) 265
Amazon Simple Notification
    Service (SNS) 171
Amazon VPC 31
Amazon Web Services (AWS) 3, 4, 257
    account, creating 41
    additional users, creating 43, 44
    Cloud9 environment, navigating 46, 47
    infrastructure, managing approaches 116
    offerings, for monitoring 170
    offerings, for observability 170
    on-prem IT landscape, extending with 11
    root user credentials, securing 42, 43
    working with 40
Amazon WorkMail 32
Ansible modules 38
Apache Struts 195
application behavior
    data, observing 189
application components 152-154
    CDK constructs, defining 128-130
Application Load Balancer (ALB) 73
    listeners and target groups 83, 84
    web application, hosting with 81, 82
application metrics
    instrumenting, with Amazon Managed
        Prometheus 190, 191
application performance
    monitoring (APM) 169
application stack
    deploying 85
application workflow
    Lambda code, defining to
        orchestrate 130, 131
automated guardrails, for policy
    enforcement 202
Auto Scaling group (ASG) 81
    web application, hosting with 81

Auto Scaling groups 84
Availability Zones (AZs) 266
AWS account
    bootstrapping, to enable CDK
        deployments 127
    CDK stack, deploying 183
    CDK stack, deploying into 133, 134
    fully automated CI/CD
        pipeline 103, 104, 105
AWS Cloud9 integrated development
    environment (IDE) 44
    setting up, in AWS account 44, 45
AWS Cloud Development Kit
    (CDK) 17, 20, 29, 120, 121
    apps 122
    benefits 123
    construct 121
    development workflow 122
    disadvantage 123
    stacks 121
    test application, deploying 123
    versus Pulumi 119, 120
AWS CloudFormation 17, 20, 60, 244
AWS CloudFormation StackSets 252
AWS CodeArtifact 16
AWS CodeBuild 15, 224, 270
    Amazon CloudWatch event integration 97
    build environments, pre-configuring 96
    builds and tests, automating 95, 96
    Jenkins implementation, integrating 97
    private VPC resources, accessing 98
    test report integration 97
    used, for enabling continuous
        integration (CI) 93
    working 96
AWS CodeCommit 15, 246
    used, for enabling continuous
        integration (CI) 93

# Index

AWS CodeCommit, key features 94
   Amazon CloudWatch event integration 94
   approval rule templates 95
   automated code reviews with CodeGuru 95
   data protection, for compliance requirement 95
   granular security controls with IAM 94
AWS CodeDeploy 16
AWS CodePipeline 17, 212, 224
AWS Config 202, 244
AWS Control Tower 239
AWS Deployment Framework (ADF) 240
AWS DevOps, services
   CD and continuous deployment 16
   CI 14
   IaC 17
AWS DevOps services, CD and continuous deployment
   AWS CodeDeploy 16
   AWS CodePipeline 17
AWS DevOps services, CI
   AWS CodeArtifact 16
   AWS CodeBuild 15
   AWS CodeCommit 15
AWS DevOps services, IaC
   AWS CDK 17
   AWS CloudFormation 17
AWS Distro for OpenTelemetry (ADOT) 170
AWS Elastic Beanstalk 32
AWS Elastic Compute Cloud (EC2) 146
AWS Elastic Container Service (ECS) 146
   constructs 147
AWS Elastic Kubernetes Service (EKS) 146
AWS Fargate Serverless 274
AWS Fault Injection Simulator (FIS)
   used, for injecting failures 267-269
AWS Global Accelerator 270
AWS IAM Identity Center 246

AWS Lambda 32, 172, 269
AWS Landing Zone (ALZ) 239
aws-nuke 249
AWS and DevOps
   production-like environments 4-9
   scaling, with cloud 9-13
AWS Organizations 241
   maintaining, for platform development 249
   service integrations, leveraging with 244
AWS Parameter Store 69
AWS PrivateLink 67
AWS Secrets Manager 69
AWS Security Hub 206, 244
AWS Service Catalog 232
AWS services 31
   Amazon EC2 31
   infrastructure, abstracting 31
   software delivery, accelerating with platform services 32
   solution components, mapping to 8, 9
AWS Step Functions 250
AWS Transit Gateway 245
AWS User Notifications 250, 263
AWS Well-Architected Framework 259
   components 258
   pillars 260
AWS Well-Architected Lenses 259
AWS Well-Architected Tool (WA) 260
AWS workloads
   securing 202
   security assessments 208, 209
AWS workloads, security challenges 203
   cloud security responsibilities 203
   risks, identifying 203, 204
   risks, prioritizing 203, 204
AWS workloads, test strategies 205
   security in pipeline 206, 207
   security of pipeline 205

## B

backup policies  244
Bandit  217
Bicycle framework  6, 7
build environments  95
build project  96
buildSpec  96

## C

cattle
  versus pets  36, 37
CDK constructs
  defining, for application
    components  128-130
  L1 constructs (raw)  121
  L2 constructs (curated)  121
  L3 constructs (custom abstractions)  121
CDK deployments
  AWS account, bootstrapping to enable  127
CDK project
  bootstrapping  125-127
CDK stack
  deploying, into AWS account  133, 134, 183
  extending, with constructs  181
  rolling out  183, 184
CDK stack constructs
  application and database containers,
    configuring  156, 157
  defining  154
  EFS filesystem, adding  158
  EFS filesystem, mapping to
    task definition  158
  Fargate service, adding with Application
    Load Balancer integration  158, 159
  networking foundations and ECS cluster  155
  task definition, adding for ECS cluster  156

change sets  61
CI/CD  89, 90
  best practices  92
  effective branching strategy  91
  used, for enabling software delivery  91
CI/CD solution
  integration  92
  need for  92
  on-premises data center  93
  open source or commercial versions  93
CI/CD workflow, for DevSecOps
  CDK stack, deploying in AWS
    account  212-214
  code base  212
  DevSecOps pipeline target
    architecture  210, 211
  security assessments result, checking  214
  testing  209
cloud
  infrastructure elasticity, leveraging  12
  scaling with  9-13
Cloud9  95
Cloud9 environment
  navigating  46, 47
cloud abstractions
  service delivery, simplifying through  12
Cloud Development Kit (CDK)  17, 176, 262
CloudFormation  208, 248
  API call logging, with CloudTrail  66, 67
  permissions delegation, for
    resource management  65
  request flow, over network  67
  using, for hands-on deployment  72
  working  64
CloudFormation hooks  202
CloudFormation stacks
  application stack  73
  network stack  72

Index    281

CloudFormation StackSets  270
CloudFormation template  61
  conditions  63
  outputs  64
  parameters  62
  resources  61, 62
  rules  63, 64
CloudFront Edge Locations  270
Cloud Infrastructure and Platform
    Services (CIPS)  4
Cloud Native Computing Foundation's
    (CNCF's) OpenTelemetry  170
cloud operating model  24
  growth  28
  workloads, optimizing  24
  workloads, sustaining with
    traditional approach  24
CloudTrail
  used, for API call logging  66, 67
CloudWatch alarm  171
CloudWatch container insights  172
CloudWatch Logs  177
CloudWatch Metrics Insights  171
CloudWatch real user monitoring
    (RUM)  171
code base  212
CodeBuild  89
CodeCommit  89
CodeDeploy  89
  using, to orchestrate deployment workflows
    in compute environment  98
CodeDeploy, key components  98
  application  98
  deployment configuration  99
  deployment group  99
  deployment type  99
CodeDeploy, key features  99
  AWS Systems Manager  100
  EC2 Auto Scaling, integration  99

Elastic Load Balancing, integration  99
  events, monitoring with CloudWatch  100
  life cycle hooks  100
CodeGuru  95
CodePipeline  89, 100, 205
  used, for implementing
    end-to-end software delivery  100
CodePipeline, key constructs  101
  actions  101
  artifacts  103
  pipeline execution  102
  stages  101
cognitive load  231
collaboration and learning culture
  establishing  227, 228
collaborative team setup and
    culture, building  224
  values, creating  224
Common Platform Enumeration (CPE)  211
Common Vulnerabilities and
    Exposures (CVEs)  149
Communities of Practice (CoP)  227
conditions  63
constructs  17
constructs, used by ECS  147
  container configuration  147
  launch types  148, 149
  long-running tasks, exposing  148
  related containers, encapsulating  147
  task definition instance  148
container ecosystem  142
container images  40
containerized deployments
  scaling  144
container platforms
  containerized workloads, monitoring  145
  integrations, with services  145
  key responsibilities  145

## 282    Index

placement of containers, orchestrating  145
security guardrails, enforcing for
   containerized applications  145
**containers**  141, 142
**Continuous Delivery (CD)**  13, 90
**continuous deployment (CD)**  13, 90
   implementation  91
**Continuous Integration and Continuous
   Delivery (CI/CD)**  260
**Continuous Integration (CI)**  13
   enabling, with AWS CodeBuild
      and AWS CodeCommit  93
**continuous learning and enablement**
   resources  234
**Control Tower**
   used, for building Landing Zone  250-253
**Cost and Usage Reports (CUR)**  272
**Cost Efficiency pillar**  272
   automated analysis, of cost and usage
      of AWS resources  272, 273
   best practices  272
**cross-region actions**  103
**customers**  7
**Customizations for Control
   Tower (CfCT)**  239
   used, for building Landing Zone  253
   used, for deploying resources  253-255

## D

**data**
   observing, to understand
      application behavior  189
   To-Do List Manager application,
      testing load to generate  189
   visualizing, with Amazon Grafana  191, 192
**declarative approach**
   adopting  117, 118

**decorators**  159
**Delegated Admin**  248
**DevOps**  3, 4
   maturity, measuring  228-230
   versus DevSecOps  199
**DevOps ideas**
   collaborators, finding  235
   commitment, demonstrating  235
   structuring  235
**DevOps methodologies, to accelerate
   software delivery**
   Continuous Delivery (CD)  13
   continuous deployment  13
   Continuous Integration (CI)  13
   effective communication and
      collaboration  14
   Infrastructure as Code (IaC)  14
**DevOps methodology**  230
**DevSecOps**  196-199
   developers  202
   features, developing  200
   identification of issues  201
   improved compliance in regulated
      environment  200
   key benefits  199
   operations team  202
   security professionals  201
   versus DevOps  199
**DevSecOps, benefits**
   improved security awareness
      of team members  200
   reduced time to market  199
**DevSecOps CI/CD pipeline constructs**  212
**DevSecOps pipeline target
   architecture**  210, 211
   application validation  211
   code change  210
   CodePipeline execution  210

Index    283

Dockerfile build  211
Dockerfile validation  211
**digital transformation**  3, 89
**disaster recovery (DR)**  232, 257
**Distributed Denial-of-Service (DDoS) attacks**  267
**Docker**  40, 92, 142
  concepts  143, 144
  using, as container platform  143
**Docker Compose**  146
**Docker containers**  143, 144
**Docker Hub**  144
**Docker images**  143
**Docker registry**  144
**Docker Swarm**  146
**Dynamic Application Security Testing (DAST)**  208
**DynamoDB**  269

# E

**EC2 Auto Scaling service**  11
**ECS**
  test application, deploying on  150
**ECS launch types**
  ECS on EC2  148
  ECS on Fargate  148
**ECS task definition**
  sidecar OpenTelemetry container, injecting  182
**ECS Task Execution Role**  149
**ECS Task Role**  149
**EKS Anywhere**  146
**Elastic Beanstalk**
  code deployment  30
  configuration  30
  monitoring  30
  operations  30

**Elastic Block Store (EBS)**  31, 40, 257
**Elastic Compute Cloud (EC2)**  31, 40, 60, 266
  change sets  61
  concepts  60
  resources  62
  stacks  61
  template  61
**Elastic Container Registry (ECR)**  211
**Elastic Container Service (ECS)**  40, 98, 211
**Elastic File Storage**  31
**Elastic File Systems (EFS)**  40
**Elastic IP (EIP)**  78
**Elastic Kubernetes Service (EKS)**  40, 212, 267
**enablement teams**  226, 227
**end-to-end software delivery**
  actions, triggering  103
  implementing, with CodePipeline  100
**enterprise-grade architectures, with CloudFormation**
  best practices, for designing  68-70
**Equifax**  195
**EventBridge**  250
**EventBridge events**  100

# F

**Fargate**  176
**feature flags**  92
**feature toggles**  92
  working with  92
**filesystem layers**  143
**Flask**  176
**Flask application code**
  events, logging  180, 181
  modifying  179
  Prometheus metrics, enabling in application  179

**frameworks**
  using, that offer high-level abstractions  119
**fully automated CI/CD pipeline**
  AMI for application, creating  105, 106
  in AWS account  103-105
  infrastructure and application stacks, deploying  107-112
**fully managed software services**  32
  Amazon Chime  32
  Amazon WorkMail  32

# G

**Git**  93
**GitHub**  201
**GitHub Actions**  91
**GitLab**  201, 246
**GitLab Continuous Integration and Continuous Delivery**  9, 91
  architectural components  10
**GoFormation**  118
**Golang**  118
**Grafana**  170

# H

**hadolint**  218
**hands-on deployment, with CloudFormation**  72
  network architecture design, to support multi-AZ deployments  73
  web application, hosting with ALB and Auto Scaling groups  81
**Hashicorp Configuration Language (HCL)**  29, 70
**Health Insurance Portability and Accountability Act (HIPAA)**  242

**hierarchy, dashboards**
  annotate graphs  174
  building  172, 173
  dimensions, plotting  174
  time series pattern analysis, adopting  174
**high availability (HA)**  266

# I

**IAM users**
  provisioning, avoidance  249, 250
**identity and access management (IAM)**  250, 263
**identity providers (IdPs)**  246, 263
**image analysis workflow**
  testing  134-136
**image recognition application, components**  124, 125
  Amazon Rekognition  124
  DynamoDB table  124
  event integrations  124
  Lambda function  124
  S3 bucket  124
**immutable infrastructure**  37, 39
  trade-offs  40
**infrastructure**
  managing, approaches in AWS  116
**Infrastructure as a Service (IaaS)**  20
**Infrastructure as Code (IaC)**  14, 208, 262
**infrastructure components**  151
  container platform (ECS)  151
  network infrastructure (VPCs, subnets, route tables)  151
  traffic controller (Application Load Balancer)  151
**infrastructure definition generators**
  using  118, 119

**infrastructure rollouts**
  automating, with scripts  117
**integrated development environment (IDE)**  95

# J

**Java project**  95
**Jenkins**  10, 91
**Jira**  249

# K

**Key Management Service (KMS)**  264
**Kinesis streams**  100
**KMS encryption keys**  95
**Kubernetes**  92

# L

**Lambda**  250
**Lambda code**
  defining, to orchestrate application workflow  130, 131
**Lambda Insight**  172
**Landing Zone**  238, 241
  as AWS service  239, 240
  as concept  239
  as reference to deployment orchestration frameworks  240
  as solution  239
  building, with CfCT  253
  building, with Control Tower  250-253
  goals  239
**Landing Zone, considerations**  241
  config management  246, 247
  cross-account need, focusing  245
  DevOps  246, 247
  hybrid networking need, focusing  245
  operations  247
  securing, with IAM  245, 246
  securing, with security services  245, 246
  structure, defining for organizational units and accounts  241
**Linux Foundation states**  204
**listeners**  83
**logs**
  monitoring, with Amazon CloudWatch Logs  189, 190

# M

**management account**  247
**manual infrastructure management**  116
**Mean Time to Recover (MTTR)**  172
**meetup**
  reference link  234
**monitoring**  167
  AWS, offerings for  170
**multi-account architectures management, best practices**  247
  access, limiting to management account  247, 248
  Account Vending Machine, building  248, 249
  AWS organization, maintaining for platform development  249
  IAM users, provisioning avoidance  249, 250
  no-code/low-code solutions, preferring  250
  solutions, adopting  248
**multi-factor authentication (MFA)**  42
**mutable infrastructure**  37, 38
**mutual TLS (mTLS)**  198

## N

National Vulnerability Database (NVD)  200
network access control lists (NACLs)  264
Network Address Translation (NAT)  77
network architecture design, for deployment with CloudFormation
  internet gateway  74, 75
  NAT gateways  77, 78
  network stack, deploying  80
  private subnets  76, 77
  public subnets  75, 76
  stack outputs  78, 79
  Virtual Private Cloud  74

## O

observability  167, 168
  AWS, offerings for  170
  benefits  169, 170
  logs  168
  metrics  169
  traces  169
Observability Access Manager (OAM)  270
observability stack
  deploying, for test application hosted in ECS  176
  for To-Do List Manager test application  177
observability strategy
  defining, for workloads hosted in AWS  176
Open ID Connect (OIDC)  246, 250
Open Policy Agent (OPA)  208
OpenTelemetry Collector  177
Operational Excellence pillar  260
  automatic enablement, of opt-in AWS regions new accounts  261-263
  best practices  260, 261

organizational unit (OU)  242
  automation OU  242
  development OU  243
  maintenance OU  242
  security OU  242
  shared services OU  242
  suspended OU  243
Otel  170
outputs  64

## P

Packer  72
  used, for building AMI  49-52
parameters  62
Performance Efficiency pillar  269
  best practices  269, 270
  cross-account observability data, aggregating to identify performance bottlenecks  270, 271
Personal Health Dashboards (PHD)  247
pets
  versus cattle  36, 37
PHP-based Beanstalk application
  Amazon S3 bucket  25
  auto-scaling group  25
  CloudWatch Alarms  25
  EC2 instances  25
Platform as a Service (PaaS)  21-26
  code deployment  27
  configuration  27
  monitoring  27
  operation  28
platform services
  AWS Elastic Beanstalk  32
  AWS Lambda  32
  fully managed software services  32
  used, for accelerating software delivery  32

platform teams  225
production-like environments  4-8
Prometheus  170
proof of concept (PoC)  235, 237
Pulumi  208
    versus AWS CDK  119, 120
Python  118
Python Flask application  212

## R

Relational Database Service (RDS)  26, 267
Reliability pillar  266
    AWS Fault Injection Simulator, used
        for injecting failures  267-269
    best practices  266, 267
resources
    deploying, with CfCT  253-255
resources, for continuous learning
    and enablement
    local communities and user groups  234
    Workshops on AWS  234
Root Cause Analysis (RCA)  231
rules  63, 64

## S

sample OU design
    for regulated organization  243
scripts
    infrastructure rollouts, automating with  117
Security Assertion Markup
    Language (SAML)  250
security assessments result
    checking  214
    Dockerfile manifest, validating
        with hadolint  218, 219

Software Composition Analysis (SCA),
    with dependency risk  215-217
Static Application Security Testing
    (SAST), with Bandit  217
security groups
    using, to secure incoming traffic  52
Security Information and Event
    Management (SIEM)  67, 242
security in pipeline  206, 207
    Dynamic Application Security
        Testing (DAST)  208
    Infrastructure as Code (IaC)  208
    Software Composition Analysis (SCA)  207
    Static Application Security
        Testing (SAST)  208
security of pipeline  205
    data process, protecting  206
    Identity and Access Management (IAM)  205
    incident detection and
        monitoring, using  206
    unusual behaviors, detecting  205
Security pillar  263
    best practices  263, 264
    security monitoring, for
        break-glass user access  264, 265
security posture
    enhancing, of infrastructure  263
    enhancing, of workloads  263
security posture, with ECS
    container secrets  150
    ensuring  149
    kernel capabilities  150
    lock down, permissions with IAM roles  149
    network isolation, using task-level ENI  149
    security patch readiness, ensuring
        on CVE identification  149

**security professionals**
  automated guardrails for policy enforcement 202
  developers, enabling to fix and identify security issues 202
  security policies, defining for application and infrastructure 201

**security trade-offs and challenges 197**
  lack of ownership 197
  outdated security tools 198
  rapid evolution of application architecture 198
  software delivery 197

**Service Catalog 250**
**Service Catalog Tools 240**
**Service Control Policies (SCP) 244**
**service integrations**
  leveraging, with AWS Organizations 244
**service lens 171**
**service-level agreement (SLA) 233**
**service-level indicators (SLIs) 233**
**service-level objectives (SLOs) 233**
**Service Limits 247**
**ServiceNow 249**
**shellcheck 218**
**sidecar OpenTelemetry container**
  injecting, in ECS task definition 182
**Snyk states 204**
**Software as a Service (SaaS) 21, 22**
**software bill of materials (SBOM) 207**
**Software Composition Analysis (SCA) 207**
**software delivery**
  accelerating, with platform services 32
**software development life cycle (SDLC) 199**
**solid observability strategy, best practices 172**
  consistent time zones, using across all systems 174
  hierarchy of dashboards, building 172
  system's components emit events, ensuring 175
  trace identifiers, propagating 174, 175

**Solutions Library 234**
**specialist teams 226**
**stack 45, 61**
**Static Application Security Testing (SAST) 208, 211**
**static HTML template**
  preparing 161
**Step Functions 269**
**Sustainability pillar 274**
  best practices 274
**synthetic monitoring 171**

# T

**tagging policies 244**
**target group 83**
**task definition 147**
**technology**
  best practices and considerations 231-233
**template**
  synthesizing 132, 133
**Terraform 20, 29, 70, 208, 248**
**Terraform, versus CloudFormation 70**
  cloud-native services, integrations 71
  modules, for code reusability 72
  resource definition, mapping with deployment 71
  state management for deployed resources 71
  support, for programming constructs 71
  third-party provider ecosystem 70
**test application 48, 49**
  deploying, with AWS CDK 123
  working with 47, 48
**test application deployment, on ECS**
  application components 152, 153
  application dependencies, bundling for 162

architecture 150
CDK stack constructs, defining 154, 155
CDK stack, deploying in AWS account 162-164
infrastructure components 151, 152
static HTML template, preparing 161
web application code, preparing 159

**test application, hosted in ECS**
observability stack, deploying 176

**test EC2 instance**
creating 53
deploying 52
incoming traffic, securing with security groups 52
terminating 54

**threat modeling process** 203

**three tiers, cloud** 20
Infrastructure as a Service (IaaS) 20
Platform as a Service (PaaS) 21
Software as a Service (SaaS) 21, 22

**To-D0 List Manager application** 150, 176, 210
testing, load to generate data 189

**total cost of ownership (TCO)** 93, 269

**traces** 170

**transpiler** 119

**Troposphere** 118

**Trufflehog** 201

**Trusted Access** 244

**twelve-factor design pattern**
reference link 141

**Two-Pizza Team rule** 14

# V

**value stream-aligned teams** 224
**Version Control Systems (VCSs)** 93
**Virtual Private Cloud (VPC)** 47

# W

**web application archives (WAR)** 38, 98

**web application code**
Flask application and MongoDB connection, initializing 160, 161
preparing 159

**Well-Architected** 258

**workloads hosted, in AWS**
observability strategy, defining for 176

# X

**X-Ray service** 170

# ‹packt›

www.packtpub.com

Subscribe to our online digital library for full access to over 7,000 books and videos, as well as industry leading tools to help you plan your personal development and advance your career. For more information, please visit our website.

## Why subscribe?

- Spend less time learning and more time coding with practical eBooks and Videos from over 4,000 industry professionals
- Improve your learning with Skill Plans built especially for you
- Get a free eBook or video every month
- Fully searchable for easy access to vital information
- Copy and paste, print, and bookmark content

Did you know that Packt offers eBook versions of every book published, with PDF and ePub files available? You can upgrade to the eBook version at packtpub.com and as a print book customer, you are entitled to a discount on the eBook copy. Get in touch with us at customercare@packtpub.com for more details.

At www.packtpub.com, you can also read a collection of free technical articles, sign up for a range of free newsletters, and receive exclusive discounts and offers on Packt books and eBooks.

# Other Books You May Enjoy

If you enjoyed this book, you may be interested in these other books by Packt:

**AWS CDK in Practice**

Mark Avdi | Leo Lam

ISBN: 978-1-80181-239-9

- Turn containerized web applications into fully managed solutions
- Explore the benefits of building DevOps into everyday code with AWS CDK
- Uncover the potential of AWS services with CDK
- Create a serverless-focused local development environment
- Self-assemble projects with CI/CD and automated live testing
- Build the complete path from development to production with AWS CDK
- Become well versed in dealing with production issues through best practices

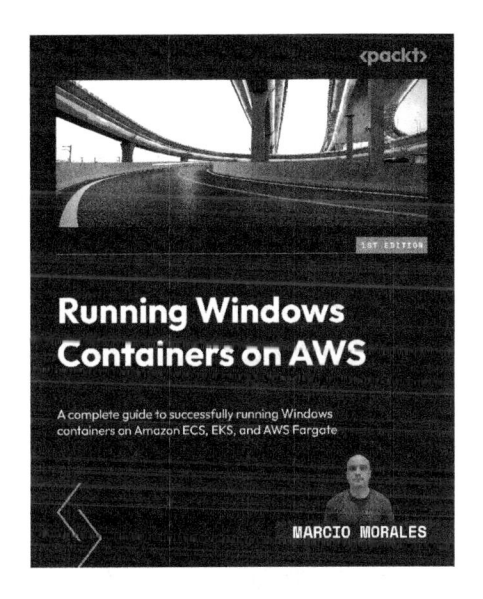

**Running Windows Containers on AWS**

Marcio Morales

ISBN: 978-1-80461-413-6

- Get acquainted with Windows container basics
- Run and manage Windows containers on Amazon ECS, EKS, and AWS Fargate
- Effectively monitor and centralize logs from Windows containers
- Properly maintain Windows hosts and keep container images up to date
- Manage ephemeral Windows hosts to reduce operational overhead
- Work with the container image cache to speed up the container's boot time

## Packt is searching for authors like you

If you're interested in becoming an author for Packt, please visit `authors.packtpub.com` and apply today. We have worked with thousands of developers and tech professionals, just like you, to help them share their insight with the global tech community. You can make a general application, apply for a specific hot topic that we are recruiting an author for, or submit your own idea.

## Share Your Thoughts

Now you've finished *AWS DevOps Simplified*, we'd love to hear your thoughts! Scan the QR code below to go straight to the Amazon review page for this book and share your feedback or leave a review on the site that you purchased it from.

`https://packt.link/r/1837634467`

Your review is important to us and the tech community and will help us make sure we're delivering excellent quality content.

# Download a free PDF copy of this book

Thanks for purchasing this book!

Do you like to read on the go but are unable to carry your print books everywhere? Is your eBook purchase not compatible with the device of your choice?

Don't worry, now with every Packt book you get a DRM-free PDF version of that book at no cost.

Read anywhere, any place, on any device. Search, copy, and paste code from your favorite technical books directly into your application.

The perks don't stop there, you can get exclusive access to discounts, newsletters, and great free content in your inbox daily

Follow these simple steps to get the benefits:

1. Scan the QR code or visit the link below

```
https://packt.link/free-ebook/9781837634460
```

1. Submit your proof of purchase
2. That's it! We'll send your free PDF and other benefits to your email directly

Printed in Dunstable, United Kingdom